T0330535

The World Economy

As globalization continues apace, market segmentations are diminishing, distance is shrinking and the boundaries between nation states are becoming increasingly blurred. National economies are closely interlinked through many channels and we rarely view things from a single country's view, adopting a global perspective instead. It is therefore imperative to understand how the world economy functions.

This book utilizes up to date empirical evidence to illuminate the mechanics of the world as a single entity. The author explores the properties of the world economy, the diverse mechanisms of interdependence, shocks and disturbances, economic processes and structures, and the institutional arrangements that guide these processes. Key topics covered include:

- world GDP, growth and global product and factor markets
- China as a new global player
- the roots and impact of financial and currency crises
- the performance of the developing countries over time (which have gained, which have lost?)
- conflicts between the national interest and global concerns (protectionism, locational competition for mobile factors of production, environmental issues)
- the institutional arrangements for the world economy (IMF, WTO).

The World Economy: a global analysis will be essential reading for students studying the world economy from the perspective of economics, finance, business, and politics.

Horst Siebert is president-emeritus of the Kiel Institute for the World Economy, Germany, and Heinz Nixdorf Professor in European Integration and Economic Policy at the Bologna Center of Johns Hopkins University, Italy.

Routledge studies in the modern world economy

The World Economy

A global analysis

Revised and enlarged third edition

Horst Siebert

LONDON AND NEW YORK

First published 2007
by Routledge
2 Park Square, Milton Park, Abingdon, Oxon OX14 4RN

Simultaneously published in the USA and Canada
by Routledge
711 Third Ave, New York, NY 10017

Routledge is an imprint of the Taylor & Francis Group, an informa business

© 2007 Horst Siebert

Typeset in Times by Wearset Ltd, Boldon, Tyne and Wear

British Library Cataloguing in Publication Data
A catalogue record for this book is available from the British Library

Library of Congress Cataloging in Publication Data
A catalog record for this book has been requested

ISBN10: 0-415-40282-4 (hbk)

ISBN13: 978-0-415-40282-8 (hbk)

Contents

Illustrations

Figures

Tables

Preface

The topic of this book is the world economy. It looks at the economy of the planet Earth as if it were observed from outer space, viewing it as a highly inter-dependent entity and analyzing global economic structures and processes as well as international institutions, relevant for these processes. In a time when the communication systems are organized globally, when we can transmit ideas from Buenos Aires to Kiel in Germany via the Internet in real time and when huge quantities of data can be exchanged between Cambridge and Hangzhou, when CNN broadcasts news worldwide, when transport costs fall, when distance shrinks and when more and more people are becoming accustomed to finding their jobs in all parts of the world, such a worldview of the economic processes and structures appears to be imperative.

In this book, we study the globalization process in its many facets and we discuss how the world economy reacts to major changes and shocks. We look at the world's gross product, its composition by sectors, at the main components of world aggregate demand and at catalysts and constraints of globalization. In Part I, we analyze the real side of the world economy, studying the world markets for goods, the adjustments to disturbances of equilibria on these markets and the role of trade. We examine the world market of the factors for production, for labor (including migration), capital, technology, and natural resources. We also study processes of economic growth, including some historical evidence and convergence.

In Part II, we look at the world's monetary and financial markets and at monetary and financial disturbances, among them currency crises. Starting with a global monetary equilibrium with different currencies, approaches are analyzed that explain the exchange rate behavior in the long run and in the short run, among them the concepts of purchasing power parity and interest rate parity as well as their interplay. Institutional arrangements of the international exchange rate system, exchange rate overshooting, optimal asset portfolios, financial bubbles and recent currency crises are further topics. Monetary and financial disturbances have a severe impact on the real sphere of the economy. An important issue is how financial crises can be prevented and which role the IMF should play.

In Part III, the book looks at the regional dimension of the world economy, in particular at developing countries and the question why some countries have succeeded in promoting their welfare through the international division of labor while others have failed. China is analyzed in detail, appplying our concepts to the real side and the monetary side of the Chinese economy. The book also analyzes regional integration in the world, including the special case of the European Union.

In Part IV, the book addresses potential conflicts between the national interest and global concerns. The idea of tensions is closely related to the classical problem of national protectionism versus free trade. It also refers to the concept of locational competition, i.e. to the phenomenon that immobile factors of production (that is labor) compete for the mobile factors (that is capital and technological knowledge). Locational competition refers to competition between governments, including competition in taxation, in the supply of public goods, and in the institutional design of countries. Using the global environment can be regarded as another area where national and global interests can clash. In order to prevent strategic (i.e. non-cooperative) behavior, an institutional order is required for the world economy in the realm of the international division of labor.

The book has developed from my regular lectures on the world economy at the University of Kiel, from my research at the Kiel Institute for the World Economy and from the discussions with my research colleagues there. It represents the continuation of my work in Kiel, with more time available without the administrative duties. If one works at a research institute like the Kiel Institute for World Economics, where many ideas are floating around, one is permanently exposed to a shifting frontier of knowledge. New problems have to be recognized quickly. Many international visitors stimulate imagination and require answers to pressing problems. Moreover, I presented the Kiel ideas at international conferences and lectures, for instance at Zhejiang University in Hangzhou, China, in Moscow and the at the Leontief Institute in St. Petersburg, at the Instituto Universitario Banco Patricio in Buenos Aires, at the Fundación Mediterránea, at Córdoba in Argentina, the Uruguay–German Chamber of Commerce in Montevideo and at the UN Commission for Latin America and the Caribbean in Santiago de Chile. Some of the paragraphs of this book have indeed been written in those and other parts of the world, often urging me to ignore the tourist attractions. I have continued to promote the Kiel view in the 'Group of Economic Analysis' and the 'Group of Economic Policy Analysis' of the European Commission, advising Romano Prodi and José Manuel Barroso as EU presidents, and in the Van Lennep Global Subsidies Initiative. I have taught the course on the world economy in the three spring semesters of the years 2004–2006 at the Bologna Center of Johns Hopkins University, and critical suggestions from students have improved the manuscript. Anticipating and erasing pitfalls for students is a marvelous incentive to improve a text. Finally new economic issues have come to the fore, among them the rise of China.

I have completely rewritten nearly all chapters for this edition. I have added new chapters on the international monetary system and on China. The chapter on the European Union has undergone major revisions. The text has been scrutinized throughout, the presentation has been improved where the previous text was unclear or too complex. All the empirical data in the tables and the figures have been updated; new institutional developments have been taken up. I also have added additional case studies, for instance on product markets (such as the car market and the pharmaceutical market), on resource markets (such as oil and coal markets), on pressure for migration, on the long term real interest rate, on inflationary experience and on subsidies as a world wide distortion.

I am grateful to many who have criticized the manuscript in its different stages and who have influenced my thoughts. I have continuously discussed the topic of the international division of labor with my colleagues at the Kiel Institute, especially with Gernot Klepper, Henning Klodt, Harmen Lehment, Rolf J. Langhammer, Joachim Scheide and Rüdiger Soltwedel, with my colleagues at the Economics Faculty of Kiel University, especially Johannes Bröcker, Gerd Hansen, Horst Herberg, Horst Raff and Thomas Lux, and with my colleagues at the German Council of Economic Advisors, who have sharpened my grasp of economic problems and of approaches to problem solving. I also had the opportunity to discuss specific issues with my colleagues Erik Jones and in particular Michael Plummer from the Bologna Center and with international colleagues, among them Jagdish Baghwati, Marty Feldstein, Gary Hufbauer, and Anne Krueger. Last but not least, my students at Kiel and Bologna, and also at the universities of Konstanz and Mannheim where I have taught before, have been a permanent challenge to present the more fascinating issues, to avoid the boring and not to hesitate to state the obvious.

A manuscript like this one is born slowly, and under pain with many roundabout processes which, unfortunately, are not always productive. I have received valuable critical suggestions fom many people. With Oliver Lorz I have discussed permanently issues of model building, with Rolf Langhammer institutional aspects of the world order; he has also given valuable hints for Chapter 10. I have received important suggestions from my student research assistants at the Bologna Center and at the Kiel Institute for the World Economy (or meanwhile at other places in the world), for which I acknowledge financial support from the Heinz Nixdorf Foundation. They have helped to find the data, prepared tables and figures and checked institutional details. I gratefully acknowledge support from Doina Cebotari on Chapters 10 and 13, from Shafik Hebous on Chapters 4, 5, 6, 11, 12, and 17, from Eduard Herda on Chapter 13, from Oliver Hoßfeld on Chapters 2, 6, and 11, from Camillo von Müller on Chapters 7, 8, and 11, from Michael Trinkus on Chapters 1, 2, 3, 11, and 17 and from Holger Wilms on Chapters 1, 8, 9, and 10. Oliver Hoßfeld has prepared some of the analytical diagrams anew, Michael Trinkus has arranged the references and checked them against the text in the chapters. Holger Wilms has read all the chapters, helped with the layout, with the harmonization of all empirical figures and, last but not least, with the technical preparation of the manuscript for the publisher.

Remaining mistakes are all mine. I hope that this book provides a fresh coherent view on the processes and structures of the world economy and gives some guidance in the actual debate on globalization, on the response of countries and their adjustment and on global institutional arrangements.

Horst Siebert

Acknowledgments

I acknowledge the following permissions to reprint illustrations used in the book (Figure 1.3): dtv (Deutscher Taschenbuchverlag) and Charles P. Kindleberger for a figure from *The World in Depression, 1929–1939*, 1973, p. 172; Routledge, London and New York, and Bernhard Heitger and Leonard Waverman for a figure from *German Unification and the International Economy*, 1993, pp. 76–77.

1   The global view

What you will understand after reading this chapter

The world economy is an exciting topic. The two oil crises of the 1970s, the Great Depression in the 1930s, the failure of Latin America in the lost decade of the 1980s, the collapse of the centrally planned economies at the end of the 1980s, the success of the Asian 'tigers' in spite of their temporary financial crises in 1997/1998 and the rise of China – these are all fascinating issues (section 1.1). The world economy is becoming more global. The segmentation of markets is being reduced. Many catalysts are at work for globalization (section 1.2). Then, the reader will be introduced to the most important variables of the world economy, notably world gross product and its composition from the production and the expenditure side as well as its regional structure (section 1.3). The world economy is in a process of continuous change. Thus, the newly industrializing countries have succeeded in becoming more integrated into the international division of labor (section 1.4). Some of them have reached remarkable places in the ranking of competitiveness (section 1.5). Rising out of poverty is the solution for the low-income countries; it is an answer to the equity issue (section 1.6). For these issues and other problems we take a global view, looking at the world as being analyzed from outer space (section 1.7).

1.1 Seven pictures of the world economy

Picture 1

Let us turn back the clock some 150 years. At that time, Japan was a closed economy without significant international relations in either the economic or the cultural field. During the Meiji Revolution in 1868, Japan opened itself consciously to the outside world. For the early periods of the opening process and of its development, it is reported that Japan started to produce spokes for imported bicycles and in this way pursued a policy of import substitution. At the end of the 1920s, Japan had become an important exporting country with a share of the world export volume of approximately 3 percent. After Japan's economic collapse owing to World War II, Japan had to start building up its economy from scratch. In 1950, Japan had a relatively insignificant position in the world economy; its share of the world export volume amounted to 1 percent. In 1986 and 1993, it surpassed 10 percent. In 2004, Japan provided about 6 percent of the world export volume, and its efficient industry poses, in spite of some problems in the 1990s, a real challenge to North America as well as Europe.

In the last twenty-five years, China has integrated itself into the international division of labor. Starting from a world market share of only 1 percent in 1980, it now accounts for 6 percent of world trade (2004). China will rise to one of the world's major economic players within the next ten years.

How does a country manage to integrate itself successfully into the international division of labor? How does an open country efficiently use its resources so that it reaches a maximum of welfare gains from trade? Which mechanisms cause an economy to produce those export goods that are demanded in the world? What does a policy concept with a consistent international orientation look like? Where are the limits of the process of economic growth through trade? Does continuing success with export goods mean that worldwide demand for the currency of the country is growing considerably, eventually culminating in an appreciation so that price competitiveness is partly diminished? How did Japan's structural problems in the 1990s affect its growth potential? What experience on catching up do we have for other countries? How will the economic core of the world economy shift in the next thirty or fifty years?

Picture 2

After 1945, the centrally planned economies of Eastern Europe were unable to reduce their development gap to the US. Whereas during the 1950s and the 1960s relatively high real GDP growth rates per capita of the communist countries could still be recorded, the 1970s are characterized by very low growth rates. During the 1980s, the communist systems collapsed. The communist countries failed to adequately provide their citizens with goods. In Figure 1.1, the relative distance to the US level of GDP per capita is denoted on the horizontal axis, growth rates are depicted on the vertical axis. High growth rates in a decade would move a country to an improved relative position to the US. Note that purchasing power parities are used; nevertheless comparisons may be distorted.

What are the reasons for this failure of the communist system? Apart from an inefficient planning system, lacking property rights and setting wrong incentives, how important was the so-called 'division of labor planned from above' for the miscarriage? How relevant was the attempt of the centrally planned socialist economies in the COMECON (Council of Mutual Economic Assistance) in Eastern Europe to exploit economies of scale in production by an explicit process of specialization? Buses for the COMECON countries were produced in Hungary, tram cars in former Czechoslovakia, and railway cars in former East Germany. This specialization, planned from above, eliminated competition between the COMECON economies, which were exempted from international competition anyway.

How can we explain why economies do not catch up? Why are some countries unable to sustain their prosperity level? Why do they even suffer a self-inflicted erosion of their economic competitiveness relative to other countries? Why did Sweden fall back from its third ranking in GDP per capital (in purchasing power parity) per capita in 1970 among the OECD countries to fourteenth ranking in 1991 (Lindbeck *et al.* 1994: Table 1.1)?

Are the three large continental countries in Europe – Germany, France, and Italy – experiencing a similar process of erosion in the 1990s and the first decade of the twenty-first century? How long can governments conceal such processes from their population? When do people, drawing comparisons with other countries, become aware of their deteriorated economic situation? Under what conditions will countries fall behind?

Picture 3

The different regions of the world experienced quite different growth performances. Instead of purchasing power parity as in Figure 1.1, we now use constant 2000 market prices. Annual GDPs at market prices are expressed in constant US dollar at the annual exchange rates. Since ten-year averages of constant 2000 prices are used, exchange rate fluctuations within a decade should be mitigated (Figure 1.2). Latin America recorded positive GDP growth rates per capita in the 1950s (not shown), 1960s, and 1970s. However, it had a negative per capita average growth rate in the 1980s, its 'lost decade.' It also was affected

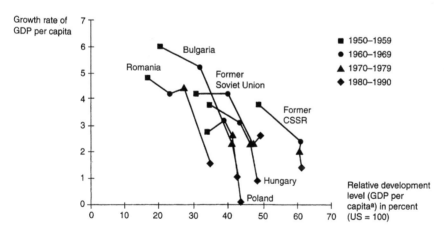

Figure 1.1 Economic growth in the centrally planned economies of Central and Eastern Europe, 1950–1990 (source: Heitger 1993, according to data from Summers and Heston 1988, 1991).

Note
a Calculated with purchasing power parity.

by currency crises. It pursued an economic policy that failed. By means of an import substitution policy, it partly excluded itself from the international division of labor. Imports were hindered, and domestic sectors were not exposed to international competition. Until the 1980s, for example, Mexico practiced a system of import licenses where, as a rule, an import license was linked to a stronger peso in a system of split exchange rates. In this way, license holders could buy imported goods at a preferential price. This system was governed by a bureaucracy, which made it possible for the politicians in charge to exert political power. Mexico did not give up this policy until the 1980s and joined the GATT only in 1986. The positive per capita growth rates of Latin American countries in the 1950s, 1960s, 1970s, and 1990s between 1 and 3 percent were not sufficient to reduce the income gap relative to the US, where the growth rate was higher.

The development of the Asian countries on the Pacific rim took a different course. Starting in the 1950s most Asian economies pursued a policy of international orientation exposing their economies to competition from abroad. On average, discrimination in favor of the domestic relative to the external sector was not prevalent. Until the Asian financial crisis of 1997/1998, the four 'tigers' (Hong Kong, South Korea, Taiwan, Singapore) had real growth rates of 6 percent (and higher) for nearly five decades. Following the currency crisis in 1997–1998, the growth rate in 1999–2003 was lower and volatile, with an average of 4.5 percent. China has had an average GDP growth rates of over 9 percent in the period 1984–2004, reaching 3 percent of US income per capita in market prices in 2004. In purchasing power parity, it is at 14 percent of the US level.

In the COMECON countries, the decline in growth rates in purchasing power parity of Figure 1.1 is confirmed when constant market prices are used in Figure 1.2. Note that in market prices the relative distance of these countries to the US is much larger than in purchasing power parities. During their transformation, the post-communist countries experienced high negative growth rates ('valley of tears'), but they now have surpassed the output level they have had at the start of the transformation shock. The data for 2000–2004 indicate that the lowest point has been surpassed. High growth rates for the first four years of the twenty-first century herald a real catch up process relative to the position of the US.

Western Europe has caught up with the United States over three decades since 1950. Starting in the 1980s the European position has been stagnant as compared the US. Since 2000 a strong US economy with high productivity growth has resulted in a marginal decline of Western Europe's relative position.

Sub-Saharan Africa shows no growth. In the period 1990–2003, the GDP per capita growth rate was at minus 0.3 percent. This is partly due to the fact that during the 1990s, population growth of 2.6 percent in this region of the world exceeded the GDP growth rate of 2.3 percent. Many countries in Africa were, and still are, caught in internal wars caused by power-hungry politicians and tribal conflicts. Severe uncertainty in the institutional set-up prevails in many economies. Corruption represents a serious distortion.

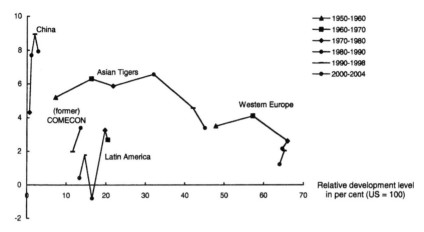

Growth rate of GDP
per capita in per cent

```
10 ┌
   │     China
    │
 8 │
   │
   │         Asian Tigers                        — 1950-1960
 6 │                                             — 1960-1970
   │                                             — 1970-1980
   │   (former)                  Western Europe  — 1980-1990
 4 │   COMECON                                   —— 1990-1998
   │                                             — 2000-2004
   │
 2 │           Latin America
   │
 0 └─────────────────────────────────────────
        10    20    30    40    50    60    70   Relative development level
                                                 in per cent (US = 100)
-2
```

Figure 1.2 Economic growth[a] in the major regions[b] of the world, 1950–2004 (source: World Bank, *World Development Indicators* March 2005).

Notes
a Real GDP per capita growth rates in market prices (constant 2000 US dollars). Annual averages of market exchange rates.
b Four 'tigers': Hong Kong, South Korea, Taiwan (excluded from 1970), Singapore.

What are the necessary ingredients for a successful growth process? Why do countries stagnate relative to others, why do some fall back? Did those countries pursuing a policy of import substitution and protection from foreign trade deprive themselves of possible development prospects and potential welfare gains? What is the relationship between international orientation and economic growth? Do open economies experience stronger growth?

Picture 4

At the time of the Great Depression in 1929–1933, the world economy experienced a massive breakdown. The volume of world trade fell to one-third of its initial level within four years. The so-called Kindleberger spiral shows how the world import volume of seventy-five countries, which can be regarded as a world trade indicator, dwindled from month to month (Figure 1.3).

What would be the effects of such a breakdown of world trade today? For instance, the US is exporting 10 percent of its GDP (2003); a fall of its exports to one-third would mean a reduction of 3 percent of aggregate demand – a severe recession. Or take Germany, which exports 38 percent of its GDP (2004). Here, a drop in the export volume to one-third would represent an 11 percent drop in aggregate demand and a devastating depression. Related questions are: will a financial crisis affect the real sphere of the economy? And if so, how?

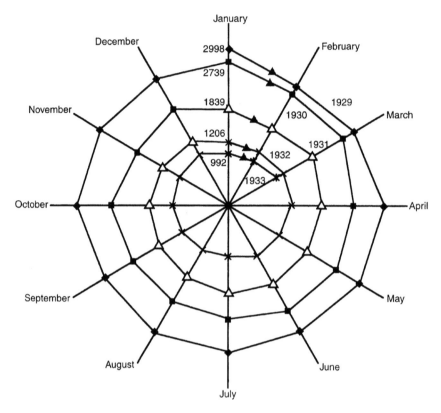

Figure 1.3 The Kindleberger spiral[a] (source: Kindleberger 1973: 172).

Note
a World import volume in million US$ gold.

What are the costs if a financial bubble bursts and what if a currency crisis hits an economy? Under what conditions can a regional currency crisis like the Asian crisis in 1997/1998, the Brazilian crisis in 1999, and the Turkish crisis in 2001 be contained? Under what conditions is contagion inevitable?

Picture 5

During the two oil price shocks in the 1970s the oil price increased nearly twentyfold compared to the 1960s (Figure 1.4). Whereas in the 1960s the oil price was significantly below US$2 per barrel of crude oil, it increased fivefold to approximately US$10 during the first oil crisis in 1973/1974. During the second oil price shock in 1979/1980, the price per barrel rose from US$2 to nearly US$40. The reason for this development was that the resource countries claimed the property rights to the crude oil reserves in their soil, even those not yet explored. In this way the seven big international oil companies ('seven sisters') were cut off from their supply sources. Under the terms of the concession contracts that were used until then, the oil firms had to pay a given percentage of their proceeds from the extracted amount of oil (royalty). De facto, they were in charge of the oil extraction and also held the right (often for a period of up to seventy years) to explore and tap new oil wells. At the beginning of the 1970s, the oil exploitation rights were transferred to the resource countries. As a consequence, the world's oil supply could no longer be allocated in the vertical hierarchy of the enterprises (extraction, refinery, transport, distribution). Instead, markets – especially the Rotterdam spot market, but later on also forward markets – increasingly took over the allocation of oil.

The impact of the oil crisis was that the capital stock, geared to the low oil prices of the 1960s, became partly obsolete, especially fuel-intensive machines in the production process and the engines of transport vehicles. The productivity of existing capital fell, reducing production, employment, and growth. At the same time, a redistribution of real income in favor of the oil-producing countries took place. The countries without oil resources, particularly the industrialized nations, had to give away more export goods per barrel of imported oil than before, their terms of trade deteriorated. In the end, the oil-producing countries had considerable petro-dollar earnings at their disposal which could not be completely absorbed by their imports. A petro-dollar recycling took place, which later became the germ cell of the debt crisis of the developing countries. Meanwhile, the oil price had reached about US$65 in the autumn of 2005, and US$100 per barrel are forecasted for future years.

How does the world economy cope with such a sudden shortage of a production factor? Which adjustment processes have to take place? Are economies that depend strongly on the import of a natural resource able to reduce their demand

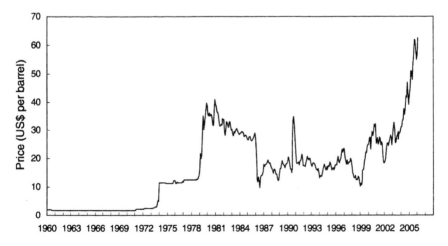

Figure 1.4 The world oil price (source: IMF, *International Financial Statistics*, March 2006, Monthly data).

for this resource in the middle and long run? Is it possible, at least partially, to substitute those resource inputs which become more expensive by other production factors? Or is import demand for oil inelastic? How is the income distribution between the production factors affected by such an adjustment process? How does the political process of countries deal with such a shortage?

Picture 6

Since the 1960s, awareness of environmental scarcity has been growing, especially in industrialized nations. In contrast to the oil crisis, this has not induced a sudden cutback of the supply of a resource but the beginning of a long-term, lengthy process in which countries change the framework for using the environment by defining new property rights. The environment is not only a national factor of endowment requiring national policy approaches; some aspects of the environment represent an international public good for which worldwide user rights as attempted in the Kyoto protocol have to be developed.

What effects does such a long-term redefinition of the institutional framework for environmental use have on the international division of labor? Do particular countries lose competitiveness in specific economic branches? Do other countries gain comparative price advantages? How are trade flows and capital flows adjusted to environmental scarcity? What solutions are offered for global environmental issues like global warming and the depletion of the ozone layer?

Picture 7

After the opening up of Central and Eastern Europe and with the integration of China into the international division of labor, a huge and radical change is taking place in the world economy. Countries well endowed with the production factor of labor are starting to participate in the international division of labor. The integration of China alone, with 1.3 billion people, means that the effective supply in the world labor market increases by one-fifth.

What impact does such an increase in the effective labor supply have on the world economy? Is it true that prices of labor-intensive goods will have to fall? Will the income of workers that have produced these goods in industrialized countries up to now have to decline as well? Will countries now take refuge in protection? To what extent will the regions being newly integrated into the world economy represent attractive markets? What stimulating effects will originate from these additional markets? Are these stimulating effects strong enough to compensate the industrialized countries, which may lose in labor-intensive goods? Will the industrialized countries as a whole gain or lose?

The common element of these seven pictures is that change is taking place in the world economy. Such a change can be a sudden shock for the world economy, like the oil price shock or the collapse of world trade and world production during the Great Depression of the 1930s. But change can also be a long-term, 'historical' process that develops gradually such as the gradual decline of the economies in Eastern Europe, the poor performance of Latin America in the decades from 1950 until 1990, and the slowly increasing awareness of the environmental problem.

1.2 What does globalization mean?

Channels of interdependence

The process of globalization has moved countries and entire regions of the world closer together; today countries have opened up and are interlinked through a number of economic and non-economic mechanisms.

In the product markets, countries trade, exchanging exports for imports. The ratio of exports to GDP, a measure of openness, differs greatly between countries. Larger countries have smaller export ratios. Using World Bank data for merchandise trade (i.e. goods provided to the world excluding services, World Bank 2005d: Table 4, 298), the US has an export share of 7 percent and Japan of 12 percent, whereas smaller economies (with smaller geographic expansion and smaller population) attain much higher ratios (Germany 33.7 percent, the Netherlands 62 percent, Ireland 57 percent, and Belgium 88 percent, all data for 2004). China, excluding Hong Kong, with 36 percent is an exception to the large-country rule (2004). If exports of services are included using World Bank country fact sheets, the shares are 9.8 percent for the US, 13.8 percent for Japan, 38.7 percent for Germany, 67.4 percent for the Netherlands, 79.5 percent for Ireland, and 39.8 percent for China, excluding Hong Kong. The European Union (EU-25) has an export share similar to that of the US if intra-EU exports are excluded (9.4 percent for 2004).

Exports and imports influence GDP, investment, and employment. Thus, countries are interlinked in the business cycles and in economic growth. A dynamic economy like that of the USs stimulates exports of other countries through its imports. A boom in the US usually leads to a boom in other countries, for instance in export-oriented Germany and Japan, by stimulating the production of export goods, then investment, and eventually consumption and employment.

In the global factor markets, capital, technology, and labor are allocated between countries. If capital leaves a country, the country's factor abundance and its production potential decline. The other country's production potential is enhanced. Capital owners may move with the capital, or ownership of capital may remain in the sending country, which then receives capital income. When a technology transfer takes place, the impact depends on whether exclusive ownership titles are defined. If so, the country to which the technology is transferred can use it exclusively; in other cases, the same technology may be used in the sending and the receiving country. In the case of labor, permanent and temporary migration (and even commuting) have to be distinguished. Remittances are a relevant phenomenon. Besides capital, technology, and labor markets, natural resources are allocated through international markets.

In the financial markets, monetary and financial transactions take place and the price of assets is determined. Apart from stock and bond markets, currency markets and money markets are essential for international linkages. Demand for, and supply of, currencies which determine the exchange rates between national or regional monies reflect trade and capital flows, for instance in the case of foreign direct investment and equity, but they also mirror bonds, bank loans, and short-term portfolio flows. Portfolios can instantaneously be changed at the touch of a button, causing capital flow reversals. Expectations are a vital factor and this type of interdependence may dissociate itself from the real side of the economy.

Besides these three basic economic mechanisms of interdependence, a fourth channel exists through environmental systems. Pollutants are transported from one country to the other, i.e. cross-border externalities exist, or all countries are affected by a global resource as in the case of global warming.

Moreover, information flows freely between most countries so that there is a 'CNN-effect' or a 'demonstration effect.' People are informed on what is happening elsewhere in the world, they observe which policies are undertaken abroad, and the psychological mood moves from one place to the other, for instance in the business cycle or during a financial crisis.

Finally, interdependencies prevail in the political arena. The policy instruments chosen in one country may have an impact on other economies; governments may wish to cooperate on specific issues, and they may opt for a regional integration or a multilateral arrangement.

Catalysts for globalization

Since the 1990s, globalization has become a key word. By 'globalization' we mean a reduction of market segmentations and the increasing interdependence of national markets. We shall now look at the catalysts for globalization.
In the world economy we can observe a whole string of tendencies that lead to globalization:

- Transport and communication costs have fallen significantly in recent decades. This holds for the traditional costs of covering distances by sea and air (which have been reduced to approximately one-fifth since the 1920s and 1930s respectively) as well as for the costs of telecommunication. For instance, a three-minute telephone call from New York to London in 1930 cost US$250 (in constant prices of 1990), in 1950 it was US$50 and in 1990 just US$3.32; the price for processing information fell from US$1 per instruction per second in 1975 to one cent in 1994 (World Bank, *World Development Report 1995*: 45). The costs have since fallen further, including the cost of using satellites and the costs for using computers as telephones.
- With regard to information technology, the world is experiencing a revolution. The World Wide Web represents a powerful global information

network. In January 2004, 11.5 billion Internet stations participated in this worldwide network. 43 percent of the households in the European Union have Internet access; in the US it is more than 50 percent (2004).

- The reduction of political tensions (e.g. the Cold War, apartheid in South Africa), regional efforts towards integration, for example in Europe, and the strengthening of multilateral trade agreements have also eliminated impediments to trade.
- The radical change in the former centrally planned economies of Central and Eastern Europe and the opening of China have integrated important regions of the world into the international division of labor. Taking India into account as well, a historical process is taking place, in which more than 40 percent of the world's population is newly integrated into the world economy. This implies that the limitation of the size of markets, which was a possible barrier for the extension of the international division of labor in the past, has become less significant.
- Most developing and newly industrializing countries have changed their strategies with regard to development and foreign trade and are now much more open. They followed a strategy of liberalization. The WTO, the successor of GATT, now has 150 members (March 2006). Sixty-two countries have joined the WTO since it was founded in 1985, including China.
- Apart from measures, which explicitly restrict trade, national regulations are increasingly being reviewed. Former governmental monopolies, for instance in the network industries, have been deregulated; publicly owned firms were privatized. Regulations are continuously adjusted in a process of institutional competition, thus reducing bureaucratic impediments further.
- The utility function of consumers now extends to a more global space. Due to information flows, personal contacts, and tourism, variables included in this function now reflect phenomena that happen in other countries. An example is the preparedness of people in Europe and the US to donate money in the case of the South-East Asian tsunami at the end of 2004.

The impact of globalization for trade

Globalization means that the segmentations of product and factor markets decline and that the interdependence of national markets increases. The allocation mechanism is working globally, so that international differences in prices will lead to arbitrage. Globalization implies that differences in supply and demand conditions of different countries can be leveled out more easily by international exchange. Market participants have to adjust to this global allocation mechanism. Firms maximizing their profits have to consider essential repercussions in worldwide markets.

Globalization of markets must not be confused with the centralization of decision processes. Increasing interdependence does not necessarily imply a centralization of decisions. Decisions are still, or even more so, made in a decentralized way. The globalization of markets and the decentralization of decisions

are supported and stimulated by new technologies for organization and communication, e.g. CAD (computer-aided design), CIM (computer-integrated manufacturing), by software that allows immediate control of the decentralized units,
by groupware that can be used by several users simultaneously. But decisions
now have to be made under different restrictions, because the options of global-
ized markets and highly mobile factors of production have to be taken into
consideration. A tightly integrated world economy, and above all the decreasing
costs for transport and communication, increases the possibility of a fragmentation of production. More fragmentation in the production process also means
that the vertical value-added chain can be sliced up and that production locations
can be changed more easily.

In combination with the fragmentation of production, the increasingly global
orientation of firms will go hand in hand with growing intra-firm trade. Foreign
direct investment (see below) as a forerunner of future trade flows will gain in
importance.

The reduction of market segmentations will not only strengthen the commodity arbitrage between different supply conditions in the traditional sense of inter-
sector trade, but it will also allow different product preferences of consumers to
play a role. Product variety is an important aspect of trade. In this respect, intra-
sector trade, i.e. trade with similar goods, will gain in significance.

Services

The increasing integration of the world economy changes the conditions for the
trade in services. By 'trade in services' we mean several quite diverse phenomena: a service like an international telephone call may actually cross a border
('cross-border supply'), consumers or firms of one country may use the service
in another country ('consumption abroad'), a service may be supplied in another
country ('commercial presence') or individuals may travel to supply their
service in another country ('presence of natural persons'). The diversity of services becomes apparent by the WTO classification list with twelve main categories (and some 148 subcategories): these are business services (professional
services like legal services, computer services, research and development services, real estate services, rental/leasing, other business services including
advertising), communication services (including telecommunication services,
audio-visual services such as motion picture production and distribution, radio
and television services), construction, distribution services, educational services,
environmental services, financial services (insurance, banking services, and
related services), healthcare services (hospital services), tourism and travel services, recreational, cultural, and sporting services, transport services (maritime
transport, air transport, rail transport, road transport) and other services.

A major distinction of service categories runs between border-crossing and
local services. This distinction is analogous to tradable and non-tradable goods.
Applying these categories, another distinction becomes relevant, namely
between 'person-disembodied' and 'person-embodied' services (Bhagwati

1984). Disembodied services, like detail engineering using computer programs, the development of software, or accounting data processing are not 'embodied' in persons. They do not require business partners to meet locally to carry out the service. For the international trading order, these services (cross-border supply) are not very different from tangible goods. Just as commodities are carried by the transport system, disembodied services cross national borders by means of communication media.

Only a slight increase in the importance of trade in services has been observed for the last thirty years. Approximately only 19 percent of world trade is trade in commercial services compared to 18 percent in 1977. This is puzzling, since about two-thirds of world output consists of services. With the advent of new communication technologies, trade in disembodied services should grow ever more rapidly. The stronger the tertiarization processes are in the industrialized nations, i.e. the increase of the share of services in GDP, the more important international trade in services should become. While it is true that a large part of world GDP is non-tradable, it is possible that a measurement problem exists for trade in services. The new communication technology and a more reliable WTO rule system for trade in services should impact favorably on the trade in services in the years to come.

Increasing interdependence of factor markets

The reduction of impediments to international mobility not only applies to commodity markets but also impacts on factor markets. Capital mobility in particular has increased in significance, especially in the form of foreign direct investment. Different causes are relevant. For example, it may be desirable to be present in an expanding market, in order to avoid transaction costs or to circumvent the political segmentation of markets due to disadvantageous foreign trade policies. Foreign direct investment also exploits comparative cost advantages slicing up the value added chain and reorganizing the geography of the production process. Expected advantages of production locations are anticipated. In this respect, foreign direct investment today is the forerunner of trade in commodities tomorrow.

Since 1973, foreign direct investment has grown considerably faster than world trade while the growth of world trade has outstripped the growth of world production, with all variables measured in real terms. World GDP increased at an average real growth rate of 3 percent per year in the period 1973–2004 whereas the world trade volume grew by an annual average of 5 percent, as measured by the volume of the world's merchandise exports (Figure 1.5). In the same period, foreign direct investment rose by 15 percent per year in real terms though its rates of change were extremely volatile and susceptible to the business cycle and political shocks as demonstrated by the sharp fall after the boom in 2000 and in the aftermath of September 11, 2001. In the tabulation of Figure 1.5 nominal foreign direct investment flows were corrected by the US Capital Equipment Producer Price Index. Annual changes since 1985 also indicate the

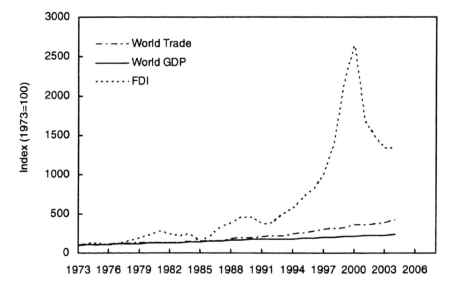

Figure 1.5 World GDP, world trade, and foreign direct investment, 1973–2004[a] (source: World Bank, *Online Database* 2005; IMF-IFS *Online Database* 2005; UNCTAD, *Online Statistical Database* 2005; own calculations).

Note

a Indices: 1973 = 100. Logarithmic scale. Foreign direct investment inflows adjusted with the US Producer Price Index of Capital Equipment. Volume of Trade: Merchandise Trade.

different speed of growth (Table 1.1). The presented figures give a clear account of the increasing interdependence of the world's economies.

With foreign direct investment accounting for 10.4 percent of total world investment in 2002 and having peaked at 21.8 percent in the boom year of 2000, real capital flows have become an important factor in the international division of labor, even compared to the world's export to GDP ratio of 24 percent in 2002 when World Development Indicator data are used. Three-quarters of the world's foreign direct investment, measured as inflows, are attracted by industrial economies (1991–2003).

Labor markets are becoming substantially more global for those with high qualifications, e.g. in research and management. For lower qualifications, labor markets remain largely nationally segmented. This is not to imply that there is no international competition between workplaces. Interdependence has an indirect effect; for instance, via trade flows and capital mobility.

International interdependence of financial markets

Besides foreign direct investment, portfolio capital has become extremely mobile; it now can be moved instantly worldwide from one financial market to another. It is estimated that the world currency markets move the volume of

Table 1.1 Growth rates of world GDP, world trade, and foreign direct investment, 1985–2004[a]

Year	World GDP	World trade[b]	Foreign direct investment[c]
1985	3.5	2.6	−2.5
1986	3.4	4.0	51.5
1987	3.7	5.5	61.0
1988	4.5	8.5	17.0
1989	3.8	6.4	18.4
1990	2.5	3.9	5.4
1991	0.8	3.7	−22.3
1992	1.1	4.8	5.9
1993	0.9	4.2	34.8
1994	2.2	9.2	13.6
1995	2.3	7.4	31.5
1996	3.3	5.0	16.1
1997	3.4	10.2	25.6
1998	2.1	4.7	44.4
1999	2.9	4.7	54.9
2000	3.8	10.4	24.4
2001	1.3	−0.6	−39.5
2002	1.6	3.5	−12.4
2003	2.3	4.8	−12.4
2004	3.7	9.0	1.4

Source: IMF, *International Financial Statistics* 2005; World Bank, *World Development Indicators* March 2005; UNCTAD, *Online Statistical Database* 2005; own calculations.

Notes
a All rates measured in percent.
b Merchandise Exports.
c FDI inflows.

world trade in about five days. In 2004, the daily average turnover on the foreign exchange market amounted to US$1.9 trillion; the gross turnover was US$2.7 trillion (Bank of International Settlements 2005). In 1986, the daily average gross turnover amounted to US$ 209 million. Admittedly, then fewer central banks (only four) reported.

Constraints for globalization

The catalysts for globalization have to be confronted with the constraints that oppose the process of globalization. First, each national economy has a large sector that is not directly exposed to the international division of labor, the sector of non-tradables. The output of this sector is not internationally traded; national production corresponds to national consumption. Globalization only affects the sector of tradable goods, i.e. the export sector and the domestic sector of import substitutes. In the larger countries or regions like the US, Japan, or the European Union, there is a strong non-tradable sector amounting to about 85 to 90 percent of GDP; in smaller countries, this sector is less important. This is confirmed by the export ratio (exports relative to GDP), which, however, only indicates the relevance of the export sector. Second, a large portion of factors of production is internationally immobile, especially low-skilled labor. Third, segmentations exist with respect to information, for instance in the financial markets. Fourth, the institutional set-ups differ, so that markets are segmented. The last two factors may explain the home bias observed in financial markets. Fifth, preferences of households and entrepreneurs differ; countries have different aggregated political preferences, different cultural identities, different legal systems, and different political processes. In this context, political demands for redistribution and social protection may put the brakes on the process of globalization. Sixth, internalizing environmental costs may lead to rising transaction costs, especially in terms of transportation costs for fossil fuels. Global interdependence in exploiting the environment becomes more apparent in the form of more devastating natural disasters, global warming, and increased scarcities of natural resources. Seventh, the fear of global terrorism increases uncertainty, affecting trade and investment. It may also lead to an increase in regulations, which limit the degree of freedom to trade and invest.

1.3 World gross product

The global sum of all production in the world is expressed by the term 'world gross product'. Here a note to the reader is required. When we look at a single country, we distinguish between two concepts: gross domestic product (GDP) and gross national income (GNI). Gross domestic product is the product generated by the factors of production located in a country, including foreigners working in the country and capital in the country even if owned by foreigners. Gross national income is the income accruing to all citizens of a country including income from work for international commuters and temporary migrants (less than 180 days per year) and capital income earned in foreign countries. GNI, formally called gross national product (GNP), measures total value added from domestic and foreign sources claimed by residents.

For individual countries, GDP and GNI can diverge. Thus, a country whose labor and capital are used abroad receives wage and capital income from abroad and has a higher GNI than GDP. On the world scale, GDP and GNI yield the same total when summed up over all countries, as (at least so far) no factor of production is active outside planet Earth. In this regard we could use the term 'world product'. However, since we have become used to the term 'GDP' (gross domestic product) and since we will continuously be comparing the country view to the worldview in this book, we will use the term 'world gross domestic product,' or 'world GDP'. Where GDP data are not available, GNI data will be applied.

The world gross product amounted to US$40.9 trillion in 2004 (World Bank 2005d: 297). Low income countries had a GNI per capita of US$825 or less in 2004. Countries with high income had a GNI per capita larger than US$10,066 or more. Middle income countries were between US$826 and US$10,065 (World Bank 2005d, p.289). Note that the world's gross national income is measured at US$39.8 billion, somewhat lower than GDP.

Viewed from the production side, services, with a share of 68 percent, are the most important sector of the world domestic product. The industrial sector contributes 28 percent and agriculture 4 percent (Table 1.2). Countries with a low per capita national income are heavily specialized in agriculture. Countries with high income have a relatively large share in services.

Viewed from the expenditure side, private consumption contributes the largest share to the world gross domestic product, with 62 percent. Gross investment is at about 21 percent and government consumption at 17 percent. Countries with a middle income show a higher share in gross investment of 27 percent. They are growing due to their strong capital formation. These countries also have a positive external balance of goods and services. This means that their savings amount to 29 percent of GDP. Low income countries have a negative current account; they finance part of their investment through capital imports, i.e. their savings rate is at 19 percent of GDP. The external balance can be defined as the difference between savings and investment.

The regional structure of the world domestic product is shown in Figure 1.6: the gross domestic products of the economies with a lower, middle or higher income rank at US$1.2 trillion, US$6.9 trillion and US$32.7 trillion, respectively. In 2004, the US contributed 29 percent to the world domestic product, Japan 11 percent, Germany 7 percent, the UK and France each 5 percent, and Italy 4 percent, respectively. The European Union (EU-25) produces about

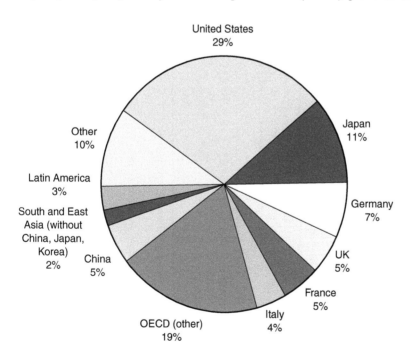

Figure 1.6 Regional structure of the world's gross domestic product, 2004 (source: World Bank, *World Development Report* 2005; own calculations).

Table 1.2 World domestic product 2004, components in percent

	Production approach by sectors			Expenditure approach			
	Agriculture	Industry	Services	Private consumption	Government consumption	Gross capital formation	Current account
Low income countries	23	25	57	69	12	22	−3
Middle income countries	12	33	55	58	13	27	2
High income countries	2[a]	28[a]	68[a]	63	18	20	0
World	4[a]	28[a]	68[a]	62	17	21	0

Source: World Bank, *World Development Report 2006*: 297.

Note

a Data for 2003: *World Development Indicators 2005*.

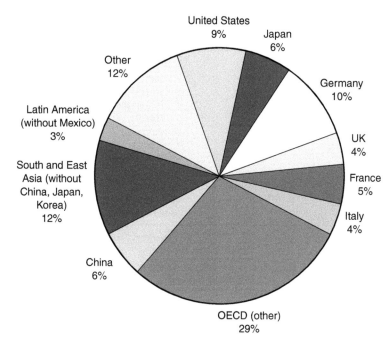

Figure 1.7 Regional structure of world trade, 2004 (source: World Bank, *World Development Indicators* 2005; IMF, *International Financial Statistics*, September 2005; own calculations).

30 percent. China accounts for 4.7 percent of the world domestic product (data after the 2005 revision).

The world market shares (Figure 1.7) differ from the production shares. This is due to the fact that large economies have a large domestic sector (non-tradables). For exports including services and using IMF data, the US had an export share of 9 percent in 2004, Germany 10 percent and Japan 6 percent (Japan had reached 9.6 percent in 1993). China accounts for 6 percent, a higher share than France (5 percent), the UK (4 percent) and Italy (4 percent). The data for merchandise exports differ slightly (WTO 2005: Table 1.5).

Product structure of total world trade of US$11 billion consisted of merchandise trade (US$8.9 billion) and services (US$2.1 billion). Manufactured goods are the overwhelmingly traded products, accounting for US$6.6 billion with fuels and mining products coming second at US$1.3 billion; trade in agricultural products amounts to US$7.8 billion.

With its US$12 trillion economy, the US is the largest country of the world measured in terms of gross national product. China is the largest country measured in terms of population (Table 1.3).

Table 1.3 The ten largest countries of the world

GNP (billion of US$ 2004)			Population (millions, 2004)		
1	United States	11,668	1	China[a]	1,296
2	Japan	4,374	2	India	1,080
3	Germany	2,391	3	United States	293
4	China[a]	1,930	4	Indonesia	218
5	United Kingdom	1,831	5	Brazil	179
6	France	1,755	6	Pakistan	152
7	Italy	1,452	7	Russia	143
8	Canada	839	8	Bangladesh	140
9	Spain	830	9	Nigeria	140
10	Mexico	613	10	Japan	128
	For information:	12,627		For information:	458
	European Union[b]			European Union	

Source: World Bank, *World Development Report* 2006, *China Quarterly Update* 2006.

Notes
a   China excluding Hong Kong, Macao and Taiwan. Data after 2005 revision.
b   Eurostat, *The statistical database* published by the European Commission, states that the EU-25 had a GPD equal to 10,370.8 billion euros.

1.4 Economic change in the world economy

The world economy is in a process of permanent change. Since 1980, economic growth has been at about 3 percent per year (Table 1.4). The GDP of low-income countries increases at a higher rate of 4.5 percent, the four Asian 'tigers' grew at 6 percent and at a somewhat lower rate after the financial crisis of 1997/1998, China has a growth rate of more than 9 percent (Figure 1.8). The industrialized countries have a lower growth rate of 2.6 percent since 1990. The transformation countries in Central and Eastern Europe and Russia have experienced negative growth rates during the period of transformation. Note that the process of economic growth in the world economy is influenced by business cycles.

Since 1970, the developing and newly industrializing countries as a whole have succeeded in integrating themselves into the international division of labor. Their contribution to world merchandise trade has grown from 19 percent in 1975 to 35 percent in 2004 (Figure 1.9). In particular the newly industrializing countries of Asia and the Pacific rim managed to realize high gains. They significantly increased the share of industry products in their total merchandise exports, e.g. Singapore from 34 percent (1965) to 85 percent (2004), including re-exports. The world market share of the four 'tigers' (Hong Kong, Singapore, South Korea, and Taiwan grew from approximately 3 percent in 1975 to 8.5 percent in 2004, reaching 10 percent in 2000 (Figure 1.10)). China increased its world market share from 0.9 percent in 1979 to 6.5 percent in 2004. In comparison, sub-Saharan Africa, with a world market share of 1.8 percent, remains the poorhouse of the world for the time being.

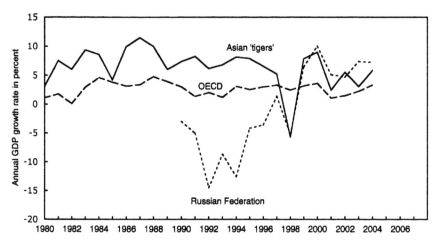

Figure 1.8 Growth in the world economy, 1980–2004[a] (source: World Bank, *World Development Indicators* 2005).

Note
a Asian 'tigers': Hong Kong, Singapore, South Korea, and Taiwan.

Table 1.4 GPD average growth rates, 1980–2004

	1980–1990	*1990–2000*	*2000–2004*
World	3.3	2.6	2.5
Low-income countries	4.4	3.4	5.4
Middle-income countries	2.8	3.6	4.4
High-income countries	3.4	2.4	2.0

Source: World Bank, *World Development Report* 2002, 2006.

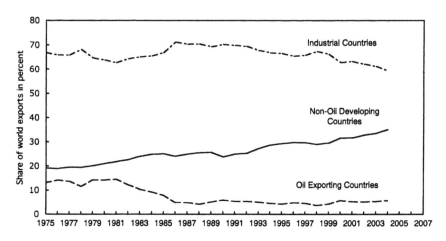

Figure 1.9 Shares of world exports, 1975–2004: Industrial countries and developing countries (source: IMF, *International Financial Statistics*, CD-ROM, January 2006).

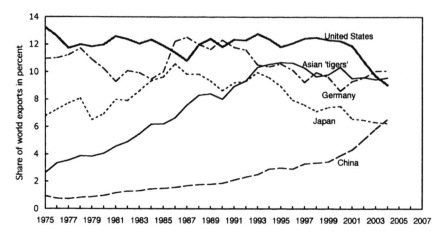

Figure 1.10 Share of world exports[a], 1975–2004: United States, Germany, Japan, China, Asian 'tigers'[b] (source: IMF, *International Financial Statistics*, CD-ROM, January 2006).

Notes
a Merchandise exports.
b Asian 'tigers': Hong Kong, Singapore, South Korea, and Taiwan

1.5 A ranking of competitiveness

Several organizations compile rankings of competitiveness for all countries of the world. For instance, the World Economic Forum (2005) has developed a ranking of competitiveness for 103 countries from surveys and statistical information. The index underlying the ranking is composed of three component indices: the technology index measuring economically effective innovation or effective transfer of technology as well as the quality of the communication infrastructure; the public constitution index measuring corruption as well as contract and judicial certainty; and the macroeconomic environment index measuring macroeconomic stability, country rating, and government waste. In this context, the Growth Competitiveness Index itself measures factors that contribute to a high growth rate in GDP per capita. The small open economies are positioned at especially high places. It is somewhat surprising to find Germany ranked only at position 13 (Table 1.5).

1.6 The equity issue

Nearly two-fifths of the world's population, 2.3 billion people, live in low-income countries (2004). These are countries with an annual gross national income per capita of US$825 or less. Equity is not only an issue in that income distribution is uneven between countries. It is also uneven in each country. Thus,

Table 1.5 Growth competitiveness ranking, 2005

Country	Competitiveness ranking	Country	Competitiveness ranking
Finland	1	Austria	21
United States	2	Portugal	22
Sweden	3	Chile	23
Denmark	4	Malaysia	24
Taiwan	5	Luxembourg	25
Singapore	6	Ireland	26
Iceland	7	Israel	27
Switzerland	8	Hong Kong SAR	28
Norway	9	Spain	29
Australia	10	France	30
Netherlands	11	Belgium	31
Japan	12	Slovenia	32
United Kingdom	13	Kuwait	33
Canada	14	Cyprus	34
Germany	15	Malta	35
New Zealand	16	Thailand	36
Korea	17	Bahrain	37
United Arab Emirates	18	Czech Republic	38
Qatar	19	Hungary	39
Estonia	20	Tunisia	40

Source: World Economic Forum, *The Global Competitiveness Report* 2005–2006, Table 2.

in the low-income countries a larger proportion of the population lives below US$1 per day, for instance 70.8 percent in Nigeria and 35.3 percent in India.

The crucial question is how these low-income countries can get out of their poverty and out of a situation where malnutrition, a high mortality rate of children, and a low literacy rate prevail and where the burden of disease makes it difficult to participate successfully in the international division of labor (World Bank 2005d). Historically, economic growth has been the vehicle through which the economic situation of many groups has improved in the developed countries over the last 200 years. Following this approach, growth continues to be the way out of poverty and low income. How much inequality is acceptable to stimulate growth is a heavily debated issue.

1.7 The global dimension

The subject of this book is the world economy. The book does not concentrate on a single open economy, i.e. an economy linked to other countries through trade or capital flows. Instead, it provides a global analysis of the structures and processes in the world economy, as if the world were looked at from outer space. In a time when the communication system is organized globally, when we can communicate from Buenos Aires in Argentina to Kiel in Germany over the

Internet and when huge quantities of data can be exchanged between Cambridge and Hangzhou in the blink of an eye, when CNN broadcasts news worldwide, when transport costs become less and less significant and when more and more people become accustomed to finding their jobs in all parts of the world, such a worldview of the economic processes and structures appears to be imperative.

Thus, the paradigm prevailing here is an analysis of the world as a whole. The world is first of all interpreted as a single entity. This is true for the macro-economic aggregates of the world economy, like the world's domestic product and the main components of world aggregate demand. It also refers to macro-economic approaches to explain processes in the world economy, like cyclical movements or economic growth. In contrast to such a macroeconomic view, other aspects are rather microeconomic; for instance, an analysis of the world markets for goods, including adjustments to disturbances of equilibria on the commodity markets. In a similar way, this also holds for the world market's factors of production, for the capital market, the labor market, and the resource market. A specific issue is the world money market and the financial markets. The volatility of financial and currency markets has an impact on the real sphere of the economy, and a crisis may spread from one country to another. A related question is how a financial crisis can be prevented. In a further step, this global view can be abandoned to analyze different regions of the world, like developing countries or specific countries of interest such as China. In such a more disaggregated outlook, processes of regional integration, including those of the European Union, are also of interest. Finally, it is fascinating to examine the role, which is left for national economic policy in the world economy today, to look at potential conflicts between the national interest and global concerns and to study the institutional arrangements, which should be developed for the world economy.

Part I

The world product and factor markets and economic growth

Being interested in the world economy, we have to answer the question of how the division of labor is carried out and how development and growth processes can be explained. We first analyze the division of labor under static conditions. In a paradigm of allocation, markets are important, notably product markets (Chapter 2) and factor markets (Chapter 3). Second, we study how the division of labor in the world changes over time and how the process of economic growth can be explained (Chapter 4).

2   The world product markets

What you will understand after reading this chapter

The reduced costs of economic distance and the integration of the newly industrializing countries as well as of the new market economies have changed the
equilibrium of the world product markets. The supply of commodities has
increased and at the same time new markets have arisen. In order to examine
these effects, we first look at world product markets and the world market equilibrium on the product markets (section 2.1). We then study how the world
market equilibrium changes. A change can come about by a reduction of trade
barriers (section 2.2). Another important story is that the rising labor supply
through the integration of China and India (section 2.3) affect international production and specialization, trade flows, the terms of trade, world market equilibrium, as well as factor income and employment. The most important theorems
on the international division of labor will be briefly summarized (section 2.4).
Shifts of demand also play a decisive role (section 2.5). While this approach
explains trade with different products, i.e. between different sectors (inter-sector
trade), empirical analysis tells us that the overwhelming part of trade between
industrial countries is trade with similar products (intra-sector trade) because
high-income people love product variety. The implications of this approach for
the world economy are analyzed; they are quite different from the inter-sector
trade approach (section 2.6). Another relevant question is whether markets are
contestable when economies of scale exist (section 2.7). Trade in services, tradable and non-tradable goods, and hierarchy versus markets represent other
empirical phenomena (section 2.8). Finally, the export structure of countries and
the influence of the real exchange rate on exports are reviewed (section 2.9).

2.1 The world product market equilibrium

Properties of the world product market

From an international perspective, it is interesting to study world product
markets, for instance the world oil market or the world coal market (see case
studies). The analysis of these and other product markets leads us to answer

questions like the following: to what extent is such a market integrated world-wide and to what extent is it segmented? Where does production take place? Do we have a vertical structure of production? Is the value-added chain of production sliced up? What are the backward and forward linkages of production? To what extent is production separated spatially from demand, i.e. what is the role of trade? Does the industry consist of vertically integrated firms? Or do markets perform the allocation of production and investment decisions? What are future trends of an industry? And which major factors influence these trends? In which sectors will production and investment shift to developing countries? And in which sectors will the developing countries drive out production in the industrialized economies?

The concept of the world market equilibrium

The world product markets are in equilibrium if there is no excess demand or excess supply. We express this condition with:

$$E_i^W = C_i^W - Q_i^W = 0 \tag{2.1}$$

Excess demand E_i^W, that is the difference between demand C_i^W and supply Q_i^W, must be equal to zero for each good i. Then, the world market is cleared. The prices on the markets must adjust in such a way that this condition is satisfied. When supply or demand conditions on a world market change, the price has to change as well.

In a world market equilibrium not only has the excess demand for a commodity to be equal to zero. In addition, it must hold that firms have found their profit maximum with their supply and households their utility maximum with their demand. For firms, this condition is fulfilled if the commodity price ratio corresponds to the marginal costs ratio. To clarify this, we introduce the concept of the world transformation curve (curve *VWX* in Figure 2.3). It indicates – for a given factor endowment and technology – the maximum production quantity of good 1 for a given production quantity of good 2. The marginal rate of transformation (i.e. the slope of the transformation curve) dQ_2/dQ_1 indicates the opportunity costs of producing an additional unit of good 2, measured in units of good 1 forgone. Q_i denotes units of good i. It shows to what extent it is possible to produce more of a good by means of diverting the factors of production away from the other good. The marginal rate of transformation corresponds to the ratio of marginal costs. The commodity price ratio $p = p_1/p_2$ also indicates the relative valuation of the two goods by the households. From the supply side of the economy an equilibrium exists if the commodity price ratio corresponds to the marginal rate of transformation $p = p_1/p_2 = |dQ_2/dQ_1|$. In Figure 2.3, the commodity price ratio p is given by a straight line with the angle ?. It corresponds to the quantity ratio Q_2/Q_1, in this way indicating how many units of good 2 can be exchanged for one unit of good 1.

The quantities of the two goods produced at equilibrium point *W* amount to the world domestic product. Valued with the relative price *p* and measured in units of good 1, the world domestic product is given by the distance *OT*. Measured in units of good 2, the world domestic product is shown by the distance *OY*.

The point of production on the world transformation curve depends on the demand conditions, because demand and supply together determine the relative price that clears the market in accordance with equation 2.1. The relative price of the equilibrium can be determined with the usual demand–supply diagram or with the help of the Marshall–Mill offer curves.

Case study: the world oil market

As an example of a world good market, the world crude oil market with the observed prices for a barrel of oil and the traded quantities is shown in Figure 2.1. In the 1960s, demand increased and supply expanded; the price

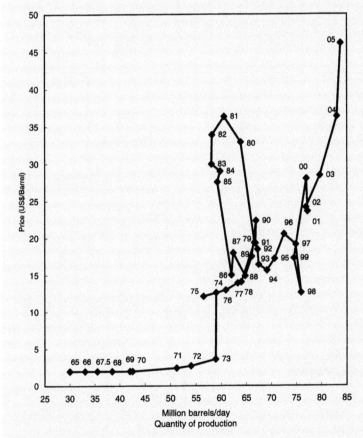

Figure 2.1 World oil market (source: OECD, *Economic Outlook*, No 77 2005).

remained nearly constant. In the two oil crises of 1973/1974 and 1979/1980, supply remained constant and even declined during the second crisis, whereas prices jumped upward and quadrupled in each of the two oil crises. In the early 1980s, prices fell. Since 1998, the oil price rose again while the quantity increased a little. In 2005, the oil price approached the US$50 mark, reaching over US$60 in some weeks. Supply increased only marginally.

The supply curve of coal

Figure 2.2 shows another example of a world product market, the long-term world supply curve for hard coal. On the horizontal axis the mining capacity is shown. The mining costs vary significantly between different suppliers from US$12 per (metric) ton in China to US$195 per ton in Germany. In this context, we have to distinguish between extraction costs for open-pit mining (o) and for underground mining (u). The supply curve shown comprises 85 percent of the worldwide mining capacity.

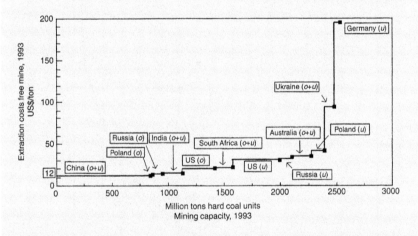

Figure 2.2 World supply curve for hard coal, 1993 (source: Bundesanstalt für Geowissenschaften und Rohstoffe 1995).

Demand–supply diagram

In Figure 2.4a, the relative price $p = p_1/p_2$ is shown on the vertical axis in the usual market diagram. The quantity of good 1 is depicted on the horizontal axis. If the relative price p is high the demand for good 1 is low; with the relative price going down demand for good 1 increases (along the demand curve $C_1^W(p)$). The supply curve can be derived graphically from Figure 2.3. The point of zero production of good 1 corresponds to the point X' in Figure 2.4 (point X of the

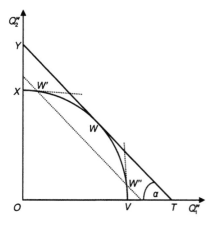

Figure 2.3 World transformation curve and world market equilibrium.

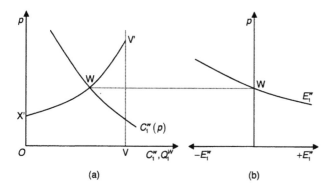

Figure 2.4 Relative price in the equilibrium.

transformation curve in Figure 2.3). The point of the maximum production of good 1 corresponds to the point V' in Figure 2.4 (point V in Figure 2.3); the positive slope of the supply curve represents the increasing marginal rate of transformation, that is the increasing marginal costs of the production of good 1. Moving along the supply curve corresponds to moving along the transformation curve. The relative price in equilibrium is determined by point W at the intersection of the supply and the demand curve. In Figure 2.4b, the excess demand for good 1 is derived from the horizontal difference between the quantities demanded and supplied.

Offer curves

The world market equilibrium can also be described by the Marshall–Mill offer curves. For this concept, the world market is divided into two regions, Home

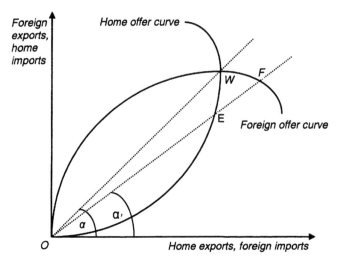

Figure 2.5 Equilibrium with the Marshall–Mill offer curves.

and Foreign. In Figure 2.5 the home and foreign offer curves are shown (in this context good 1 is the home export good and good 2 the foreign export good). The offer curve of a country indicates how many units of the import good have to be offered to a country in exchange for its export good. The shape of the offer curve of a country is determined by the following factors:

- The substitution effect: with an increasing relative price of the export good domestic demand for this good decreases and demand for the import good rises correspondingly. This effect causes the slope of the offer curve to increase; the slope is positive and remains so.
- The income effect: the rising relative price p means an increase in real income for the home country, because it gets more units of the import good for one unit of its export good. This means that its terms of trade improve. With higher income, demand for each of the two goods increases; ceteris paribus, the country provides less export goods. Consequently, the income effect runs counter the substitution effect. It causes the curve to bend backwards and the slope to eventually become negative.
- The increasing marginal production costs of a good: when moving along the transformation curve of a country the marginal rate of transformation increases. This indicates that the opportunity costs of a good increases with the amount being produced. Therefore, the positive slope of the offer curve increases. This effect vanishes when the point of full specialization is reached.

As long as the substitution effect dominates the income effect, the offer curve has a positive slope. When the income effect dominates, the curve bends backwards. The equilibrium is reached at point *W* at a relative price *p* that is given by the tangent of the angle α. At point *W*, excess supply of the export good of the home country and excess demand of the import demand of the foreign country are identical. The market is cleared. Along the straight line with the gradient α′, however, the points *E* and *F* signal that at the given relative price the home country's trade offer does not correspond to the offer of the foreign country. There is excess demand for good 1 and excess supply of good 2. Consequently, the relative price *p* must rise to restore equilibrium.

The law of one price

The world market can be characterized by the law of one price. This is Jevons's law. If no trade barriers exist and if transport costs equal zero, that is if markets are not segmented, the same price must be observed everywhere for a homogeneous good. Certainly, this is a significant simplification to the real world, because there are trade barriers and transportation costs. However, the concept helps to make an important aspect perfectly clear, namely spatial arbitrage. As long as there are price differentials it is worthwhile to arbitrage them away by moving goods from one location to another.

2.2 The reduction of trade barriers and the world market equilibrium

The reduction of trade barriers, for example as a result of lower transport and communication costs, means that arbitrage is intensified and that efficiency gains rise. The world transformation curve moves outward.

The world transformation curve is derived from the transformation curves of each individual country. Figure 2.6 shows the special case of two countries. In order to keep the argument simple we assume that initially both countries are in autarky. Alternatively, the initial situation may be interpreted as having some trade, but the level of trade can be expanded if market segmentations are reduced. The transformation curves are drawn in such a way that the production points *A* and *A** of the two countries in autarky coincide in one point. In this case, world production is given by point *O**. The states of autarky *A*, *A** in the two countries do not represent a world market equilibrium, because relative prices differ and because without trade barriers it is worthwhile for the home country to produce more of good 1 (i.e. moving in the direction of an increased production of good Q_1 on its transformation curve to point P). At the same time, it is worthwhile for the foreign country to produce more of good 2 until the price ratios in the two countries are brought in line with each other. This is the case at point *P* in Figure 2.6. The marginal rates of transformation in the two countries correspond to each other, and they correspond to the uniform price ratio in the world economy (straight line *p*). In point *P* output in the world economy is higher ($O*' > O*$). In this way the world as a whole gains from the transition from autarky (or from a low level of trade) to trade (or to more trade).

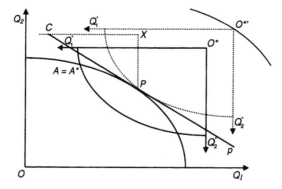

Figure 2.6 Trade barriers and world transformation curve.

It can also be shown that each country gains from the higher level of trade, i.e. when the segmentation of markets is reduced. Take the home country and compare its budget space in the initial situation *A* and in the new situation *P*. In autarky, the home country has no other choice but to consume in point *A*. With free trade, the home country consumes on a point along line *p*. Its budget space has increased; it enjoys a higher welfare at point C. It exports CX of good 1 and imports XP of good 2. This trade triangle allows the country to have a consumption point C different from its production point P. Trade is an option to supply or demand goods at the given world market price. It offers welfare gains; otherwise, a country could always choose the state of autarky. Gains from trade will even occur if the other country behaves in a protectionist way (Free Trade for One Theorem).

Countries will trade, if in autarky they have relative price advantages. For instance, in the intersection point A=A*, we have $p < p^*$. The slope of a tangent to the transformation curve in the home country at point A is smaller than the slope of a tangent to the transformation curve of the foreign country at point A*. Then the home country has a comparative price advantage in good 1 and it will export commodity 1. Accordingly, the foreign country has a relative price advantage in good 2 and will export this good. Relative price advantages are due to advantages in factor endowments and in technology. They also reflect a low domestic preference for a good that is valued more dearly abroad.

Note that in the real world economic decisions of households and firms depend on absolute price advantages, but absolute price advantages are related to relative price advantages. Here the exchange rate comes into play. Take the case when the home country has an absolute price advantage for commodity 1, i.e. its autarky price p_l is lower than abroad $p_l < p_l^* e$ where *e* is the exchange rate, for instance €/$. The exchange rate is the relative price of monies; it indicates how many units of euro have to be spent to obtain one US-dollar (or how many euros you get in exchange for one unit of US-dollar). It makes the product price expressed in different currencies comparable. Let the foreign country have an absolute price advantage for commodity 2, i.e. $p_2^* e < p_2$. Combining the two conditions for absolute price advantage, we have:

$$p_1/p_1^* < e < p_2/p_2^* \qquad (2.2)$$

where the price ratios are nominal ratios, i.e. nominal prices of the same product in different currencies. If the exchange rate establishes itself between the nominal prices, we have $p_1/p_1^* < p_2/p_2^*$ and consequently $p_1/p_2 < p_1^*/p_2^*$. This condition denotes the relative prices in both countries instead of nominal prices. Thus, the exchange rate transforms relative price advantages into absolute price advantages. Looking only at trade and neglecting capital flows, a country needs foreign currency in order to pay its imports. With demand for foreign currency being derived from import demand, an absolute price disadvantage of a country drives up the value of the foreign currency. It can be shown that the exchange rate establishes itself according to equation (2.2).

After the most important characteristics of the world market equilibrium have been discussed, it will be explained in the following how the world market equilibrium adjusts to disruptions.

2.3 The impact of an increase in the labor supply

Effect on the world product market equilibrium

The world economy is in a state of permanent change. World market equilibrium may change gradually or abruptly. Thus, the equilibrium is disturbed, if the supply of a production factor changes. The price of an important resource such as oil may shoot up or factor abundance may change gradually; for example, if the pollution of the environment is increasingly taken into account. Another relevant case is the increase in the world labor supply which currently occurs with the integration of China, India, and the former centrally planned economies into the world economy. Assume that these countries were completely segmented from the world in an initial situation. Let them then participate in the international division of labor. Integrating them in the international division of labor means that the world transformation curve shifts outward more in favor of the labor-intensively produced good 2 than in favor of good 1 (Figure 2.7). Consequently, more of this good can be produced.

Let us conduct a thought experiment. Assume that the relative price p between the two goods remains constant for the moment; the world market equilibrium then moves from point W to point W''. The production of good 1 falls, the production of good 2 increases. If consumers associate an increase of good 2 with a lower marginal utility of a unit of good 2 and a decrease of good 1 with a higher marginal utility of a unit of good 1, then the relative price of the initial position will not be a market equilibrium. In other words, at the old price there is an excess supply of good 2 and an excess demand for good 1. Consequently, the price of good 2 has to fall (by a little) and the price of good 1 to rise (by a little).

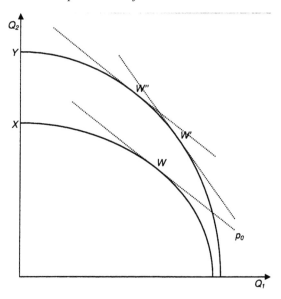

Figure 2.7 Increased labor supply and world transformation curve.

This means that the relative price p has to rise and in this way a new point of equilibrium W' will be realized. This point must be situated to the north-east of the initial equilibrium W if the transformation curve shifts in favor of good 2. The quantity ratio Q_2/Q_1 increases compared to the initial position (assuming for instance homothetic preferences).

In the demand–supply diagram, the increased labor supply can be expressed by a downward shift of the supply curve of the labor-intensive good, in relation to the relative price of this good (Figure 2.8). The relative price of the labor-intensive good 2 is $p_2/p_1 = 1/p$, which is the reciprocal value of the relative price of good 1 that has been used as a numeraire. With a given relative price OW there is an excess supply TW of good 2. Therefore, this cannot be an equilibrium and the relative price $1/p$ must fall to OW'.

When determining the new equilibrium point W' it must be taken into account that besides the additional supply or production effect an income effect is relevant as well. The income effect results from the rise in world domestic product. This means that income increases and that the demand for good 2 rises (the demand curve moves upwards). Assuming that the production effect dominates the income effect, the excess demand curve moves downwards and the relative price changes to the disadvantage of the labor-intensively produced good and in favor of the non-labor-intensively produced good.

Equilibrium in the industrializing and the industrial country

In order to show the adjustment process in separate regions of the world economy, let us divide the world into relatively capital-abundant industrialized

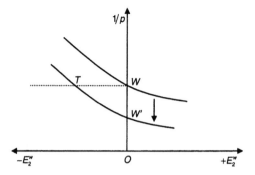

Figure 2.8 Increased labor supply and relative price.

countries and newly industrializing countries with relative labor abundance such as China. According to their comparative advantage, the industrial countries export the capital-intensively produced good 1 and import good 2. For the representative industrializing country the increased labor supply means that its terms of trade improve (p rises). The situation analyzed here differs from the oil crises of the 1970s. There is not a shortage of an important foreign production factor, with the supply deficit negatively affecting the terms of trade of the industrialized country. Instead labor supply increases.

The industrial country specializes even further in the production of the capital-intensive good. The point of production moves from P to P' (Figure 2.9a). The new trade triangle indicates the more favorable terms of trade. The country reaches a higher utility level (the indifference curve in point C' is further away from the origin than the indifference curve in point C).

The newly industrializing country (China) gains as well. Its terms of trade $p_2^*/p_1^* = 1/p^*$ improve. It moves its production from P^* in autarky (Figure 2.9b) to $P^{*'}$ and reaches consumption point $C^{*'}$ (higher than C^*). Note that demand for the labor-intensive product is increased, that more of this good is produced and that wages rise in the newly industrializing country.

Equilibrium with a third labor-abundant country

Consider now a third group of countries: the newly industrializing countries without China, for instance Bangladesh. They export labor-intensively produced goods and now have to face competition from the newcomer China (Figure 2.9c). The terms of trade p_2^{**}/p_1^{**} of this group of countries decrease; they respond by moving their production point from P^{**} to $P^{**'}$. Note that the trade triangles of this group of countries ($P^{**}B^{**}C^{**}$) and of the industrialized countries (PCB) must be identical in the initial situation, if China is assumed to not have traded in the initial situation.

If we do not only look at an isolated labor supply increase, other factors can increase real income position of this group of newly industrializing countries; for example, if there is technological progress in the production of the export good 2 or if demand for the export good of the newly industrializing countries increases strongly owing to world economic growth.

The volume effect

An important aspect of a new equilibrium is the volume effect of the larger world market. Since real income in the developing countries will rise when they participate in the international division of labor, their import demand for the products of industrial countries will increase. This stimulates the industrial countries' exports. This volume effect is an important element of the gains from trade, which arises in addition to the specialization effect; it improves the industrial countries' terms of trade. To take an example: when the Iron Curtain fell, Germany very quickly exported about 10 percent of its exports to the transformation countries in Central and Eastern Europe, as much as to the US. The volume effect is also highly relevant in the case of China, whose demand for investment and agricultural products as well as for energy and natural resources represents a demand stimulus for other countries.

Adjustment of production quantities and factor demand

Globalization does not only mean that segmentations of product markets are reduced and that the law of one price for goods is getting more relevant. In addition, the factor markets are also moving closer together. At any rate, this is valid for production factors that are mobile internationally, but it can be shown that the law of one price is also valid for the immobile factors including labor. This result is brought about by trade.

Given a set of assumptions, factor prices will be brought in line with each other by trade, even if the factors are internationally immobile. Again, we start with the assumption that important population-abundant regions of the world are integrated into the international division of labor. This is equivalent to an increase of the world factor supply. In Figure 2.10, the rectangle $OCO'B$ characterizes the factor endowment of the world (industrialized countries plus developing countries) before the integration of labor-abundant Central and Eastern Europe, China, and India. In this endowment box (Edgeworth box), the slopes of the lines k_1 and k_2 show the capital intensities of the two sectors 1 and 2. The capital intensity defines how many units of capital are used per unit of labor in the production of a good. These factor intensities are determined by the wage-interest ratio, that is by the factor price ratio. The lengths of the lines (OW and OZ) are proportional to the production volumes of the two goods.

By integrating new labor-abundant regions into the world economy the factor endowment box of the world is enlarged by the rectangle $O'DO''E$. If we assume that the wage-interest ratio – and along with it the factor intensities – remain constant, then the additional labor supply causes an extension of the production of good 2 from Z to Z'. The production of the capital-intensive good is reduced from point W to W'. If we only take an increase of the labor supply into

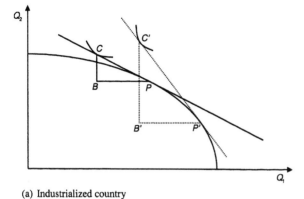

(a) Industrialized country

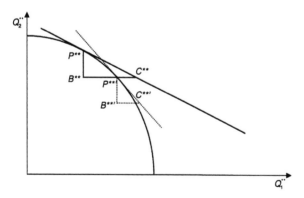

(b) Newly industrialized country (China)

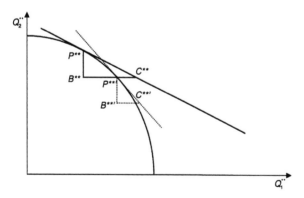

(c) Newly industrialized country (without China)

Figure 2.9 Increased labor supply and welfare in industrialized and newly indus-
     trializing countries.

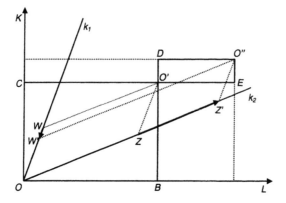

Figure 2.10 A change in factor endowment.

account (and not an increase of the capital supply as well), then, if a constant relative price of the goods is assumed, the production of the capital-intensive good will clearly decrease. This is the Rybczinski theorem. If the regions that have been newly integrated into the world economy possess a capital stock in addition to their labor supply, the change in the production of good 1 is not clear if a constant relative price of the goods is assumed. However, as the newly integrated region is relatively labor-abundant compared to the rest of the world, the relative production Q_1/Q_2 falls (from OW:*OZ* to *OW′:OZ′*).

Adjustment of relative factor prices

Until now our argument has followed the Rybczinski theorem and assumed that the wage-interest ratio remains constant. This implies that the capital intensities in both sectors remain constant, too. However, as shown above, an increase in the world labor supply results in an increase in the supply of the labor-intensive good 2. As a consequence, the price of good 2 must fall and the relative price p must rise. As the relative product price and the factor price ratio are connected with each other this means that the wage–interest ratio must fall (if good 2 is the labor-intensive good).

We can explain this relationship with the help of the Harrod–Johnson diagram which is based on the Heckscher–Ohlin model (Figure 2.11). Let us assume perfect competition and a linear–homogeneous production function. Then the capital intensity rises with an increasing wage–interest ratio. Labor will be replaced more and more by capital. This relationship is valid for both sectors. In Figure 2.11, sector 1 is more capital-intensive than sector 2. Let us assume that the wage–interest ratio rises. Then, the relative production costs for the labor-intensively produced good 2 increase. Consequently, the relative price p of the capital-intensively produced good falls.

We can also argue in another way: let us assume that demand changes in favor of good 2. This increases the incentive to produce more of the labor-

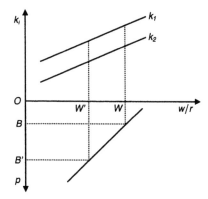

Figure 2.11 Commodity price ratio and factor price ratio.

intensive good 2. Demand for labor increases and the wage–interest ratio rises. Therefore, the Harrod–Johnson diagram has the shape that is shown in the lower part of Figure 2.11. These relationships are valid in both countries, because we assume that the same technology is used everywhere.

The distance *OW* in Figure 2.11 characterizes the wage-interest ratio in the world economy in the initial position. This wage–interest ratio corresponds to the commodity price ratio *OB*. If the labor supply in the world increases when labor-abundant countries are integrated into the international division of labor, the labor-abundant countries find it favorable to produce more of the labor-intensive good. For the capital-abundant country it is favorable to specialize more strongly in the production of the capital-intensive good. On balance, the wage–interest ratio must fall to *OW'*. The relative price *p* rises to *OB'*, that is the labor-intensively produced good becomes relatively cheaper.

If the world market equilibrium is disturbed by an increase of the labor supply, the system will adjust until a new equilibrium is found. With the new uniform relative price, the world consumption point and the world production point on the world transformation curve are determined. It is further determined which commodities are traded between the different regions of the world, in this way evening out the differences in the factor endowments. The relative product price is determined on the product markets. The new factor price ratio is found as well, and the factor intensities that characterize production in the world are determined (Figure 2.12). In this way we have a new 'integrated' world market equilibrium. Note that in Figure 2.11 the slope of the curve between the relative product price and the relative factor price varies with the assumption which of the sectors is capital-intensive and which is labor-intensive. The slope of the curve is negative if our previous assumption on the capital intensity of the goods is reversed, i.e. if good 2 is assumed to be capital intensive and good 1 labor intensive.

We have shown that the wage rate in the newly integrated labor-abundant country (China) rises. Consequently, the real wage-interest ratio has to decline

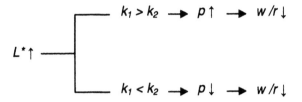

Figure 2.12 Chain of effects of an increased labor supply.

over-proportionally in the industrialized countries. The Harrod–Johnson diagram in Figure 2.11 can be redrawn for the two-country case. Then $p < p^*$ indicates a relative price advantage for the industrial countries in favor of the capital-intensively produced good and price advantage for industrializing country for the labor intensive product, i.e. $1/p^* < 1/p$. This corresponds to $1/r < 1^*/r^*$, i.e. a relative labor abundance for the industrializing country. In a new equilibrium, the relative product prices and the relative factor prices have to be equal.

Important aspects in economic reality

In reality, there will never be a perfect equalization of commodity prices and factor prices. There will always remain some potential arbitrage possibilities, because not all segmentations of markets will be eliminated. However, there is an ongoing process which tends to equalize relative prices. Besides remaining segmentations, other aspects have to be taken into consideration which are not included in the very simplified Heckscher–Ohlin model used here. This is true for the assumption of the same technology in the two regions of the world as well as for the assumption of homogeneous production factors. In the real world, countries have different technologies embodied in their capital stock. This means that some countries have a more efficient capital stock. This raises labor productivity in the industrial countries. Moreover, labor is not homogeneous, because in the real world labor represents different levels of technological knowledge (human capital). Therefore, labor productivity (for example, in the industrialized countries) is higher than elsewhere. Consequently, there cannot be a perfect wage equalization.

The approach used here looks only at a comparative-static change of an increased labor supply. Other approaches have to complement this picture. For example, the newly industrializing countries could succeed in building up a capital stock and in attracting capital and technology from abroad, which improves the productivity of labor, if they pursue a suitable policy. Then a growth process starts and, as a consequence, real income and real wages in the newly industrialized countries rise. This happens in addition to the effect of the increased demand for labor due to specialization in the newly industrialized countries. As empirical data show, real wages in these countries rise. For instance in China, real wages rose 12.9 percent per year in the period 2000–2004 (World Bank, Country Fact Sheet: *China*, December 2005).

Finally, the Heckscher–Ohlin approach merely explains the inter-sectoral division of labor. Under comparative-static conditions, one sector of a country expands, whereas the same sector of the other country shrinks. According to the paradigm of intra-industry trade, this need not be the case (see below).

Quantity adjustment with rigid factor prices

If the factor price ratio does not react to the changed scarcity conditions, the factor quantities, particularly employment (and unemployment), have to adapt. This is exactly what happens in the 'European' model of the labor market (or the 'Continental' model, as it applies especially in France, Germany, and Italy) with a relatively rigid wage rate. As a simplification, we look only at three regions of the world:

1   the labor-abundant countries that are newly taking part in the international division of labor, where the wage rate rises due to the specialization in labor-intensive products;
2   the US, where wages adapt flexibly so that full employment is achieved;
3   Continental Europe with its inflexible labor markets and a rigid relative factor price, where (as a consequence) the adjustment process is carried out via employment changes.

If there is an excess supply on the world labor market, this imbalance is 'corrected' by the price effect in the US and by the quantity effects in Europe. Figure 2.13a shows the European endowment box. The factor price ratio and therefore the factor intensities remain constant. Europe has to reduce the production of the labor-intensive product 2 by $H'F'$. If at the same time the capital-intensive production is expanded by HE, this results in unemployment EO'.

In contrast to the European model, the relative factor price adjusts in the American model (Figure 2.13b). Here, the wage–interest ratio (w/r) falls. The capital intensity in the two sectors decreases from k_1 (k_2) to k'_1 (k'_2) and full employment is reached. In reality, it is not the wage rate of all workers, but the wage of the less qualified that goes down.

2.4 The most important theorems

The adjustment process in the world economy can be summarized by the following theorems. Originally, these theorems were related to the transition from autarky to trade; in our context we apply these theorems to the change from an initial position with foreign trade to a new situation where an increased labor supply is integrated into the world economy. It is assumed that full employment is reached by flexible factor prices.

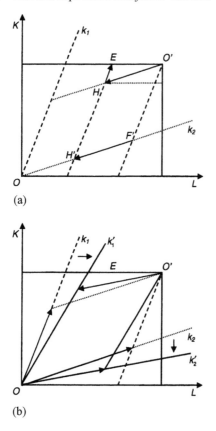

(a)

(b)

Figure 2.13 (a) The European model of unemployment (a) and the American model of employment (b).

- *Jevons's law of one price.* If transaction costs are left out of consideration, then there will be a uniform price for one good in the world market. The characteristics of the world market equilibrium is that the product markets are in equilibrium and that therefore the profit-maximizing product supply of firms corresponds to the utility-maximizing product demand of households. This equilibrium is established by a uniform relative price ratio.
- *Heckscher–Ohlin theorem.* A country has a comparative advantage to export the good that uses its relatively abundant factor of production intensively. An increased labor supply in a labor-abundant region of the world means that this region exports the labor-intensive good and expands the production of this good; the capital-abundant region exports the capital-intensive good and expands the production of that good.
- *Gains from trade.* A country entering the international division of labor and opening up has gains from trade, i.e. from specializing on the production of the good with a comparative advantage. It reaches a higher utility level due

to two effects: its terms of trade improve and the volume of trade increases (the trade triangle becomes larger).

The other countries already participating in the international division of labor and trading with the newcomer will also gain by specializing on products for which they have a comparative advantage. For them, the world market is enlarged. Their terms of trade improve. Countries already participating in the international division of labor and producing the same product set as the entrant are likely to experience a loss, unless they are compensated by a rise in demand due to the volume effect caused by the entrant.

- *Rybczynski theorem.* With given relative product prices, the increase of a factor supply leads to an increase in the production of the good whose production is relatively intensive in that factor. This result illustrates one aspect of the Heckscher–Ohlin theorem. The incidence of an exogenous increase of a production factor is described by a partial equilibrium analysis.

- *Stolper–Samuelson theorem.* The rise of the relative price of one good results in an increase of the real price of the factor that is used intensively in the production of that good. The real price of the other factor falls. In the labor-abundant region of the world, the demand for labor increases and the wage rate rises. In the capital-abundant industrialized nations, the real interest rate rises and the real wage falls. The income share of labor in the labor-abundant region rises. In the typical industrialized country, the income share of capital increases.

- *Factor price equalization theorem.* Trade of final products leads to a complete equalization of relative factor prices. The real factor prices adjust as well. Relative product prices adjust. The labor-abundant country exports more labor-intensive products and this drives up wages. The capital-abundant country exports more capital-intensive products and this drives up the interest rate.

2.5 Demand shifts and world market equilibrium

If the preferences in the world move in favor of one of the goods, this will have an impact on the trade equilibrium. Let us assume that a change in preferences in favor of good 1 disturbs the old equilibrium at point G (Figure 2.14). At the old relative price (p: OG), excess demand in the world for good 1 is positive (GG'), the market is not cleared. Point G', reflecting the increased preferences, cannot be realized. Since there is a positive excess demand $E_1^W(p) > 0$ in G', the relative price of good 1 must rise in order to reduce demand for good 1 and increase the production incentive for this good. A new equilibrium will be realized at point G''.

In this new equilibrium the relative price p is higher. If we assume good 1 to be the capital-intensively produced good, then the wage–interest ratio must fall correspondingly. The income share of labor declines.

A similar effect as a preference shift in favor of a commodity is an increase in world income, including a rise in income in the newly integrated regions. This

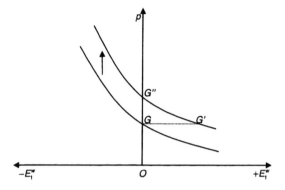

Figure 2.14 Demand shift and international trade.

income effect depends on the income elasticity of the product in question; if this elasticity is positive, the income effect implies an increase in the price of commodity 1.

Case study: China's impact in the market for natural resources

In the world market for raw materials, natural resources and agricultural products, China with 1.3 billion people and high annual real GDP growth rates of nearly 10 percent in the last twenty years has a strong impact. For instance, with a sturdy increase in investment in equipment and in buildings China developed a huge appetite for steel, accounting for 27 percent of the world's steel consumption in 2003. This share was at 17 percent in 1992. About 60 percent of the increase in the world's steel consumption in 2005 was attributed to China. The implication of such an increase in demand is that other countries experience a price increase for steel and related products, for instance coke. Thus, the price of steel scrap, around US$100 per ton in the period 1999–2002, rose to US$250 in 2003 when China strongly increased its imports. New demand drives out old demand. China's petroleum consumption stands at about 8 percent of the world's consumption. Its cotton consumption is 27 percent of global consumption, for wheat the percentage is 17 percent. It imports about 35 of the world's soybeans imports.

China also has an impact on a resource for which a scarcity price has not yet been established globally; the environment. China produces 4.5 billion tons of CO_2 (2004), more than the EU-25 with about 3.6 billion tons, and less than the US with seven billion tons. It has doubled its CO_2 emissions since 1980. If a global price for CO_2 emissions would exist, it would be apparent that China drives up the scarcity price of using the environment.

The general phenomenon behind the China case is that economic growth in the developing countries will increase the demand for raw materials, energy, and agricultural products. This will raise the price of these products, partly crowding out the demand of other users, including the industrial economies. Population growth will have the same effect.

2.6 An alternative approach: Intra-sector trade

In the philosophy of the Heckscher–Ohlin approach, trade is explained as exchanging different goods against each other, for instance textiles from the developing country against machinery from the industrial country, or oil from the resource country against fancy consumer durables. Economic reality, however, shows us that that the overwhelming part of trade occurs between high-income countries and is of a different nature than the one described above. French cars are exchanged against Italian cars, Korean IT products against US IT products, German machinery against Japanese machinery. This is trade with similar products, i.e. in the same sector, of course with different individuals as buyers (intra-sector trade). This type of trade is observed between high-income countries because high-income people love product variety. Besides differences in consumer preferences, this approach has assumptions on the production process that are different from the Heckscher–Ohlin model. Most importantly, the implications for the world economy differ.

Imperfect competition

Until now the analysis has been characterized by the assumption of perfect competition: market participants on the world product markets are so numerous that the individual firm in a country cannot influence the price and must accept it as given. This premise becomes doubtful if the average costs of production fall with an increased quantity of production and if product preferences bring about specific market segments.

Increasing returns to scale

Constant average costs are the result of constant returns to scale, i.e. of a linear-hogeneous production function. By multiplying the use of all production factors by a factor λ (for example by 2), the production result is also multiplied by λ (for example by 2). If the production activity is compared to putting a flower in a flowerpot, then any number of flowerpots can be put side by side, and the production is multiplied according to the number of flowerpots. Adding an identical second factory to an existing factory therefore leads to a doubling of output. This relationship no longer holds if there are increasing returns to scale, i.e. if $Q\lambda^\alpha = F(\lambda K, \lambda L)$ with $\alpha > 1$. Then a doubling of the inputs multiplies output by more than 2. Therefore, in the case of increasing returns to scale the production becomes less costly if the quantity produced increases. The firm moves downwards along the falling average costs curve (Figure 2.15).

Increasing returns to scale or falling average costs can be explained, for example, by a learning curve (learning by doing). Empirical studies, e.g. for the construction of large airplanes, show a learning rate of 0.2, which means that unit costs are reduced by 20 percent if the accumulated output is doubled. But falling average costs are also caused by production processes requiring a minimum input of production factors, for example, because the input of capital must exceed a minimum size due to the characteristics of the production process. In all these cases, there are fixed costs of production which are more profitably spread over the units of output with an increased production quantity. Falling average costs may apply to specific production units (e.g. the shop level) or they may appear on the plant level because with several shops it is possible to fragment the production process or to have a better risk-spreading. Finally, increasing returns to scale can be linked to the firm level; minimum advertising budgets for building up a reputation for a product or better liquidity can be mentioned as examples.

Increasing returns to scale can also be explained by positive spillovers. Let K^j, L^j represent factor inputs of firm j. Then output Q^j of firm j may also depend on the capital stock K of the industry (of all the firms) with $Q^j = F^j(K^j, L^j)?K^\zeta$; where K may represent the capital stock as a measure of accumulated experience from learning by doing or knowledge capital. ζ indicates the impact of the industry's capital stock on a firm's output. Whereas the part F^j of the production function may be linear-homogeneous, the function as a whole can exhibit economies of scale. The marginal productivity of capital in firm j then also depends on the industry factor K with $F_K^j(K^j, K)$.

According to this approach, the spatial dimension of knowledge capital is an important question:

1   If it is industry-specific, each firm of an industry in a country benefits from the knowledge capital of other firms in the same industry.

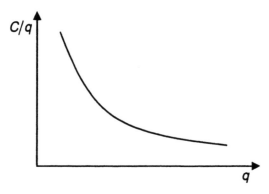

Figure 2.15 Falling average costs.

2   If it is localized, then firms in a region benefit from the knowledge capital accumulated in the region, but knowledge capital may extend to many sectors. An example is a qualified regional labor pool as in the Swiss Jura where the clock industry built up the dexterity of people that could later on be used by light metal industry. Similar phenomenon could be observed in the clock industry of the Black forest.
3   Spillovers may also occur worldwide. Then K relates to knowledge capital existing in the whole world.

Increasing returns to scale and falling average costs imply that perfect competition changes into imperfect competition: a firm may become a monopolist or an oligopolistic structure may arise.

The limits of increasing returns to scale

The argument of increasing returns to scale should not be overestimated. It should not be forgotten that central planning in Eastern Europe was based on the supposed supremacy of increasing returns to scale; the idea was to exploit the falling costs, for instance by producing refrigerators in one plant for the whole COMECON. In the end, this strategy to make use of increasing returns to scale failed. There are quite a few reasons why increasing returns to scale do not grow without limit. With larger organizational units, flexibility will be lost and management costs will rise. Moreover, important restrictions can weaken the advantages of large dimensions, for example missing opportunities to expand at the actual location or a lack of employees with the necessary qualifications. In the end, missing competition leads to a loss of efficiency.

Case study: the international division of labor in central planning

In the times of central planning in the Soviet bloc, the international division of labor was not left to a bottom-up process of a competitive process. Trade flows were decided centrally by international agreement. The general idea was to exploit economies of scale in production to ensure low prices. The basic assumption was that producing refrigerators in one plant of the COMECON (Council for Mutual Economic Assistance) would drive down production costs. Thus Hungarians produced autobuses, Czechs streetcars and East Germans wagons for the Trans-Siberian Railroad. The specialization could not be based on labor costs which was the underlying Marxian theory of value these days. It was influenced by expected production costs and had to be integrated into the nation's central planning. Moreover, specialization was determined by political considerations. Although the COMECON countries could observe scarcity prices in the world economy, they did not apply the correct scarcity prices. The most important drawback was that central planning and economic cooperation took the place of a competitive process. Thus, the system did not have incentives to find better solutions. Countries such as Hungary eventually became more and more oriented to the international market and tried to introduce international scarcity prices. But these approaches could not reform the COMECON until it finally collapsed in the late 1980s.

Different product preferences

Apart from increasing returns to scale, product preferences are a second reason why world markets can be imperfect. People do not have the same preferences everywhere. They do not all want to consume the same homogeneous product. Thus, China eventually got rid of the Mao look. These product preferences mean that market segments are defined by households with a preference for a specific product. Consumers are prepared to pay a relatively higher price for the specific good they want best ('ideal variety'). We can arrange households a–h along a commodity axis indicating proximity or distance between goods according to individual preferences (Figure 2.16). Assume all households have the same income. Then the continuum a–h indicates the demand side of a market with different product preferences. Consider two firms x and y which produce goods c and g. Firm x may also cater for preferences a, b, d, and e, but it cannot produce these goods with the same quality c; it may compete with firm y with respect to products e and f. Depending on the average cost curve of firms and on distance costs in terms of product quality, firms may serve a larger or a smaller market segment. In reality, preferences of consumers may be concentrated on some goods. Also, goods with similar characteristics may be easily substituted against each other so that they form a cluster of relatively similar goods. On the commodity axis, there may be substitution gaps between groups of goods; according to preferences, goods may not be sufficient substitutes. Consequently, the market form of imperfect competition prevails under such conditions.

The importance of intra-sector trade

The combined effect of economies of scale and preferences for different goods on the size of markets is ambiguous. Economies of scale pull in the direction of large markets because average costs fall; preferences for different products pull in the other direction working towards market niches for specific products and for market segmentation. This means that extremely large production units are not necessarily the outcome of both forces. This also has implications for location and trade.

While increasing returns to scale work towards a situation where the production would be concentrated at a few places or even at one single spot, product preferences have the consequence that market segments are defined and that

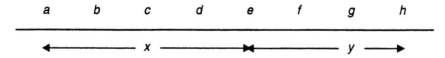

Figure 2.16 Commodity axis and firms.

these market segments limit the exploitation of increasing returns to scale. Product preferences of consumers thus prevent production from concentrating in a single spot; on the contrary, they cause production to be spread over many firms and thus over a wide area. Then, intra-sectoral trade takes place because the individual firms, each filling a certain market segment, produce for their own country as well as for abroad. Exploiting increasing returns to scale is limited by the demand for different product varieties and distance costs.

A significant part of the product flows between countries with a high per capita income is not an exchange of products between different sectors, but exchange within the same sector. It can be argued that the love for variety increases with per capita income. Increasing returns to scale and product preferences are two reasons why we can observe such intra-industry or intra-sector trade.

More than half of the trade between the industrialized nations is intra-sector trade. With a wide delimitation of sectors on the two-digit level, intra-industry trade reaches 75 percent for Germany and 61 percent for the US (Table 2.1). It explains a little less than half the trade of Japan. On the three digit-level, the coefficients are only slightly smaller. Historically, intra-industry trade has grown strongly. In the German case, the coefficient has increased from 0.41 in 1961 to 0.75 in 2004. With a rise in income, an increasing importance of the intra-industry trade can be observed. This is also observed in the case of regional integrations like the European Union. Note that the coefficient for a sector becomes zero if the sector is a pure export sector ($Im_i = 0$) or a pure export sector ($X_i = 0$). It is zero for the whole economy if all sectors have intersector trade. It is 1 if the export value of a sector corresponds to its import value.

Table 2.1 Intra-industry trade[a]

	1961	*1971*	*1981*	*1991*	*1996*	*2001*	*2004*
US	0.4695	0.5271	0.4953	0.6556	0.6721	0.6615	0.6160
Germany	0.4102	0.5735	0.6115	0.7500	0.7277	0.7434	0.7464
Japan	0.2453[b]	0.2743	0.2010	0.3385	0.4310	0.4704	0.4572[c]

Source: OECD, *International Trade by Commodities Statistics, CD-Rom.*

Note
a Intra-industry trade of each country with the world, calculated with the Grubel–Lloyd index (*GL*), two-digit level $GL = [\Sigma_i[(Ex_i + Im_i) - |Ex_i - Im_i|]/\Sigma_i (Ex_i + Im_i)]$.
b 1962.
c 2003

An additional theorem

The analysis presented in this section allows us to add an important theorem to the list of the previous theorems.

- *Intra-sector trade.* When we allow for love of variety of consumers (and of firms) and also for economies of scale in production with imperfect competition, countries gain from exchanging similar products. Increased trade does not require sectors to shrink in the same way they do in the Heckscher–Ohlin context. Since the love for variety increases with higher income, high-income countries have more intra-sector trade. With growing income, developing countries will more and more be able to participate and to benefit from this type of trade.

Two different approaches to explaining trade

So far, we have discussed two very different approaches to explaining the international exchange of goods. The hypothesis of the inter-industry trade in the sense of the Heckscher–Ohlin approach explains the exchange of different goods, the exchange of wine and cloth, or of crude oil and machines, that is the trade between sectors. Against this background, trade is therefore predominantly dependent on the differences in the production conditions, especially the factor endowments. The hypothesis of intra-industry trade, on the other hand, emphasizes the exchange of similar products, for example the exchange of certain cars for different cars or of a certain wine for different wine. Here, trade is based on increasing returns to scale in the production process and on differences in product preferences; different consumers want different products.

The perspective of intra-industry trade increases the acceptance of the international division of labor: while in the inter-industry approach, countries can only gain advantage from the international division of labor by allowing sectors with a relative price disadvantage in the country to shrink, intra-industry trade means that the same sector can expand in different countries owing to an intensified division of labor. Although an individual branch must also shrink in this approach, other branches of the same sector can grow. This makes adjustments less painful. Specifically, the impact for labor is different. Employment or wages in a specific sector do not have to decline with more trade.

The most important implication of the intra-sector approach is that with rising income in the developing countries, intra-industry trade will play a larger role in the world economy. This means that both the developing countries and the industrial countries can move on a higher level of welfare without the necessity of shrinking sectors.

2.7 Contestable markets

Monopolies and international oligopolies

Increasing returns to scale mean that, in theory, large production facilities arise. This implies at the extreme that single suppliers (monopolies) or few suppliers (oligopolies) will prevail. Oligopolistic firms can either be in a Cournot quantity competition (with, as a rule, a homogeneous product) or in a Bertrand price competition (with a heterogeneous product). In this context, the assumptions about the strategy variable of a supplier, especially how he or she reacts to the actions of the other supplier, is relevant. In the Cournot quantity oligopoly, each supplier takes the quantity supplied by the other producer as given and decides on its own supply quantity. In the Bertrand oligopoly, the price of the other suppliers is taken as given and then one decides on one's own price. In a two-stage game, the production capacity is determined first; then price competition starts. Oligopolistic market forms are the starting point for strategic trade policy (Chapter 14).

Barriers to market entry

Most of the capital that has been invested in a firm is no longer malleable and cannot be used in any other way. This capital represents sunk costs. Firms that are established on a market have two strategic advantages in comparison with a potential newcomer: as part of their capital used has sunk, they no longer necessarily have to take these capital costs into account in order to calculate their prices. The new entrant, however, must first of all incur these fixed costs before he can actually enter the market. Sunk costs give the established firm a short-term competitive advantage. Apart from sunk costs, the established enterprise can have an advantage because it has gained production experience and has already moved downwards on the average costs curve, e.g. owing to learning effects. This stresses the advantage of an early start. Enterprises that are established early on the world market have the opportunity to gain experience, to make use of learning effects and to attain lower average costs with their accumulated production.

The contestability of markets

Markets are contestable in the sense that a market entry of a new supplier could be imminent. This limits the maneuvering space of an incumbent firm in its price setting. In Figure 2.17 the position of a monopolistic supplier with a falling average cost curve is shown. If the firm is in a monopolistic position it may produce at point M on its average cost curve with a monopoly profit MF. Point M is determined by marginal revenue (not shown in Figure 2.17) and marginal costs being equal. If a newcomer enters the market, the firm can no longer capture demand DD alone. For the monopolistic supplier, the demand function rotates downward to $D'D'$. If the market is sufficiently contestable, profit will be driven to zero (point S').

Whereas the established supplier does not have to consider his sunk costs in the short term and has an advantage to a new supplier who must finance the use of fixed capital, there are no sunk costs in the long-term. That is because in the long-term the established firm must renew its capital. Then it has to decide whether to redirect the earned depreciations to another investment purpose. This means that the renewal of the depreciated capital must pay off. Besides sunk costs, a newcomer must take into account the lower average costs of the incumbent supplier owing to the production experience it has gained. But if the established firm exceeds its scope for setting its price, a newcomer can successfully enter the market. Therefore the established enterprise is restricted in the use of its monopoly position by the imminent market entry of a potential competitor. In addition, it is possible for the newcomer to undermine the pre-eminence of the established enterprise with a better technology. An example are Apple, Microsoft, and other software and PC firms with respect to the dominant player IBM in the 1970s. Meanwhile IBM has sold its notebooks to Lenovo. Another example are the new suppliers of mobile telephone services with respect to the incumbents with stationary technology.

It is difficult to come up with examples for monopolistic or oligopolistic world product markets that are actually not contestable. Unambiguously there is an dyopoly with high barriers to enter the market in the construction of large-capacity airplanes with the two suppliers Airbus and Boeing-McDonnell-Douglas (the latter came into existence by a merger in 1996). Other world markets, however, can be characterized as contestable markets; for example, the world automobile market or the semiconductor market. It is important to note that the lifespan of the products has decreased significantly, for instance in the semiconductor market. This implies that for new entrants market entry is easier and competition is intensified.

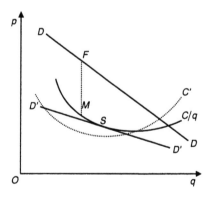

Figure 2.17 The incumbent and the newcomer.

Case study: the world car market

The world car market can be considered to be a contestable market with some oligopolistic structure. The production process is well known, but cost cutting is possible and product quality can be improved. Firms traditionally first serve their home market and then the foreign markets. If one looks at the number of cars produced in 2004, five firms cover 61 percent of the market, namely General Motors (17), Ford (14), Toyota (12), Volkswagen (10) and DaimlerChrysler (8). In 2005, Toyota overtook the American producers putting General Motors in the second rank.

The global car market is characterized by remarkable changes. Most of the firms of the industrial countries lost market share. General Motors had a share of 23 percent in 1999, Ford 17 percent. New suppliers from Korea entered the world market, cars are now produced in nearly all larger countries and soon China will be competitive as an exporter. The dominance of the Japanese car producers in the early 1990s was countered by the American and German producers with an improved product and with innovations of the production process, including the integration of IT software. Firms also attempted to increase their profitability by mergers and acquisitions, to some extent with limited success. Moreover, car producers in the industrial countries sliced up the value added chain by outsourcing and off-shoring and by optimizing the networks with their input suppliers, reducing costs. The car industry thus is an example of the continuous change in the world economy, including the shift of competitiveness of locations and the spatial reorganization of the production process. It also is a demonstration of imperfect competition where the love for variety of consumers plays an important role and allows firms to produce for their specific market segments.

Case study: the pharmaceutical market

The pharmaceutical market has sales of about US$0.5 trillion worldwide (2005) with the main sector being ethical products, including typical medicinal products such as antibiotics, cardiovascular drugs and lifestyle pharmaceuticals (sales data from industry). The other sectors are generic pharmaceuticals, i.e. substitutes of existing products, over the counter products and biopharmaceuticals. The top ten companies cover 46 percent of the world market, 70 percent of the ethical products. North America represents about half the world market, Europe one-fourth, Japan about one-eighth. China as well as India are not only important sources for raw materials used in the pharmaceutical industry but are gaining importance as sites for research and development and as customers.

High research and development expenditures to find new products characterize the pharmaceutical industry which is a knowledge driven industry. It spends about 16 percent of revenue for R&D and is highly innovative with about fifteen breakthrough innovations each year. Biotechnological knowledge is an important leverage for new entrants to find new biopharmaceuticals and for structural change of the industry. It is expensive to finance the research program and the necessary worldwide advertising campaign to market a product. Products are typically patented and there is limited time to use the market potential since the patent is usually granted for twenty years, a period of time which begins with the first test of a substance. International property rights as defined in the WTO framework are important conditions. New products have to be licensed by the regulatory authorities, for instance the Food and Drug Administration in the US. Governmental regulation, institutional arrangements of the health sector, for instance buying power of governments and health maintenance organization, the increasing role of generic substitutes and the emergence of biopharmaceuticals and genome revolution are the typical phenomena of the industry.

The biggest players are Pfizer with a turnover of US$52.5 billion in 2004 and an R&D spending of US$7.7 billion, Johnson and Johnson US$47.3 billion (R&D spending of US$5.2 billion), Bayer with a turnover pf US$39.2 billion, Glaxo-Smith-Kline with US$38.2 billion, Sanofi-Aventis US$33.4 billion and Novartis US$28.2 billion. Traditional chemical enterprises such as BASF no longer have the expertise to develop the new line of pharmaceutical products; they cannot finance the huge entry costs including R&D and marketing the new products. Although research costs are very high, the pharmaceutical industry is one of the most profitable ones where a company like Pfizer made a profit of US$11.4 billion in 2004.

The race for the technological lead

Markets are also contestable if enterprises compete for new knowledge, i.e. if they engage in a research and development race (Grossman and Helpman 1991a). Enterprises of individual countries try hard to find new products and new production technologies by means of research and development in order to become the market leader in the corresponding markets. Research and development may be interpreted either as an independent industry or as an element of industrial firms of the high-technology field. The output of the research and development industry, i.e. new products and new technology, can be regarded as an input to the manufacturing industry. The research and development process is driven by the profit prospects in the industry. This means that new technological knowledge is generated in a competitive process. Technological progress is endogenous, being the result of competition.

In such an approach, firms compete with their research and development expenditures for world market shares. This has implications for trade. The manufacturing industry can be subdivided in this context into a high-technology field and a traditional industry. The high-technology industry is characterized by the market form of an international oligopoly with profit prospects owing to technological leads or by the market form of monopolistic competition, whereas the traditional industry can be characterized by perfect competition with constant returns to scale. While in the high-technology field essentially intra-industry trade takes place, the traditional industry is the basis for inter-industry trade. Besides inter-industry and intra-industry trade, international trade also encompasses the exchange of technological knowledge.

2.8 Other relevant empirical phenomena

Trade in Services

Export products are usually conceived as consumer or investment goods being produced in the manufacturing sector. This notion forgets that the service sector plays a huge role in modern economies, accounting for about 70 percent of the high-income countries' GDP (see Chapter 1). Whereas some services are local and non-tradable, others are border-crossing. The export of tradable services can be explained by similar models as the export of commodities, depending on production costs, accumulated experience, preferences, income levels, and market structures. The main difference to the trade of products is that tradable services are quite a different output of the production process than commodities. They come in a variety of forms, as person-embodied or person-disembodied services, or in the forms of cross-border supply, consumption abroad, commercial presence, and presence of natural persons (see Chapter 1). In the production of tradable services, the human factor and knowledge play an important role in establishing a comparative advantage. Under that limit, both the Heckscher–Ohlin approach and the intra-sector model of trade with imperfect competition can explain the trade in services. A country with a comparative advantage in new technologies, for instance in IT, will also be able to export services in this area. A similar argument applies to countries with important financial centers as New York or London or with a strong insurance industry. Similarly, the acceptance of the Anglo-Saxon law for international contracts or the Anglo-Saxon dominance of the movie or music industry play a role.

Empirically, the importance of export of services differs a lot between countries. For the US, services account for 29 percent of their exports (2004); this share is even higher for the UK with 35 percent, possibly due to financial services. In contrast, services account for 15 percent of French and 13 percent of German exports. These figures reflect the importance of the service sector in the Anglo-Saxon economies.

Tradable versus non-tradable goods

Apart from internationally tradable goods there are non-tradable goods, i.e. goods which – by definition – must be produced in the country where they are consumed. For these goods there can be only a national (or regional) market equilibrium; national excess demand or national excess supply do not represent feasible equilibria. If we combine the export goods and the import substitutes of a country into a composite tradable good (which is possible if the relative price between the export goods and the import substitutes remains constant), then an economy can produce tradable (Q_T) and non-tradable (Q_{NT}) goods as shown by a transformation curve (*TT* in Figure 2.18). If the relative price p_T/p_{NT} between tradable and non-tradable goods is given (by tan α), then the point of production *P* is determined as the tangential point of the relative price line and the trans-formation curve. The market equilibrium for non-tradable goods requires that the quantity supplied (*OB*) corresponds to the quantity demanded. This is the case for the straight line *BD* in Figure 2.18. If the country obtains a credit *PD* from abroad (budget line *p′*) it can realize a higher point of consumption on the straight line *BD*. Note that in this diagram a trade triangle cannot be drawn.

Globalization applies only to the goods that are tradable. Globalization is not valid for the non-tradable goods that are produced for purely national (or regional) demand. Here international competition can only have indirect effects; in fact, there are two relationships. First: non-tradable goods define the opportunity costs of the tradable goods, because they attract production factors that could otherwise be used for the production of the tradable goods. If the pref-erence for non-tradable goods increases, the production point *P* moves to the left, and therefore fewer production factors are available for tradable goods. Depending on the factor intensity of the non-tradable goods, there are effects on the comparative advantages of the country. Second: owing to decreasing trans-port costs and declining barriers to trade, more non-tradable goods turn into tradable goods; thus goods that were previously non-tradable can be exported owing to lower transport and communication costs. This is even the case for a whole lot of disembodied services (like engineering services). Therefore,

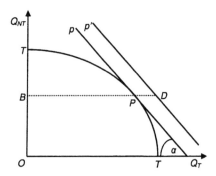

Figure 2.18 Relative price between tradable and non-tradable goods.

globalization means that the line of distinction between tradable and non-tradable goods is shifted. This implies that the transformation curve is moved outward with a bias: the area of Q_{NT} shrinks and the area of Q_T expands (this effect is not shown in Figure 2.18).

Hierarchy versus markets

Goods and resources can be allocated through markets or within firms. Markets can replace firms; that is, there are hierarchies or vertical integrations. A firm can be interpreted as a network of explicit and implicit contracts that combines different production factors. Following institutional economics, a firm can also be defined as an organizational unit with lower transaction costs than on markets: a transaction will be carried out within a firm if the transaction costs within the firm are lower than on the markets. The dividing line between firms and the market therefore is determined by the level of the transaction costs.

Firms can be integrated vertically by including production levels that precede or follow the production process within the firms. They take advantage of backward and forward linkages, i.e. the value-added chain. For example, the large crude oil companies (the 'seven sisters') were integrated vertically before the first oil crisis in 1973; concession contracts, often for a period of fifty to seventy years, guaranteed their access to the natural resources, also to the undiscovered resources of the resource countries. The firms had transport capacities at their disposal, and they owned refineries and distribution networks in the industrialized countries. In the 1970s, the extraction rights were passed to the resource countries and therefore the vertical integration of the enterprises was broken up. The spot markets (for example, in Rotterdam) gained in importance and forward markets were established. Markets replaced vertically integrated firms.

2.9 The changing pattern of world trade

Shifting comparative advantage and relocation

In the course of time, location conditions and therefore trade flows change. Different mechanisms are responsible for this effect: some economies, for instance the newly industrializing countries, succeed in improving their factor endowments (acquired comparative advantage instead of natural comparative advantage). For example, the savings rate and the investment rate of some newly industrializing countries of South-East Asia amount to 30 percent or more, resulting in a strong increase of the capital stock. Apart from physical capital, also the endowment with human capital can be strengthened in the course of time, by investing in education. As a third factor, the infrastructure can be improved by building new roads, airports, and better telephone networks. In addition, the diffusion of new knowledge causes an improvement of the locational conditions in developing countries.

At the same time, processes take place in the industrialized countries that reduce the competitiveness of some sectors. The desire for a higher labor income causes some labor-intensive products to become unprofitable. The extension of the social security systems leads to a rise of labor costs. Moreover, a society can get lethargic: for example, people could shy away from taking entrepreneurial risks or from opening the educational system to competition.

Export structure and market share of countries

If we aggregate a country's position on all these specific world product markets of the world we obtain a picture of a country's specialization. This includes information on whether a country is heavily specialized on a few specific export goods and thus is exposed to risks in these markets or whether its product structure of exports is more evenly balanced thus spreading the export risk

Information on the export structure may also relate to the issue whether exports are in the high-tech, medium-tech or low-tech category. Technology intensity is defined as a part of R&D expenditure relative to product sales (high tech: >10; medium tech: 4.9–0.9; low tech: <0.7). Figure 2.19 exhibits this information for the US, Germany, Japan, France, and the United Kingdom. The export position has been calculated using RCA coefficients, i.e. revealed comparative advantages.[1] The US strongly specializes in high-tech exports (2004). France and the United Kingdom also have a revealed comparative advantage in this area. Germany and Japan have their comparative advantage in medium-tech

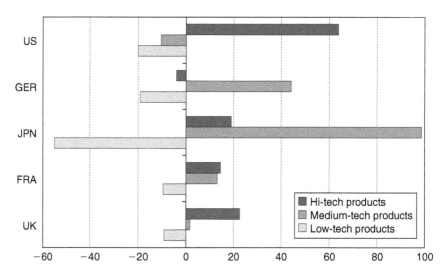

Figure 2.19 Technology intensity[a] and comparative advantage, 2004 (source: Siebert 2005b: Table 3.4, updated with OECD 2005, ITCS International Trade by Commodities Statistics).

Notes

a RCA indices according to technology intensity.

products; Japan also has an advantage in high-tech goods. Compared to 1999, Japan has gained a comparative advantage in high tech, Germany has reduced its disadvantage.

Exports and the real exchange rate

Exports are influenced by many factors such as the income level and income growth abroad and the business cycle. A crucial determinant is the exchange rate (e) which we have defined as the price of the foreign currency: how many units of the home currency, for instance euro (€), have to be given up for one unit of US-dollar ($), i.e. $e = €/\$$. An increase in the exchange rate, i.e. $\hat{e} > 0$, means a devaluation of the euro, since one has to give up more euros to get one US-dollar or gets less dollar for one euro. Accordingly, $\hat{e} < 0$ means an appreciation. Exports are also influenced by price differentials between countries. Consequently, it is not the nominal, but the real exchange rate:

$$e^R = eP*/P$$

that influences exports. In empirical work with exports to many countries, the real effective exchange rate is relevant, being defined as the (geometrically) weighted average of the real exchange rates of a country such as the US versus their trade partners. The weights x_i then are the relative trade volumes for the different export goods i.

$$e^R = \frac{eP*}{P} = \frac{(e_1 P_1*)^{x_2}}{P} \cdot \frac{(e_2 P_2^*)^{x_2}}{P} \cdot \ldots \cdot \frac{(e_n P_n^*)^{x_n}}{P}$$

Real exports change in line with the real effective exchange rate. Thus, US real exports fell slightly with a real appreciation of the US dollar in the early 1980s, and they increased with a real depreciation. The US-dollar depreciated the late 1980s until the mid 1990s (Figure 2.20). In the 1990s, real exports increased whereas the real effective exchange rate fell (the US dollar appreciated in real terms in the late 1990s. This may have been due to the IT revolution. The US gained competitiveness. Since 2002, we have a real depreciation of the US-dollar and an increase in exports.

Figure 2.21 exhibits exports of the UK and the real exchange rate of the British pound. The interdependence seems less pronounced than in the case of the US. The pound devalued in the period 1981–1987, but real exports rose only after 1984. They continued to rise until 2004, in spite of the fact that the pound appreciated until the early 1990s and that it appreciated again after 1996. The strong real devaluation of the pound in 1992, when Britain left the European Exchange Rate Mechanism, had a positive impact on real exports.

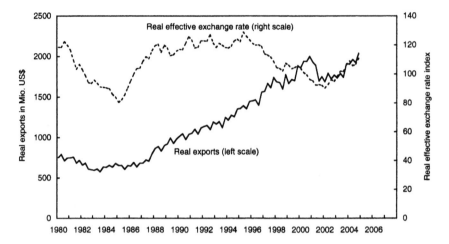

Figure 2.20 Exports[a] and the real exchange rate[b]: the US (source: International Monetary Fund, *International Financial Statistics*, CD-ROM, September 2005. Own calculations).

Notes
a Real exports, adjusted with export prices. Base year 2000.
b The real effective exchange rate is the inverse of the real effective exchange rate index published by the IMF. Base year 2000.

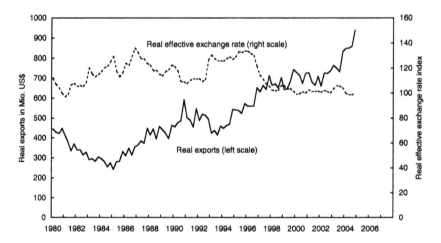

Figure 2.21 Exports[a] and the real exchange rate[b]: the UK (source: International Monetary Fund, *International Financial Statistics*, CD-ROM, September 2005; own calculations).

Notes
a Real exports, adjusted with export prices. Base year 2000.
b The real effective exchange rate is the inverse of the real effective exchange rate index published by the IMF. Base year 2000.

3   The factor markets in the world economy

What you will understand after reading this chapter

Besides the markets for goods, the factor markets play a decisive role in the paradigm of the world economy. Equilibrium of the world economy also requires the factor markets to be in equilibrium. If this equilibrium is disturbed, the world economy has to adjust. The adjustment processes in the world factor markets are thus of great importance. The world labor market has to find an equilibrium between the demand for and the supply of labor; migration and trade are important adjustment mechanisms (section 3.1). The other crucial factor market is the world capital market, bringing the demand for and the supply of new real capital, i.e. savings and investment, into balance (section 3.2). Important questions are whether national capital markets are segmented and how close is the relation between national investment and national savings (sections 3.3 and 3.4). Historically, some countries have developed from net debtors to net creditors. This is the debt cycle hypothesis (section 3.5). For a given production technology, the prices of labor and capital are related to each other in a factor-price frontier (section 3.6). In a knowledge society, the world market for technological knowledge has great importance. Moreover, the world market for natural resources including energy, oil, and the environment has gained great relevance (section 3.8). Finally, shocks on the factor markets are dealt with (section 3.9).

3.1 The world market for labor

Labor market equilibrium

Applying the concept of a world market for labor as a production factor, as we did for goods, we have to compare the world demand for labor and the world supply of labor. An equilibrium exists where:

$$E_L^W = D_L^W - S_L^W = 0 \tag{3.1}$$

holds. Labor demand is driven by the marginal productivity of labor (F_L) which is given by the supply of labor, but also by the capital stock used and by the technology applied, according to the production function, $F_L(L,K)$. Labor demand is determined by the behavior of profit maximizing firms; they demand labor if the marginal productivity of labor is higher than (or equal to) the costs of labor, the real wage. It is a derived demand, being determined simultaneously in the profit maximum with the profit maximal supply of the firm. Labor supply is seen influenced by the utility maximization of households in the choice between leisure and work. It is a negative function of the real wage. Thus, the real wage is the crucial variable bringing the labor market into equilibrium.

If a disequilibrium exists, the wage rate has to bring about a new equilibrium. For instance, when the population in the European cities in medieval times were decimated by the plague or by wars (as in the Thirty Years War in Germany in 1618–1648), the wage rate rose considerably. When new territories were settled as in the US, Canada, and Australia in the nineteenth century, the factor land and new capital had to be equipped with labor, and the real wage rate could rise. With China entering the international division of labor and providing more labor to the world's production process, ceteris paribus the wage rate has to fall globally. This tendency may be offset or even changed positively by gains from trade and by more capital accumulation. When the two oil crises made part of the existing capital stock obsolete, labor productivity was affected negatively, and wages came under pressure.

The world's labor supply curve

Arguing with a homogenous and perfectly mobile labor supply (as above) is a first step in the economic analysis, but the assumption of a homogeneous and perfectly mobile world supply of labor represents a simplification: the demand for workers is spatially concentrated, but workers are, on average, immobile and are not able to satisfy a local excess demand elsewhere. For the curves of labor demand and supply in the world labor market, we therefore have to take into account that the demand and the supply of labor are spatially fixed. The labor markets of the world will thus be characterized by regional segmentation. Taking this into consideration, a simplified labor supply curve of the world can be developed (World Bank, World Development Report 1995, Figure 18.1). In this concept, labor supply depends on the annual income in US dollars, the segments of this curve being valid only for particular regions of the world. For each segment, labor is homogeneous, receiving the same real wage. In Figure 3.1, the horizontal distance between the particular lines indicates the size of the labor supply of the relevant regions in the overall world labor supply in 2003. For simplicity, wages are measured by the region's share in global GDP; this ignores distributional issues between capital and labor. In Figure 3.1, Chinese labor earns 4 percent of world GDP, the US receives 30 percent.

Segmentation and wage differences

If workers are spatially internationally immobile and inhomogeneous concerning their qualification, then national labor markets are segmented, and wage differ-

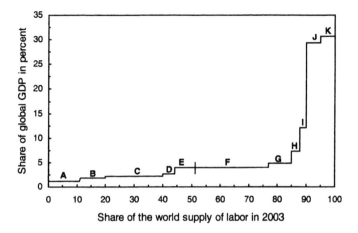

Figure 3.1 The supply curve of the world market for labor, 2003 (source: World Bank, *World Development Indicators* 2005; own calculations).

Notes
A – sub-Saharan Africa; B – East Asia; C – South Asia; D – North Africa and Middle East; E – Eastern Europe and West Asia; F – China; G – Latin America and Caribbean; H – OECD (excluding USA, Japan and EU-15); I – Japan; J – EU-15; K – USA.

ences exist. But besides differences in qualification, or human capital, workers in a particular country can also benefit from a better endowment with physical capital or from locally immobile technological knowledge that enables them to be more productive. Such differences of endowment conditions have to be distinguished from policy-induced market segmentations, e.g. immigration laws. Finally, preferences for a certain location can be so strong that people accept lower wages.

Migration as an adjustment mechanism

Looking at the world's supply curve of labor with different wage levels, the idea of a world labor market represents quite a simplification. In the real world, people migrate between regions of the world that offer different income levels and options to live. According to estimates of the International Organization for Migration (2005) for the year 2000 (data are published every five years), 175 million people, or nearly 3 percent of the world's population, live in countries in which they were not born (stock of migrants). Seventy-seven million had migrated to the OECD countries, fifty-seven million to the middle income countries and fifteen million had migrated to the sub-Saharan African countries, representing internal migration in the continent. Net immigration in 2000 to the OECD countries amounted to twelve million, emigration from the least developed countries was 1.7 million. In the period 1995–2000, 4.5 million left the low-income countries and 9.5 million the middle-income countries, whereas fourteen million immigrated to the high-income countries (World Development Indicators 2005: 364). Besides this border-crossing migration, there is internal migration in larger countries. For China where about 60 percent of the population live in rural areas (2004), annual migration from rural areas to the urban centers is high; for 1999 it was estimated at sixty-seven million (Zhao 2005).

Historically, migration flows in the nineteenth century went into the colonies and former colonies and since the sixteenth century to Latin America. The property rights of the ochtochtonic population were not respected. There were major migration flows by the Islam in the seventh century (North Africa and Spain) and by Nordic and Germanic tribes to the Mediterranean in the third to the sixth century AD. In all these cases, migration was coupled to conquering a foreign territory.

Case study: the pressure for migration

In the fall of 2005, five sub-Saharan Africans have been killed and fifty others wounded as they and hundreds of others scaled tall fences in a bid to enter Melilla, a Spanish enclave on Morocco's northern coast. Migrants from sub-Saharan countries undergo immeasurable sufferance in order to get into Spain and into the EU via Melilla and Ceuta, another Spanish enclave. They, as others trying to enter Italy via the small island of Lampedusa, traverse the Saharan desert accepting risks for their lives in order get a into a better income situation. Coming, for instance, from Mali with an income per capita at purchasing power parity of US$980 per year (or from Nigeria with US$930 per year) and seeing the option of an income per capita of US$25,070 per year in Spain at purchasing power parity, the risks even of losing one's live dwindle compared to a twenty-fivefold increase in income. Such potential gains represent a strong motivation for migration. It will remain so, unless the economic situation in sub-Saharan Africa improves.

Migration and wage equalization

The most important effects of migration can be analyzed in a model with two regions. Then a simple interpretation of the world labor market is obtained under the following assumptions. Assume labor to be perfectly mobile internationally and to be homogeneous especially as far as qualifications are concerned. Furthermore, the labor supply is assumed to be exogenously given and constant over time. Under these assumptions, the world market for labor can be represented as shown in Figure 3.2. OO^* is the world supply of labor, allocated between the home country, or Home (OC), and foreign countries, or Foreign (O^*C). Home's labor demand curve (F_L) shows a higher marginal productivity than the corresponding curve of Foreign (F_L^*). The two markets are assumed to be segmented; the home wage of CA is higher than the foreign wage CB.

If the wage difference *BA* is sufficiently high, foreign workers find it worthwhile to migrate into the home country. Consequently, world production can be extended. Migration generates additional production represented by the triangle *BAE* (Harberger triangle). Home's additional production is *AEDC*, whereas Foreign's production is reduced by *BEDC*. Owing to the migration, the factor endowments of the two countries change. Home increases its supply of workers, requiring the Home wage to fall. In the new equilibrium (point *E*), all home workers receive a lower wage. Foreign loses labor, and all foreign workers receive a higher wage.

Migration has an impact on the distribution of income. In Home, capital gains the area *HAEG*. Labor loses *HAFG*. *AEG* is the part of the efficiency gains of the Harberger triangle that goes to capital. The migrants gain the area *FEJB*. The foreign country loses workers and GDP. Since labor becomes more scarce, the wage of those remaining in the foreign country will increase.

Workers may migrate permanently, temporarily, or even commute. Permanent migrants usually send remittances to their families, so that GNI of the foreign country is higher than its GDP. Remittances in 2005 to developing countries amounted to US$167 billion (World Bank staff estimate); this is higher than the level of development aid, amounting to US$79 billion (World Bank 2006c: 88). For quite a few countries, remittances play an important role. Thus, Moldova receives remittances amounting to 27 percent of its GDP (2004). For Lesotho, the percentage is 26, for Haiti 25, for Jordan 20. Total remittances to all countries are estimated at US$232 billion.

Migration of people can be viewed as an adjustment mechanism similar to trade and the flow of capital. It partly evens out differences in income per capita. It thus is similar to commodity arbitrage.

Depending on the stimulus or motives for migration, we distinguish different types of migration. In demand-pull migration, the stimulus for migration comes from the immigration country where labor is scarce and where economic opportunities are ample (compare the open space in the US in the nineteenth century, Germany in the 1960s). In supply-push migration, i.e. poverty-driven migration, the poor conditions in the home country more or less force the migrants to leave their country such as the disappointing potato harvests in Ireland, again in the nineteenth century. Asylum seekers migrate in order to escape political prosecution, freedom seekers change to other countries for love of freedom. In social welfare migration, migrants exploit the benefits provided by the welfare state of the immigration country.

The impact of migrants depends on several factors. Very often, young, dynamic, daring, and entrepreneurial people migrate. They then are likely to improve productivity in their host country considerably. Who will migrate also depends on the immigration policy. Thus, the immigration country may explicitly look for qualified people. Whether migrants succeed depends on whether the immigration country is an open society, where vertical social and income mobility is accepted. Markets tend to help the immigrants, whereas societies with a rigid institutional structure and decisions based on informal closed networks do not. Open labor markets represent a means of integration.

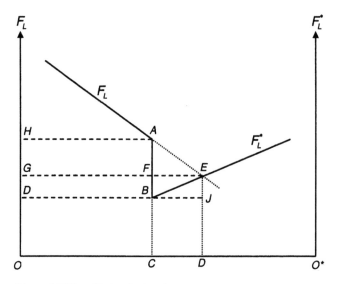

Figure 3.2 The effects of migration.

Integration of migrants

Migrants cannot only contribute economically to their host country, they can also enrich the host country culturally by bringing in new capabilities and new customs. An important condition for such fecundation is that the host country is open to new ways of life and that the immigrants are open to integrate themselves as individuals. The immigrants then are absorbed by the host country. This approach has been the concept of the multicultural societies in European immigration policy. Apparently, this approach does not work if immigrants are not prepared to integrate themselves. The murder of Pim Fortuyn in 2002 and of Theo van Gogh in 2004 in the Netherlands and the uprisings in the *banlieues* in France in 2005 have cast doubt on this approach. It seems that more or less isolated ethnic and religious groups have coexisted without integration.

In contrast to this approach, most immigrants to the US had and still have the American Dream, i.e. to be successful in their new environment. Vertical mobility, moving up the income ladder, is a powerful means of integration. The market economy in the US made it easy for ethnic minorities to succeed. In contrast, in European societies a once given status plays a more important role. Moreover, unlike in the US, continental countries in Europe also experience welfare migration. Moreover, a rigid labor market with a lacking lower segment such as in Continental Europe makes it more difficult to integrate foreigners; as a consequence they have a high unemployment rate and a larger proportion of social welfare recipients. Problems arise when third generation immigrants, deprived of economic opportunities and sticking to their ethnic and religious background, voice their dissatisfaction. The UK approach to immigration policy seems to be different from the continental approach. It does not intend to integrate immigrants individually but accepts groups of immigrants and only aims at not discriminating against these groups.

Terrorism has a strong impact on migration. Immigration presupposes open societies. With the threat of terrorism, the immigrant is seen as a potential terrorist, a sleeper to become active when called upon. If terrorism continues to be a threat to immigration countries, they are likely to become less open.

Movement of goods instead of migration

Even if labor is completely immobile internationally, there can be a tendency to the equalization of real wages through international trade, with goods assuming the role of migration. The country that is relatively rich in capital specializes in the production of capital-intensive goods, causing the price of capital goods, i.e. the real interest rate, to rise and the real wage to fall. Under appropriate model conditions, a convergence or even a complete equalization of real wages occurs (see Chapter 2).

Population growth

The world labor supply also depends on population growth. An increase in population translates into a higher labor supply. Official UN forecasts of 2002 estimate that in 2050 the world's population will have increased from 6.3 billion in 2003 to 8.9 billion in 2050. Urbanization will rise from 2.86 billion (in 2000) to five billion in 2050. About half of the world's population will live in urban centers. The increase in population will not be spread evenly over the regions of the world. Continental Europe and Japan especially are expected to see a decrease in their population. The birth rate is not sufficient to keep the population constant. At the same time, longer life expectancy will mean that the average age of the population rises. Ageing will be less pronounced in the US economy. Population decline will increase the pressure for migration or other adjustment mechanisms.

3.2 The world market for capital

On the world capital market, the equilibrium between savings and investments is determined. Savings means abstaining from consumption, investment means accumulating capital. Demand and supply of new capital meet on the world capital market. The share of gross investment is 21 percent of the world gross product (2004, see Table 1.2). With a world gross product of approximately US$40.9 trillion (World Bank 2005d: Table 3), the world capital market consequently has a volume of about US$8.6 trillion per year. Since we are here looking at savings and investment this sum does not refer to financial markets but to the market for 'real' capital.

The productivity of abstaining from consumption

On the capital supply side, people abstain from consumption, i.e. they save. The demand for capital is determined by production. From the production side, it is possible to produce additional units of goods in period 1 through capital formation in the preceding period 0. Not consuming a cow today means that the cow is still available for consumption tomorrow and that on top of this it has calved as well. As Robinson Crusoe abstains from walking to the remote source of fresh water, and as he produces a bucket during the time, he suffers thirst. But he also spares himself the frequent walk to the water source in the next period and then has more water per unit of time at his disposal. Abstaining from consumption, i.e. investing, has a positive productivity. In the next period, $1 + F_K$ units of a good are available instead of one unit, F_K indicating the marginal productivity of capital (of abstaining from consumption).

In Figure 3.3, the transformation curve shows the possibility of transformation over time. The marginal rate of transformation $|dQ_1/dQ_0|$ indicates how many additional units of output are possible in the second period (distance *HI*) if one unit of consumption is abstained from in the first period (distance *TH*). The marginal rate of transformation in time results, on the one hand, from a

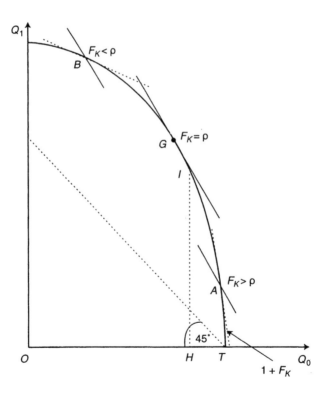

Figure 3.3 Transformation in time.

unit of a good not consumed today being preserved and being available for consumption in the next period (storing). But, on the other hand, abstaining from consumption is also linked to a productive detour or a roundabout method (Marshall 1890), yielding a positive marginal productivity per unit of consumption abstained from.

The transformation curve ranks all investment projects in the world according to their marginal productivity of capital F_K. Those projects with the highest marginal productivity are located on the lower part of the transformation curve, so that the first unit of capital invested has the highest marginal productivity. The more capital is invested, the lower is the marginal productivity of an additional project. The increasing marginal rate of transformation thus indicates the declining marginal productivity of additional units of capital. The opportunity cost of abstaining from consumption rises. The rate of return of investment (i.e. of non-consumption) is F_K. Through non-consumption, $1 + F_K$ units of the good are available in the next period. This is the benefit of waiting. The marginal rate of transformation in time $|dQ_1/dQ_0|$ must correspond to the relative price of the two goods in time, p_0/p_1; this relative price is of the dimension Q_1/Q_0. It shows in which quantitative relation a good is intertemporally exchanged on the market. Thus, from the production side of the world economy:

$$\left| \frac{dQ_1}{dQ_0} \right| = 1 + F_K = \frac{p_0}{p_1} \tag{3.2}$$

has to hold.

The cost of abstaining from consumption

Abstaining from consumption involves costs of waiting. These opportunity costs are generated by shifting consumption to the future. If the household had only the one unit of a good at its disposal tomorrow that it abstains from today, and if it would assign the same utility to this situation as to the initial situation, it would have no preference for the present period.[1] But if it values this unit less, because it will be consumed only in the future, the future consumption has to be discounted with the rate of time preference, ρ. The rate of time preference indicates how the future consumption is evaluated in comparison to consumption today. It is the factor used to discount consumption in the future in comparison to consumption today. For the rate of time preference:

$$\rho = \left| \frac{dC_1}{dC_0} \right| - 1$$

holds, where $|dC^1/dC^0|$ is the marginal rate of intertemporal substitution. It measures the quantity of consumption necessary in the second period to compensate the household for abstaining from one unit of consumption in the first period.

The time preference rate of consumption ρ is not identical to the utility discount rate δ. The preference rate of consumption in time ρ expresses how the future consumption has to be discounted, whereas the discount rate of utility δ expresses how the future utility has to be discounted. This is the 'impatience'. The discount rate of utility is, as a rule, assumed given as constant over time, whereas the rate of time preference varies with the consumption level. If future consumption is higher than present consumption, an additional unit of consumption yields less satisfaction in the future than it creates in the present.

The rate of time preference ρ is thus determined by two factors. One is the impatience of households (or individuals). A household generally values future satisfaction of its needs lower than the immediate satisfaction. This impatience is represented by the discount rate of utility δ. The second factor is intertemporal consumption smoothing: because of a diminishing marginal utility of consumption, a household wants to stretch consumption over time. In a long-term growth equilibrium, where consumption does not change anymore, the rate of time preference ρ equals the discount rate of utility δ. Thus (in models where consumption increases over time) the discount rate of utility can be regarded as the lower limit of the rate of time preference. Therefore, the literature often speaks only of the discount rate δ.

What does this mean for the consumption and saving decision of households? Consumers are indifferent about consuming today or tomorrow if the utility of a unit consumed today and the present value of the utility of a unit consumed tomorrow are equal in their judgment. For households, the relative price has to correspond to the marginal rate of substitution in time and thus be equal to the ratio of the marginal utilities in both periods.[2] The marginal rate of substitution in time thus measures the consumption quantity that is necessary to compensate the household for abstaining from one unit of consumption in the first period. Thus, from the consumption side of an economy, the price ratio between consumption today and consumption tomorrow has to be equal to the marginal rate of substitution and the ratio pf marginal utilities. (Note that the marginal utility of the future is discounted by $1+\delta$).

$$\left|\frac{dC_1}{dC_0}\right| = 1 + \rho = \frac{U'_0(C_0)(1+\delta)}{U'_1(C_1)} = \frac{p_0}{p_1} \tag{3.4}$$

Equilibrium between the benefits and the costs of abstaining from consumption

Summing up the conditions for the production and consumption sides, it follows that:

$$\left|\frac{dQ_1}{dQ_0}\right| = 1 + F_K = \frac{p_0}{p_1} = \frac{U'_0(C_0)(1+\delta)}{U'_1(C_1)} = 1 + \rho = \left|\frac{dC_1}{dC_0}\right| \tag{3.5}$$

The marginal rate of transformation (tangent to the transformation curve) and the marginal rate of substitution (tangent to the indifference curve) have to be equal (point G in Figure 3.3; the indifference curve is not shown).

In Figure 3.3, point A cannot be an optimal point, as the marginal productivity of capital is higher than the rate of time preference ρ. The benefit of waiting, i.e. the additional production, is higher than the costs of waiting, i.e. the loss of utility through abstaining from consumption. Analogously, point B is not an optimal point, as the marginal productivity of capital is smaller than the rate of time preference. Here the benefit of waiting is less than the costs of waiting. The optimum is reached in point G.

The position of the optimal point G varies with the rate of time preference. If the rate of time preference ρ is high, abstention from consumption is relatively low. Then, the equilibrium point G moves downward on the transformation curve. If the rate of time preference is low, abstention from consumption is higher. Then, the equilibrium point G moves upward.

Marginal productivity, time preference rate, and market interest rate

The marginal productivity indicates how, from the supply side, investing yields a return (through a productive detour or a roundabout process); the time preference rate expresses what, from the consumption side, the consumers demand for abstaining from consumption. The relative price p^0/p^1 for the product in the two periods expresses the intertemporal relative price. For this relative price, $p^0/p^1 = 1 + r$ holds, where r is the market interest rate. The equilibrium for capital formation in the world capital markets thus requires $F_K = \rho = r$.

In equilibrium, the market interest rate r has to be equal to the marginal productivity and the rate of time preference. As we shall see later on, in intertemporal approaches and also in models of growth, we distinguish between long-term equilibria and adjustment paths to long-term equilibria (Chapter 4). The market for capital has to be in equilibrium in the long-term situation as well as during transition to it.

The demand–supply diagram of the world market for capital

The relationship between the benefits and the costs of waiting can also be illustrated in a different representation of the world capital market (Figure 3.4a). On the vertical axis, the marginal productivity of capital (F_K), the rate of time preference ? and the (real) interest rate r are shown. On the horizontal axis, the levels of investments (I) and savings (S) are shown. The demand curve for new capital contains projects with different marginal productivities. Projects with a particularly high marginal productivity are located in the upper part of the F_K curve. When these projects are complete, projects with a lower marginal productivity of capital become worthwhile. The F_K curve is thus the demand curve for new capital in the world economy. It results from the demand curves of the individual countries. The curve is obtained by horizontally adding the curves of the individual economies. Regarding the world market, all feasible projects in the world are ranked according to their profitability on this curve. It represents the demand side of the capital market with different investment prospects.

The supply curve shows the abstention from consumption that the households of the world are ready to accept at different world-market interest rates. One may also imagine that this supply curve for new capital represents households or countries with different rates of time preference. Countries or households with a low rate of time preference offer abstention from consumption, i.e. real savings, even at a very low real interest rate. If the real interest rate rises, more households or countries supply savings.

The equilibrium lies in point *G*, where an equilibrium real interest rate is determined and the demand for new capital equals the supply of new capital. Investment projects with a lower marginal productivity are not carried out whereas the investment projects with a higher marginal productivity receive a capital user (demand-side) surplus. They have a marginal productivity that is higher than the real interest rate required in the market equilibrium. Concerning the supply curve, the potential savings of households or countries requiring a time preference rate (respectively a discount rate) higher than the market-clearing real interest rate do not become effective. Countries or households with a lower time preference receive a supplier surplus.

These relations can also be represented as a curve of excess demand for new capital depending on the interest rate (Figure 3.4b). At high real interest rates, excess demand is negative, i.e. there is too much abstention from consumption; at low real interest rates, excess demand is positive, i.e. too much capital is demanded.

In Figure 3.4, the flows of a period are taken into account, i.e. the investments, the abstention from consumption, the savings. This figure can also be applied to the aggregated demand for capital over all periods and the aggregated savings over all periods. In this interpretation, the capital stock is indicated on the horizontal axis. If capital already in existence can be employed flexibly, both representations are equivalent.

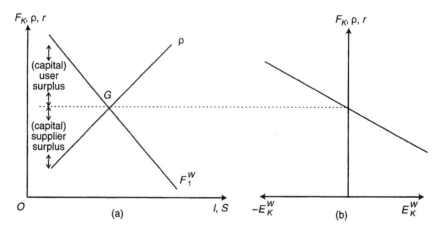

Figure 3.4 The world market for capital.

Tobin's q

Tobin's q represents an evaluation of a country's capital goods (or of its existing stock of capital). In the above model, the stock of capital is determined by the condition $F_K = r$, assuming that capital can be reallocated at negligible costs. In the long run, this may indeed be the case. In the short run, however, adjustment costs arise with the reallocation of capital. This has effects on investment behavior. Consider a firm maximizing its profit over a time period and facing adjustment costs for its capital. Then, the installed capital enters the investment calculation of the firms at a shadow price with adjustment costs playing a role. Tobin's q can be regarded as an expression of this shadow price. It is defined as:

$$q = \frac{\text{Market value of the capital installed}}{\text{replacement cost of the capital installed}} \tag{3.6}$$

If $q < 1$, the market value lies below the replacement costs, and it does not pay off to replace the capital good once it is depreciated. It is not worthwhile for a firm to take up new capital from the capital market. The firm reduces its capital stock. If $q > 1$, it is worthwhile to renew a capital good. Then it pays off to use more capital and to attract it from outside.

Tobin's q permits us to link the investment decision to the stock market, as the market value of the capital installed can be indicated by the valuation of shares. The replacement costs of the installed capital are given by the price index for investment goods. Thus the rate of change $\hat{q}$ of Tobin's q is:

$\hat{q}$ = share index (e.g. Dow Jones) rate of change – rate of change of the price index for investment goods.

If, for example, the share index rises, perhaps because optimism spreads in an economy, because of lowered corporate taxes, a technological breakthrough recorded or more favorable export opportunities, the rise of Tobin's q signals better investment opportunities. The formulation with Tobin's q is perfectly compatible with the neoclassical approach of marginal productivity. If the marginal productivity rises through technological progress, the market value of capital will increase, q exceeds 1 and it pays off to invest. With positive expectations, q rises as well. The appeal of the q approach is that the investment behavior of firms is linked to the valuation of the firms through the stock market.

Capital allocation for two countries

An alternative representation of capital accumulation on the world market for capital explicitly considers two regions of the world (two countries; Figure 3.5). It is assumed here that the marginal productivity of the capital stock in the two countries is higher than the discount rate δ (which is relevant in the long-run). We assume the two countries to have a uniform discount rate. Figure 3.5 shows

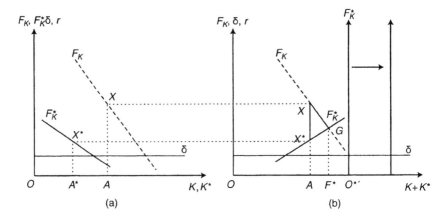

Figure 3.5 Optimal allocation of capital.

the curves for the marginal productivity of capital for the home and foreign countries. It is assumed that due to technological knowledge the home country has a higher marginal productivity of capital. It has accumulated the capital stock OA with the corresponding marginal productivity of capital AX. The foreign country has a less favorable productivity curve, a smaller capital stock OA^* and a lower marginal productivity of capital A^*X^*. The capital productivities of the two countries are higher than their discount rate δ.

The information contained in Figure 3.5a is rearranged in Figure 3.5b. The curve for the marginal productivity of the home country has been duplicated from Figure 3.5a, the home country has realized a marginal productivity according to point X, and it has accumulated the corresponding capital OA. The curve of marginal productivity for the foreign country is arranged in the 'inverse' direction, originating at point O^*. Figure 3.5b is drawn such that the straight line OO^* represents the sum of the capital stocks OA of the home country and of the foreign country O^*A. With the present capital allocation between the two countries, a gap between their marginal productivities results. The points A and A^* can thus not be a world market equilibrium. Similarly to the market for goods, the possibility of arbitrage exists. This is expressed by the Harberger triangle XGX^*. It is worthwhile to transfer capital from the foreign country to the home country. The equilibrium point is reached in point G in Figure 3.5b, the foreign country having transferred an amount AF of capital to the home country.

Point G balances the differences in the marginal productivities of capital. It represents, however, only a short-term equilibrium, as the marginal productivity of capital exceeds the discount rate. It is thus worthwhile to accumulate capital. The total stock of capital OO^* rises. Capital accumulation can occur in the home country as well as in the foreign country. For simplicity, let us assume that the capital stock rises only in the foreign country, equal to an amount of the straight line $O^*O^{*'}$. Notice that the position of the foreign country's curve of marginal productivity F^{**} moves to the right, along with the point of origin $O^{*'}$. The equilibrium is attained at the intersection of the curves of marginal productivity on the δ line (the new equilibrium is not shown in Figure 3.5b). The point of origin $O^{*\prime}$ moves until the marginal productivity in both countries equals the discount rate δ.

3.3 Global demand for capital interpreted as national excess demands

In the previous analysis, we started out from the assumption of a uniform world market for capital. An alternative concept is to assume that, as a first step, single countries attempt to achieve a balance between the demand for new capital and the abstention from consumption. If there is excess demand for capital in a country, this excess demand then, as a second step, becomes effective on the world market. The world demand for new capital is then the sum of the countries' excess demand for new capital (E_I) and thus $D_I^W = \Sigma_j$ for $E_I^j > 0$. Correspondingly, the word's supplied savings S_I^W are the sum of all countries' excess supply, and thus $S_I^W = \Sigma_j E_I^j$ for $E_I^j > 0$.

In principle, this formulation leads to the same result as a uniform view of the world market for capital. The formulation is helpful because it can be specified with the help of the countries' current account balances. A current account deficit means that an economy receives more goods, services, property income, and unilateral (free) transfers in one period than it gives away. Thus, resources amounting to the level of the current account deficit are transferred into the country. Capital imports take place. A current account surplus means that a country gives away more goods, services, and transfers than it receives in one period. Resources are exported. Capital export takes place.

Looking at a current deficit from a financing point of view, a current account deficit means that a country uses more goods than it produces. Absorption exceeds production; this has to be financed from abroad (Siebert and Lorz 2006: Chapter 12). The financing restriction can be explained as follows. Let us start with the equation for national income $Y = C + I + G + X - Im$ (*C*: consumption; *I*: investment; *G*: government expenditure; *X*: exports; *Im*: imports). A country may receive unilateral transfers from abroad (or may provide transfers), for instance development aid or transfers of the European Union for its members. Adding the transfer balance, *Tr*, on both sides, we have:

$$Y + Tr = C + I + G + X - Im + Tr \qquad (3.7)$$

If taxes *T* (which are supposed to contain the indirect taxes as well) are subtracted from both sides of equation 3.7, it follows that the current account balance $X - Im + Tr$ equals $S - I + (T - G)$. The current account balance thus equals the surplus of savings over investments. Taking into account government savings (i.e. the government budget surplus), we have:

$$S - I + (T - G) = X - Im + Tr$$

This is the financing restraint of an open economy. In a model with two countries, the current account balance and the capital account balance are determined simultaneously; they are two sides of the same coin. A country with a current account deficit does not have enough savings to finance its investments. A country with a current account surplus saves more than it intends to invest.

If the world consists of two countries only, the home country and the foreign country, the balances of the two countries' current accounts must add up to zero in each and every period. If Home has a current account deficit in period 0, meaning that it is not able to fully finance its investments and therefore it has to import capital, indebting itself, Foreign has to have a current account surplus of a corresponding amount in the same period, exporting capital and granting a loan. Let us now introduce the time aspect and assume that there are only two time periods. Then Home has to obtain a current account surplus in period 1 to be able to repay its debt. Home's current account is thus intertemporally balanced, but it has been able to consume more goods in period 0 than it would have been able to, based only on its own production capacity. In return, it has to pay goods back in period 1. Correspondingly, this results in a current account deficit for Foreign in period 1, as it can now live off means received from credit loan repayment. For Foreign, the current account is intertemporally balanced as well. This intertemporal mechanism of balances is represented in Table 3.1.

In Figure 3.6, the national markets for capital are shown. In autarky (point *A*),

Table 3.1 Intertemporal mechanism of balances

	Home	*Foreign*
Period 0	Current account deficit, import of capital, indebtedness	Current account surplus, export of capital, loan
Period 1	Current account surplus, export of capital, debt repayment	Current account deficit, import of capital, debt repayment received

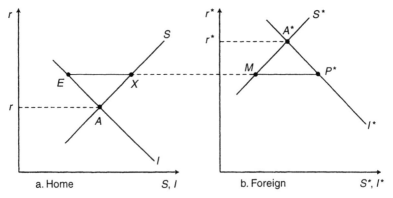

a. Home   b. Foreign

Figure 3.6 Current account balances and national capital markets.

Home's interest rate is relatively low, whereas Foreign has a relatively high interest rate (point A^*). With free movement of capital, a uniform world market for capital exists. Home exports capital (EX) and has a current account surplus. Foreign imports capital (MP) and has a current account deficit.

3.4 The relationship between national investment and national savings

The Feldstein–Horioka paradox

Feldstein and Horioka (1980) found out that the national capital markets are of considerable importance for the clearing between capital demand and capital supply. For a panel of twenty-one OECD countries and the time from 1960 to 1974, they found a high correlation between the national savings rate and the national investment rate with a regression coefficient close to 1. The rates were calculated as averages for the total period of fifteen years and also for sub-periods of five years. The simple OLS (ordinary least squares) regression $(I/Y)_i = \alpha + \beta \, (S/Y)_i$ for the 21 countries $(i = 1, \ldots , 21)$ and the fifteen-year period yields a regression coefficient β of 0.89 for gross savings and of 0.94 for net savings. Similar coefficients were found for the five-year period. These coefficients can be interpreted as savings retention coefficients. With perfect capital mobility one would have expected no relation at all between the savings rate and the investment rate, β thus equaling zero. However, since the coefficient is closer to 1 than 0, the hypothesis $\beta = 0$ has to be rejected. The results of Feldstein and Horioka suggest that national capital markets have considerable weight and that only small excess demands and supplies are balanced on the world market for capital. Perfect capital mobility does not exist.

In Figure 3.7, savings rates (share of gross savings in GDP) and investment

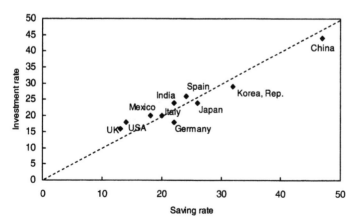

Figure 3.7 Gross savings shares and gross investment shares in GDP in selected countries, 2003 (source: World Bank, *World Development Indicators* 2005).

rates (share of gross investment in GDP) in 2003 are shown for selected countries. As can be observed, the values for most countries lie close to a straight line with an angle of 45°.

Recent tests show that the close relation observed by Feldstein and Horioka has become less tight. Based on annual data for 1960–1988, Sinn (1992a) has shown for twenty-three OECD countries that the long-term average of the relationship between the national rates of savings and investment has declined considerably, especially since 1973 (the coefficient of the regression equation is 0.68 for the 1980s). This indicates that international capital mobility has increased. More recent studies for the period 1970–2000 find a coefficient of 0.636 for twenty-eight OECD countries (Georgopoulos and Hejazi 2005); the home bias decreases with a time trend.

The world market for capital as a peak balancing device

One approach to determining world excess demand for capital is to add up national excess demand. The volume of the excess demand for new capital can be observed from the sum of the negative current account balances. Summing up the negative current account balances of the 133 countries featured in the World Development Report 2006, the total deficit for the year 2004 amounts to US$320 billion. Putting the current account deficits into relation with the world national product yields a value of only 0.78 percent of world GNP. According to this figure, the peak balancing function of the world capital market, measured against the current deficits, makes up for only a small portion of the world national product. Gross savings, however, amount to 18 percent of the world domestic product. Thus, in this approach only 8.5 percent of gross investment in the world economy is financed through international (real) capital movements. Data of foreign direct investments, reported in Table 3.2, suggest a somewhat higher, but basically similar, dimension for the annual average of US$521 billion in the period 1991–2003. Older sources indicated that the current account deficits of individual countries tended to be in the range of 2–3 percent of GDP (see Bosworth 1993). However, recently individual countries had larger current account deficits, for example the US with 5.6 percent of GDP in 2004 and Portugal with 6.9 in 2005 and even more than 10 percent of GDP in 2000 and 2001. High deficits of up to 5–6 percent of GDP may be observed in currency crises (see Chapter 8).

Capital flows run mainly between the industrialized countries. About three-quarters of the world's foreign direct investments are capital inflows into the industrialized countries (annual average for 1991–2003). The annual share of the developing countries has risen slightly in the same period (from 26 to 32 percent, Table 3.2). The portfolio investments (transactions in shares and bonds and also in money market instruments and derivatives) flow overwhelmingly (93 percent) in the industrial countries. Portfolio investments differ from direct investments in the way that the investor is not durably interested in the firms in which he or she is investing.

Table 3.2 Gross capital inflows (billion US$)

		1991	1995	2000	2002	2003	Annual average[a]
World	Direct investment	154.4	329.2	1,517.1	702.6	553.9	521.0
	Portfolio investment	466.4	604.3	1,511.0	1,049.8	1,687.1	843.5
	Other investment	104.4	756.9	1,306.5	664.6	1,244.8	638.2
	Total	725.2	1,690.5	4,334.6	2,417.1	3,485.8	2,002.7
Industrialized countries	Direct investment	113.7	206.1	1,250.3	521.6	376.1	377.2
	Portfolio investment	418.3	541.7	1,415.9	1,019.3	1,570.0	765.4
	Other investment	36.7	564.3	1,272.5	659.0	1,159.4	594.6
Developing countries	Direct investment	40.7	123.2	266.8	181.0	177.8	143.8
	Portfolio investment	31.0	52.7	81.1	19.1	97.1	64.1
	Other investment	64.1	150.7	32.6	−14.3	85.4	24.3
Latin America	Direct investment	13.1	30.3	78.6	45.7	35.9	43.3
	Portfolio investment	26.0	12.4	4.4	−10.4	5.4	18.1
	Other investment	4.5	40.0	5.4	−2.9	−38.5	2.8
Asia[b]	Direct investment	20.8	69.1	140.9	81.9	86.0	68.7
	Portfolio investment	3.7	30.1	69.4	14.3	73.3	30.5
	Other investment	36.9	63.0	−4.6	−10.6	39.6	−3.7
Eastern Europe[c]	Direct investment	2.7	7.9	17.6	16.0	16.9	9.8
	Portfolio investment	0.8	5.1	−1.9	11.0	12.1	8.8
	Other investment	3.7	31.9	18.4	14.1	59.9	15.9

Source: IMF, *Balance of Payments Statistics* September 2005; own calculations.

Notes
a Annual average for the years 1991–2003.
b Asia: does not include Hong Kong and Taiwan.
c Eastern Europe: includes Malta, Turkey and Cyprus.

Considerable capital inflows for particular countries

Even if the world market for capital in general only seems to balance peaks between savings and investments, capital inflows can gain a considerable importance for particular countries and in particular periods. For instance, in 1995 the share of foreign direct investments (gross inflow) in gross investment attained more than 50 percent in Hungary and reached nearly 40 percent in Chile in 2004. In the period 1991–2004, Hungary attracted 27 percent of its gross investment through investment from abroad, for Chile it was 24 percent.

Once more: the benefits of capital flows

Similarly as trade, capital flows have benefits for the countries exporting and importing capital (Neely 1999). First, for the capital-exporting country, a higher income can be earned investing abroad than investing at home, i.e. capital

Table 3.3 Inflow of foreign direct investment, as percent of gross investment

	1991	1995	2000	2001	2002	2003	2004	Annual average[a]
China[b]	3.9	15.4	10.3	10.5	10.4	8.6	8.0	11.3
Czech Republic	n.a.	14.7	32.4	33.6	43.2	8.3	15.3	19.8
Hungary	20.9	53.7	25.2	32.3	19.8	11.9	18.4	27.3
Poland	2.0	15.5	23.8	14.9	11.4	10.7	14.3	13.2
EU-15[c, d]	5.1	6.8	41.4	22.6	23.7	19.7	n.a.	14.8
Argentina	8.8	12.1	22.6	5.7	17.6	8.4	13.9	14.5
Brazil	1.5	3.4	28.2	22.7	19.6	11.3	15.3	12.7
Chile	11.0	16.5	31.2	28.2	17.8	28.2	39.2	24.0
Mexico	8.1	20.6	13.6	22.3	12.3	9.6	12.2	13.0
Korea	1.0	0.9	5.8	2.5	1.5	1.8	4.1	2.4
Malaysia	22.4	10.8	16.4	2.5	14.5	10.8	n.a.	14.8
Thailand	4.9	3.0	12.5	14.6	3.3	5.7	3.3	8.7
USA[c]	2.4	4.5	16.0	8.3	3.8	2.9	n.a.	6.7

Source: IMF, *International Financial Statistics*, CD-ROM, September 2005; UNCTAD, *World Investment Report* 2005; UNCTAD, *Major FDI-Indicators*, Online FDI-database 2005.

Notes
a Annual average: for the years 1991–2004. For China 1991–2002.
b China without Hong Kong SAR, data missing for 2003 and 2004.
c Data missing for 2003.
d Data for the EU-15 FDI flows include internal capital movements in the EU.

productivity is larger abroad $F_K^* > F_K$ or the interest rate in the world capital market is higher than productivity at home $r^W > F_K$. Second, capital flows also allow consumption smoothing over time. For instance, a society facing an aging population can invest abroad today in order to enjoy an income in old age. Third, the capital-importing country has the benefit of accumulating capital earlier than it would be possible through its own savings, i.e. $F_K^* > r^W$. The country can produce more. For instance, the US imported capital in the nineteenth century to build up its capital stock. Fourth, consumption smoothing can prevent the impact of a severe economic downturn or a natural disaster. These arguments are similar to those of the gains from trade. Capital flows exploit differences in countries' characteristics, such as age structure of the population, savings behavior, investment opportunities and risk profiles. Moreover, capital flows are linked to technology transfer and can increase the competitiveness of the capital- importing country. Capital controls will be discussed in Chapter 9, the impact of the exit option of capital for the capital-exporting country is analyzed in Chapter 15.

Capital flows versus labor migration

Capital flows, the migration of people and trade can be viewed as three different adjustment mechanisms evening out differences in income per capita. If capital flows to lower income countries, emigration is not necessary (jobs to the people). Capital imports tend to enhance the competitiveness of the export sector. Then, capital mobility is a substitute for labor mobility. Similarly, exports of labor-intensive products by a labor-abundant country will raise real wages and will make it unnecessary to emigrate. Historically, both labor and capital have moved to a country as in the case of the US in the nineteenth century.

Case study: the long-term real interest rate

The long-term real interest rate is the price that clears the capital market. A possible indicator is the nominal interest rate of long-term bonds, corrected for the inflation rate. In principle, inflationary expectation should be used for correction. Since they are often not known, the consumer price inflation rate is applied. In theory, the real price of capital should depend on capital scarcity or abundance, economic growth and the business cycle.

Figure 3.8 exhibits the real interest rate of the US during the period 1956–2004, calculated as the yield of ten-year government bonds minus the inflation rate measured as the consumer price index. The US real interest rate can be considered to be an indicator of the world's real interest rate even if market segmentations may play a role. The average US rate for this period has been 2.68 percent. The high real interest rate in 1984 (8.12 percent) can be seen as a consequence of the Reagan boom attracting foreign capital to the US. The rate then fell to 1.59 percent in 2004.

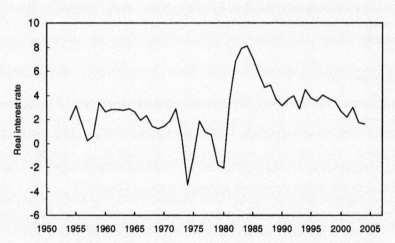

Figure 3.8 Long-run US real interest rate[a] (source: IMF, *International Financial Statistics* 2005).

Note

a Ten-year government bond yield year minus the inflation rate measured by the consumer price index.

During the two oil crises, the real rate became negative (with minus 3.48 in 1974 and minus 2.5 in 1980). One reason is the high inflation rate due to the two oil shocks. Another is that there was an excess of capital supply in the aftermath of petro dollar recycling. The real rate of the UK shows a similar pattern. The real interest rate moves with the business cycle and economic growth. It is surprising that China's entry into the world economy and the increase in the world labor supply has not lead to a systematic increase in the real interest rate. This could have been expected with a temporary decline in the world's capital labor ratio from some long-term equilibrium.

3.5 The debt cycle: from net debtor to net creditor

The debt cycle

In its historical development, an economy can go through a debt cycle (Siebert 1987, 1989). It begins as a 'young' debtor because capital imports are worthwhile due to $F_K > r$. The marginal productivity of capital exceeds the world market interest rate, for instance when considerable investment opportunities exist in a country. Through capital imports, a stock of capital is built up in the debtor country. This increases the production possibilities. From the additional production, interest payment and debt repayment can be financed so that debt decreases in the course of time. At some point in time, the country moves into a creditor position.

Debt half-cycle

An economy will not always succeed in going through a full debt cycle from debtor to creditor. The expected marginal productivity of capital may be overestimated, or the foreign debt may not be used for capital formation, but to finance the government budget and, in the end, for consumption, e.g. to finance social programs or election promises. Then the commitment of the foreign debt weighs heavily on the economy. From a country's budgetary restriction $\dot{V} = I - S + rV$ (with V: foreign debt; $\dot{V} > 0$: new indebtedness) it follows that reducing debt ($\dot{V} < 0$) at a given investment level (I) and given interest payments (rV) requires high savings if a country has accumulated high foreign debt. This is equivalent to the statement that there has to be a high export surplus for a country to be able to pay interest and repay its foreign debt.

Case study: the US and the UK debt cycle

An example for a debt cycle is the development in the US. Especially during the time of the railroad boom (1840–1870), the US attracted foreign capital. At some point foreign debt was more than 20 percent in relation to its gross domestic product (Figure 3.9). The debt amount was then reduced and the US became a net creditor from 1914 onwards before moving into a net debtor position again in 1985. In Figure 3.9, two different statistical sources are used for the US, but their results show similar tendencies. The United Kingdom had a net creditor position in the world economy until the beginning of the twentieth century; afterwards it got into a net debtor position which was partially reversed by the oil discoveries in the North Sea.

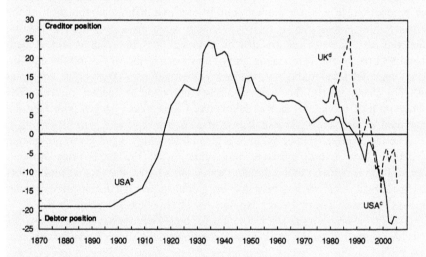

Figure 3.9 Debt cycle of the US and the UK.[a]

Notes
a Net financial asset position in percent of gross domestic product.
b Data from Holtfrerich and Schötz, 1988.
c US data from IMF, *International Financial Statistics* 2006; US Department of Commerce, Bureau of Economic Analysis, *International Investment Position*.
d UK: IMF, *International Financial Statistics* 2006; own calculations.

3.6 The factor-price frontier

Owing to the production function, a unique relationship exists between prices of the different production factors. Intuitively, a factor's marginal productivity under a given production function can increase if less of this factor is employed; it can also increase if more of the other factor is employed. The marginal productivity of the increasingly employed factor then falls. The real factor prices correspond to the marginal productivities. We have $r^R = r/p = F_K(K,L)$ for the real rental rate of capital and $w^R = w/p = F_L(L,K)$ for the real wage rate. Taking the price of one factor as given determines the maximally possible price of the other factor because of the production function. The factor-price frontier describes this relationship. It is the locus of all combinations of real factor prices which are feasible with a given production function and thus with a given technology. For a substitutional, linear-homogeneous production function, the factor-price frontier is shown in Figure 3.10. Thus in point A, the real wage rate falls (when labor input increases) and the real interest rate rises (when capital input is reduced). Note that this factor-price frontier is a possibility set of real factor prices, defined from the production function. Only a specific point on this curve represents an equilibrium, once the supply of the factors is given.

Assuming a production function for the world, there is an interdependence between the real interest rate (r^R) and the real wage (w^R) under given conditions of production. In a factor market equilibrium, one distinct combination of the conceivable combinations is realized on both factor markets (point A). Assume that the real factor prices are just high enough for full employment of both factors in the world. If the labor supply now rises in the world and the equilibrium wage falls due to this rise, the real interest rate rises (from point A to point B). The change of real factor prices already described in Chapter 2 occurs. The integration of economies rich in labor, like China, thus changes both absolute and relative real factor prices in the world economy.

The factor-price frontier assumes a given technology, i.e. a given production function. In a two-dimensional representation of the factor-price frontier, technology is a given and a hidden factor. If we take into consideration that technological progress is stimulated by globalization, the factor-price frontier moves outwards. The real wage can thus rise (from point B to point C).

The factor-price frontier is also valid for single economies or regions of the world. Depending on the production technologies, the frontier may be different

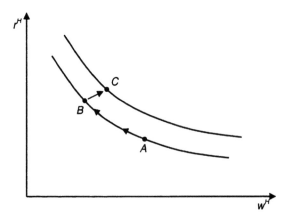

Figure 3.10 The factor price frontier.

for different countries. With the factor-price frontier we may also show what it means for a country if capital moves out of a country: the real interest rate rises, the real wage falls. Locational competition for the mobile capital thus has consequences for labor as a production factor.

3.7 The world market for knowledge and technology

In the knowledge economy, ideas have become an important factor of production. Ideas or knowledge refer to fundamental theoretical concepts, to products, methods of production, software, and to information itself. In such an economy, activities relate to the production of knowledge or information, to selling ideas, to processing information, and to the diffusion of knowledge and information.

Knowledge can be a public good (used in equal amounts by all), an open access resource (its use being available to everybody) or a private resource. The first two categories apply to fundamental concepts such as basic discoveries in the natural sciences. For other forms of knowledge an important aspect is that property rights can be defined that make ideas private property – through patents, copyrights, or trademarks. Patents protect the inventor and the innovator and represent an incentive to search for new technological knowledge. The duration of a patent must be chosen in such a way to keep the search incentive alive; it should not be so long to establish a monopoly. The duration of a property right depends on the length of the product cycle and varies considerably between sectors. For instance in the IT sector, where some products have a half-life of one year only, property rights have to be defined differently from the pharmaceutical sector. In the Uruguay Round the WTO established TRIPs (Trade-Related Aspects of Intellectual Property Rights) in 1994 – an agreement intended to secure the recognition of property rights among its member countries.

Given private property rights, ideas can be marketed. This happens not only in the form of new products such as new seeds, investment goods embodying new technology or software. Companies like the French consumer electronics firm Thomson and the UK technology firm BTG can make more profits by selling ideas through patents than building products themselves (*International Herald Tribune*, October 3, 2005). They market ideas directly. Knowledge is not only linked to the typical industrial production process and to technical knowledge of the traditional type, it is also coupled with services. This relates for instance to data processing, communication and movies.

Internationally, ideas can be traded between countries. Whereas some of these transactions may be intra-firm flows of ideas, knowledge can also be bought and sold between countries. The technology balance of countries shows who is a technology exporter and who is a technology importer. It includes payments for licence fees, patents, purchases of technology and know-how as well as research and technical assistance. The technology balance of the US and the UK show a surplus amounting to 0.26 and 0.7 percent of the country's GDP, (Table 3.4) whereas Germany's balance exhibits a slight deficit of 0.05 percent

(2003). France and Finland have a positive technology balance (OECD 2005b: 74–75). The EU balance is negative.

In order to analyze how the production of technological knowledge may be influenced, one can look at the inputs of the process of producing new knowledge, i.e. R&D expenditures, the number of graduated engineers, and patent applications. Unfortunately, we do not know exactly how the production function of new technological knowledge looks like. Consequently, the inputs may only be understood as potential candidates of explanation. Moreover, the data may not be comparable. For instance, the number of patents represents only the patents registered at one of the major patent offices; it reflects different shares of residents (in the US 52 percent, in Japan 76 percent, Germany 26 percent).

In terms of the number of patents, the US, Germany, and Japan have high application rates (Table 3.4). Approval rates are different, for instance about one-half in the US and one-sixth in Japan. Japan spends a high proportion for R&D in terms of GDP (3.15 percent); the US and Germany spend lower rates. Sweden has a unusually high proportion of 4.27, the UK a low one of 1.89 percent.

It should be noted that innovation not only depends on the factors mentioned so far such as patents and R&D spending. It also is strongly influenced by human capital which is a precondition for finding and implementing new technology. It is reported that China graduates in excess of three times more engineers in applied sciences – electrical, industrial, bio-chemical, semiconductor, mechanical and power generation – than bachelors degrees than the US university system (*Herald Tribune*, 30 December 2003).

3.8 The world market for natural resources

Natural resources, including oil and other sources of energy, are an important input into the production process. Shortages of these inputs affect the productivity of the other factors of production.

Oil in the factor-price frontier

The considerations on the factor-price frontier above can analogously be applied to natural resources as a production factor. Taking natural resources (R) into account as an additional production factor in the production function $Q = F(L, K, R)$, the demand for resources is determined by the real resource price (nominal resource price v divided by the product price p) being equal to the marginal productivity of the resource (F_R): $v/p = F_R$. Thus, the world market for resources can be represented in a diagram similar to Figure 3.1.

In the two-dimensional factor-price frontier, natural resources are a hidden factor. A sudden resource shortage (for example, during the oil crisis in the 1970s) can be interpreted as a shift of the factor-price frontier (in Figure 3.10) to the left. The existing capital stock being adjusted to low oil prices becomes partly obsolete as oil prices rise. The marginal productivity of capital and labor

Table 3.4 Indicators of technological performance

	Number of patents[a]		Number of patent applications residents 2003[c]	R&D as percent of GDP by 2003[b]	Number of full-time researchers 2003[d, e]	Technology balance in percent of GDP 2003[e]
	Applications	Approvals				
USA	350,000	200,000	198,339	2.60	1,261,227 (9.3)	0.26
Europe (EU-15)	180,000	50,000	176,144	1.95	1,046,547 (6.1)	
Germany			80,661	2.55	264,721 (6.9)	−0.05
UK			33,671	1.89	157,662 (5.5)	0.7
Japan	400,000 (10.4)	60,000	371,495	3.15	675,330	0.2
China			40,346	1.22	675,000[f] (1.1)	

Notes
a Data from *Herald Tribune* October 3, 2005.
b Word Bank, *Development Indicators* 2005.
c OECD Science, *Technology and Industry Scoreboard 2005*: 190.
d Per 1,000 employees in parentheses.
e OECD, *OECD in Figures* 2005.
f *China Statistical Yearbook* 2004.

falls. This means that the real factor incomes for capital and labor are reduced. In the course of time, this movement of the factor-price frontier to the left can be partly reversed if technological progress, e.g. opening up new energy resources and saving energy, moves the factor-price frontier outwards again.

Case study: World oil production and oil exports

World production of oil was at 83.2 million barrels per day (mbd) in 2005. The largest producers were the OPEC countries with 29.6 mbd of which Saudi Arabia produced 8.9 mbd, the former USSR countries (10.6 mbd) and the US (5.4 mbd, all 2004). OPEC which had reached 50.5 percent of world production in 1975 accounts for 29.6 percent of world production (2004). OPEC's role was reduced because new sources of oil supply in the Gulf region, in the North Sea, in Alaska, in Russia, and in Kazakhstan came on stream. OPEC's reserves, including those reserves which are only profitable at a price of US\$75, are estimated at 896,659 mbd. A constant production of 30 mbd would last for 82 years. Such a calculation may be misleading, however, because it neglects the production in non-OPEC countries, the increase in demand over time and supply disruptions in the case of political crises.

Large oil consumers are the US (20.6 mbd), Japan (5.1 mbd), and China (6.4 mbd). For comparison, Germany consumes 2.6 mbd (all figures 2004). Net oil exports of the oil exporting countries amounted to 38.3 mbd. The biggest exporters were Saudi Arabia with 9.5 mbd, the former USSR countries with 7.6 mbd, and Norway with 2.6 mbd.

As in other markets of natural resources, China has an impact on the world oil market. With a production of 3.6 mbd and a consumption of 6.6 mbd in 2005, it had an import demand of 3.6 mbd. In 2001, its excess demand was only 1.4 mbd. This means that China as as booming region of the world crowds out other users and drives up the oil price. Whereas it stimulates economic growth in the world through its imports, it forces other countries to adjust to the new price situation on the petroleum market. This process will continue.

Depletion

A special problem with natural resources is depletion. We distinguish between non-renewable resources (oil) and renewable resources (wood, fish populations). When non-renewable resources are in finite supply and when substitution is not possible, they may eventually be exhausted. The optimal rate of resource extraction over time is therefore a decisive issue. When resources are renewable, the issue is how the rate of renewal and the rate of withdrawal have to interplay in order to secure an optimal pattern of resource use over time (see Chapter 4).

Environmental constraints

Another issue is allocating the environment for competing uses. The environment can be interpreted as a public good for consumption and as a receptacle for wastes such as emissions. The allocation problem relates to the environment as national resource as well as to the environment as a global resource (Chapter 15).

3.9 Changes on factor markets and world market equilibrium

A new equilibrium in the world factor markets has to be found when supply and demand conditions change. Such changes may occur abruptly and then appear as shocks to the world economy or they make take place gradually. Here are some cases:

- A technological breakthrough leads to an increased demand for capital. The capital demand curve on the world market for capital moves upwards. The interest rate rises.
- Higher growth in a large country of the world or in one of the world's important regions can exercise demand pressure on a natural resource, raising its price. The same effect can be observed in the case of stronger growth, e.g. due to a higher growth path or during a recovery in the business cycle.
- A shortage of natural resources as in the two oil crises in the 1970s makes the natural resource more expensive. It reduces the marginal productivity of capital. The interest rate falls. Also the marginal productivity of labor falls, the real wage goes down or does not increase as much as before.
- Institutional changes can influence the factor markets as well. In the large countries of Continental Europe, a high level of unemployment has developed over the past thirty-five years owing to the institutional setting of the labor market. Another example of the impact of institutional arrangement is the introduction of capital-funded old-age insurance systems in the world; this stimulates savings and reduces the interest rate.

4 Growth processes in the world economy

What you will understand after reading this chapter

The previous chapters have analyzed the world markets for goods and for factors of production. This chapter continues the global economic view, looking at the way growth processes take place in the world economy. The historical record of the last two centuries shows a continuous upward movement in income per capita interrupted by two world wars and the hyper-inflation of the 1920s and the Great Depression of the 1930s (section 4.1). Growth processes overlap with cyclical movements (section 4.2). The driving force of economic growth is the augmentation of production factors, comprising capital accumulation, population growth, and technological progress. Institutions defining incentives and constraints are an important factor (section 4.3). Capital exports and imports play a decisive role in the growth processes of open economies (section 4.4). We discuss why openness is important (section 4.5). Localization factors are surveyed (section 4.6). Empirical evidence suggests the relevance of capital accumulation for growth (section 4.7). An intensely discussed topic is whether economic processes are characterized by divergence or convergence (section 4.8). Economic growth is a process with many features different from the neoclassical approach (section 4.9). To conclude, some special aspects of the world economy's growth process such as resource scarcity are dealt with (section 4.10).

4.1 Economic growth: the historical record

The world economy is not static, but dynamic in character. In the course of time, various changes take place. In the last 200 years, a sizable increase in per capita income of the early industrialized countries can be observed (Figure 4.1). However, the two world wars, the European hyper-inflation in the 1920s and the Great Depression halted the increase in economic welfare.

A decisive question for growth processes is whether economies are open or closed. Historically, there seems to be a relation between the openness of an economy and economic welfare. In the countries that were industrialized earliest, gross national product has risen with growing openness. The two world wars

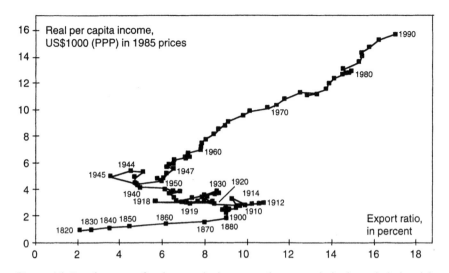

Figure 4.1 Development of real per capita income and export ratio in the early industrialized countries,[a] 1820–1990 (source: Maddison 1992; own calculations).

Note

a Australia, Austria, Belgium, Canada, Denmark, Finland, France, Germany, Italy, Japan, Netherlands, Norway, Sweden, Switzerland, United Kingdom, United States.

of the twentieth century reduced the openness; they represent a period of decline
and stagnation. This also holds for the 1920s and early 1930s, whereas after
1945 a continuous upward movement begins.

A rich source of historical data on economic growth in a long-run economic
perspective is specified in Maddison (2001). For instance, growth in China and
Europe is compared for two millennia. The book also looks at the impact of
Europe on the world economy in the second millennium and in the second half
of the last century.

4.2 Global economic growth and cyclical movements

Cyclical fluctuations

In the world economy, as well as in a national economy, long-term growth
processes are characterized by cyclical movements. In Figure 4.2, a growth trend
with cycles is shown for the G7 countries, the larger OECD industrialized
nations. Real gross national product oscillates around a trend. The recessions of
1974/1975, 1982/1983, 1986/1987 (mini recession), 1992/1993, and 2003/2004
in the industrialized countries are clearly visible. Economic growth is thus not
constant over time, but varies with the ups and downs of economic activity.

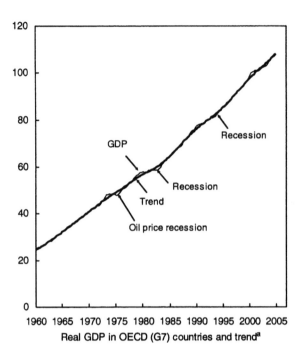

Real GDP in OECD (G7) countries and trend[a]

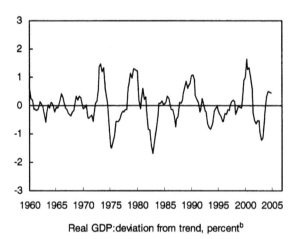

Real GDP:deviation from trend, percent[b]

Figure 4.2 Growth and business cycle in the G7 countries (source: OECD, *Main Economic Indicators*, current volumes).

Notes
a Index 2000 = 100.
b Hodrick/Prescott filter (smoothing factor 1,600).

GDP growth varies with world trade. A strong increase in world trade (in real terms) as with 10.4 percent (merchandise trade) in 2000 is associated with a strong growth rate of world production (GDP growth rate at 3.8 percent, see Table 1.1). A lower growth of world trade, even if not negative as in 2001 with only 0.1, goes together with a slow GDP growth rate (2.4 percent). For the industrial countries it meant a recession.

Cyclical movements are not necessarily synchronized in the world economy. One region of the world may be in a recession while other regions are in an upswing. In this case, different regional factors are responsible for the cyclical movements, such as home-made and specific problems in one region, a weakening of impulses of growth in one area of the world or structural issues specific to one region only. The cyclical situation in a big country spills over to other economies (international business-cycle interlink). Thus, the US accounting for nearly 30 percent of world GDP has a strong impact on other areas including Europe. If a worldwide disturbance (like the oil crisis in the 1970s) occurs, the world business cycle evolves in a rather synchronous way, resulting in a uniform world business cycle.

The processes of economic growth are accompanied by crises and other disturbances. The disintegration of the world economy in the 1930s, for example, went together with a breakdown of the world economy characterized by a significantly negative growth rate (see the Kindleberger spiral in Figure 1.3).

Crises

Whereas periods of increasing integration in the world economy, like the two decades after World War II, went along with high growth rates, the oil crisis of the 1970s partially devalued the existing capital stock that was contingent on low energy prices. This lowered the marginal productivity of capital, with the consequence that growth collapsed. At the same time, the export revenues of the OPEC countries increased considerably. With higher purchasing power, this increase led to a redirection of trade flows, to trade balance surpluses of the OPEC countries, to the accumulation of financial assets, and to a redirection of financial flows (petro-dollar recycling). Other disturbances had their effects on the growth process as well, like the Korean War which led to a boom with strong price rises, and the Vietnam War, where the strong expansion of the money supply in the United States ended in the inflation of the Bretton Woods system's anchor currency and, finally, in the collapse of this system. The debt crisis of the 1980s cut the Latin American countries off from real capital inflows. In real terms, a temporary transfer of capital in favor of the industrialized countries took place ('capital flowed up the hill'). The collapse of the centrally planned economies in the late 1980s lead to an output decline, and the post-communist economies went through a deep valley of adjustment. In 1997 the Asian countries experienced a financial crisis with negative growth rates, high current account deficits, currency devaluations and serious adjustment problems.

Case study: the Swedish crisis

In 1992, Sweden was hit by a severe crisis (Lindbeck *et al.* 1994). The GDP growth rate became negative (1991: −1.08 percent; 1992: −1.28 percent), the unemployment rate quadrupled from 1.7 percent in 1990 to 8.2 percent in 1993 within three years, the public sector deficit rose to 12 percent in 1993 and the current account deficit was at 2.8 percent of GDP in 1992 (6.3 percent in 1993). The short-term interest rate was at 500 percent during September 16–22 in order to prevent capital outflow. The financial system was at risk. In 1991, Sweden had fallen to rank fourteenth among the OECD countries in GDP per capita in purchasing power parity terms.

Many causes account for the crisis. There was a disequilibrium between the current account and internal stability and a collision between the exchange rate and domestic inflation. High nominal wage increases were offset by a depreciation of the exchange rate, but not completely. Nominal wages in the 1980s increased by 7–8 percentage points more than labor productivity, and productivity growth declined. This implied a cost rise. The inflationary development was accentuated by a high credit expansion made possible by the financial market deregulation of the 1980s. Public sector spending had reached 70 percent of GDP in 1992.

Some impulses of growth

Technological breakthroughs like the first industrial revolution in Great Britain in the eighteenth century represent an impulse for world economic growth. This also holds for the settlement and the industrialization of new areas such as North America. Moreover, changes in a country's economic policy, such as the institutional reforms in China since 1979, can influence growth processes worldwide. In most of these cases, a redirection of investment flows takes place.

Case study: Kondratieff cycles

Basic innovations can be interpreted as stimulating long-run growth cycles lasting for half a century. Such basic innovations change the technological structure of an economy comprehensively. While it may be somewhat arbitrary to pin down the timespan of such basic innovation waves, five Kondratieff cycles, named after the Russian economist Nikolai Kondratieff, can be distinguished:

1   Kondratieff (1800–1850): steam engine
2   Kondratieff (1850–1900): steel, railroads
3   Kondratieff (1900–1950): electro-technology, chemistry
4   Kondratieff (1950–1990): automobile, petro-chemistry
5   Kondratieff (1990–2020): information technology, biotechnology.

Originally, the idea was an attempt to describe the behavior of nineteenth century economies, especially their prices including raw material prices, wages, interest rates, bank deposits, and foreign trade. A wave of about fifty years was seen as having an expansionary and a contractionary phase. Technology was seen as leading the way out of a contraction. Later on, it was associated with the Schumpeterian concept of creative destruction (1934).

4.3 The driving forces of growth

World production function

Following at first a global view, i.e. of the world economy as a whole, a possible approach to the analysis of growth processes in the world economy is a world production function

$$Y = F(L, K, T, R, ..; \text{In})$$

where the world product Y depends on the production factors labor (L), capital (K), technological knowledge (T), resources (R) and other production factors, among them institutions (In). Therefore, the growth equation:

$$\hat{Y} = G(\hat{L}, \hat{K}, \hat{T}, \hat{R}, ..; \text{In})$$

can be derived; according to this the growth rate of the world product is a function of the growth rates of labor, capital stock, technological knowledge, natural resources, and other production factors. As an alternative indicator, we refer to an increase (or decrease) of per capita output ($y = Y/L$) when analyzing world economic growth, as it is a measure for people's provision with goods and thus a rudimentary measure for welfare.

   Such a formulation of a world production function is certainly interesting for historical analyses, where the importance of particular growth factors like capital accumulation, population growth, technological progress, or changes of the natural resources supply can be investigated. The world production function and the growth equation represent a general framework for an economic analysis and can also be the basis for econometric studies. In the ideal case, however, a formulation like this requires us to be able to empirically measure with sufficient accuracy the inputs of a world production function, like the world's capital stock, the world's labor supply, and its technological knowledge. This is impossible at the moment. We thus have to content ourselves either with applying the production factors and the growth equation to the world as a whole in a rather general interpretation, or to refer to the growth processes of particular regions of the world where outputs and inputs can be measured accurately. In both cases, it is worthwhile to further investigate the role of the particular determinants of growth.

Growth through capital accumulation

A first approach to explaining growth refers to capital accumulation in the context of neoclassical growth theory (Solow 1956).

Capital accumulation does not concern a static look at the allocation of capital in one period, i.e. a flow equilibrium (as in Chapter 3), but the accumulation of capital over time. In such an intertemporal context, we distinguish between a long-term equilibrium and the time path to the equilibrium. In a long-term equilibrium (steady state) all variables grow at the same rate and the ratios between these variables remain constant. A special case is the stationary state where the equilibrium growth rates of all variables equal zero. The time path indicates how an economy moves from the initial situation to the long-run equilibrium.

Pure capital accumulation without population growth or technological progress is the simplest case of growth. The world accumulates capital and a higher capital stock means more output, i.e. growth. The process of accumulating capital continues until the marginal productivity of capital and the discount rate (of utility, δ) are equal. Using a per capita version of the production function $y = f(k)$ with y being output per capita and k being the capital intensity (capital per capita) we have as an optimality condition for capital accumulation $f_k = \delta$ (Figure 4.3). As long as $f_k > \delta$, capital is accumulated; when $f_k = \delta$ (point G), capital accumulation comes to a halt (stationary state). Note that a simple version of the per-capita production function is $y = k^\alpha$ with $\alpha < 1$. α is the production elasticity of capital.

According to this concept, the world moves downwards along the negatively sloped marginal productivity-of-capital curve. The growth rate of gross national income, however, falls with increasing capital formation (increasing k) because each additional unit of capital has a lower marginal productivity. In the long-term equilibrium (point G), the growth rate is then zero because no further capital is built up.

Let the discount rate now approach zero, i.e., $\delta \to 0$. Then, the marginal rate of capital productivity also approaches zero. Point G approaches the horizontal axis.[1]

Real capital and human capital

Besides real capital (K), human capital (H) can also be regarded as a production factor of its own, comprising the skills, the capabilities and the knowledge of workers. All these characteristics are influenced by formal education and by 'learning on the job.' Furthermore, a traditional factor 'labor' (L: simple labor) is regarded as input. The production function, e.g. of the Cobb–Douglas type, then takes the form $Y = K^\alpha H^\beta L^{1-\alpha-\beta}$ instead of $Y = K^\alpha L^{1-\alpha}$. Obviously, the weight

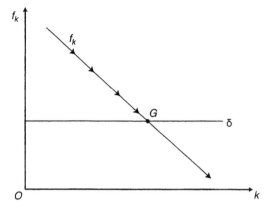

Figure 4.3 Optimal accumulation of capital.

of the traditional factors, labor and capital, measured by the elasticities of production α and $(1 - \alpha)$, changes. Under the assumption of perfect competition, the factors' elasticity of production corresponds to their shares of national income. With the share of labor in national income being $1 - \alpha = 0.7$, the production elasticity of labor is estimated by that value in the traditional Cobb–Douglas function (and the share of capital at $\alpha = 0.3$). By taking human capital into account, the share of traditional labor is reduced, whereas the importance of capital formation (including human capital) increases. The formation of human capital in the form of education requires abstaining from consumption, i.e. saving, like the formation of real capital. Saving thus becomes increasingly important. If we correspondingly define a broad notion of capital K^H: (K, H) that comprises real and human capital, this factor is attributed a weight of $\alpha + \beta$.[2] Empirical studies show that this elasticity of production $\alpha + \beta$ is 0.7 or higher and that traditional labor's elasticity of production lies at 0.3 and lower (Mankiw 1995). Income differences between economies can thus be explained not only by differences in the provision with physical capital, but also by different qualities of human capital, especially a different impact of education systems (years of schooling, universities).

Population growth

Taking population growth into account as well and assuming a discount rate near zero, a long-term equilibrium would be reached when the marginal productivity of capital (f_k) and the growth rate of the labor supply (n) are just equal, i.e. $f_k = n$ (point G in Figure 4.4). Each additional worker is equipped with additional capital. This follows from the neoclassical growth model and is called the 'golden rule of capital accumulation.' It ensures the highest per capita income possible in the long-term equilibrium. This golden rule is not valid, however, if a

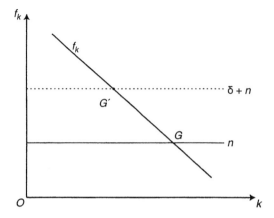

Figure 4.4 Optimal capital accumulation, time preference, and population growth.

positive discount rate is explicitly assumed.[3] With a higher capital stock per worker, it would indeed be possible to achieve a higher domestic product, but due to the positive discount rate, the economy is not willing to wait for it. With a positive discount rate, less capital is accumulated (point G' in Figure 4.4). The rule for optimal allocation is $f_k = \delta + n$. Here we have an analogy to renewable resources where it would be possible to achieve a maximum extraction quantity ('maximum yield') at a discount rate of zero, but owing to a positive discount rate, the resource stock that is being held is smaller. Analogously, less capital is accumulated (Blanchard and Fischer 1989: p. 45; Siebert 1983: Chapter 5).

The optimum time path for consumption and capital

The position of the long-term equilibrium and the adjustment path leading to the equilibrium can be represented in a c–k diagram. The long-term equilibrium is defined by per capita consumption (c) and the capital stock per capita (k) no longer changing. This means $\dot{c} = 0$ and $\dot{k} = 0$ where a dot indicates the change of a variable over time. Per capita consumption does not change any more when the condition $f_k(k) = \delta + n$ is satisfied (where δ and n are constant).[4] From this condition follows that in the c–k space, the c curve is a vertical line since $f_k(k)$ is determined by $\delta + n$ (Figure 4.5). From the system's equation of motion $\dot{k} = f(k) - c - nk$, it follows for $\dot{k} = 0$ that $c = f(k) - nk$, meaning that with k increasing, c first rises on the $\dot{k} = 0$ curve (if $f_k > n$), but then decreases again due to falling marginal productivity ($f_k < n$). At a positive discount rate $\delta > 0$, point G' will result in the world economy in long-term equilibrium. Note that for $\delta > 0$, point G would be reached. The positive discount rate implies a lower capital formation. Note that Figure 4.5 also holds for renewable resources where c is resource withdrawal from nature and $f(k)$ represents a production function of a natural resource stock k (e.g. a regeneration function of a forest or a fish population)

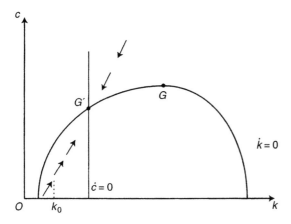

Figure 4.5 Long-term equilibrium.

with $f^k > 0$ below a natural equilibrium k^* and $f^k < 0$ above k^*. Point G then corresponds to the maximum yield.

As a rule, the growth rate decreases with a growing capital stock per capita, owing to decreasing marginal productivity. Every additional unit of capital has a smaller output effect. If we look at an economy where only the accumulation of real capital plays a role as a growth factor, capital formation comes to a stand-still in the long-run; a stationary state is reached. This holds, for example, with a per capita production function $y = k^\alpha$ with $\alpha < 1$.

Technological progress

If technological progress is present and if labor input is measured in efficiency units $\tilde{A} = a(t)A$, a figure analogous to Figure 4.4 results in the simple Solow-type model, where n has to be replaced by the term $n + x\epsilon \approx \tilde{n} + \epsilon$ (where ϵ is the rate of technological progress and $x = -cu''/u'$). In this case as well, a positive discount rate causes the accumulation of capital to come to a stop earlier. In Figure 4.4, new technological knowledge moves the marginal productivity of capital curve upward, shifting points G and G' to the right. Technological progress thus prevents a 'walking down the marginal productivity of capital curve.'

Endogenous growth in technological knowledge

Marginal productivity does not necessarily fall if the production function shows increasing returns to scale. This is Romer's (1986) concept of knowledge capital ($K^{H,}$ see also Grossman and Helpman 1991a). With capital formation per worker in an enterprise (k), knowledge capital per unit of labor $K^H = \varphi(k)$ develops as well, and this capital can also be used in other enterprises, i.e. capital accumulation in one firm has positive effects in other enterprises. For the marginal productivity of capital, we then have $f_k(k, K^H)$; that is, the marginal productivity of capital is positively affected by knowledge capital. Assuming $\varphi(k) = k^\gamma$, the production function takes the form $y = k^\alpha \varphi(k) = k^{\alpha+\gamma}$. Here, the traditional production function shows constant returns to scale for labor and capital and thus a decreasing marginal productivity of capital intensity k^α ($\alpha < 1$). The production function as a whole, however, has increasing returns to scale. This is related to technological knowledge being not a private commodity with rivalry in its use, but a public commodity, e.g. software that can be used in various places without the occurrence of rivalry. If the effect discussed here is strong enough and if ? + γ approaches 1, decreasing marginal productivities of capital disappear completely.

What drives the determinants of growth?

To explain growth processes, it is important to know what drives the determinants of growth. One of the drivers, capital accumulation, depends on the savings and on the expected return on investment. A country having a low time preference rate will tend to have higher savings. High rates of return are an incentive to invest and to build up a capital stock. Institutional arrangements such as a pay-as-you-go system or a capital-funded system influence the volume of savings. Technological progress depends on investments into research and development. High expected profits from research and development are an incentive to invest and to innovate. In the Romer model (1986), for example, the profit expectations in the high-technology industry drive the expenditures for research and development. The development of the growth determinants has thus to be explained endogenously.

The historical shift from physical capital to intangible capital

Historically, different growth factors were the driving force in the growth process; the importance of growth factors has shifted considerably over time. Looking at the US as an example (David 1999), working capital was the source of growth in labor productivity at the beginning of the nineteenth century; fixed (physical) capital took the leading role in a process of capital deepening in the later part of the nineteenth and the earlier part of the twentieth century. In the later part of the twentieth and the start of the twenty-first century, intangible capital (knowledge capital) with investments in education and training became the dominant growth factor.

Institutions

The institutional set-up of an economy, such as the rule of law, tax laws, economic and political liberty, and the independence of the central bank, plays an important role in determining the income level and economic growth. It defines the rules, the restraints and the incentives and consequently affects economic behavior, including such important growth determinants as investment, innovation, and human capital formation. Stability in the institutional set-up gives confidence while failures in the institutional arrangement mean uncertainty with a negative impact on the economic process. Indeed, it is fair to say that countries with an unstable institutional environment have had low growth rates, for example sub-Saharan African countries with internal conflicts. The role of institutional arrangements was stressed by the German *Freiburg* school of the ordo liberals in the 1940s and is now highlighted by institutional economics (Helpman 2004; Rodrik *et al.* 2004).

Other growth factors

Openness and localization, other important factors, will be studied in later sections. Other growth factors may also be relevant. Thus disease burdens in underdeveloped countries play an important role in explaining current variation in income levels and economic growth. Ecological aspects also play a role.

4.4 Capital importers and exporters

Let us now study open economies that do not have to rely on their own savings for their investments, but can import capital. Similarly, other countries may export capital. In order to determine whether a country is a capital importer or exporter, the interaction between the marginal productivity (f_k), the discount rate (δ), and the world market interest rate (r) has to be discussed.

Efficiency gains through capital movements

If the marginal productivity of capital and the discount rate in a country are higher than the world market interest rate, i.e. $f_k = \delta > r$, it is worthwhile to import capital from the world market for capital (Figure 4.6a). If, however, the discount rate is lower than the interest rate in the world market for capital, it is worthwhile to export capital (Figure 4.6b). The capital importer gets an advantage (in the case of $\delta > r$) by passing from autarky to free capital mobility: with capital from the world market, they can produce more in their home country (point *G* instead of point *A*). The importer pays interest on the imported capital amounting to the rectangle *CBGD* and additionally produces the area *CAGD*. The part of the production that additionally remains for the importer is the triangle *BAG*. This is the advantage from importing capital.

The capital exporter also has an advantage by passing from autarky to free capital mobility. He produces less than in autarky, but receives a higher income from interest. The exporter gains the area *GFA* in Figure 4.6b.

Figure 4.6 exhibits an equilibrium in only the short-run. In the long-run, the current account has to be balanced for the two equilibrium solutions *G*, so there is an intertemporal budget restriction to be respected. To balance its current

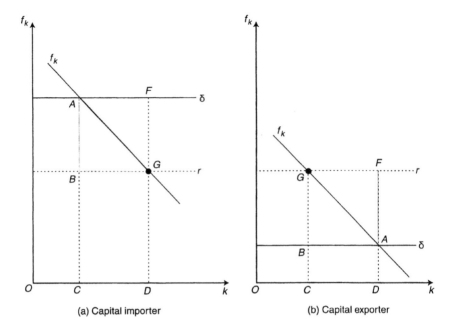

Figure 4.6 Long-term equilibrium with capital import and capital export.

account in the future, the debtor country thus has to fulfill its interest obligations by exporting goods to the creditor country. For the capital-importing country, gross domestic product exceeds gross national product which can be interpreted as gross residents' product. In the long-term equilibrium, it cannot use its whole production for consumption, but has to set some part aside for paying interest and repaying debt (see Appendix 4.A).

Possible scenarios of capital accumulation

If all countries in the world have the same discount rate and if one country has the highest capital productivity, capital will be accumulated first in this country. The country with the highest capital productivity grows fastest at first, causing marginal capital productivity to fall gradually so that eventually capital accumulation becomes attractive for the other countries as well.

Let us now look at a situation where initially all countries have the same marginal productivity of capital, but one country has a lower discount rate. This country will be more inclined to abstain from consumption. This results in a consumption level that is lower at first, but also in faster capital accumulation owing to higher savings. Because of this, it can consume more later on: its consumption increases faster in time. The other countries, on the other hand, have a high discount rate and are thus more impatient. They start with a higher consumption level, but they build less capital, and their consumption increases more slowly in time.

If all countries have different discount rates, the country with the lowest discount rate determines up to which point capital is accumulated in the world economy.[5] The country with the lowest discount rate provides capital until its discount rate and the real interest rate are equal, then its consumption stays constant. For the other countries, $\delta > r$ holds, and consumption decreases in the course of time. In a simplifying model context, the patient country finally accumulates all the capital of the world.

Taking different discount rates, different population growth rates, and different rates of technological progress into consideration, the implications for the capital market become very complex. Under *ceteris paribus* assumptions, the country with the low discount rate remains the world's net creditor, and this result should not change if, owing to population growth, the debtor country needs more capital and has a high national discount rate. A country with strong technological progress can also indebt itself to the country with the low discount rate. The technological progress may be strong enough to finance the interest service in favor of the creditor country.

4.5 How important is the openness of economies?

Economic growth is related to the openness of economies. Figure 4.7 gives an insight. It illustrates a group of developing countries that are identified as post-1980 globalizers in terms of the increase in their trade to GDP ratios. The 16 countries are: Argentina, Brazil, China, Colombia, Costa Rica, Hungary, India, Jordan, Malaysia, Mexico, Nicaragua, Paraguay, Philippines, Thailand,

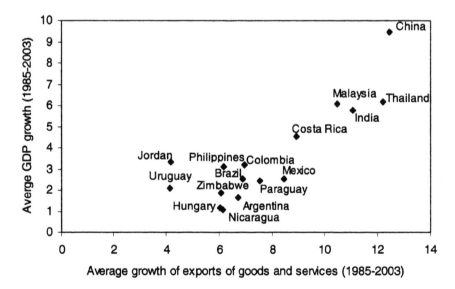

Figure 4.7 Growth of exports and GDP for post-1980 globalizers (source: World Bank, *World Development Indicators* 2005; own calculations).

Uruguay, and Zimbabwe (Dollar and Kraay 2004). For these countries, the growth rate in the period 1985–2003 is linked to openness. Open countries have a higher growth rate. A similar figure (not shown) is obtained for a group of early industrialized countries for the period 1870–1990, using Maddison (1992) data. The growth rate of GDP per capita is then linked to openness, measured as the rate of increase of the export ratio, i.e. of the share of exports in GDP. Except for the two world wars and the inter-war period, the export ratio increases, and the growth rate of the gross domestic product per capita rises. Exports are beneficial to economic growth.

There is a variety of mechanisms through which growth occurs in an open economy. The first to be mentioned here are traditional gains from foreign trade with final products, generating a higher national income and welfare. In the course of economic development, countries manage to gain comparative price advantages through the formation of real and human capital. The comparative advantages of endowment change; and these advantages can be influenced by policy ('acquired comparative advantage'). At the same time, some comparative advantages migrate away from industrialized nations to the developing countries, e.g. because production no longer pays off owing to increasing factor costs (like labor costs or regulation). Gains of specialization add to the welfare gains; especially, economies of scale (learning effects) are of relevance. A wider variety of products is made possible. The hypothesis of the product cycle also explains why production moves away from industrialized countries (via a diffusion of knowledge from the innovator to the imitators) and eventually finds its locations worldwide. The intensification of competition that is related to foreign trade (with the consequence of falling costs and new technological knowledge discovered) results in higher growth as well.

If trade with capital goods is also taken into account, additional effects result. Debt allows the import of capital goods so that the capital stock can be accumulated faster; the economy moves on a higher growth path towards the long-term equilibrium. Competition in the production of capital goods is intensified so that efficiency gains can be expected. The sectoral resource allocation between research and development on the one side and production on the other is improved through trade with capital goods, leading to a higher long-term growth path with income gains. In the long-term equilibrium, a higher per capita production is reached. Finally, the international diffusion of technological knowledge, like the trade in patents and the flow of ideas, is a channel through which the growth process can be influenced favorably in open economies.

4.6 Localization factors and geography

Economic activities are not uniformly distributed in space (Krugman 1991). One reason is that space itself is not homogeneous, but structured by resource deposits, agricultural areas, natural highways like valleys and rivers, focal points like natural harbors, settlement possibilities, and other factors. Thus, the physical geography plays a role in the growth process. For instance, land-locked countries do not have the option of using maritime transportation and depend on land logistics (Sachs 2003).

Beside these basic locational advantages, advantages of agglomeration play an important role as factors that constitute spatial structure. These concern positive external effects between economic activities, referring to technological as well as pecuniary external effects. This comprises spatially limited diffusion processes related to new technological knowledge (spillover, spatially bound knowledge capital), informal or formal information networks delimited in space and 'proximity advantages,' e.g. between enterprises and politics. A case in point is the labor market. If a region has a qualified labor supply at its disposal (historical examples: the Swiss Jura and the Black Forest in Germany for the watch industry, Baden-Württemberg in Germany for precision engineering), it is easier for the enterprises to rely on a pool of qualified workers. If a region is occupied by enterprises that demand similar qualifications, such a region is attractive for qualified workers simply because they do not depend on just one company to find a job. They have the option of switching to other companies, and thus their risk of becoming jobless is smaller.

Transport costs are another factor that has structuring effects on space. They determine the size of the market. The decline of transport costs increases the size of the market. The reduction of virtual distance in the internet improves the size of networks.

Once a certain structure is given, like the existence of a city with a homogeneous area around it, it can be shown that rings of economic activity develop around the city as a function of transport costs (Thünen 1826); other things equal, businesses with high transport costs will settle near the city (Alonso 1964).

Furthermore, the historical development of the spatial structure is path dependent. The spatial structure given in a specific moment of time is the base for economic decisions that for their part have spatial effects in the future. Thus, the future spatial development is in some way shaped by the original structure. Old locations have the advantage that various investments have already been made there, comprising real capital of the companies, durable consumption goods of the households (real estate), and infrastructure capital (roads, harbors, universities). The costs related to these are partly 'sunk costs'; production stays at the old location, even if these costs can no longer be covered.

In contrast, a new location does not have the sunk-cost advantage. It has to compete with an old location that can neglect the sunk costs in locational competition. As the capital stock of a region is, in a disaggregated view, defined by a variety of capital goods, the decision about choices of location for the individual capital good is dispersed on the time axis. As a consequence, decisions about the location of capital goods that are currently installed at an old location and need replacement have to be made again and again. If a capital good stays at an old location, chances improve for another capital good at that place to be renewed there as well.

However, sunk costs cannot justify a location permanently. At some time, the marginal productivity of investments may decline so much or the locational quality elsewhere may improve so strongly that a change of location becomes worthwhile, despite sunk costs.

During the process of economic development, self-amplifying factors may occur that lead to the development of growth poles, especially if a region can attract resources owing to advantages of location and agglomeration (polarization). The growth process in the world economy is then seen as taking place in a large set of regional growth clusters. During the further development, such growth poles then radiate out to other regions and pull them along. Here, the question arises of whether a process of convergence will come about or whether economic development is finally accompanied by divergence (see below).

On a more aggregated scale of the world economy, the concept of the center (or core) and periphery plays a role. Over the last century, the two centers of Europe and North America have been distinguished. In the twentieth century, a third center or growth pole in Asia, with Japan, the four or six 'tigers' and China, has appeared beside the two centers of North America and Europe.

4.7 Empirical evidence: capital formation

The variety of the approaches to explaining economic growth presented here has produced a considerable literature striving for empirical scrutiny. The task of empirical work is to analyze which of the growth factors described above has which effect on the growth rate. This can be done by studying time series and looking at the relationship of a specific factor or many factors and the growth rate in a specific country or by analyzing data that are pooled for many countries. In pooled data sets, structural relationships are sought that hold for many countries. It is not surprising that the results of empirical studies differ, for instance whether openness, the quality of institutions or physical geography has a more important impact on growth and the income level. The findings of an econometric study crucially depend on the following:

1   the specification of the model;
2   the sample selection;
3   the time period used;
4   the method used in estimation;
5   the used proxy (trade or institution indicator for instance).

A specific problem in empirical studies is that erosion processes such as the decline of the communist countries take a long time, and there is not very much movement in the data. It is then difficult to discover an erosion process.

Let us look at the importance of capital formation as a growth factor and then study the convergence hypothesis. Economies with a high marginal productivity of capital should, other things being equal, be characterized by a strong capital formation. Capital is also needed if the population increases, to equip the additional workforce with machines. Moreover, strong technological progress will lead to high investment activity. We can expect a high investment activity to be

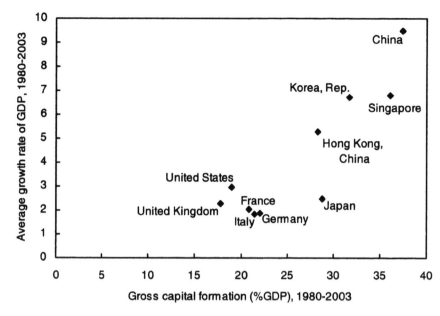

Figure 4.8 Gross capital formation and growth rates in selected countries, 1980–2003 (source: World Bank, *World Development Indictors* 2005).

linked to high growth rates because the capital stock is an important ingredient of the growth process. The higher the gross capital formation relative to GDP, the stronger is the growth rate. The thesis that the average growth rate is positively related to the share of investment in GDP is empirically corroborated (Figure 4.8). It is remarkable that three of the four tigers, with investment shares of significantly above 25 percent in the years 1980–2003 have had annual growth rates of over 6 percent; a similar story holds for China with an investment share of nearly 40 percent.

4.8 Catching-up processes in the world economy: convergence or divergence?

The convergence hypothesis

The marginal productivity of capital falls with growing capital accumulation. Consequently, the contribution of a unit of capital to growth decreases as well. We thus have to expect the growth rate to fall with capital accumulation. This argument can also be pointed in another direction: as poor countries have a small capital stock, they should – all other things being equal – have a higher marginal productivity of capital and thus a higher growth rate than rich countries with better capital equipment. The hypothesis thus is: 'Poor countries grow faster.' Differences in income are then (at least partly) leveled out in the course of time.

In the extreme case, we should – with a fully integrated world market for capital and without differences in risk – expect that there cannot be any differences in the marginal product of capital. In the simplest of models with perfectly mobile capital and identical production technology everywhere, the international capital mobility would have to lead to an almost immediate equalization of growth rates. This cannot be observed empirically, however. One reason is that there is no perfect capital mobility. In reality, the international capital mobility performs a balancing function only at peaks, as the discussion of the Feldstein–Horioka (1980) result in Chapter 3 has shown. In addition, there are other factors that are specific for a certain country and explain differences in economic growth; these factors particularly comprise the institutional set-up and the growth of technological knowledge.

In the very long-run, differences in marginal productivity should be impossible even under imperfect capital mobility if we assume identical production technologies and institutions. In this case, there would be absolute convergence, i.e. output per worker would, in the long-run equilibrium (steady state), be equal in all countries. In the simple neoclassical model of the Solow type, though, absolute convergence is only reached if the exogenous data for the long-run equilibrium, like population growth (n) (if it is exogenously given), the savings rate and human capital are identical. Regarding different long-term equilibria, we have to make corrections for these differing exogenous conditions.[6] This is why we speak of conditional convergence, where the different exogenous conditions of different countries are taken into account. Then, neither do countries reach the same long-term equilibrium nor are the per capita incomes equalized between countries.

Some formulae of convergence

To get an impression of the time required for convergence, we take a look at two economies with constant growth rates g (home country) and g^* (foreign country) of per capita income. Note that this represents a simplification because on a growth path to a long-run equilibrium the rates would change. Assuming that Home has a lower initial per capita income than Foreign, i.e. $y_0 < y^*_0$, the convergence rate $\hat{\alpha}$ satisfies $\hat{\alpha} = \hat{y} - \hat{y}^* = g - g^*$. If Home grows at a rate of $g = 5$ percent and Foreign at $g^* = 2$ percent, the income difference is leveled out at a rate of about 3 percent per year.

The duration of the absolute convergence (t) is calculated by setting the per capita incomes of the two countries in t equal, so that:

$$y_t = y^*_t \Leftrightarrow y_0 \, e^{gt} = y^*_0 \, e^{g^*t}$$

with:

$$t = \frac{\ln(y_0 / y^*_0)}{g^* - g} = \frac{\ln(y_0) - \ln(y^*_0)}{g^* - g}$$

where the income ratio is expressed in natural logs. With a growth difference $g-g^*$ of three percentage points and an income level at 30 percent in the original situation (e.g. $y_0 / y_0^* = 0.3$), it takes forty years until both countries have the same per capita income. With a growth difference of four percentage points it takes thirty years. For the half-life of the income difference:

$$t_{\text{half}} = \frac{0.5\ln(y_0/y_0^*)}{g^* - g}$$

holds.[7] With a growth difference of three percentage points and an income level of 30 percent in the original situation, it takes seventeen years until the income differential is halved, i.e until the 50 percent level is reached. Starting from 40 percent, it takes 7.4 years to reach 50 percent. In these statements, absolute convergence and half-life depend on the original situation (Table 4.1).

This type of calculation has been applied to East Germany. The calculations told us that we had to expect a long-term adjustment process. In 1991, the East German region (excluding West Berlin) was at about one-third of West Germany's GDP level of production. If an adjustment to 80 percent of the West German level would have been set as a target and if the East German growth rate exceeded West Germany's growth rate by five percentage points, the level of 80 percent would have been attained in eighteen years, i.e. in 2009. With a growth rate differential of 3 percent, we would have had to wait until 2120, i.e. for twenty-nine years.[8] Unfortunately, East Germany has not been growing at a higher rate than West Germany since 1997. The East German per capita income level (of the population, not identical to per capita of the employed) – with Berlin included – was at 67.1 percent of the West German level (or 72.0 percent of the German level) in terms of GDP in the year 2003.

Table 4.1 Time required for convergence

Percentage points of lead in growth (%)	Half[a]: difference of per capita incomes halved in … years			Absolute convergence[b] in … years		
	Starting from an original level of					
	30%	40%	48%	30%	40%	50%
1	51	22.3	4	120.4	91.6	69.3
2	25.5	11.2	2	60.2	45.8	34.7
3	17	7.4	1.4	40.1	30.5	23.1
4	12.7	5.5	1	30.1	22.9	17.3
5	10.2	4.4	0.8	24.1	18.3	13.9
6	8.5	3.7	0.7	20.1	15.3	11.6

Note
a Calculated according to the formula:

$$t_{\text{half}} = \frac{0.5 \ln(y_0 / y_0^*)}{g^* - g}$$

b Calculated according to the formula: $t = \ln(y_0 /y_0^*)/(g^* - g)$.

Convergence between regions

Thus far, the analysis has been simplified in the sense that the growth rates of two countries or regions are assumed to be fixed. In the adjustment period of the neoclassical model, the growth rate changes, however, when approaching the steady state. Strictly speaking, convergence addresses the question whether the actual per capita income is converging against the per capita income in the long-term equilibrium. In this formulation, the average growth rate per year over a period spanning from the initial period 0 to the steady-state period T is given by the growth rate x in the long-term equilibrium and the 'distance' of the per capita income in the steady state $\tilde{y}$ from the original situation y_0 (Barro and Sala-i-Martin 1995: 81).[9]

$$\hat{y} = \frac{1}{T} ln\left[\frac{y(T)}{y_0}\right] = x + \frac{1}{T}(1 - e^{-\beta T})ln\left[\frac{\tilde{y}}{y_0}\right]$$

The further the per capita income in the initial situation is away from the income in the steady state, the higher is the average growth rate over the period from 0 to T. β is the rate of convergence. At a constant rate of convergence β, the expression $(1/T)(1 - e^{-\beta T})$ approaches zero if T approaches infinity. The growth rate is then dominated by the steady-state rate (x).[10]

The Barro rule

Barro and Sala-i-Martin (1992) have applied these considerations to the regions of the US for the period from 1880 until 1988. Their result was that the differences between the regions were leveled out at a rate of 2 percent per year. This is the so-called Barro rule. At a rate of convergence of 2 percent, it takes about thirty-five years until the difference of per capita incomes between regions is halved. As the regions of the US surveyed by Barro are relatively similar, we can assume that they approach the same long-term equilibrium (steady state) in the long run. These results suggest that catch-up processes exist, but that these processes require considerable time.

Convergence of early industrialized countries

For the period from 1870 until 1979, Maddison (1982) concludes that early industrialized countries with a high per capita income had smaller growth rates of per capita income whereas economies with a lower per capita income showed a higher growth rate. The regression[11] yields (L: number of workers, standard error in parentheses):

$$log\left(\frac{Y_{1979}}{L_{1979}}\right) - log\left(\frac{Y_{1870}}{L_{1870}}\right) = 8.46 - \underset{(0.09)}{1.00} log\left(\frac{Y_{1870}}{L_{1870}}\right),$$

$$R^2 = 0.88$$

The slope of −1 means that for every percent that a country's per capita income was below the average in 1870, the cumulated growth rate in the period 1870–1979 was higher by 1 percent. According to this result we thus observe a long-term convergence, in fact an absolute convergence. A critical objection to this is that the country selection is biased in the sense that the examined countries have a high per capita income today as well. If instead countries are examined that do not have a high per capita income today, but did in 1870 (thus additionally taking into account, among others, Argentina, Portugal, and Spain), and if Japan is excluded from the observation as a one-off case, we can at best speak of a convergence that is only weak.

Convergence in the OECD countries

If we take the OECD countries – and thus the industrialized countries – into account, a negative relation between the level of the growth rate and the per capita income results as well, but the differences for the period from 1870 to 1993 are leveled out at a rate of only 1 percent compared to 2 percent in the Barro estimates for regions of a country (Figure 4.9). Inside an economy, the catch-up processes are thus, as a rule, stronger than they are between countries. Since World War II, the European economies and Japan have grown significantly more strongly than that of the US. In 1990, the income differences per capita of 1950 had been reduced by well over a half (Obstfeld and Rogoff 1996: 455).

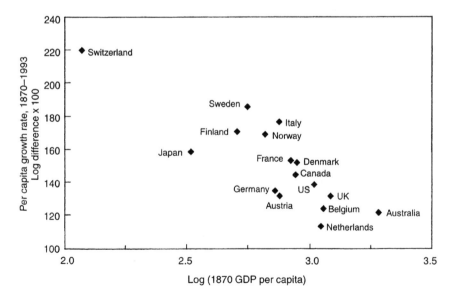

Figure 4.9 Convergence in the OECD countries, 1870–1993 (sources: De Long 1988, Maddison 1982; own calculations).

Convergence in the European Union

For the fifteen countries of the European Union excluding Luxembourg as an outlier, convergence of per capita incomes with a convergence rate of 1.07 percent for the period 1961–2003 can be observed (Figure 4.10). If the countries of southern enlargement Greece, Spain, and Portugal are excluded from the calculation in addition to Luxembourg, the conversion rate jumps to 1.86 percent. Older studies for the period 1960–1995 show a convergence rate of 1.4. As countries in a regional integration like the European Union have an intermediate position between regions of an economy and the nation states like OECD countries, the catch-up processes in regional integrations (like the EU) are not as swift as between the regions of a country (2 percent), but faster than between the OECD countries (1 percent). Thus, the Barro rule differs with respect to the level of disaggregation and the level of institutional integration. Regions with a common institutional framework of a nation have a high rate of convergence. Autonomous countries have a much lower convergence. Countries belonging to a regional integration like the EU are in between. As the regression coefficients for different subsets of countries show, the results are somewhat arbitrary.

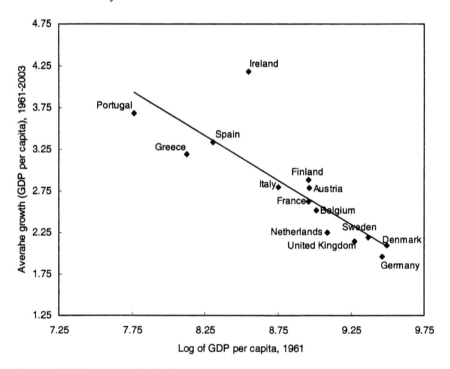

Figure 4.10 Convergence in the European Union[a] (source: World Bank, *World Development Indicators* 2005).

Note
a Excluding Luxembourg.

Divergence between industrialized countries and developing countries

Convergence does not occur any more, however, if the number of countries is greatly increased. In a study of ninety-eight countries, a moderately positive regression between growth rate and development level results (Barro and Sala-i-Martin 1992). This means that countries with a higher income level grow (moderately) stronger. Divergence prevails instead of convergence; accordingly, industrialized countries and developing countries grow apart. For the developing countries as a whole, again convergence cannot be found. This image presumably changes if some countries like the African countries south of the Sahara (and possibly some Latin American countries) are excluded. A possible explanation for the fact that convergence cannot be observed in these cases is that the parameters of technology and of resource endowment are very different. Economic policy plays an important role as well, as in the misorientation of Latin America in the four decades until 1990. The countries are then characterized by different long-term equilibria.

Absolute and conditional convergence

Conditional convergence refers to the fact that not all factors of economic growth are identical between countries and regions, but that differences in initial factor endowments exist that are permanent. For instance, cultural differences could be such a factor. Then, the country or region in question cannot reach the same steady state as other areas. The steady state is conditional upon the endowment difference. If, however, the initial differences in factor endowments can be overcome by accumulation in the course of time, the same steady state can be reached; we speak of absolute convergence.

Convergence clubs

Empirical analyses suggest that convergence can be more easily shown for a subset of countries and for a subset of regions of a country. Some countries or some regions diverge; if these are excluded from the analysis of a set of countries or regions, the convergence process is stronger.

Sigma convergence

So far, the discussion about convergence has been based on the catching-up rate of the per capita income. This is called 'Beta convergence.' Sigma convergence, on the other hand, refers to the coefficient of variation of the per capita income expressed in logs. We have Sigma convergence if the per capita income coefficient of variation for a group of regions (or countries) decreases. Beta convergence and Sigma convergence are different measures. Beta convergence is geared to the growth rates of the per capita income over a period; Sigma convergence refers to the variance of the per capita incomes at two points in time. The two measures thus do not lead to identical statements about convergence processes: regions with a low per capita income can grow so strongly (high Beta convergence) that at the end of a period of comparison the variance of the per capita income is higher than at the beginning (Sigma divergence).

4.9 Growth as a process

Growth is a dynamic process where the accumulation of factors of production plays a major role, i.e. the accumulation of physical capital, of human capital, and of technological knowledge. The accumulation of these factors drive the growth process, either steadily or in a step-wise fashion. Accumulation means that normally there is a ratchet effect in the growth process so that the level of production reached in one period is the floor for the process in the next period. Growth is a process which, if disturbed, will tend to resume. Besides this concept of accumulation, there are constraints for the process; it is possible that growth factors become weaker over time. There is an immense diversity of historical experiences (David 1999), a wide diversity of outcome. Here are some aspects of the growth process.

A Schumpeterian process

Unlike in the model concept of a steady state, things do not grow in equal proportion; rather, there is some imbalance and an increase in diversity which keeps the process going. The process does not go smoothly, there is boom and bust, up and down, and there is a tremendous structural change in which existing sectors disappear and new sectors come into existence. In a Schumpeterian (1934) process of creative destruction existing capital becomes obsolete. The economy and society undergo profound changes, growth transforms society.

Growth leaders and countries that fall back

The analysis of catching-up and convergence processes says something about how fast economies close in on the countries with the highest level of wealth or the highest growth rate. But studies about catch-up processes do not answer the question how an economy manages to take the leading role in the growth process of the world economy (like the US relative to the UK in the last two centuries) and to reach a very high level of production per head. Apparently, a country has, in this case, the possibility to activate growth factors in some special manner.

The opposite picture is that countries fall back, either absolutely or relatively. It is by no means a given fact that growth processes of economies go on and on. There can be stagnation and decline. Some examples are the centrally planned economies in the 1970s and 1980s until the systems finally collapsed, but also Sweden in the period 1970–1992, the UK after 1945, or Argentina which figured among the ten richest countries of the world at the end of the nineteenth century.

The new frontier

In the stagnation thesis of Alvin Hansen as illustrated by his student Higgins (1959), the lack of a new frontier is the major reason for stagnation. In Hansen's view, extending to the west in US history was such a new frontier opening up new investment opportunities, and his fear was the lack of such a frontier in the future. Technological breakthroughs and the integration of the world economy with an increase in the size of the market may represent such a new frontier.

Path dependence

Initial conditions, like the capital stock per worker given in the initial situation (k_0) which determines output per head and thus the starting point for the growth process, can play a more important role than in the neoclassical model. Even in the neoclassical model some aspects of endowment may not be overcome in the growth process and economies may reach a different long-run equilibrium and, consequently, may move on a different growth path. But the initial level may have even greater importance. Thus, the technological knowledge available at a certain moment of time determines the direction in which the technology will develop. Localization factors are another important example. In this sense, growth processes are path-dependent. Added to this, the determinants of an initial constellation can interact. If a combination of factors is what matters in the initial situation, economic policy may have to start at several points simultaneously to reach a more favorable growth path. In that sense of path dependence, history matters.

Thresholds and the poverty trap

A different case of path dependence is that thresholds exist which must be overcome for growth to take place. Countries can find themselves in a trap of weak growth from which they cannot find their way out. These aspects are relevant, for instance, for growth processes in developing countries. Here, the path dependence of economic development plays a special role; a big push may be necessary to get out of a trap (Chapter 10).

Open societies

The organization of societies is an important aspect determining the growth process. Whether societies are closed or open in the sense of Popper (1945) is of major relevance for the growth process. An open society allows choice and individual freedom. This implies decentralization and subsidiarity. It also implies competition as the principal element of organizing a society. Competition can be interpreted as a discovery device (Hayek 1968) helping to find new technological, economic, and institutional solutions. The alternative to competition is a corporativistic approach where corporations like trade unions and employers' associations play a decisive role in decision-making. As a rule, this means that insiders have an important weight in decision-making, that the status quo is protected and that new avenues, especially if unknown and uncertain, are often not pursued.

Self-enforcing institutional weakness

In Asia, the industrialized countries of Europe that fall back in their growth performance were (before the Asian crisis in 1997/1998) ironically named NDCs, or newly declining countries, following the newly industrializing countries (NICs). Some of the industrialized countries, most prominently the major countries in continental Europe, France, Germany, and Italy, have become rigid in their institutional structures; they seem to be unable to modernize their incentive systems, and of the conflicting aims of equity and efficiency they have chosen equity. This leads to an Olson-type inflexibility (Olson 1982). Internal institutional constraints make these countries incapable of reforming the social insurance systems or their regulatory framework of the labor market. Institutionally, they have started a silent erosion of their competitiveness.

Aging societies

In many countries, such as in Germany, in Japan and – not to the same extent – in the US, a population has to be expected in the next decades that will live longer and will be older on average. At the same time, the changing age structure is related to a decrease in population. All this causes a change in the demand structure (e.g. lower demand for housing, higher demand for leisure services and medical supply), a lower supply of labor and changed demands on the old-age insurance systems. These and other changes have feedback effects on the growth processes.

4.10 Particular topics of economic growth

Resource shortage

The stock of natural resources (Z) changes over time, satisfying:

$$\dot{Z} = -R + g(Z)$$

where $\dot{Z}$ denotes the change of the resource stock in a period, R represents the resource extractions from nature in a period and $g(Z)$ is a natural growth function for renewable resources. In the case of non-renewable resources, this function is dropped, and the resource stock (Z) declines according to the equation $\dot{Z} = -R$ in every period.

Starting with a production function that contains natural resources as a production factor, the decisive question is whether the natural resource can be substituted. If this is not the case, nothing can be produced without natural resources, so that $Q = F(L, K, R = 0) = 0$. If substitution is possible, the non-renewable natural resource is substituted by other factors, and the production does not come to a standstill when the natural resource cannot be utilized any more.

Sustainable development

The question of sustainability is relevant for the growth process. This is the issue whether the process can be kept up for a long time (mathematically until infinity) or whether it will meet constraints that will make an ever-lasting growth impossible. Such constraints can be the depletion of natural resources or the limited capacity of the environment as a sink of pollutants such as CO_2-emissions. The decisive question is whether new technologies can be found substituting dwindling natural resources or preventing emissions. From the point of view of a production function, the substitutability of factors is crucial. If factors are substitutable, the preservation of a given stock of resources is not required in a concept of sustainable development. It is then sufficient to pass a stock of many production factors on to the future generation, with natural resources eventually being replaced by real (and human) capital.

Appendix 4A: Capital movements and the time path of consumption

In Figure A4.1, the long-term equilibrium of a capital-importing country is represented in the c–k diagram. G characterizes the long-term equilibrium without capital import and thus in autarky. Starting from the capital endowment of the original situation k_0, this equilibrium is reached through own savings. This takes time. Compared to the autarky situation, a capital-importing country can reach the consumption level G' faster by importing capital instead of saving on its own (G). But in the long-term equilibrium, this country has to pay GG' for debt service and debt acquittance. Its long-term consumption level is lower; through own savings it could have reached a higher consumption level (point G), but waiting for it would have been longer, meaning a loss of utility. The mirror image is the capital-exporting country that reaches a higher consumption level (Maurer 1998).

The two-country case is represented in Figure A4.2. It is assumed that the productivity of the capital stock per capita f_k is lower in the home country, e.g. owing to its lower level of technology (lower part of the diagram). At a capital stock per capita of k^0, the marginal productivity of capital in the home country is higher than in the foreign country which is assumed to have a capital stock per capita of $\tilde{k}^*$. Thus, the home country imports capital. In the long-term equilibrium, the home country pays interest and acquittance (distance GG'), implying that in the long run it can consume only less than it produces. The foreign country provides capital to the home country, receiving capital income for it in the long run (distance $S*S*'$). For simplicity it has been assumed that in the original situation, the foreign country was in a steady state already (point $S*$).

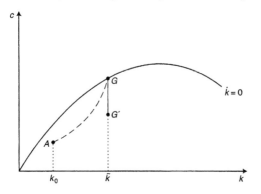

Figure A4.1 Growth path of a capital-importing country.

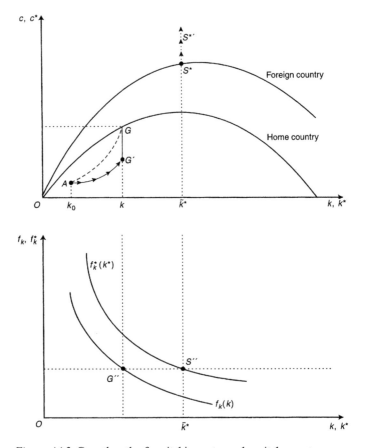

Figure A4.2 Growth path of capital importer and capital exporter.

Part II

Monetary and financial disturbances in the world economy

In Part II, we introduce money, different currencies, and financial markets into the international division of labor. We analyze how economic processes in the real economy are affected by monetary phenomena. If money were a veil it would have no impact on the real sphere of the economy. Since money is more than a veil, the real economy is affected by such phenomena as inflation and hyperinflation, exchange rate fluctuations, and changing trends in the exchange rates as well as financial and currency crises. The correct institutional arrangement for a currency system is a major question. Another important issue is how financial and currency crises come into existence and how they can be prevented.

5 Global money and currency markets

What you will understand after reading this chapter

In national economies as well as in the world economy, money plays an important role, as a unit of measurement, as a medium of exchange and as a store of value. Money reduces the costs of transactions. Its invention, i.e. the transition from an exchange economy to a money economy, must be interpreted as an important innovation to lower the costs of transaction. In the following, we start with a thought experiment assuming that there is a world money market with only one currency (section 5.1). As a result, some simple conditions can be derived for an equilibrium on the global money market. But in reality this standardized money does not exist and thus the prices of currencies, the exchange rates, play an important role. In the long-run, the exchange rate is likely to follow purchasing power parity (section 5.2), but in the short-run it is determined by interest rate parity (section 5.3). The exchange rate may overshoot in the short- and the medium-run (section 5.4). Expectations are an important factor (section 5.5). Some empirical evidence on purchasing power parity and deviations from it in the short-run is presented (section 5.6).

5.1 Global monetary equilibrium and national monetary policy

A thought experiment: world market equilibrium for a uniform currency

If there were a single currency for the world economy, an equilibrium of the world money market would require excess demand to be effectively zero for this currency, which we shall assume is the dollar:

$$E^\$ = L^\$(i, Y, P, \ldots) - M^\$(\cdot) = 0 \tag{5.1}$$

where E is excess demand for money, L nominal demand for money and M nominal money supply. If there were a disequilibrium, the factors influencing money demand and money supply, e.g. the interest rate (i) and world domestic

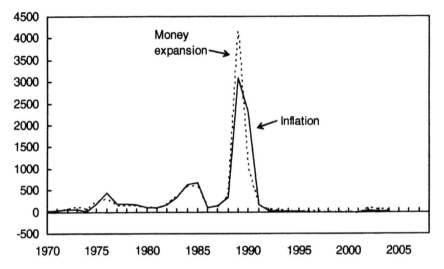

Figure 5.1 Money expansion and inflation, Argentina, 1970–2004 (source: IMF, *International Financial Statistics* 2005).

product (*Y*), would have to change until an equilibrium is reached. Thus, an excess money supply requires the interest rate to rise (for instance by the central bank selling bonds) in order to increase the opportunity costs of holding money and thus reduce the demand for money. Money demand would also be lower if national income falls, for instance in a recession. An extreme excess money supply (a monetary overhang) can be removed if the world price level (*P*) were to increase; then the given money supply would be devalued in real terms. The disequilibrium would be undone through inflation. Then, the price level can be seen as a positive function of the money supply, i.e. $P = f(M)$.

As an example consider the increase in the money supply of Argentina in the four decades since 1970 (Figure 5.1). It shows that the increase in the inflation rate corresponds to an increase in the money supply. For instance, an increase in the money supply by 4,169 percent – a forty-twofold increase – in the year 1989 was accompanied by an increase in the price level by 3,006 percent. The price level was stable during the currency board period 1991–2001, and it rose again to an inflation rate of 25.9 and 13.5 percent in the years 2002 and 2003, respectively.

Money as a means of transaction and as a store of value should be stable. Central banks therefore steer the money supply in a way such that the increase in the price level does not surpass a target, for instance 2 percent in the case of the ECB. In order to be non-inflationary, an increase in the money supply should not exceed the increase in the production potential. Following a more refined approach, it should not exceed the increase in the production potential permanently. A temporary overshooting may be permissible if one can be sure that the price level will come down again, for instance in the case of a temporary price shock. Moreover, a trend of a reduced velocity of money of about 0.5 percent per year, i.e. a trend of a higher transaction demand relative to nominal GDP as observed in Germany in the 1990s, would justify a somewhat higher expansion of the money supply. In contrast to this approach of steering the money supply (which presupposes that money demand is determined by a stable function, including a stable trend), a central bank may use inflation targeting (as the bank of England does) in which it publishes an inflation forecast and attempts to steer inflationary expectations through such a forecast. Or it practices a more informal approach of monetary policy which is not rule-based as the Fed did during the Greenspan years.

Why do we need stable money?

To fix a monetary disequilibrium by raising the price level as discussed in equation 5.1 is a rather technical answer to a disequilibrium problem. It means that a monetary disequilibrium is cured by inflation which itself is a major disturbance of an economy.

Inflation means that savings of people are destroyed. This represents a severe uncertainty in the lives of people, for instance in their consumption smoothing during their lifecycle. By destroying the accumulated savings (i.e. wealth), efforts to undertake precautionary savings for old age are annihilated and renouncing on consumption has been in vain. This runs counter to the incentives needed in an aging society in which people take individual precautions for their old age and do not rely on the government. The intertemporal allocation of resources is distorted, since it is worthwhile to hold on to physical assets such as land and buildings instead of selling them. Physical asset owners are privileged. There is an incentive to over-invest. Moreover, inflation has serious redistribution effects and is unjust. Those who can invest in physical assets can protect themselves against inflation, the recipients of nominal payments such as wage earners or pensioners experience a real income loss because the nominal payments are not automatically adjusted to the inflation rate. Inflation thus hurts people with lower income. Inflation means that taxes increase over-proportionally since they are linked to a nominal tax base and not to a tax base in inflation-adjusted values. De facto, government levies an inflation tax, a phenomenon that has been relevant during the high inflation periods of Latin American countries. The inflation tax represents an implicit expropriation by the government. Finally, hyperinflation with high rates as in the case of Germany in the 1920s can lead whole groups of society into poverty, can destabilize voting behavior as in the Weimar Republic and can be the reason for political instability.

It is therefore necessary to have reliable institutions, that make sure that money is stable. The rule that governments are not allowed to monetize their debt is such an imperative. This condition, however, is not sufficient to keep money stable. Governments with high debts will attempt to influence the interest rate policy of the central bank, so to say a hidden form of monetizing public debt. Therefore, central banks have to be independent. Moreover, there must be some limit on the level of public debt and on new public debt, for instance through constitutional requirements.

Case study: inflationary experience in the world economy

The price level in the world economy has changed at quite different speeds in the past. Looking at the industrial countries since World War II, we see a relatively stable price level in the Bretton Woods era with an inflation rate of about 2.5 percent for the US as an average for the period 1949–1971 (Table 5.1). One exception was the Korean War in 1950–1953 when the increase in the US price level was over 10 percent. The other exception was the Vietnam War (1965–1975). Eventually the price level rose in the US to 4.2 percent in 1968 and then to more than 5 percent. The US increased its governmental expenditures; its budget deficit rose, reaching 2.5 and 2.7 percent of GDP in 1967 and 1971, respectively. On August 15 1971, President Nixon enunciated the end of the convertibility between the US dollar and gold. The US was no longer willing to provide a stable anchor currency for the Bretton Woods system. The system of fixed exchange rates collapsed.

In the 1970s, the change in price level in the industrial countries was quite high, amounting for instance to 11 percent in the US and 12 percent in Japan in single years. The industrial world was characterized by a high inflation rate in the 1970s, the major reason being the two oil crises. For instance, trade unions tried to recuperate the quadrupling of the oil prices in the first and the second oil crisis by high wage increases in the European countries. Even higher inflation rates prevailed in many developing countries.

In the 1980s and the 1990s the inflation rate has come down. The industrial world was no longer exposed to the oil price shock, and the philosophy of monetary authorities changed. Inflation was not seen any more as a solution to economic problems. Monetary authorities followed a more stability-oriented monetary policy. Many central banks switched to a policy of steering the money supply. At the start of the 1980s, market participants were used to high inflationary expectations. Thus, the central banks had to change these expectations. They did this by raising the nominal interest rate. For instance, when Fed Chairman Paul Volcker had taken office in August 1979, the monthly short term interest rate rose to 20 percent by early 1980. I remember discussions at the MIT round table, when an increase in the money supply led to an increase in the short-term rate, contrary to the textbooks; and I heard Paul Samuelson arguing that the increase in the money supply apparently was smaller than anticipated by the markets. The high rates then lead to a stabilization recession in the first Reagan years, and this was the price to get rid of the inflationary expectations and the inflationary environment. Since the late 1990s, inflation targeting became fashionable as monetary strategy. While inflation of consumer prices was prevented, a new disturbance appeared, financial exuberance with the risk that bursting financial bubbles negatively affect the real side of the economy.

Table 5.1 Average inflation in selected countries

	USA	Japan	UK	France	Germany
1950s	1.8	3.0	3.5	6.2	1.2
1960s	2.3	5.4	3.5	3.9	2.4
1970s	7.1	9.1	12.6	8.9	4.9
1980s	5.6	2.5	7.4	7.4	2.9
1990s	3.0	1.2	3.7	1.9	2.4
2000–2004	2.6	−0.5	2.5	1.9	1.5

Source: IMF, *International Financial Statistics* and *World Economic Outlook* 2005.

The equilibrium on the global monetary market with two currencies

In order to understand the impact of a monetary disturbance, let us analyze the effect of an excessive increase in the money supply. Let us start with a single money in a two-country world. Of course, in the real world there is no single global currency. But we can imagine two countries that couple their currencies so firmly that the legally different currencies are perfect substitutes. During the time of the gold standard, national currencies almost came close to this scenario. To keep the argument simple, let us assume the exchange rate between two national currencies to be equal to one, so that the two countries' quantities of money $\tilde{M}$ and $\tilde{M}^*$ can be added up to the total quantity of money in the world $\tilde{M}^W$, i.e. $\tilde{M} + \tilde{M}^* = \tilde{M}^W$. The quantity of money in the world is given exogenously and is shown in Figure 5.2 by the straight line WW'. A single point of this straight line shows how the quantity of money in the world is allocated to the two countries.

The equilibrium allocation of the quantity of money in the world is determined by the demand for money in the two countries. Assume that the nominal demand for money is determined by transaction purposes only, i.e. it is governed by nominal national income ($L = kp_1Y$ for the domestic country and $L^* = kp^*_2Y^*$ the foreign country; see Ethier 1995). This is in accordance with the Cambridge equation. For simplicity let us assume that the coefficients of transaction k, k^* are equal in the two countries. Real national incomes in the domestic country (Y) and in the foreign country (Y^*) are considered to be exogenously given. Moreover, it is assumed that the domestic and the foreign country are both completely specialized in the production of their export goods. Then, the equilibrium of the money market in the domestic country is given by $\tilde{M} = kp_1Y$. For the foreign country it is $\tilde{M}^* = kp^*_2Y^*$.

Dividing the conditions for the national equilibria by one another, the equilibrium allocation of both quantities of money between the two countries is given by:

$$\frac{\tilde{M}^*}{\tilde{M}} = \frac{kp_2^*Y^*}{kp_1Y} = \frac{Y^*}{pY}$$

(5.2)

In the monetary equilibrium, the ratio between the two quantities of money ($\tilde{M}^*/\tilde{M}$) is determined by the ratio of the national incomes and the relative price p of two goods $p = p_1/p^*_2$. National income is determined on the supply side in the real sphere of the economy. The relative price is established in the equilibrium on the global product market, i.e. in the real sphere. In Figure 5.2, the equilibrium ratio of the quantities of money is given by the angle α of the straight line ON, where $\tan \alpha = Y^*/pY$.

The equilibrium on the global monetary market and the real economic equilibrium

In the world market equilibrium, the transaction demand for money has to be equal to the world money supply (equation 5.3). All variables in the demand-for-money equation 5.3 are determined in the real sphere of the economy, except for the domestic price level (p_1). Consequently, the domestic price level is proportional to the quantity of money in the world, $\tilde{M}^W$. As the quantity of money expands, the domestic price level has to rise as well. According to the quantity theory of money, the expansion of the quantity of money influences the price level.

$$k(p_1Y + p^*_2Y^*) = kp_1(Y + Y^*/p) = \tilde{M} + \tilde{M}^* = \tilde{M}^W$$

(5.3)

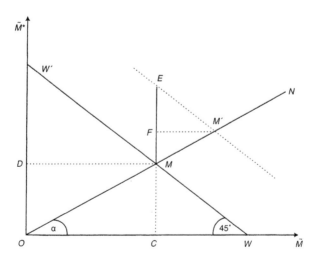

Figure 5.2 Equilibrium of the quantity of money in a world with two currencies.

Under the assumption of two currencies with a fixed exchange rate, the increase in the price level is not limited to the domestic country. The price level in the foreign country increases as well. The money market equilibrium (point M in Figure 5.1) is coupled to the real economic equilibrium. If, for example, the foreign country raises its quantity of money (by the distance ME), the world money market line is shifted outward. In point E, foreigners keep a larger quantity of money than they need for their transactions. They get rid of this excess money by demanding goods from the home country. The home country has a surplus in its balance of trade; thus its quantity of money is increased. Therefore, the domestic price level has to rise. The foreign country has a balance of payments deficit; its money surplus is reduced. At the end of the adjustment process, the same real economic equilibrium (point M' on the expansion path) is reached for both currencies, but the price level of both countries has increased.

This simple formulation makes it clear that a national monetary policy that expands the money supply excessively beyond the production potential leads to an increase of the price level, i.e. to inflation. Under the conditions of the model, inflation also occurs in the country in which monetary policy has not changed the money supply. This country has imported inflation. But still, in this approach, money is a veil. The expansion of the money supply has no impact on the real economy.

5.2 The exchange rate and purchasing power parity

The exchange rate

What has been vaguely described so far as the ratio between two currencies is the exchange rate. The exchange rate e is defined as the ratio of a unit of one currency per unit of another currency. It is the relative price of monies. Using the euro (€) and the dollar ($) as an example, we choose the dimension €/$. It indicates how many euros have to be given up in order to obtain one unit of US dollar (or how many euros one obtains for one unit of dollar). In the previous section, we assumed a constant exchange rate of one-to-one between the two currencies.

From the very simple scenario of a fixed exchange rate in the previous section, we can derive an obvious conclusion: whenever two national currencies have a fixed exchange rate, a stable price level in both countries can only exist if the real money supply stays in line with real economic conditions. Under static conditions, the relative money supply is determined by the relative price of national outputs and by the ratio of national incomes. In a growing economy, the relevant point of reference for the increase in the money supply, which is equivalent with price level stability, is the growth of the production potential.

In the following, the exchange rate is no longer regarded as fixed but as flexible. In trade equilibrium, the law of one price is valid:

$$p_1 = p^*_1 e \quad \text{with the dimensions } €/Q_1 = (\$/Q_1) \cdot (€/\$)$$

where Q_1 is the quantity unit of commodity 1. From this, the exchange rate results as:

$$e = p_1/p^*_1 \qquad \text{as well as} \qquad \hat{e} = \hat{p}_1 - \hat{p}^*_1 \tag{5.4}$$

where $\hat{}$ indicates the rate of change. Equation 5.4 is the purchasing power parity condition, with p_1 and p^*_1 being interpreted as price levels of the two economies. A currency like the euro depreciates, which means that e rises, if the price level increases more in Europe than in the US; it appreciates, which means that e decreases, if the price level increases less in Europe than in the US.

Consider now the case of complete specialization of both countries, for instance if the home country (Europe) specializes in good 1 and the foreign country (the US) specializes in good 2. Then the exchange rate can be defined as the relative price for two currencies where p_1 and p^*_1 can again be interpreted as the price level in the two countries. But besides the prices for goods 1 and 2, the relative price p also has to be taken into consideration; it is once again defined by the world market equilibrium. Hence, the exchange rate is now defined as:

$$e\left[\frac{\text{€}}{\$}\right] = p_1[\text{€}/Q_1] / p^*_2[\$/Q_2] \cdot p[Q_2/Q_1] \tag{5.5}$$

According to the concept of purchasing power parity, fluctuations of the exchange rate can be explained by the variation of the ratio of the two currencies. Equation 5.5 is shown graphically in Figure 5.3b. The tangent of α is given by $1/p$. Thus, the exchange rate is given by purchasing power parity.

Monetary equilibrium with flexible exchange rates

Let us now look at the monetary equilibrium with flexible exchange rates. If both sides of the money market equilibrium condition of the foreign country are multiplied by the exchange rate, we get $e\tilde{M}^* = kep^*_2Y^*$. Dividing the conditions for the national equilibria by each other, we obtain:

$$e\frac{\tilde{M}^*}{\tilde{M}} = \frac{kep^*_2Y^*}{kp_1Y} = e\frac{L^*}{L} = \frac{Y^*}{pY} \tag{5.6}$$

Equation 5.6 describes the monetary equilibrium of the domestic and the foreign country with explicit consideration of the two currencies (i.e. of the exchange rate). The product of the exchange rate and the relative money demand is a constant. With a given relative price p, with given national incomes in the domestic and the foreign country, and with a given money supply in the two countries, there is only one exchange rate e at which the money supply of both countries is equal to the demand for money: the product of the exchange rate and the relative money supplies is constant, Y^*/pY.

In Figure 5.3a, monetary equilibrium is shown with two currencies and a flexible exchange rate. The horizontal axis depicts the money supply of the two countries as a ratio. The distance OG denotes the exogenously given relative

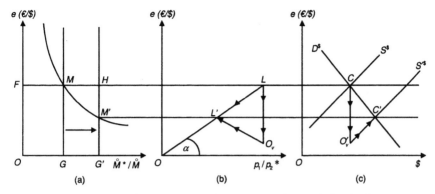

Figure 5.3 Monetary equilibrium, purchasing power parity, and the foreign currency market.

money supply between the foreign and the home country $(\tilde{M}^*/\tilde{M})$; the vertical line GM shows the relative supply. The curve through MM' indicates the relative money demand. Equation 5.6 can also be written as a hyperbolic equation $eL^*/L = a$ with the constant $a = Y^*/pY$. The monetary equilibrium M is marked by the point of intersection of the two curves.

The equilibrium in the real economy is described in Figure 5.3b. According to equation 5.5, there is a unique relation between the exchange rate and the ratio of nominal prices p_1/p^*_2 for a given relative price which is determined in the exchange equilibrium, i.e. $e = p_1/p^*_2\, p$. This relation is determined by $\tan \alpha = 1/p$ or line OL in Figure 5.3b. It portrays purchasing power parity.

Assume, now, that the money supply $\tilde{M}^*$ rises in the foreign country (USA). Then the foreign currency ($\$$) is devalued and the long-term equilibrium moves from M to M'. The expansion of the money supply also results in an increase of the goods prices in the foreign country. In Figure 5.3b, the economy moves from point L to point L'. Thus, we have two changes: the price level in the foreign country rises and its currency depreciates. The currency of the home country appreciates and by this the domestic (European) price level is insulated against the expansion of the money supply in the foreign country.[1]

The foreign currency market and the balance of payments

Monetary equilibrium and purchasing power parity are also related to the foreign currency market and to the balance-of-payments position of a country. The foreign currency market explains the demand for and the supply of the foreign currency ($\$$) as a function of the exchange rate (Figure 5.3c). It is assumed here that the supply curve of the foreign currency has a positive slope and does not bend backwards. Excess demand for the foreign currency $E^\$$ is defined by the difference between demand for US dollars and the supply thereof.

$$E^\$(e) = D^\$(e) - S^\$(e) \qquad (5.7)$$

Demand for and supply of US dollars can easily be explained if we consider commodity exchange only and neglect capital flows. Then US dollars are demanded by European importers (IM^{EU}) in order to pay for their imports. And US dollars are supplied by Americans who want to import goods from Europe (IM^{US}); they supply US dollars in order to get euro. Thus, excess demand in the foreign currency market is equivalent to a balance-of-trade disequilibrium with:

$$E^{\$} = D^{\$}(e) - S^{\$}(e) = IM^{EU} - IM^{US} = IM^{EU} - X^{EU} = \text{trade balance} \qquad (5.8)$$

if it is assumed that the world consists of two countries only and that US imports are identical to EU exports ($IM^{US} = X^{EU}$). An excess demand for dollars ($E^{\$} > 0$) is equivalent to a deficit in the European trade balance, an excess supply of dollars ($E^{\$} < 0$) is equivalent to a deficit in the US trade balance.

Assume now that the US money supply is expanded. At a given exchange rate OF, this disturbs monetary equilibrium M in Figure 5.3a. It also leads to an excess supply of foreign currency (US dollar), CE in Figure 5.3. This is equivalent to a trade deficit for the US. Americans swap excess money (which they do not want to hold) for European goods. This process takes time. The US dollar depreciates and the price level in the US rises until the excess money supply disappears (point M' in Figure 5.3a). The purchasing power parity reaches its new equilibrium (point L' in Figure 5.3b), the foreign exchange market clears (point C' in Figure 5.3c) and the deficit in the trade account disappears.

Purchasing power parity: a first glance

Our analytical considerations have shown that an expansion of the money supply does not only affect the price level but it may also lead to a depreciation of the currency. Figure 5.4 shows that a high inflation rate was more or less accompanied by a depreciation of the Argentinean peso. As can be seen from Figure 5.1, an expansion in the money supply of Argentina went along with an increase in the price level. Whenever the money supply increased, for instance in 1989 by 4,169 percent, the price level went up (by 3,006 percent) and the peso was devalued by 4,736 percent. In 2002, the increase in the price level by 25.8 percent was accompanied by a devaluation of 206 percent. These observations correspond to equation 5.4. We will look at other examples of excessive increases in the money supply in Chapter 10. Purchasing power parity will be reviewed in more detail in section 5.6.

5.3 Interest rate parity and portfolio equilibrium

Capital flows and the exchange rate

So far we have assumed that the exchange rate is determined by trade only. If capital movements are taken into account, the demand for US-dollars reflects

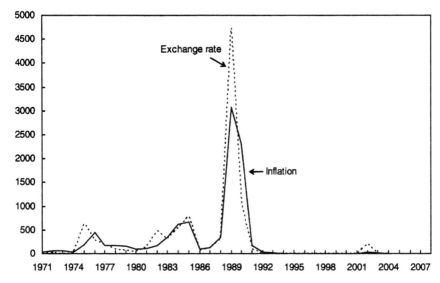

Figure 5.4 Inflation and the exchange rate change (in percent), Argentina 1970–2004
(source: IMF, *International Financial Statistics* September 2005).

European export of capital (to buy US bonds, equities or to repay debt owed to the US) and the supply of US-dollars mirrors US-demand for euro for buying European bonds, equities or to repay debt to Europeans. Taking into account capital flows only, an excess demand for US-dollars in equation 5.9 then means a capital account deficit of the euro area and a capital account surplus of the US. An excess supply of US-dollars means a capital account deficit of the US.

$$E^\$ = D^\$(e) - S^\$(e) = K_X^{EU} - K_X^{US} = \text{capital balance} \qquad (5.9)$$

The trade flow and the capital flow view

Equations 5.8 and 5.9 describe two different views of the drivers of the balance of payments, the trade flow view and the capital flow view. These are often seen as competing explanations. In the real world, economic agents take decisions that affect both the current account and the capital simultaneously. A decision of the household sector of a country to import commodities (affecting the current account) means also that a decision to save or to finance consumption by credits is taken (affecting the capital and financial account). A decision of the enterprise sector to import investment goods simultaneously includes a decision to finance the investment, either through enterprise savings, through savings of the domestic households or through credits from abroad. The consumption and savings decisions of households (and the government) and the investment decisions of firms (and the government) mean that capital imports are necessary.

Thus, a negative current account may be financed by capital inflows, i.e. by a positive capital account (compare the US in 2005). And a positive current account may mean that the export surplus is used for capital exports, i.e. it is accompanied by a negative capital account (Japan in 2005).

When both the current account and the capital account are determined simultaneously, for instance in decisions of residents, it is not worthwhile to ask the question which account is in the driving seat, dominating the balance of payments. However, taking into account the full set of all economic agents influencing the current and capital account, different agents at home and abroad affect the two accounts. Thus, foreign investors may want to invest in equity or real estate of a country. Such a decision is independent of the trade flows. Not all economic decisions affect the two accounts simultaneously.

Change in reserves

The sum of the current and the capital account is mirrored in a change in international reserves. If both the current account and capital account are positive, the country accumulates international reserves (China in 2005): excess demand for foreign currency then includes the accumulation of international reserves (equation 5.10):

$$E^\$ = D^\$(e) - S^\$(e) = IM^{EU} - IM^{US} + K_X^{EU} - K_X^{US} + \text{accumulation of foreign}$$
reserves   (5.10)

If both the current account and the capital account are negative, the country loses reserves. It finances an import surplus and a capital outflow from accumulated reserves.

An example are countries in a currency crisis when capital inflows reverse. In such a case the country loses reserves. Taking Brazil as an example, the current account deficit increases in the years prior to the currency crises in 1999, and Brazil loses reserves in the years 1995 and 1996 (Table 5.2). Without the inflow of funds from the IMF, it would also have lost reserves in 1998 and 1999.

Interest rate parity

Capital flows occur if a portfolio equilibrium is disturbed. A portfolio equilibrium with respect to domestic and foreign financial assets (such as bonds) exists when the expected rate of return on assets in the home country is equal to the expected rate of return on assets in the foreign country.[2] The rate of return on financial investment in the home country is given by the domestic interest rate $1 + i$. If a euro is invested abroad, it has to be transformed into US-dollars, i.e. we have to divide 1 (or the amount placed abroad) by the spot rate e^0. This gives us the equivalent amount in US-dollars. With an interest rate i^*, this gives us an income $(1 + i^*)/e^0$ at the end of the period in US-dollars. Changing this into

Table 5.2 Brazil: balance of payments and change in currency reserves (billion US$)

Year	Current account	Capital and financial account	Reserve assets [a]	Use of IMF credit, loans, and exceptional financing	Errors and omission
1995	−18.1	29.6	−13.0	−0.05	1.5
1996	−23.3	34.0	−8.3	−0.35	−2.0
1997	−30.5	25.4	8.3	−0.03	−3.2
1998	−33.9	20.4	7.0	9.30	−2.9
1999	−25.4	8.4	7.8	8.98	0.2
2000	−24.2	29.6	2.3	−10.24	2.5
2001	−23.2	20.3	−3.3	6.72	−0.5
2002	−7.6	−3.5	−0.3	11.58	−0.1
2003	4.1	0.3	−8.4	4.90	−0.9
2004	11.6	−3.0	−2.2	−4.30	−2.1

Source: IMF, *International Financial Statistics* 2005.

Note
a Technically, the accumulation of reserves has a negative sign in order to balance the balance of payments. A positive sign (not shown) denotes a loss of reserves.

euros again, i.e. multiplying with the expected exchange rate e^e at the end of the period gives us the rate of return on investment in the foreign country. It is defined by the foreign interest rate plus the expected appreciation gain. Thus interest rate parity requires:

$$1 + i = (1 + i^*)e^e/e^0 \qquad (5.11)$$

This is also simplified and written as:

$$i = i^* + \hat{e}^e \qquad (5.12)$$

Here $\hat{e}^e$ indicates the expected rate of change of the exchange rate, i.e. the expected devaluation ($\hat{e}^e > 0$) or appreciation ($\hat{e}^e < 0$). The expected rate of change of the exchange rate is defined as $(e^e - e_0)/e_0$. The interest rate refers to short-term or long-term financial assets.

If the domestic currency is expected to be devalued within the next year ($\hat{e}^e > 0$), then investing in the foreign country has the advantage that the money invested is worth more at the end of the investment period. If, for example, a devaluation by 2 percent of the domestic currency is expected, then for the portfolio equilibrium a domestic interest rate of 5 percent is compatible with a foreign interest rate of 3 percent. Therefore, in the portfolio equilibrium the foreign interest rate can be correspondingly lower than the domestic interest rate. If, in contrast, an appreciation ($\hat{e}^e < 0$) of the domestic currency is expected to take place, then the investment in the foreign country suffers a loss in value. The foreign interest rate has to be correspondingly higher.

5.4 Exchange rate overshooting

The exchange rate has to adjust, i.e. a currency has to depreciate or appreciate, when at a given exchange rate excess supply or excess demand exists in the foreign exchange market. If the disequilibrium in the foreign currency market is due to an excessive money supply; that is, if the money supply has increased significantly more than it should relative to the growth of the productive potential, there are several ways in which the imbalance can be reduced. One mechanism is by goods arbitrage in the sense of purchasing power parity, as described above.

A disequilibrium can also be eliminated by capital flows, especially by restructuring a given portfolio (Dornbusch 1976). In this case, an overshooting of the exchange rate may occur if the prices of goods are sticky in the short-run. Consider a monetary expansion in the foreign country ($\tilde{M}* \uparrow$). This implies that people in the foreign country hold more money than they want to. Their portfolio is not optimal. There is an excess supply of foreign currency in the system ($S^\$ \uparrow$). They react and adjust their portfolio. Instantaneously, they demand bonds of the foreign ($D^{b*} \uparrow$) and bond prices in the foreign country rise ($p^{B*} \uparrow$). The interest rate in the foreign country falls ($i* \downarrow$) and demand shifts to the bonds of the domestic country ($D^B \uparrow$). As a result, the demand for the domestic currency increases abruptly ($D^\$ \uparrow$). Consequently, the foreign currency is immediately devalued ($e \downarrow$) as a result of the change in the money supply (point O^v in Figure 5.3b).

Note that the interest rate parity implies the overshooting of the exchange rate. In equation 5.11, interpret e^e as the exchange rate expected in the long run equilibrium, i.e. determined from equation 5.6 as:

$$e^e = \frac{Y*}{pY} / \frac{\tilde{M}*}{\tilde{M}} \tag{5.13}$$

This exchange rate e^e is given. Consider now the adjustment period t in which $i*$ $< i$, while the exchange rate has not yet changed. According to the interest rate parity of equation 5.9, $1 + i = (1 + i*)e^e/e_t$, we must have $e_t < e^e$ because with $i*$ $< i$ the right-hand side of equation 5.9 is smaller than the left-hand side unless the currency of the foreign country depreciates and e_t falls abruptly. This means that we have an overshooting of the exchange rate relative to a long-run equilibrium.

Only gradually does this devaluation have an impact on the flows of goods. Devaluation improves price competitiveness of the foreign country, which then develops an export surplus. Domestic importers have to obtain foreign currency which works against the devaluation of the foreign currency. The price level in

$$\tilde{M}* \uparrow \; \rightarrow \; S^\$ \uparrow \; \rightarrow \; D^{b*} \uparrow \; \rightarrow \; p^{B*} \uparrow \; \rightarrow \; i* \downarrow \; \rightarrow \; D^B \uparrow \; \rightarrow \; D^e \uparrow \; \rightarrow \; e \downarrow$$

Figure 5.5 The incidence chain of an increase in the money supply.

the foreign country rises. Finally, purchasing power parity is reached again (movement from point O^v to point L'). Apparently, the exchange rate can deviate from purchasing power parity in the short-run. It can overshoot temporarily.

Note that the eventual long-run equilibrium of the exchange rate according to purchasing power parity is not a sufficient intertemporal fix point to prevent overshooting. Even assuming that people know that the purchasing power parity holds in the long run, the time needed to reach the long-run equilibrium allows the short-term flows to deviate from the long-run equilibrium.

5.5 The role of expectations

Exchange rate change expectations

If the condition for the portfolio equilibrium is not fulfilled, the portfolio is adjusted, which implies capital flows. If, for instance, $i > i^* + \hat{e}^e$, then the rate of return on portfolio investment in the home country is higher than in the foreign country. Such a situation arises if a devaluation of the foreign currency may be anticipated, because a less favorable economic development is expected in the foreign country, or because of greater political instability or rising public debt with the expectation of policy uncertainty. Another possible reason for the anticipation of a devaluation might be an excessive increase in the money supply of the foreign country. All these factors will be an incentive for adjusting the portfolio in favor of the domestic assets.

The interplay between interest rate parity and purchasing power parity

Purchasing power parity and interest rate parity interact. The interest rate parity $i = i^* + \hat{e}^e$ determines the capital flows, the purchasing power parity determines the exchange rate expectations, $\hat{e}^e = \hat{p}^e - \hat{p}^{e*}$. Combining both equations, price level expectations enter into interest rate parity, so that $i = i^* + \hat{p}^e - \hat{p}^{e*}$ holds (Figure 5.6). If people expect a stronger rise of the price level in the foreign country than in the home country, they expect a devaluation of the foreign currency. Of course, the anticipation of the exchange rate change is not determined by changes in the price level only, but also by a number of other factors, e.g. by political instability, high budget deficits and large debt. But usually these factors also have a long-term effect on the price level.

An example for the interplay between the interest rate parity and the purchasing power parity was the European Exchange Rate Mechanism (ERM) in the European Monetary System (EMS) before EMU started. On the one hand, interest rate imparity set into motion capital flows as soon as economic policy of a single country erred away from the stability target. The markets quickly required a premium on the national interest rates and eventually induced a devaluation of the national currency. Therefore, interest rate parity determined the pain of instability; it served as a control mechanism.

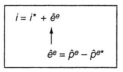

$$i = i^* + \hat{e}^e$$

$$\uparrow$$

$$\hat{e}^e = \hat{p}^e - \hat{p}^{e*}$$

Figure 5.6 Interest rate parity and purchasing power parity.

On the other hand, purchasing power parity shaped the exchange rate expectations, which entered into interest rate parity. If a larger price differential between countries developed, market participants expected that the exchange rate would have to be adjusted. Governments anticipated the consequences of a stability-averse policy which were made explicit by this mechanism, and consequently governments had to aim at stability. An example of this controlling mechanism is the economic policy situation in France in 1983. The Mitterrand government had to completely reverse its economic policy approach which had led to budget and balance-of-payments deficits, a rising price level and a devaluation of the French franc.

Case study: defending a pegged exchange rate by interest rate policy

A country that wants to defend its weak currency may have to take recourse to high interest rates in order to prevent portfolio capital from leaving the country. A case in point is the 500 percent short-term interest rate that Sweden used in the days of financial crisis in September 1992 in order to prevent the outflow of short-term capital and in order to defend the Swedish krona. In early 2001, the short-term interest rate in Turkey was raised to 5,000 percent in order to prevent the devaluation of the Turkish lira. Another example is the high real interest rate of 30 percent of Brazil prior to the devaluation of the real, the national currency, in January 1999.

Applying interest rate parity, a high interest rate differential $i - i^*$ is needed to compensate devaluation expectations with respect to the domestic currency. Assuming a given expected depreciated exchange rate at a future date t, e_t, interest rate parity $i - i^* = (e_t - e_0)/e_0$ indicates how high i must be in order to prevent e_0 from rising. For example, if the expected exchange rate e_t : 100 and if the spot rate e_0 : 5 is to be defended and if the interest rate i^* is given as 6 percent, the domestic interest rate must be chosen as 25 percent in order to prevent a capital outflow, so that $25 - 6 = (100 - 5)/5$.

In August 1998, the Russian rouble was devalued (the exchange rate rouble/US dollar increased). There was an attempt to prevent the devaluation of the rouble by high nominal interest rates up to more than 100 percent in the spring of 1998. Such a high interest rate, however, did not prevent the rouble from being devalued (Figure 5.7).

In the case of South Korea, it seems that a high interest rate relative to the US has (together with other measures and an IMF stand-by credit) helped to keep the Korean won from depreciating further (Figure 5.8). The reason for the different outcome in Korea can be seen in better fundamentals relative to Russia.

Defending an exchange rate by a high interest rate poses quite a burden on an economy. Private investment including construction is suppressed, and this impedes economic growth. Therefore, such a policy can only be followed temporarily in order to establish confidence. A policy of high interest rates is not sustainable in the long-run. Eventually, the exchange rate must be in line with the fundamentals.

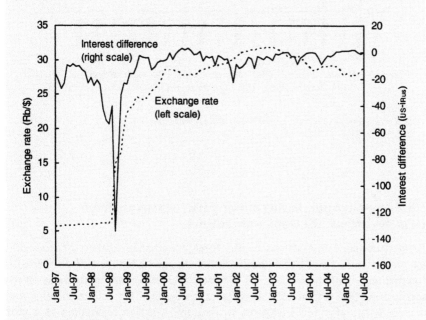

Figure 5.7 Russia: interest rate[a] and exchange rate with respect to the US, 1997–2005[b] (source: IMF, *International Financial Statistics* 2005).

Notes
a Russia: money market rate; United States: federal funds rate.
b Monthly data.

continued

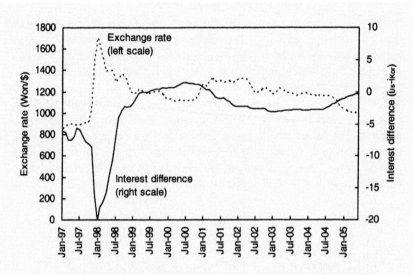

Figure 5.8 Korea: interest rate[a] and exchange rate with respect to the US, 1997–2005[b] (source: IMF, *International Financial Statistics* 2005).

Notes

a Korea: money market rate; United States: federal funds rate.

b Monthly data.

5.6 Long-term purchasing power parity versus medium-term deviations: the empirical evidence

Foreign currency transactions on the foreign exchange markets of the world amount to a volume of US$470 trillion annually, including derivatives (Bank for International Settlement 2004). Of this total, 143 trillion are transactions on the spot market (see Chapter 6).[3] This figure is corrected for double counting and exchange rate changes. Compared to this, the world trade volume of a year (merchandise exports plus imports) amounts to only US$19 trillion (2004), only 1/25th of the currency transactions. Thus, all sorts of capital flows undisputedly can influence the exchange rate more strongly than the transactions of goods. Therefore, the exchange rate does not follow purchasing power parity in the short-run. Empirically, we observe such divergences from purchasing power parity.

For the DM/$ exchange rate a remarkable deviation can be found for the time from 1980 to 1985 when the US dollar appreciated, but in the long-run the exchange rate between the deutsche mark and the US dollar follows purchasing power parity (Figure 5.9). Purchasing power parity is calculated as the German consumer price index to the US consumer price index with the index of 2000 set equal to 1.0. Since the DM was replaced by the euro, for the period 1999–2004

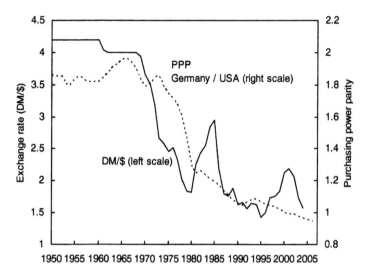

Figure 5.9 Exchange rate DM/$[a] and purchasing power parity[b] (source: IMF, *International Financial Statistics* 2004 and *World Economic Outlook* September 2005).

Notes
a Consumer price index Germany to consumer price index US, 2000 = 1.0, annual averages.
b For the period 1999–2004 the official conversion rate between the DM and the euro is used to calculate the DM/$ rate.

the official conversion rate between the DM and the Euro was used to calculate the DM/$ rate.

An approach to empirically determine the purchasing power of currencies is to study how much of a commodity basket a unit of currency can buy. A well-known example is the 'Big Mac' parity published by *The Economist* (Latest January 12, 2006). If a Big Mac costs US$3.15 dollars in the US and US$3.51 in the euro area, using the actual exchange rate, the euro is overvalued by 10 percent. The implied purchasing power parity is 0.90. With a burger in China costing US$1.30, the Chinese renmimbi is undervalued by 59 percent.

Similarly, a measure of the differences in price levels for the GDP between countries can be constructed. This is done by calculating the rates of currency conversion that eliminate the differences in price levels between countries (OECD National Accounts 2006: 264.) These rates are purchasing power parities (PPPs). PPPs for European countries are annual benchmark results calculated by Eurostat. PPPs for non-European countries are OECD estimates. The PPPs are given in national currency units per US dollar. The price levels and volume indices derived using these PPPs are then rebased on the OECD average.

Note that you cannot simply relate price indices of different countries to one another since they do not relate to an identical basket. Even choosing an identical base year (=100) does not mean that the price index relates to the same basket.

As an alternative to determining price level differences, one looks at changes of the price level over a long period of twenty years, taking the averages over these longer periods. Then a correlation between changes of the exchange rate and differences between inflation rates becomes visible. In Figure 5.10, the annual average depreciation or appreciation rates of some currencies including the DM, the yen, the won, and the euro currencies with respect to the US dollar and the annual average inflation differentials are shown for the period 1980–2004. For the euro area currencies, the period is 1980–1998. For the DM the full period 1980–2004 is used, applying the official conversion rate between the DM and the euro to calculate the DM/$ rate.

The currencies lie along a line where the exchange rate change mirrors the inflation differential. The Italian lira, the Korean won, and the Swedish krona depreciated relative to the US-dollar; the yen, the Singapore dollar, and the Swiss frank appreciated. The DM did not change its value to the US dollar in spite of a lower inflation rate of more than 1 percent. Even with some deviations from a straight line, purchasing power parity is valid for this time period. Purchasing power parity by and large reigns in the long-run. This should be no surprise since in the long-run all sorts of instability will eventually be reflected in the price level of a country and thus in the exchange rate.

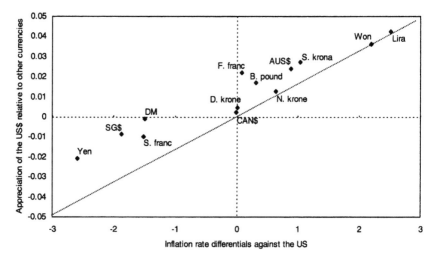

Figure 5.10 Inflation and exchange rate changes of some important currencies, 1980–2004[a] (source: IMF, *International Financial Statistics* and *World Economic Outlook* September 2005).

Notes

a Annual averages of the period ranging from 1980 until 2004. For the euro area currencies: average 1980–1998, except for the DM. For the DM in the euro area, the official convergence rate was used. SG$: Singapore dollar.

Purchasing power parity here is not interpreted in its absolute form where the level of the exchange rate and the price levels are shown but in its relative form looking at changes in the exchange rate and relative inflation rates (see equation 5.4). In such an empirical approach, it is not necessary to determine the level of prices and the exchange rate; we only analyze rates of change. More accurate analyses should not study the prices of all goods, but only of those goods that are traded. Only for those goods arbitrage can equalize prices (Taylor and Taylor 2004). Moreover, it would be better to consider producer prices instead of consumer prices, because consumer prices can be distorted by taxes, tariffs, and other trade barriers.

If purchasing power parity holds and if nominal exchange rate changes even out price differentials over time, the real exchange rate would not change in the long-run. This follows from the definition of the real exchange rate (see Chapter 6). However, productivity effects, wealth effects, different policy environments, aging populations, and other forces all could affect the real exchange rate. Consequently, purchasing power parity would have to be corrected for these factors. Moreover, the Balassa-Samuelson effect leads to an appreciation of the real exchange rate (see Chapter 6).

Purchasing power parity holds for the exchange rates in the long-run of ten or twenty years, but when a disturbance occurs a deviation from this long-term tendency takes time. Empirical studies show that divergences from a filtered trend are reduced only by a rate of 15 percent per year. The half-life, i.e. the time period in which the divergence halves on average, is three to five years (Rogoff 1996). At the same time, the short-run divergences are high and volatile.

6 International exchange rate systems

What you will understand after reading this chapter

This chapter deals with institutional arrangements for exchange rates. Countries can choose different exchange rate regimes. The exchange rate, i.e. the relative price of monies, is determined in the foreign exchange market (section 6.1). Countries are in different balance of payment situations, requiring different types of exchange rate adjustments (section 6.2). Several options are available in choosing the exchange rate system; they differ with respect to the type of nominal anchor, the type of goal (nominal anchor versus real target) and the amount of sovereignty to be given up, i.e. whether a unilateral or a multilateral approach is followed (section 6.3). Unilateral strategies for single countries are dealt with in section 6.4. The historical experience of multilateral approaches is presented in section 6.5; multilateral options are discussed in section 6.6. Finally, we deal with specific policy issues such as choosing the right exchange rate (section 6.7).

6.1 The global foreign exchange market

The leading currency

In the international foreign exchange market, the US dollar is the dominating currency, the euro, newly established in 1999, coming in second place. Of the total transactions in the international currency markets, 89 percent have the US dollar on one side of the transaction, 37 percent the euro. The yen and the sterling follow with 20 and 17 percent, respectively. The daily average turnover on the foreign exchange market amounts to US$1.9 trillion (April 2004). This figure is adjusted for double counting; the gross turnover is US$2.7 trillion. Spot market transactions account for US$620 billion, outright forwards for US$208 billion, foreign exchange swaps for US$944 billion. The average daily turnover in the over-the-counter derivatives market is US$2.4 trillion. The by far most traded currency pair in 2004 was the dollar/euro – amounting to 28 percent of global turnover; the dollar/yen accounted for 17 percent and the dollar/sterling for 14 percent (Bank for International Settlements, March 2005). Thirty-one percent of total turnover is done in the UK; this means that London has retained its historical position. The next in the rankings are the US with 19 percent, Japan with 8, Singapore with 5, Germany with 5, and Hong Kong with 4 percent.

Of the total reserve holdings of all central banks in 2004 that can be allocated to a currency (identified reserves), about 65.9 percent are held in US dollars, 24.9 percent in euros, 3.9 percent in Japanese yen, and 3.3. percent in British pounds (IMF 2005a: Table I.3). Total reserves including unaccountable reserves total US$ 2.4 trillion. Euro holdings only amount to a value of US$626 billion. However, they have been constantly increasing and more than doubled since 1999. Yen and pound sterling holdings amount to less than US$100 billion each.

Most currencies, including the major ones – the US dollar, the euro, the yen, and the British pound, float against each other. The foreign exchange market can be viewed as a wheel of floating currencies to which the pegs and the managed floats are attached (Figure 6.1). Out of the currencies of the 184 member coun-

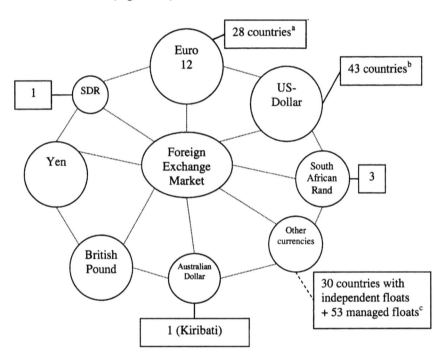

Figure 6.1 The foreign exchange market (source: IMF, *Annual Report on Exchange Arrangements and Exchange Restrictions* 2005b).

Notes
a Four of them within a currency board. Also included are the seven member countries of European Exchange Rate Mechanism II (Cyprus, Denmark, Estonia, Latvia, Lithuania, Malta, Slovenia).
b Two of them within a currency board, seven use the US dollar as only legal tender.
c Two more countries (Bhutan and Nepal) peg their currency to the Indian rupee, which itself is a managed float (and which is counted as one of the fifty-three managed floats here). A further country (Belarus) is pegged to the Russian rouble, which also is a managed float. One more country (Brunai) is pegged to the Singapore dollar (again a managed float). Seven other countries restrict the flexibility of their home currency against another basket of currencies.

tries of the IMF and of three non-members,[1] forty-three currencies are pegged to the dollar (including managed floats) and twenty-eight to the euro. Thirty other countries let their currencies float independently, fifty-three have a managed float. Every restriction of flexibility of a currency with respect to another one including dollarization has been considered a peg (but except managed floats). Most of the Asian countries use the dollar standard where their currencies are linked to the US dollar. Since mid-2005, China applies a basket for its renmimbi, reflecting the weight of its trading partners (see Chapter 11).

A few currencies are strictly fixed to another currency such as the Hong Kong dollar, whose monetary base must be backed by US dollars at a fixed rate, and the Estonian kroon to the euro. The Estonian kroon also participates in the European Exchange Rate Mechanism II.

The three major currencies of the world: a historical review

Prior to World War I, the British pound was the dominating currency of the world economy. Its decline in importance reflects the loss of the relative position of the British economy and the rise of other economic countries. Since the end of World War II, appreciations and depreciations of the three major currencies of the world today – the US dollar, the deutsche mark (and from 1999 the euro), and the yen – reflect fundamental changes in the three major economies in the last fifty-five years. These include differences in economic growth, long-term shifts in comparative advantages and in trade flows, switches in capital flows as well as other phenomena such as asynchronous business cycles among the countries and differences in stabilization policies, i.e. in monetary, fiscal, and wage policies. Moreover, institutional changes are relevant.

In the 1950s, 1960s, and 1970s, the catching-up process of Germany, the European economies, and Japan, all affected by World War II, and the growth of their exports worked towards an appreciation of the deutsche mark, other European currencies and the yen vis-à-vis the US dollar. During the 1950s and 1960s, the exchange rates between the US dollar and the deutsche mark and between the US dollar and the yen were revalued at certain intervals, but remained relatively stable due to the Bretton Woods system. From 1970, both currencies appreciated against the US dollar (Figure 6.2a). In the 1970s, Japan was exposed more intensively to the two oil crises than other countries, so that the yen had to depreciate temporarily vis-à-vis the deutsche mark. In the first part of the 1980s, the US dollar appreciated. After 1985, the deutsche mark and the yen gained value relative to the US dollar. In light of the IT boom in the US, the US dollar appreciated again. After 1980, the deutsche mark appreciated against the yen.

Taking the ECU as the predecessor of the euro and converting it into euros with the conversion rate of 1:1 at the start of the euro, the ECU/euro appreciated against the US dollar from the mid 1980s to 1995, then depreciated until 2000 and appreciated afterwards. The ECU/euro appreciated against the yen until 2000, then depreciated (Figure 6.2b).

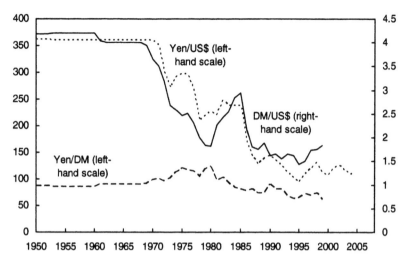

(a) US$, deutschmark, and yen

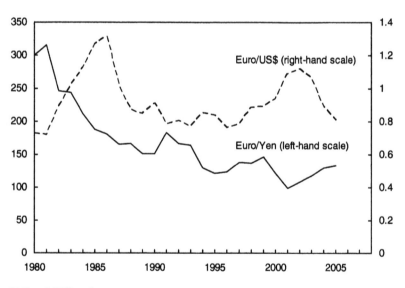

(b) Euro [a], US$, and yen

Figure 6.2 US dollar, euro[a], deutschmark, and yen (source: IMF, *International Financial Statistics* 2005).

Note
a For the euro, the exchange rate of the ECU is used from 1978 to 1998 with the official conversion rate.

Case study: will the euro drive out the dollar?

At the start of the twenty-first century, the US dollar is the leading currency of the world. Today, official holdings of foreign currencies by
central banks are overwhelmingly in US dollars (see above). But such a
leading position is not guaranteed. At the beginning of the twentieth
century, the British pound was the dominating currency. In a slow process
after 1914, the US dollar gained more and more importance. After World
War II it had overtaken the pound. Factors having a positive effect on the
international status of a currency are a large share in international output,
trade, and finance of the currency's country (or region in the case of the
euro), deep and well-developed financial markets, confidence in the currency's value and positive network effects of the currency.

Chinn and Frankel (2005) study under which conditions the euro may
overtake the US dollar. They extrapolate an empirical equation that they
estimated for the period 1973–1998. Their result is that the euro will
surpass the US dollar as leading international reserve currency if the UK
and all the other EU members (of the EU-25) join the European Monetary
Union by 2020; the euro then will overtake the US dollar a few years later.

Foreign currency market

As already discussed, the exchange rate e is the relative price of monies that is
determined by demand for and supply of a foreign money, let us say the US dollar.
Let us again define $e = €/\$$. The exchange rate then indicates how many euros you
have to pay to buy one dollar and how many euros you get for one dollar. Assume
the world consists of two regions only and let them be the US and the euro area.
Then demand for and supply of US dollars reflect the demand for and supply of
US dollar for goods (which appears in the trade balance) and the demand for and
supply of US dollar for capital flows. The result is the change in the foreign currency position, as discussed in equation 5.10, which is reproduced here:

$$E^\$ = D^\$(e) - S^\$(e) = IM^{EU} - IM^{US} + K_X{}^{EU} - K_X{}^{US} + \text{accumulation of reserves}$$
$$(6.1)$$

In the real world, the picture looks more complicated. Currencies are demanded
for services like royalties and interest payments and for unilateral transfers. Consequently, IM^{EU} stands for the euro area's total demand for US dollars in the
current account. Likewise, IM^{US} is the US dollar supply (i.e. the US demand for
euro) of all positions in the current account. Moreover, capital flows include all
sorts of transactions; for instance market participants hedge positions and speculate with currencies. These transactions are part of the capital and financial
account. Moreover, the real world is more complicated than a two-region case
with two currencies. There are more currencies than the US dollar and the euro.

In addition to the demand for and the supply of foreign currencies for trade and capital flows, central banks follow an explicit strategy with respect to their reserves. Thus, they may demand foreign currencies in order to build up their reserves. This means that they drive up the price of the reserve currency and lower the price of their own currency. Reserves may also be used to finance a deficit in the sum of the current and the capital and financial account.

6.2 External balance

Countries can be in different balance of payments situations. In the surplus-surplus category, where both the current and the capital account are in surplus, countries can use both types of surpluses to build up reserves (China, Korea, Japan, see Table 6.1). Surplus–deficit countries use the current account surplus to finance the capital account deficit, i.e. the import of capital (Germany, euro area). The current account surplus may be large enough to accumulate reserves. Deficit-surplus countries finance the current account deficit with capital inflows. If capital inflows are strong enough, the country can even accumulate reserves. A deficit-deficit country has to finance the two deficits by the depletion of its reserves. For instance, Brazil lost reserves of US$8 billion in 1997 prior to its 1999 currency crisis (see Table 5.2). Thailand lost US$9.9 billion in reserves in 1997, the year of its currency crisis.

Table 6.1 Countries in different balance of payment situations, 2004 (billion US$)

	Current account		Capital and financial account		Change in reserves[a]		Errors and omissions
Surplus-surplus countries							
China	surplus	68.6	surplus	110.7	accumulation	−206.1	26.8
Japan	surplus	172	surplus	17.7	accumulation	−160.8	−28.9
Korea	surplus	27.6	surplus	8.3	accumulation	−38.7	2.8
Surplus-deficit countries							
Germany	surplus	103.4	deficit	−121.8	reduction	1.8	16.6
Euro area	surplus	58.7	deficit	−2.4	reduction	15.5	−71.7
Deficit-surplus countries							
Australia	deficit	−40	surplus	41.9	accumulation	−1.1	−0.8
Portugal	deficit	−12.7	surplus	12.6	reduction	1.9	−1.8
USA	deficit	−665.9	surplus	611.2	reduction	2.8	51.9
UK	deficit	−41.9	surplus	25.9	accumulation	−0.4	16.4

Source: IMF, *International Financial Statistics* 2004.

Note
a Technically, the accumulation of reserves has a negative sign in order to balance the balance of payments. A positive sign denotes a loss of reserves.

External balance, the nominal and the real exchange rate

The nominal exchange rate is a price that helps to clear the foreign currency market. In principal, the exchange rate should adjust in such a way that an imbalance in the balance of payments is reduced. However, exports and imports in the current account, an important element in the excess demand for a currency, are not a function of the nominal exchange rate alone. Since the competitiveness of firms also depends on the relative price levels in the countries considered, it is the real exchange rate that determines the trade and the current account. As already discussed in Chapters 2 and 5, the real exchange rate is defined as:

$$e_R = eP^*/P \qquad (6.2)$$

where P^*, P are the respective national price levels being used as correction factors of the nominal exchange rate. The real exchange rate denotes the real price of products of the foreign country, i.e. of a country's export goods in terms of its imports. It has the dimension:

$$\frac{Q}{Q^*} = \frac{€}{\$} \cdot \frac{\$}{Q^*} / \frac{€}{Q} \qquad (6.3)$$

Therefore, it depicts the relation between the quantities of the domestic good (Q) and the quantities of the foreign good (Q^*), i.e. the ratio at which domestic goods can be exchanged for foreign goods. It tells us something about the purchasing power of the domestic good. Thus, the real exchange rate is a relative price. In the simple two-goods model, in which a country trades the domestic good Q for the foreign good Q*, the real exchange rate has the inverse dimension of the terms of trade (Q^*/Q), i.e. we have $e_R = 1/p$.

Countries that want to remove a current account deficit have to perform a real devaluation. They offer more of their export good Q per unit of the foreign good Q*. Thus, they put a higher real value on their export good, domestic demand for export goods is reduced; domestic supply of exports is stimulated. From the

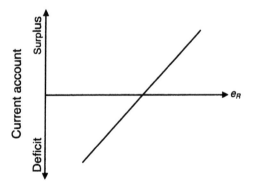

Figure 6.3 The real exchange rate and the current account.

point of view of the euro area as the domestic country, e_R rises. The relationship between the real exchange rate and the current account is shown in Figure 6.3. A high real exchange rate, i.e. a depreciated currency, means that it is easier to export, and the country will have a surplus in the current account. With a real appreciation (i.e. e_R falls), the surplus will be reduced and eventually a deficit arises. (see also Figures 2.20 and 2.21). Assume the US has a higher inflation rate ($\hat{P}*$) than the euro zone ($\hat{P}$). This means we have $\hat{P} < \hat{P}*$ instead of $\hat{P} = \hat{P}*$ initially. Then e_R rises, and the euro area experiences a real devaluation whereas in the US we have a real appreciation, crowding out its export sector.

An alternative definition of the real exchange rate

In an alternative interpretation, the real exchange rate is defined in terms of the prices P_T and P_{NT} of tradables (Q_T) and non-tradables (Q_{NT}):

$$e_R = eP_T/P_{NT} \tag{6.4}$$

where P_T is the price of tradables in foreign currency and P_{NT} is the price of non-tradables in domestic currency. The dimension is:

$$\frac{Q_{NT}}{Q_T} = \frac{€}{\$} \cdot \frac{\$}{Q_T} / \frac{€}{Q_{NT}}. \tag{6.5}$$

A real appreciation ($e_R < 0$) means that the price of non-tradables increases more than that of tradables. The economy will have an incentive to produce more non-tradables, and so a balance-of-payments surplus will be reduced.

External and internal balance

While changes in the real exchange rate can bring the current account into balance, they also have an impact on aggregate demand and internal equilibrium. Consequently, the real exchange rate has to satisfy the condition that internal equilibrium is established. In a simple Keynesian approach, the equilibrium conditions can be illustrated by the curves of the goods market equilibrium, of asset market equilibrium and for a zero balance in the current account.

The curve of the goods market equilibrium GG must satisfy the goods market and the monetary equilibrium. If at a given equilibrium, a real depreciation occurs, exports will be stimulated and output Y will increase. Consequently, the curve of the goods market equilibrium GG slopes upward.[2] The curve of the asset market or portfolio equilibrium AA must satisfy interest rate parity and monetary equilibrium. If at a given equilibrium output Y increases, transaction demand for money will rise, the interest rate will rise and this will lead to an appreciation. Consequently, the AA curve slopes downward.[3] If the current account has a zero balance and Y increases, import demand rises and in the new equilibrium the exchange rate has to depreciated. Consequently, the CA–CA curve has a positive slope.[4]

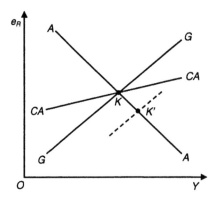

Figure 6.4 Internal and external equilibrium.

Policies affecting the external equilibrium will influence the internal equilibrium. For instance, an expansionary fiscal policy will shift the asset curve to the right since it will expand output. The new equilibrium will be at K' instead of K. If there was a deficit in K to start with, the deficit will be increased in K'.

Note, that in a more realistic approach, the internal equilibrium depends not only on the real exchange rate, but also on the real interest rate and the real wage rate. Moreover, in the Keynesian model the influence of the real exchange rate is only captured on the demand side. Supply side effects are not taken into consideration.

The concept of an equilibrium real exchange rate

Since the real exchange rate is a relative price that brings exports and imports or tradables and non-tradables in line with a macroeconomic equilibrium, the concept of the equilibrium real exchange rate has some prominence in economics. The real exchange rate depends on the model used. First, the trade flow approach and the capital flow approach have to be distinguished. Second, related to this but not identical to it, the distinction between the long-run and the short-run plays a role. Third, the richness of the model in terms of variables included is relevant.

Take the model used in Chapter 5. From equation 5.5 we have:

$$\hat{e}_R = -\hat{p} \tag{6.6}$$

In the long-run, the real exchange rate has to move in the opposite direction of the relative commodity price. If preferences shift or if relative supply conditions change, for instance in the case of technological change, capital accumulation or population decline, the real exchange rate has to adjust so that a new macroeconomic equilibrium is reached. In terms of Figure 5.3b, this means that tan α of ray ON changes.

This long-run relationship between the real exchange rate and the fundamentals according to the trade flow approach may be different if long-run or short-run capital flows are relevant and if temporary phenomena lead to overshooting or bubbles. As a very simple relationship we have, from equations 5.6 and 6.6:

$$\hat{e}_R = \hat{e} + \hat{M}^* - \hat{M} + \hat{y} - \hat{y}^* \tag{6.7}$$

Consider the case where the nominal exchange rate is fixed ($\hat{e} = 0$) and where the money supply in the home country ($\hat{M}$) expands by much more than the production potential ($\hat{y}$), with the foreign country expanding its money supply according to its production potential ($\hat{M}^* = \hat{y}^*$). Then, the price level of the home country will rise, and the home country will experience a real appreciation that will hurt its competitiveness. Such a development would not be consistent with an equilibrium. Instead, the nominal exchange rate would have to adjust. In contrast, with $\hat{e} = \hat{M} + \hat{y}$, there would be no impact on the real exchange rate.

Whereas it is already difficult to precisely determine the equilibrium real exchange rate on the theoretical level (as establishing equilibrium in the balance of payments and in the macroeconomy), complexities increase if the equilibrium real exchange rate is to be found out empirically when specific conditions come into play (see section 6.7). Nevertheless, this is an important policy question.

Case study: global imbalances

The US current account deficit amounted to US$804.9 billion in 2005 and again sharply increased compared to the previous year value (US$668.1 billion). As a share of GDP, the US current account deficit rose from 5.7 percent in 2004 to 6.4 percent in 2005.

Such a high US current account deficit may be interpreted as having the positive aspect of representing demand for other countries' products since the US soaks in their goods. At the same time, such a deficit, financed by capital inflows and by Asian central banks' demand for US dollar reserves, is a fragile situation. If market participants are no longer willing to provide credit and if central banks stop acquiring dollar reserves or start selling them, adjustment becomes inevitable. The situation cannot persist forever; it entails the risk of an unwanted, abrupt, and hefty decline in the US dollar. This would represent an economic earthquake for the world economy, causing massive repercussions. In such a scenario of a hard landing, the exports of other countries to the world's largest economy would collapse, which would put the exporting regions of the world into a severe recession. Moreover, wealth of holders of dollar assets will be destroyed.

A solution to this imbalance consists first in a controlled (not abrupt) devaluation of the US dollar, choking off US import demand and stimulating US exports. Note that in this scenario other countries receive a weaker demand stimulus and world growth would be lower. Since exports and imports are steered by the real exchange rate, the US would need a real dollar depreciation. And since the elasticity of exports and imports with respect to the real exchange rate is small for the US, a real depreciation of 20–40 percent may be necessary (Ahearne and von Hagen 2005). They also estimate that a nominal depreciation of 30 percent would bring a loss of wealth amounting to 10 percent of the rest-of-the world's GDP, given US dollar holdings of US$9.3 billion by the rest of the world.

As a second avenue, a reduction in the US budget deficit lowers domestic absorption and may eventually find its way into lower import demand. However, it does not represent a direct constraint on US import demand. Third, monetary policy plays a role in the adjustment process. An increase in the US interest rate keeps up external financing but reduces domestic US demand at the same time. One reason for the high external deficit was the easing of monetary policy after the stock market crash in 2000/2001 when the Fed set the interest rate at 1 percent. In mid-2005, the Fed has reversed its policy and raised the rate in a series of steps to 5.25 percent. Fourth, a higher savings rate in the US would help to alleviate the problem. Also, if the US would save energy or allocate the environmental costs of global warming to its energy users, it would reduce its current account deficit. Fifth, growth in Europe, being brought about by institutional reforms in innovation policy and human capital formation, labor markets and social security systems, would be a welcome stimulus for the US and for the world economy and would help to get the US out of its current account deficit. Realistically, a combination of all these factors would facilitate to reduce the risk of a major disturbance of the world economy.

A sixth avenue of adjustment relates to the current account surplus countries in East and South-East Asia of US$325 billion in 2004, of which Japan has a surplus of US$172 billion and China of US$69 billion. The oil-exporting countries had a surplus of US$194 billion due to the high oil price; the euro area's surplus stood at only US$58.7 billion. It is argued that if the Asian countries would apply a free float instead of the US dollar standard, appreciating their currencies, US exports would be stimulated and Asian exports to the US be reduced. As a consequence, the burden of adjustment for the European countries would be lower. If they leave their currencies unchanged or even let them depreciate, Europe will face a higher burden of adjustment because there is a stronger pressure for an appreciation of the euro. In a disequilibrium one of the relative prices of money has to adjust. Thus, Asian exchange rate policy determines whether Europe has to bear a larger adjustment burden.

Often, bilateral current account deficits of the US with the respective regions are used as arguments. Surprisingly, however, the 2004 US bilateral trade deficits, for which data are available (IMF 2005a) are not too different from those of other regions of the world. The US trade deficit with Japan amounted to US$ 65 billion, with China US$ 80 billion (and US$ 111 billion including Hong Kong), with the European Union US$ 87 billion and with the oil-exporting countries US$ 64 billion. This suggests that a unilateral appreciation of the renmimbi by China would not solve the US problem; rather a depreciation of the US dollar with respect to all the currencies seems necessary.

It is a highly debated question whether Asian countries, above all China, should appreciate their currencies (on China see Chapter 11). One argument says that the Asian countries have excess savings (i.e. a savings glut) and that it is normal that they use them to build up financial wealth abroad. It is also pointed out that they have to built up wealth abroad since they do not have appropriate public pension systems in place. Moreover, China uses accumulated foreign reserves to clean the balance sheets of its banks from the non-performing loans from time to time.

Of course, if savings in Asian countries were to fall, excess savings in the world would decline and the US would have to adjust. Finally, if the euro gains a stronger position as an international reserve currency and if Asian central banks would hold more euros, the euro would appreciate, taking away pressure from the US dollar. All these arguments show that the task to reduce the US current account deficit is a complex issue in which many aspects are relevant. To only look at the bilateral Asian surplus with the US is not sufficient.

6.3 Choosing the exchange rate system

The wish for stable exchange rates

Regarding money as an innovation which lowers transaction costs, the volatility of exchange rates reduces the intended reduction of transaction costs. Volatility of the exchange rate can mean different things: first, exchange rate movements can deviate in the short-run (monthly, up to one year) from a long-term trend or a somehow defined frame of reference. Second, the exchange rate can follow a trend for some years and then switch to a different trend, changing for instance from appreciation to depreciation. Third, the exchange rate can change abruptly and to a large degree when a currency crisis occurs. All three types of volatility cause transaction costs. Whereas short-term deviations from a longer trend may be hedged to some extent, a trend reversal has the consequence that trade flows and direct investment flows have to adapt to the new currency relations. This means that product specialization, factor allocation and the sectoral structure of countries have to adjust. A currency crisis wipes out savings, destroys financial wealth, affects the balance sheets of banks and firms and ends up in a decline of

GDP. The transaction costs arising from high volatility are the main reason why policy aims at stable exchange rates. The choice of an institutional arrangement for the exchange rate therefore is of major importance.

The basic choices

In establishing an exchange rate system, a country has several options. To restrain trade and capital flows is not an appropriate solution; then the country renounces on the gains from trade and capital flows (see Chapter 9). A first viable option relates to the nominal anchor. The country can choose the price level as its nominal anchor or the exchange rate. If it chooses the price level, it can direct its own autonomous monetary policy and can enjoy seigniorage. Given the monetary policy of other countries, the movement in the exchange rate reflects economic processes. The price levels at home and abroad affect trade flows, influencing the demand for and the supply of foreign currency. They also impinge on inflationary expectations, which in turn change capital flows. All this feeds into the exchange rate. Consequently, once the price level has been chosen, the country is no longer free in its exchange rate. If, as an alternative, the country chooses an exchange rate as its nominal anchor, for instance in a hard peg, it is no longer free in its price level. If its price level changes with a higher rate than abroad, real appreciation will hurt its exports and, since such a situation is not sustainable, eventually capital will flow out for fear of depreciation. Again, given monetary policy in other countries, the country that chooses the exchange rate can no longer determine its price level autonomously. Thus, there is an interdependence between the two potential nominal anchors. You cannot have both at the same time.

In any case, choosing a nominal anchor does not imply that an internal and external balance is guaranteed without conditions. It is real prices that have to bring about internal and external equilibrium. These are the real exchange rate as the relative price between export and import goods or tradables versus non-tradables, the real interest rate and the real wage rate.

A second option refers to the choice of nominal anchors versus a real target. A country cannot choose real prices, since real prices have to respond to specific economic situations in order to restore equilibrium in the markets. In the real target approach, the nominal exchange rate is seen as a policy instrument that affects internal equilibrium, i.e. output and employment (Corden 2002: 26). The country does not explicitly choose an exchange rate target (or an inflation target) but uses the nominal exchange rate to bring about internal equilibrium.

An example is the Swedish policy in the 1980s prior to the 1992 crisis. Trade unions pushed up the nominal wage rate so that the real wage increase was higher than productivity growth for the given price level. The ensuing cost increase would have made firms uncompetitive. This would have implied unemployment. In order to prevent this, the currency was devalued bringing about a rise in the price level. This then meant a fall in the real wage. Another example of this approach is the IMF policy applied in the 1970s, 1980s and also in the

1990s in the case of balance of payments problems and currency crises: conditionality for credits included a recommendation to devalue (besides reducing public budget deficits). Lowering the deficit means to trim down absorption and nominal devaluation stands for changing the relative price between tradables and non-tradables in favor of the tradables in order to enhance the incentive to produce tradables. This then stimulates exports and helps to come closer to an external balance. Apparently, this approach, rooted in the Keynesian model, is not possible with a fixed exchange rate as the nominal anchor.

Both examples are somewhat exceptional. In Sweden, devaluation was used as a correction of the trade union's wage policy, playing with the money illusion of trade union members. In the end, the perceived wage increases did not occur in real terms. Devaluation so to say corrected an institutional deficiency. In the case of the IMF, the approach was applied when the balance of payments or currency crisis had already broken out. These two examples do not suggest that the real target approach is too promising.

Yet in other examples the approach has more relevance. Thus, it can be argued that the anchor currency of the world, the US dollar, can follow a strategy of benign neglect, in which the authorities of the leading currency country do not worry too much about the external value of the currency. The goal then is to use the currency to enjoy gains through seigniorage, through capital gains by a future devaluation of the US dollar (albeit at the cost of losing credibility) and to see the (low) external value as a stimulus for growth. ('The dollar is your problem and our currency'.) In the real target approach, countries may use an undervalued currency as an instrument to stimulate exports and thus to promote economic growth as was the case with the German mark in the Bretton Woods system and as today is reproached to China with respect to the renmimbi (see below).

A third alternative is between a unilateral and a multilateral approach. In a unilateral option, the country chooses an exchange rate approach, given the monetary and financial policies used elsewhere. It takes the international environment as given. This is an option that small countries can follow. In the multilateral approach, a country joins a rule system such as the Bretton Woods system. It binds itself accepting a set of rules; possibly it can influence these rules. The multilateral system is supposed to provide monetary and financial stability for a group of countries or internationally. The opportunity costs of this approach are that the individual country cedes sovereignty, as happened in the gold standard or as it applies to the European Monetary Union. Whereas in these institutional arrangements the nominal exchange rate is fixed or placed into a band, the real exchange rate has to bring about equilibrium in the internal and the external balance.

Crucial interdependencies

In choosing the exchange rate, the policy-maker must be aware of several interdependencies given by the markets. These interdependencies can be considered as constraints for the choice of currency system.

First, there is an interdependence in the price levels. Differences in price levels will be evened out through trade in the long run, and they show up in exchange rate changes (purchasing power parity). Second, there is an interdependence in the interest rates. Differences in interest rates will be leveled out through capital flows, real interest rate differences through the mobility of real capital (and price changes), nominal interest rate differences through portfolio flows subject to exchange rate expectations (interest rate parity). Third, there is an interdependence between the price level and exchange rate expectations. Given capital mobility, this interdependence has been summarized as the impossible trinity – to simultaneously have fixed exchange rates, capital mobility, and a monetary policy dedicated to domestic goals.

Fourth, there is an interdependence between the nominal and the real exchange rate. A nominal devaluation will not be successful if its effect is eaten up by an increase in the price level. Then a real appreciation undoes the nominal depreciation. A devaluation tends to be followed by a price effect. Less goods are imported and more are exported. If this feeds into wage demands, a cost push inflation will follow. Thus conditions, for instance with respect to a competitive environment, must prevail that keep prices from rising.

Fifth, there is an interdependence between the real exchange rate, the real interest rate, and the real wage rate. If the real exchange rate is sluggish, a higher real interest rate can force the country to adjust, albeit with a cut in real output. An example would be a member country of a monetary union experiencing an asymmetric negative supply or demand shock. If the required real appreciation cannot happen due to sticky prices of the non-tradables, capital may leave the country so that the real interest rate has to rise in order to hold the capital. This, however, would aggravate the problem and force the country to adjust. Similarly, rigid wages may imply a higher real rate of return, i.e. a higher interest rate, also forcing the country to adjust. Or a rise in the real wages not covered by productivity growth would lead to a loss of competitiveness and to current account deficit, eventually requiring a real depreciation.

The limits of intervention

A central bank can intervene in the foreign currency market in order to defend an exchange rate. However, there are limits. In the case of a run on the currency (or an undesirable depreciation), the central bank can sell foreign reserves thus driving up the demand for the currency. This implies that the money supply declines and the interest rate rises. A higher interest rate affects investment and aggregate demand; thus there are costs to defending an exchange rate. In order to prevent the interest rate effect, the decline in the money supply may be sterilized if the central bank buys domestic bonds, thus withdrawing liquidity from the non-banking sector. In full sterilization, the money supply, the interest rate, and the exchange rate remain unchanged. This type of intervention has its limit when the central bank runs out of international reserves. As a matter of fact, when the loss of reserves gets known, this may intensify the process of losing reserves (Corden 2002). Note, however, that the exchange rate is affected in models that explain the exchange rate via the bond market.

If a central bank wants to prevent the appreciation of its currency, it can buy foreign reserves by selling domestic currency. This increases the money supply which then would lead to inflation. The interest rate falls. In order to avoid these effects, the central bank can sell domestic bonds in order to mop up the excessive money supply. This strategy finds its limit in that the central bank accumulates domestic liabilities which makes its position more risky.

The criterion of credibility

An important element of choosing an anchor is credibility. If the chosen anchor is not credible, monetary stability is not established. Then inflationary expectations and expectations of a depreciation start to creep into the system, and eventually market participants anticipate the impact of these expectations.

At the core of credibility is the independence of the central bank: money must be de-politicized. If it is not, politicians will make use of the central bank, either in monetizing public debt or, if this is judged as foul, in framing it to keep interest rates low so that the burden of public debt is not too heavy.

6.4 Unilateral exchange rate strategies: approaches for individual countries

In the following we distinguish between approaches that individual countries can follow and multilateral institutional arrangements that several countries or, in the extreme, the world economy can strive for. In this section, we look at options for individual countries.

Countries can choose from a menu card of quite different exchange rate policies ranging from a free float to using a foreign currency as legal tender (dollarization). These different options can be arranged in a continuum being defined by different shades of monetary sovereignty and dependency (Figure 6.5). Some of the approaches only represent nuances of one another.

Floats

In a free float, the currency of a country is determined exclusively by the currency market. The monetary authorities do not intervene in the foreign exchange market, nor does economic policy attempt to influence the external value of a country's money in international negotiations or through communication policy.

A managed float is characterized by interventions of the central banks

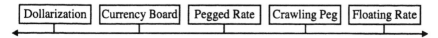

Figure 6.5 Different unilateral exchange rate systems.

supplying a country's currency or buying it up in order to influence the exchange rate. For instance, the central bank offers the currency in the foreign exchange market in order to reduce its price. Or it buys up its currency, given up accumulated international reserves, in order to stabilize or augment the currency's external value.

A unilateral target zone attempts to keep the exchange rate in a band. Such an approach comes close to a free float if the band is very wide and if the wide band has a very short memory so that older dates do not have an influence. However, it belongs to the category of pegs and can even be a hard peg if the band is tiny and the memory is long. It is not sufficient for a target zone to officially declare its existence. Credibility is crucial. If market participants do not have sufficient confidence in the band, the currency will shoot beyond the limits of the band.

Pegs

In a peg a country ties its currency to the currency of another country (single peg) or to several currencies (basket peg). Forty-three countries have pegged their currencies to the US dollar, twenty-eight to the euro. Most Asian countries have implicitly pegged their currencies to the US dollar (Asian dollar standard, McKinnon 2005).

The advantage of pegs is that producers and consumers face stable currency prices, relevant for their trade, assuming the peg can deliver stable expectations. In a peg, a country follows an exchange-rate-oriented monetary policy, which means it chooses the exchange rate as a nominal anchor. This implies that monetary policy has to influence the domestic price level in such a way that the exchange rate remains stable. Following the equation of purchasing power parity, $\hat{e} = \hat{P} - \hat{P}*$, the policy aims at an exchange rate change $\hat{e} = 0$. If the currency of the foreign country is used as an anchor, the rate of change of the foreign country's price level P* is regarded as the point of reference, i.e. $\hat{P} = \hat{P}*$. The domestic price level P follows the foreign price level. In the pre-euro era, Austria, Belgium, and the Netherlands were examples of such an exchange-rate-oriented monetary policy, holding their currencies in a constant ratio to the deutsche mark. An exchange-rate-oriented monetary policy is normally only carried out by smaller countries. Larger economies prefer to determine their price levels themselves. If larger economies pursue an exchange-rate-oriented monetary policy, at least one country has to provide a stable currency as a nominal anchor (anchor currency).

A peg will not succeed if the follower is unable to keep the change of its price level in line with the leading country, i.e. if $\hat{P} > \hat{P}*$. Then, its rate of return falls, capital leaves the country and the currency has to be devalued. Moreover, other aspects of economic policy, for instance the countries' fiscal policies, have to be in line. Thus, in the pre-euro era Austria's wage policy prevented price increases that would have led to inflationary pressure on the exchange rate.

In a basket peg, a country ties its currency to the currencies of its main trading partners, often in proportion to their absorption of the country's exports. For instance, China has used such a basket peg since 2005.

A crawling peg is applied when it is expected that the inflation rate in a country will tend to be higher than abroad over a longer period of time. Then the exchange rate is brought in line with the inflation differential, normally with a pre-announced rate of change of the exchange rate $\hat{e}^P$. It may be used when a country wants to get out of a hyperinflation or after a currency reform. For instance, the post-communist countries Poland and the Czech Republic applied the approach in the early and mid-1990s. It is chosen when a stringent stabilization policy which would be necessary for a constant exchange rate is unlikely to be kept up. Credibility of the pre-announced rate is crucial. This approach runs into problems, if the pre-announced rate $\hat{e}^P$ is smaller than the price differential $\hat{P} > \hat{P}*$. Then the system does not hold.

Whereas in a regime with pre-announced changes in the exchange rate the adjustment of the exchange rate takes place automatically, it is adjusted on an ad hoc basis in an adjustable peg. In a multilateral context the Bretton Woods system can be characterized as an adjustable peg.

In a truly fixed peg, the currency is definitively linked to another currency. No changes are made in the exchange rate.

Currency boards and dollarization

A currency board is a special form of an exchange-rate-oriented monetary policy. In such an approach, the domestic currency has to be covered completely by foreign currency reserves at a given rate. The central bank binds itself to provide domestic money only to the extent that foreign monetary reserves are available. To gain credibility in such a policy, the foreign currency can be authorized as legal tender in contracts. In a currency board, the domestic currency has to be as stable as the foreign currency, or it is driven out of the market. Argentina had followed this approach since 1991; it had to give up the policy of a currency board in 2001 (see Chapter 8). Hong Kong uses a currency board tying the Hong Kong dollar to the US dollar. Estonia also has pursued a currency board approach since 1992.

The approach of the currency board can only be chosen by small countries. They follow another country completely in their monetary policy. They use the other currency as an anchor, because they cannot provide monetary stability themselves. Thus, they import the stability of the anchor currency as Argentina did in 1991 after its inflation rate had soared to four digits. The country completely renounces an own independent monetary policy and gives up seigniorage.

An important condition for a currency board is that the internal markets of the currency board country, including the labor market, are flexible. The country must be able to digest external shocks by price adjustments, i.e. by a real depreciation. This is especially important if the country is very sensitive to external shocks. For instance, a currency is difficult to sustain if the country is a resource exporter and if resource prices are volatile internationally. The currency board country will also run into difficulties if the foreign currency chosen appreciates. This will make the country's exports uncompetitive. A related problem arises for investment, if the central bank of the chosen currency raises the interest rate, in order to choke off excess demand. The currency board country thus suffers through the business cycle of its currency provider. Moreover, serious problems will arise if the anchor country's performance differs from the currency board country's most important export markets. Institutional arrangements are necessary to ensure that the currency board system is not disturbed by a banking crisis or by an overexposure to public debt, neither through the federal government nor the provinces.

In dollarization, the foreign currency is used as legal tender in day-to-day operations. The country no longer issues its own money; it does not have a central bank.

Which currency regime for which country?

It has been argued in the literature that countries can only choose the corner solutions, either a free float or hard peg. Solutions in between would not be viable in the end, it is suggested. Against this bipolar view, an analysis of existing exchange rate systems shows that indeed a multitude of approaches have been used in the world economy. These approaches may be appropriate under given conditions and they tend to be stable for some time. They run into problems if credibility is lost and expectations of a depreciation start to creep in. Thus, countries can choose their own exchange rate system (Frankel 1999). As stated in the title of Frankel's article, 'No single currency regime is right for all countries or at all times.'

6.5 Multilateral approaches: the historical experience

In a multilateral approach, the spotlight is not on the option of a single country, but instead on the monetary stability of a group of countries or of the international monetary system. Such approaches represent an institutional framework, i.e. a set of rules, on which a group of countries agree. The countries joining such a rule system cede sovereignty to a multilateral system, giving up their monetary authority, or parts of it. Their benefit consists in having a stable monetary environment with more or less stable exchange rates. This is especially relevant for export-oriented economies. We have empirical experience with four approaches, the gold standard, the period of egotistic approaches with monetary disintegration, Bretton Woods and flexible exchange rates.

The gold standard

The gold standard was established in the nineteenth century. In 1821, the obligation was introduced for the Bank of England to redeem bank notes into gold coins. In the Bank Charter Act of 1844, the obligation of redeeming was guaranteed by cover clauses. Later on, other countries joined the gold standard, like Germany (1871), the US (1879), and Japan (1897).

To redeem the bank notes into gold meant that the central banks had to exchange the money in circulation for gold at any time at a legally fixed ratio. As a result, gold became a means of international payments and constant exchange rates existed. Let us argue in terms of actual currencies, dollars and euros. Since the currencies had fixed ratios to a unit of gold (Q^G), i.e. $€/Q^G$ and $\$/Q^G$, the ratio between the currencies $€/\$$ was fixed as well. The decisive task for the central banks was to credibly stick to the official parity between gold and the domestic currency. Therefore, it was important to keep sufficient gold reserves. This was guaranteed if the balance of payments was in equilibrium.

Figure 6.6 can be used to explain the effects of the gold standard in the nineteenth century. Suppose, for instance, that the US dollar declined in value, e.g. because of a rising supply of US dollars shifting the supply curve to the right. Starting from an equilibrium point E, with flexible exchange rates a new equilibrium E' would be reached by the devaluation of the US dollar.

But this cannot happen in a gold standard. If the dollar is sufficiently devalued, the market participants will be able to use the low-valued US dollars to buy gold in the US, transport it to Europe and change it into high-valued euros. Because of these transactions, there is additional demand for US dollars in terms of gold exports AB from the US; this means a US capital export. The exchange rate e cannot sink under the so-called 'lower gold point.' Then it would be worth exporting gold from the US. The lower gold point depends on the costs of transportation, insurance, and interest payments: it indicates the lowest possible exchange rate. The upper gold point has a corresponding effect: if the exchange rate increases, i.e. if the euro is devalued, from a certain threshold onwards it is worth changing dollars into euros; arbitrageurs would buy gold with the euros purchased in Europe and transfer it to the US.

If the appropriate institutional rules for a gold currency are chosen, the

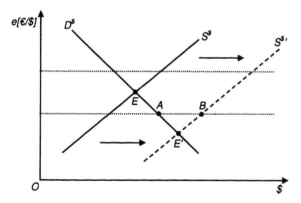

Figure 6.6 Exchange rates within a band.

exchange rate will find its equilibrium between the upper and the lower gold point. Thus, the exchange rate is stable within a small band. The arrangement includes self correction. Through the outflow of gold, the money supply is reduced so that the price level in the US will fall. In Europe, the money supply increases and the price level rises. Adjustment is symmetric. When a country loses reserves (gold), another country gains reserves.

The system collapsed at the beginning of World War I in 1914 when countries had to expand their expenditures for military purposes. Only the US remained on the gold standard, albeit with many restrictions. The other countries went back to individual exchange rates. Attempts to revive the gold standard after World War I failed (see below). It is now agreed that a gold standard does not represent a viable alternative today. One argument is that countries could not follow their own independent monetary policy. Stabilization policy would also not be possible. The other argument is that such a system would give huge windfall profits to gold producers like Russia and South Africa. Finally, a gold standard only guarantees a stable price if the relative price of gold to a basket of goods remains constant. If more gold is discovered, the relative price of gold to a basket of goods would fall, implying an increase in the price level. It is also not recommendable to peg a currency to a commodity basket.[5]

Monetary disintegration in the inter-war period

The period between the two world wars was characterized by disintegration of the monetary-financial system. Germany experienced a hyperinflation in 1923. It had to pay high costs of reparations due to the Treaty of Versailles and the government was heavily indebted. Government expenditures were financed by the printing press. From August 1922 to November 1923 the price level rose by a factor of 1.02×10^{10}.

After World War I many countries tried to re-establish the gold standard. In 1925 the UK followed, pegging the pound to gold at its pre-war parity. Since the UK had a higher price level in 1925 than before World War I, it moved into the gold standard with an over-valued exchange rate. This reduced its competitiveness and led to a depression in the UK. Choosing the pre-war parity meant a real appreciation of the pound with a negative effect on the economy.

In order to make it possible for smaller countries to participate in the gold standard, they were permitted in the conference of Genova in 1922 to hold reserves (instead of gold) of those countries whose reserves consisted of gold only. This implied that the UK de facto was the bank of other countries. Due to its economic weakness, however, the UK could not play this role. With low reserves it could not withstand a run of other countries on its reserves. The system did not have a lender of last resort. In 1931, the UK gave up the gold standard after smaller countries had left it already in 1929 and 1930.

This was preceded by the stock exchange boom in 1928 in New York, which absorbed financial means and reduced means available on the bonds market. Capital flows that financed countries like Germany ran dry. Since these countries could not find finance, they stopped to service debt. The world financial system received a serious blow.

With the Great Depression in the most important countries, a grave disintegration of the international monetary system and of the world trade order set in. Countries went into a downward spiral of competitive devaluations in order to regain competitiveness. Thus, when the US returned to the gold standard in 1934, they defined a new parity of gold with US$35 per ounce, whereas they had left the standard in 1933 with US$20.67 per ounce. This was a substantial devaluation. Other countries like France attempted to defend their exchange rate by imposing tariffs and trade restrictions. Besides cumulative depreciations the 1930s were characterized by strong interventions into the system of international exchange. The inter-war period has shown that an institutional framework for the international monetary system is a significant precondition for a prosperous international division of labor.

The Bretton Woods system

In 1944, forty-four countries reached an agreement on the post-war international monetary system in Bretton Woods, New Hampshire, USA. Like GATT, which was established in 1948, the Bretton Woods exchange rate system was created in order to establish a stable institutional environment during the period of reconstruction after World War II. While GATT aimed at a rule-based system for trade, Bretton Woods attempted to establish stable exchange rates. The system came into force in 1946. The anchor currency was the US dollar. The central banks (not individuals and private banks) could change their dollar reserves into gold at the US central bank, at fixed exchange rates. In order to join the International Monetary Fund, each country had to establish a parity to the US dollar (or to gold). The governments had to keep the exchange rates of their currencies within a margin of +1/−1 percent. Since each currency's exchange rate was fixed to the dollar, cross rates (for instance between the deutsche mark and the British pound) were fixed as well.

Central banks had to intervene to keep the exchange rate in the predetermined range. Consequently, central banks needed reserves. Only in the event of fundamental imbalances were exchange rate adjustments allowed to leave that fixed margin: international agreement was required for this. Temporary deficits in the balance of payments were to be balanced by loans from the International Monetary Fund. In contrast to the gold standard, monetary adjustment was asymmetric. If a country gained reserves this did not mean that other countries lost reserves. This is due to fact that reserves were provided by the anchor country (on the position of a reserve country, see below).

Initially, the Bretton Woods system was characterized by a dollar shortage. Countries in Europe and Japan desperately needed dollars to pay for imports. Eventually, these countries became competitive and earned dollars through their exports. Most of them then had current account surpluses. The constant exchange rate had the negative effect that they imported inflation from abroad.

From time to time, they had to appreciate their currency. This used to be a major affair; consultation was necessary and a political agreement had to be reached for appreciations over 5 percent. Moreover, the exchange rate had become a political price for the export industry. Prior to an immanent appreciation, 'hot money' would flow in; alas, the volume of speculation was low relative to speculative money flows in later periods, for instance in the devaluation of the British pound in 1992.

The Bretton Woods system collapsed in 1971 when the convertibility of the US dollar into gold was given up; the US no longer sold gold to foreign central banks. A band of 4.5 percent on both sides was introduced which was given up for completely flexible rates in 1973. The US, under the pressure of high budget deficits as a consequence of the Vietnam War, was no longer willing to provide a stable anchor, i.e. a stable leading currency. The system had moved to a situation of the dollar glut.

It is now agreed that a return to Bretton Woods-type system is impossible due to the role of portfolio flows. Capital mobility now plays a completely different role than in the 1950s and the 1960s when the capital accounts were not yet liberalized and currencies were only made convertible in cautious steps by allowing first convertibility for foreigners and eventually later on for residents.

The experience of the flexible exchange rate system

When floating exchange rates were introduced after the Bretton Woods system was given up, it was expected that flexible exchange rates would insulate countries against monetary and other shocks and thus contribute to stability. The price of this system was expected to be a greater variance in the exchange rate. It is now agreed that day-to-day volatility has increased since Bretton Woods. Not surprisingly, also the month-to-month volatility of bilateral exchange rates has increased sharply, which can be illustrated with the help of the following two currency pairs: deutsche mark against US dollar and yen against US dollar.[6] For the deutsche mark against US dollar pair, month-to-month exchange rate volatility in the flexible exchange rate system is about 4.5 times as high as in the Bretton Woods system. For the yen–US dollar pair month-to-month volatility increased even more, by a factor of fourteen.

Also the variability of the exchange rate for longer periods has increased compared to Bretton Woods. In the period from January 1980 to December 2005 the ECU/euro depreciated by 21.1 percent against the US dollar and 144 percent against the yen. In the same period, the US dollar depreciated by 102 percent against the yen. However, this longer-run variability does not mean volatility in the sense of fluctuations; the change in the exchange rate also reflects long-run trends. The larger changes in the exchange rates are the other side of insulating countries against shocks in other countries. Another observation is that the current account deficit of the anchor currency (and some other countries) have increased.

By and large, the flexible rates have insulated national economies in the larger countries against foreign shocks. In evaluating the system of flexible exchange rates, it is fair to note that this system has experienced major shocks including two oil crises and the rise of oil prices in the early 2000s, the fall of the Iron Curtain and German unification, many currency crises including the Asian crisis, the Reagan expansion, and the Japanese bubble. Exchange rate changes have helped in the adjustment to these shocks that had a different nature than in the time of Bretton Woods due to the high mobility of portfolio capital. We can state that flexible exchange rates have helped to absorb these shocks. For instance, the Reagan stimulus of the US economy in the early 1990s led to a stark appreciation of the US dollar. However, this appreciation stimulated foreign exports and reduced US exports, thus self-correcting the shock. The system of floating rates has stabilizing properties. Note that most currency crises in emerging markets were linked to pegs, including crawling pegs.

Floating rates shifted the relative weight between monetary policy and fiscal policy, giving monetary policy greater relevance in fighting inflation. Flexible exchange rates make fiscal policy less efficient in fighting unemployment if we use a Mundell–Fleming model. When the exchange rate is constant, fiscal expansion leads to a rise in national output and employment and to an increase in the interest rate. While this reduces investment as a secondary effect, it induces capital inflows. The balance of payments improve. Thus fiscal policy can reach two targets, internal (more employment) and external equilibrium. Two objectives are in harmony. With flexible rates, the increase in the interest rate leads to an appreciation, dampening the expansionary effect of fiscal policy. In contrast, flexible rates make monetary policy more efficient since monetary expansion reduces the interest rate which then requires a deprecation due to capital outflows. The depreciation is an additional stimulus for exports. Under constant exchange rates, however, monetary policy reduces the interest rate, driving out capital and aggravating the goal conflict between more employment and external equilibrium. Thus, moving from constant rates to floating rates limits the power of the finance ministers whereas it increases the influence of central bankers. Of course, Mundell–Fleming is a rather simple model, since it does not include variable prices, inflationary expectations, and changes in the exchange rate expectations due to fiscal policy. Moreover, the long-run effect of government debt is neglected. In the Reagan presidency, fiscal expansion led to the expectation of an appreciating dollar which then stimulated capital flows to the US and appreciated the dollar. This overshooting, however, must eventually be corrected.

The system of floating rates goes together with lower inflation rates. Unfortunately, a reduction of unemployment in the major continental European countries cannot be observed. To reach this target, one needs real exchange rate changes, including flexible real wages.

6.6 Multilateral approaches: available options and idealistic ideas

We have empirical evidence on multilateral exchange rate regimes including the reasons why they eventually failed such as the gold standard. This experience is

Figure 6.7 Multilateral exchange rate systems.

the basis from which new approaches can be attempted (Figure 6.7). One such approach is the European Monetary Union.

The low-inflation central bank dominated system

The actual monetary system is a hybrid system with several elements. Looking at the three major currencies, the foreign exchange markets determine the exchange rates; there are no exchange rate targets. Swings in the exchange rate like in the DM–US dollar rate or the euro-dollar rate occur and are only corrected over time. The exchange rate responds to asymmetric business cycles in the major regions, to differences in growth prospects as well as in economic policies.

The additional element to a free float is that the central banks in the three major regions or countries – the Fed, the ECB, and the Bank of Japan – have by and large followed a policy to bring down inflationary expectations since the early 1980s and to keep the inflation rate low. This also holds for the Bank of England. In this environment, the Fed has a leadership role, setting the stage for inflation in the world economy. None of the other larger central banks will tend to surpass the implicit inflation target of the Fed, i.e. allow a higher inflation rate. However, it can also be argued that the Bundesbank with the pre-euro system around the DM and now the ECB represent a check on the Fed's behavior. The ECB has a more ambitious price stability target than the Fed, one aspect being that the new institution and the new currency have to establish reputation and confidence. Thus, the Fed is not completely free in choosing its inflation target; it is restrained. In this concert of central banks, the Bank of Japan has not been concerned with inflation since 1990. It has been pumping liquidity into the Japanese system in order to fight deflation. It could even intervene to bring down the value of the yen. Under these conditions there somehow is a nominal anchor for the world economy, consisting in low inflationary expectations and in a low inflation rate. This low inflation system is a central bank created system. It is a soft system, albeit with rules.

The exchange rate is the policy domain of national policy-makers, not the central banks in most countries. Governments have the right to determine the exchange rate regime. For instance in the euro area, the European Council, the central decision-making body of the EU, has the right to conclude formal agreements on exchange rate systems with non-EU members (by unanimity) and it may (by qualified majority) formulate the general orientation for exchange rate policy (Article 111 EU Treaty). The ECB would be involved by recommendation or by consultation. The Eurosystem conducts foreign exchange operations according to Article 105 and consistent with the provisions of Article 111 of the EU Treaty. In the US, the Treasury, in consultation with the Federal Reserve System, has responsibility for setting US exchange rate policy, while the Federal Reserve Bank New York is responsible for executing foreign exchange market interventions. In Japan exchange rate policy has been assigned, by law, to the Ministry of Finance and not to the Bank of Japan.

Political exchange rate decisions or orientations can, however, be incompatible with an independent central bank. Actually, exchange rates are de facto determined by the markets, given the monetary policy of central banks. Interventions are used from time to time, for instance to smoothen or even to influence the exchange rates. An example is the 1987 Louvre Accord in which an attempt was made to appreciate the yen and the deutsche mark. Central banks can lean against the wind, however they cannot establish an exchange rate that runs counter to economic fundamentals. Once they have decided in favor of a price level as their nominal anchor, the exchange rate is determined. In times of an imminent crisis, such as 11 September 2001, they can provide liquidity in order to prevent uncertainty from arising. Yet another example is the rescue of the investment fund Long Term Capital Management in 1998 which the Federal Reserve Bank of New York organized in order to prevent a crisis.

The exchange rates seems to be on slack reins, changing a lot. However, exchange rates are not completely free nor erratic. They are determined by the inflation rates in the major regions of the world, due to the stability target of the three central banks. If these stability targets were given up, the system would most likely degenerate. It is a fragile system.

Apparently, there are corrective mechanisms in the system. If countries are in synchronous boom, high interest rates dampen economic activity (due to monetary braking). If a country's or a region's boom is asymmetric to other countries or regions, high interest rates (due to monetary braking) and appreciation (due to a positive business cycle outlook and capital inflows) dampen economic activity and appreciation spreads the boom to other countries.[7] If countries are in a synchronous recession, low interest rates stimulate economic activity. If a country's or a region's recession is asymmetric to other countries or regions, it has more leeway in its monetary policy. Low interest rates (due to monetary expansion) and depreciation encourage economic activity.

This system has some similarity to the McKinnon proposal (1982). According to this concept, exchange rates can be stabilized by a coordination of national monetary policies. The world quantity of money should increase according to the quantity rule of money. If a currency gets under pressure to depreciate, then monetary expansion of this country has to be reduced, whereas a currency with a tendency for an appreciation would need a more generous monetary expansion.

Macroeconomic coordination

Game theory tells us that countries can have benefits from macroeconomic coordination. For instance, fiscal policy may be more effective if undertaken jointly. Therefore global macroeconomic coordination between the major currencies, the US-dollar, the euro and the yen, is proposed. Such a coordination is also suggested as an important role for the IMF in order to reduce the current imbalances (discussion in the spring meeting of 2006). However, the political economy of macroeconomic coordination has its flaws. A crucial issue is which model is to be used in order to determine the policy instruments. Often, a simple Keynesian demand management approach is applied, for instance pushing for a coordinated demand package between the US, Europe, and Japan as in the second part of the 1980s to put the Japanese and German economy under steam. This seems to be a rather simple or even naïve approach. Moreover, structural questions such as how countries should react to an oil price shock, who has to raise energy prices, and which policy instruments to use against unemployment remain unanswered (flexible wages as in the US versus an inflexible (or rigid) labor market as in the European social model of the three large continental countries). Furthermore, countries have different policy goals and they may be in different political cycles. Finally, macroeconomic coordination may be used to put the blame on the other country; it may also be used to put the burden of adjustment on the other country. Exchanging information on policy instruments to be applied in individual countries is helpful (barometric coordination). An institutional rule-system when public goods are involved as in trade (WTO) and the prevention of currency crises (IMF) is appropriate.

Multilateral target zones

In multilateral reference zones or target zones, the exchange rate is allowed to only fluctuate within a band. The exchange rate should only deviate from the (real) equilibrium exchange rate within a limited range. Coordination of monetary and stabilization policies has to ensure that the limits of the range of fluctuations are not surpassed. As long as monetary policy and the other fields of economic policy of the countries involved do not contradict the credibility of the band, the exchange rate can be kept in the target zone. But as soon as the markets doubt the credibility of the band, such a system has a destabilizing effect.

If the limit of the band is reached, the central banks have to intervene. Consider an initial equilibrium E in Figure 6.6 and let the supply of the foreign currency ($) increase; for example, because of an excessively rising money supply in the US. The supply curve of US dollar shifts to the right. This means that, without an intervention, the US dollar will be devalued and the euro will be revalued (point E'). Such a devaluation of the US dollar can be avoided if the central banks intervene by demanding additional foreign money to the extent of line AB in exchange for domestic money.

Two major problems arise with reference zones:

- Who has to intervene at the limits? If the ECB supplies euros and buys US dollar in order to defend the exchange rate, this means that the money supply of the ECB is de facto steered by a foreign central bank, the Fed. If the foreign central bank expands its money supply excessively and the foreign currency is threatened with devaluation, then the ECB would have to supply euros accordingly. But, in the end, this would imply that the ECB would be heteronymous in its monetary policy. The way out of this dilemma is that the intervention has to be undertaken by the central bank whose currency is under pressure. This was the basic rule of the European Exchange Rate Mechanism. It is unlikely that such a system which requires to cede monetary sovereignty can be agreed upon.
- How to determine the reference standard of the real equilibrium exchange rate? On a theoretical level, an equilibrium exchange rate has to be established ex ante. In this respect, a model has to be available that includes all relevant definitions of the equilibrium exchange rate and also identifies the factors that could change the expectations of market participants (see section 6.7). On a practical level, a political agreement of the sovereign states has to be achieved in order to determine the equilibrium exchange rate.

Case study: the European Exchange Rate Mechanism

The European Exchange Rate Mechanism, a forerunner of the euro, can be interpreted as a system of reference zones. The intention was to keep the exchange rate within a band. It was a distinct combination of interest rate parity, which determined the capital flows, and of purchasing power parity, which defined the expectations for the exchange rate. In their monetary policies, but also in their fiscal policies, all participating countries were interested to keep their currencies stable and to prevent devaluations. The additional risk premium for a less stable price level, i.e. a higher interest rate and the threat of devaluation, represented a burden for the countries and, therefore, national policy attempted to minimize that risk. This system managed to keep the exchange rates stable during 1987–1992 (Figure 6.8). When the exchange reached the band, the central bank of the currency endangered with depreciation had to intervene. It could receive a credit line from other central banks. Sometimes the Bundesbank intervened as well.

However, it proved that real economic changes had to lead to an adjustment of the exchange rates when they did not affect all countries in the same way and when changes were adequately strong. German reunification was such an asymmetric shock. Real interest rates in Germany rose because of investment opportunities in East Germany and because of a

higher national debt. The other countries suffered an unwanted real appreciation. This added to problems already existing. For instance, Italy saw an
increase in the wages and in prices of non-tradables, but prices of tradables could not rise and profits of its export industry were squeezed. This
was a distortion in favor of non-tradables. For these reasons, the exchange
rates had to be adjusted. Italy and the UK left the European Exchange Rate
Mechanism in 1992 (September 16), the Italian lira devaluating by some
30 percent, the British pound by 32 percent. (Italy returned later.) For the
UK, a too-high entry rate had been chosen in 1990, so that the British currency was overvalued. The Spanish peseta, the Portuguese escudo and the
Irish pound were devalued. The French franc stayed within its band, being
defended by the Bundesbank. The intervention volume of the Bundesbank
reached DM90 billion in September 1992. For the remaining currencies,
the band of +2.25 percent was raised to +15 percent in 1993. The lira and
the peseta then stayed at their devalued level.

With the monetary union in place, only those EU countries outside the
euro area, the so-called pre-ins, participate in the ERM-II, except the UK.

Exchange rate zones can induce speculation by making it less costly to
speculate. The costs of speculation are relatively low as soon as the limit
of the band is reached. If a speculator can expect realignments, i.e. an
adjustment of the target rates, then this implies a high expected return on
investment. If the realignment does not take place, possible losses are
limited. If, for example, a devaluation is imminent (by a shift of the supply

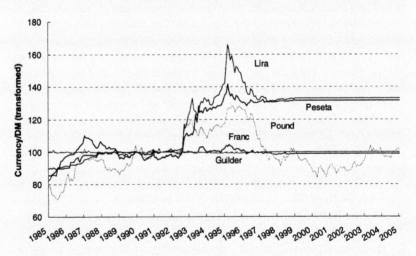

Figure 6.8 Exchange rates in the EMS[a] (source: Deutsche Bundesbank, monthly
reports; own calculations).

Note
a January 1990 = 100.

curve for the foreign currency to the right in Figure 6.6), investors can speculate on an adjustment of the exchange rate. Accordingly, they will buy the currency to be appreciated (in 1992 deutsche mark) and finance this by a credit in foreign currency, which is to be repaid later in a weaker currency. Or they will sell foreign currency now at a future date that they themselves will buy in the future at a lower price (selling short). Once the realignment has taken place, they will make a profit. If there were no realignment, investors would have to cover only the interest costs for some days. As demand for buy the currency to be appreciated is increased by speculation, any intervention of the central bank to defend the old rate was made more difficult.

Monetary union

In a monetary union, a common money is established whose supply is steered by a common central bank. In the euro area, the money supply process has been de-nationalized and put into the hands of a European institution. At the same time, the money supply process remains de-politicized as during the Bundesbank times since the ECB is independent (see Chapter 13).

While the nominal exchange rate is constant (since there is only a single currency instead of several ones), real exchange rate changes are needed in order to restore internal and external equilibrium. In the case of an economic shock asymmetric to a member country, a hierarchy of adjustment mechanisms can set in (Mundell 1961). First, capital and labor can leave the region, increasing the per capita income and employment for those that remain. Second, since cross-border labor mobility is low in Europe, a real depreciation in the crisis country is necessary. This is brought about by a fall in the price of non-tradables and by lower land prices and wages. Third, if the real exchange rate cannot perform the task of adjustment because wages are sticky, transfers between member states become necessary. Without them, economic divergence, for instance in unemployment, becomes too large.

The dream of a universal money

Mundell (2003) pushes the idea of a global universal money, a monetary union between the US dollar, the euro, and the yen. He suggests six steps to develop such a common money in the dollar, euro, and yen area:

1   decide on a common price index;
2   set an inflation target;
3   set an upper and lower limit for the exchange rate;
4   establish a joint monetary committee to decide on monetary policy;
5   make an arrangement for sharing seigniorage and;
6   close the exchange rate margins (p. 28).

Once such a system is in place, the final step would be introduce the INTOR, a new world currency. The INTOR would be backed by the weighted average of the three currencies for which the exchange rate have been fixed and of gold.

Unfortunately, it is not as simple as suggested. One decisive issue is that each central bank stands ready to buy the other currency at its lower limit. This, however, would imply for instance that the ECB would have to buy dollars when the Fred increases its money supply. The ECB would have to expand the money supply. It would have to import inflation and would be at the mercy of the Fed's monetary policy. The other decisive issue is that an unstable money is such an important policy instrument with such a significant impact on the citizens of a country, that governments are reluctant to give up money as a policy instrument. An example is the potential risk of citizens losing their savings by depreciation.

Looking at such a dream it is good to remind ourselves which conditions must be satisfied to have a stable international currency.

* The price levels must move with the same speed. If the price level in one country increases at a higher rate, its currency will devalue. Commodity arbitrage implies that purchasing power reigns in the long-run. Since the price level depends on the money supply, a first condition is that the money supplies expand at about the same speed, correcting for differences in the expansion of the production potential of the countries. It is a fact that the link between some monetary aggregates measuring the money supply and the price level becomes weaker, but in the end inflation continues to be a monetary phenomenon. If the link would indeed disappear completely, other monetary instruments such as the interest rate must be used to make sure that the price levels move in line.
* Exchange rates are not only influenced by commodity arbitrage, but are also influenced by capital flows, among them not only foreign direct investment but also short-term movements of portfolio capital. Capital flows are influenced by many factors, most importantly by exchange rate expectations. These are affected by interest rate differences, by inflationary expectations, changes in relative wage costs, budget deficits, and the solidity of public finance. To harmonize expectations on exchange rate changes requires to harmonize these factors.
* Historically it has not been possible to have a stable money if the fiscal situation of the state was in disarray.
* If we want to have stable nominal exchange rates, we put more adjustment needs on the real exchange rate, i.e. the relative price between non-tradables and tradables or between export goods and import goods. Such adjustments are harder to perform. Whenever the nominal and the real exchange rate diverge with a current account deficit accumulating, a currency crisis is imminent.

In the face of these conditions for a universal money, it is necessary to remind ourselves that monetary and financial disturbances had their root in policy fail-ures. Too often the triggers for exchange rate volatility are political ones reflect-ing economic policy conditions, above all failed stabilization policy, fiscal disorder, and misguided monetary policy. Exchange rate movements thus can be interpreted to represent a barometer of fundamental disturbances. It is a realistic assessment of the possibilities for the stabilization of exchange rates to empha-size national responsibility. The scenario then is as follows. Each country aims at monetary stability at home. It basically expands its money supply according to the growth of the national production potential or according to an inflation target satisfying monetary stability. Then, the price level remains stable in each country. Consequently, the exchange rates do not change as far as monetary policy is affected. However, stability orientation of monetary policy alone is insufficient to keep exchange rates stable. Fiscal policy and the whole economic policy, including wage setting, also have to be oriented towards stability. More-over, the country's time preference rate, the aging process of population, and technological progress all affect price level stability.

Thus, a solution can only consist in each individual country's keeping its own house in order and maintaining a stable domestic price level. Then, exchange rates will generally remain stable. This approach should be complemented by some minimum agreement on prudential rules for the financial sector in order to shield the overall system against instability and contagion. Summing up these points, the strategy for a stable money is: stability begins at home. Each country must attempt to have a stable money. If that is the case, a stable international monetary system will follow.

6.7 Choosing the right exchange rate

An important question for exchange rate systems is how the equilibrium exchange rate can be defined. A less ambitious question is whether a mismatch of currencies exists that has to be corrected. Of course, once an equilibrium exchange rate can be defined, misalignment can be interpreted as a deviation from the equilibrium rate. These questions are relevant when a country wants to enter a currency union or another multilateral exchange rate system. Thus, the UK re-entered the gold standard in 1925 with an overvalued rate; it also joined the European Exchange Rate Mechanism in 1990 with an overvalued currency. East Germany was united with West Germany in 1990 at an overvalued exchange rate. It also has been discussed whether Germany joined the European Monetary Union at an overvalued exchange rate. In all these cases, overvalua-tion will dampen economic activity and put a severe burden on the economy in the long-run.

Selecting the right exchange rate is not only a question of choosing the correct nominal rate. The price levels also play a role since it is the real rate exchange rate that determines internal and external equilibrium. The choice of the correct exchange rate is a thorny question for the profession, and usually economists fall back on purchasing power parity. As we have seen in Chapter 5, the empirical validation of purchasing power parity has its problems, especially if the level of the exchange rate is to be determined. However, we know already that the real exchange rate is not only influenced by trade flows, but also by capital flows. External balance in the current account and portfolio balance are relevant aspects for misalignment. For countries with a current account deficit over many periods such as the US, foreign debt and interest payments rise. When the debt burden is sufficiently high, devaluation is required to pay interest. In the longer run, the foreign debt/GDP ratio must be stable at a tolerable level (Stein 2001). For countries with a current account and a capital account surplus, there is a limit in the benefit of collecting international reserves. After all, these reserves are only paper, and the reserve currencies may depreciate. In order to determine the misalignment, we need a model of the real exchange rate and its determinants as well as the impact of the real exchange rate on internal and external equilibrium. Such a model also must include a forecast, since the real exchange rate changes over time with non-monetary factors (already discussed in Chapter 5), such as preference shifts between countries for products, changes in time preference, technological progress, and institutional innovations in the governance of the economy.

The Balassa–Samuelson effect

One aspect for such a model linked to a long-run trade flow view is the Balassa–Samuelson effect. It starts from the empirical observation (or assumption) that productivity levels and productivity growth are different in the tradable and in the non-tradable sector (Table 6.2). Typically industrial products are assumed to be tradable whereas services are considered as non-tradable. In addition, international differences in productivity levels and productivity growth should be more pronounced in the tradable sector than in the sector of non-tradables services. To simplify, assume productivity in the non-tradable sector is the same in developed and developing countries and that in the tradable sector productivity is low in (low-income) developing countries and high in (high-income) developed countries. In order to simplify consider labor productivity only. Prices of tradables must be the same due to Jevons's law of one price and purchasing power parity. Non-tradables are labor- intensive whereas tradables are intensive in other factors. Three implications follow.

Table 6.2 Assumptions of the Balassa–Samuelson effect

	Low income countries	*High income countries*
Non-tradable sector	Same labor productivity as in high income country	Same labor productivity as in low-income country
Tradable sector	Low labor productivity	High labor productivity

Lower price level in developing countries

Since the labor force in developing countries has a lower productivity in the tradable sector than in developed countries, wages in the tradable sector are lower than in developed countries. The same wages, however, are paid in the non-tradable sector. Consequently, the aggregate price level, defined as a weighted average of the prices of tradables and non-tradables, is lower in developing countries.

Real appreciation in countries catching up

If in countries catching up productivity growth in the tradable sector is assumed to be higher than in the labor-intensive non-tradable sector, the prices of tradables rise less than that of non-tradables, implying a real appreciation. This means that catching up countries get more competitive with respect to tradables over time.

Higher inflation rate in countries catching up

Since the price level of a country is defined as a weighted average of the prices of tradables and non-tradables, catching up countries tend to have a higher inflation rate than developed countries. This is due to the fact that wage increases in the tradable sector (due to productivity growth) spread to the sector of non-tradables with a lower productivity increase. This effect is relevant for currency unions. In the European Monetary Union, countries of the periphery with higher growth rates have a higher inflation rate than the core countries. This also will apply to the new EU members (that became members in 1994) once they have joined EMU. Since the ECB is oriented at the overall price level of the euro area, the attempt to keep the price level low seems to hurt the core countries.

Meanwhile it is questionable, whether the underlying observation of lower productivity growth in the non-tradable sector is justified. In a service economy, capital-intensive technological progress in important service sectors such as banking, insurance, communication and IT is high. Besides, the lines between tradables and non-tradables are becoming more blurred.

Determining the exchange rate empirically

To indicate a mismatch between currencies or to know where the equilibrium exchange rate exactly is, one has to integrate the trade flow view and look at purchasing power parity. We have already seen that looking at the price levels of two countries and the level of the exchange rate may not lead to convincing results since it is really the price levels of tradables that count. Moreover, we should look at producer prices. But even when the producer price levels for tradables and the exchange rate are in line, capital flows may influence the exchange rate following the capital flow view. Such an influence may be temporary, i.e. it may last for some years and may be corrected after a while (overshooting). Possibly, we can indicate a band for the 'right' exchange rate, but unfortunately, we do not exactly know how wide the band is.

As an example, Stein (2001) constructs a model that includes the current account and the net asset position or foreign debt. A real depreciation improves the current account. Productivity growth increases the trade surplus and appreciates the currency. Interest rate parity determines the optimal portfolio, for simplification as i=i* as in Mundell–Fleming. The current account balance drives the net asset position, a current account deficit leading to an increase in debt. This in turn requires higher interest payments which then mandates a depreciation in order to earn the foreign currency needed to meet the interest payment. Thus, there is loop in the model that connects the net asset position to the current account and to the real exchange rate.

A similar concept is used in a model in which debt influences the price level (IMF 2003: 33). In this approach, an intertemporal budget constraint of the consolidated public sector is introduced, including outstanding government debt, the nominal stock of money, the primary surplus in the current account (current account surplus excluding debt service), and the price level. In a money-dominated system, the price level is determined by the money supply; then the primary balance must adjust to maintain the government's solvency. In a fiscal-dominant regime, the primary surplus is considered as given. Then the price level is the only instrument that can make sure that the equation is satisfied. In such a regime, the price level is determined in such a way that the intertemporal budget constraint is satisfied.

In contrast to these approaches for deficit countries, Wang (2004) empirically determines the real effective exchange rate of China, using a non-linear least square approach. His results show three relevant factors:

- The relative productivity of tradable versus non-tradable goods affects the exchange rate. Theory predicts that a higher productivity growth in the tradable sector reduces the price of tradables relative to non-tradables (numerator in the definition of the real exchange rate becomes smaller): this means a real appreciation. Applying this approach to China for the period 1987–2003 and using the ratio of the consumer price index (containing many non-tradables) and the producer price index (containing mostly tradables) yields a coefficient of 1.12 in the regression analysis (Wang 2004: Table 4.1). A 1 percent increase in relative productivity growth would lead to a real appreciation of slightly more than 1 percent.
- The net foreign asset position also influences the exchange rate. An increase in foreign assets means an increased demand for a foreign currency. It can also be argued that the country that accumulates reserves can afford a trade deficit in the future. For China, a 1 percent increase in the ratio of net foreign assets to GDP leads to an appreciation of 0.9. Both lines of argument go in favor of an appreciation.
- As a third factor, openness plays a role. Whereas trade obstacles tend to

reduce the demand for a foreign currency, making an economy more open increases the demand for foreign currency and leads to a depreciation. Measuring a openness by the ratio of exports and imports to GDP, a 1 percent increase in openness leads to a 0.3 percent decline in the value of the currency.

Wang then compares the exchange rate predicted by the model with the actual rate. His approach demonstrates how difficult it is to determine the correct exchange rate ex ante. This is one of the reasons why the concepts for exchange rate policies based on the idea of an equilibrium exchange rate (Williamson 1983) are not very promising.

Specific strategies I: benign neglect of the anchor currency

A leading currency or an anchor currency comes into existence if a country has a high share of world output, trade, and capital flows. Another important condition is that the currency is stable. This means that the leading currency covers a large part of transactions taking place in the world. Such a currency has the prospect of being accepted in many countries (dollar standard, dollarization). The anchor country enjoys several advantages: it has lower transaction costs because many transactions are done in its currency. It also has the advantage of seigniorage since foreign central banks and market participants hold its currency. Moreover, the country's financial industry benefits from the currency position. Finally, it does not have to intervene in the foreign exchange market to keep a specific value of its exchange rate. This means that it can use its monetary policy for internal goals without worrying about its balance of payments deficit (or its exchange rate). It does not bear the burden of financing its balance of payments.[8] On the side of disadvantages, the competitiveness of the anchor country's industry may be negatively affected, since demand for the anchor currency as an international reserve tends to increase, letting the currency appreciate.

The anchor country may be tempted to strategically play with the external value of its currency, for instance riding out of international debt through depreciation. This would mean that wealth abroad is destroyed. The leading currency country also can follow a policy of benign neglect, not worrying too much about the impact of monetary policy on others (Bundesbank in Europe, Fed). However, the authorities of the anchor currency cannot overstretch this role since they risk to eventually lose the role as anchor.

Specific strategies II: explicit undervaluation

Countries may use a strategy of undervaluing their currency as a means to generate growth. This policy was said to be followed by Germany and Japan in the Bretton Woods era. It is also reproached to China (see Chapter 11). An undervaluation stimulates exports and reduces imports and initiates and fuels sectoral change through a decentralized market process. It is a policy instrument that is not directly visible to the voter.

Problems associated with this approach are an over-expansion of the export sector that eventually has to be corrected with high adjustment costs. There is a misallocation of resources. Moreover, the country will import inflation. Finally, such a policy may lead to depreciation spiral if other countries use the same strategy.

7   Financial crises

What you will understand after reading this chapter

Money is not a veil; monetary-financial disturbances have an impact on the real economy (section 7.1). An optimal portfolio is a delicate equilibrium, in which expectations play an important role; if they lose touch with fundamentals, a bubble may develop (section 7.2). Historic examples of financial bubbles are discussed in section 7.3. Preconditions may lead to a bubble and some mechanisms reinforce it (section 7.4). Speculative bubbles in asset prices can be modeled as the actual asset price moving away from a fundamental asset price where the system has no intertemporal fix point (section 7.5). The bursting of a bubble has implications on the real economy (section 7.6). The Japanese bubble represented a major financial crisis with a long-run impact (section 7.7). Financial exuberance in the US in the late 1990s exhibited aspects of a financial bubble (section 7.8). Financial exuberance has implications for the anatomy of the business cycle (section 7.9). A specific form of a monetary-financial disturbances are bank runs (section 7.10). Deflation is a disturbance of a different nature (section 7.11).

7.1 Monetary-financial disturbances

In a first best world, money is simply a veil of the real economy which you can withdraw, and the real economy is not affected. Money is neutral. As we have seen in Chapter 5, however, money can cause serious disturbances in the real economy which are associated with the destruction of accumulated savings and wealth and large GDP losses.

- *Inflation* (including hyperinflation) occurs when the money supply expands at a quicker pace   than the production potential.
- *Deflation* is a process in which the price level of country falls
- A *financial bubble* (asset price inflation) occurs when asset prices deviate considerably from a long-run fundamental equilibrium.
- A *currency crisis* is a specific form of a financial crisis for a currency. It occurs when the exchange rate can no longer be maintained and has to adjust abruptly to a new equilibrium.

- A *banking crisis* arises when customers withdraw their deposits and the balance sheet of an individual bank or a banking system gets into disarray.

Sometimes only one of these different forms of monetary-financial crises is prevalent, but very often different forms appear simultaneously. One form of disturbance may lead to the other. All forms of monetary-financial disturbances affect the real side of the economy. In an inflationary environment, nominal wealth is destroyed and recipients of nominal income (pensioners, workers) are the losers, whereas owners of physical assets gain. Inflation therefore is extremely unsocial. When deflation is anticipated by consumers and investors, they will postpone demand since it pays to wait when the price level falls. This will lead to a downward spiral of a reduction in demand. Deflation may lead to a recession. A financial bubble and a banking crisis will wipe out savings and nominal wealth and imply a GDP decline. Similarly a currency crisis will wipe out wealth and lead to quite a GDP loss.

7.2 An optimal portfolio

Portfolio equilibrium requires that the expected rates of return of different assets are equal. Assets may be all sorts of interest-bearing financial assets such as money market funds, bonds, or dividend paying shares. Neglecting risk and considering a closed economy, the rate of return of holding money in interest-bearing form like money market funds, i.e. the interest rate i, should be equal to the rates of return on other financial assets in a portfolio equilibrium. For instance, the rate of return on bonds is the interest rate on bonds (i_B plus the rate of change in the bond price, $\hat{p}_B$). Similarly, the rate of return on shares is given by the dividend, d, relative to the share price and the rate of change in the share price, $\hat{p}_{SH}$. Besides financial assets, a portfolio may also include real estate where the rate of return is the change in the real estate price, $\hat{p}_{RS}$. Finally, storable commodities like natural resources also have a rate of return, namely the convenience yield (here neglected) plus the rate of change in the resource price, $\hat{p}_R$. The condition for an optimal portfolio is:

$$i = i_B + \hat{p}_B = d/p_{SH} + \hat{p}_{SH} = \hat{p}_{RS} = \hat{p}_R \qquad (7.1)$$

Price changes become relevant for portfolio decisions whenever stock variables are involved. This means that commodities, factors of production, or financial assets are considered that are durable and have a longer life than a single period. In that case, an intertemporal decision has to be made as to when to sell, buy, hold or use the product or resource in question.

In an open economy, currency changes have to be taken into consideration as well. The optimal portfolio requires, for instance for shares, that the dividend plus the rate of change of the domestic share price is equal to the dividend plus the rate of change of foreign shares plus the currency gain:

$$d + \hat{p}_{SH} = d^* + \hat{p}^*_{SH} + \hat{e}^e \tag{7.2}$$

where d, d^* represent the domestic and foreign dividend; $\hat{p}_{SH}$, $\hat{p}^*_{SH}$ denote the rate of change in the price of domestic and foreign shares. In this chapter, we will study financial crises in which currency issues are not at the center and which are more or less contained to the individual country. Currency crises are discussed in Chapter 8.

A portfolio equilibrium very much depends on expectations. If people expect prices and currencies to behave according to a certain trend, their expectations will influence their market behavior, and this trading behavior reinforces the expected trend (self-fulfilling expectations). If expectations change abruptly, economic variables will adjust quickly to the new expectations unless the variables are sticky.

7.3 Case study: historic examples of bubbles

Historic famous bubbles have been the Mississippi Bubble in Paris in 1719–1720 and the related South Sea Bubble in London. Another well-documented bubble is the Dutch Tulipmania (Garber 1989, 1990). In the Tulipmania bubble, the price of tulip bulbs rose increasingly during the years 1634–1637. Some special tulip bulbs reached a value equivalent to a house.

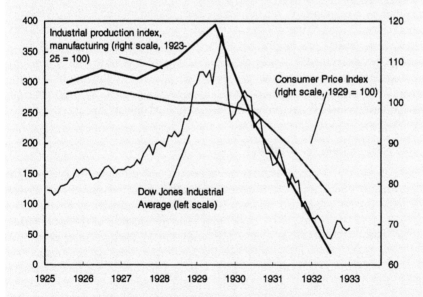

Figure 7.1 The stock market bubble and the Great Depression (source: United States Department of Commerce, *Survey of Current Business*, various issues; Pierce (ed.), *The Dow Jones Averages 1885–1995*).

At the end, the prices collapsed. There also was a railroad mania in England in 1846–1847.[1] Real estate bubbles have occurred frequently; examples are the real estate booms in Florida and in California in the 1980s. In yet another example, after the two oil crises expectations changed in the early 1980s on the excess liquidity and on the prospects of syndicated bank loans to developing countries.

More prominent examples of a financial bubble are the Great Depression in the US in the late 1920s and the Japanese Bubble of 1989 (see below). In the Great Depression stock prices in the US collapsed from an index above 350 in 1929 to 70 in 1932 (Figure 7.1). Industrial production halved in the same timespan, gross national income fell by 33 percent, unemployment jumped from 1.8 percent in 1926 to 24.9 percent in 1933.

Consumer prices fell by 20 percent, thus indicating a deflation. The Great Depression was a major shock. World trade declined and the depression spread to the European countries. The money supply, both in nominal and real terms, remained relatively constant in the second part of the 1920s; it even fell prior to 1929. Therefore, excess liquidity was not at the root of the problem.

7.4 Speculative bubbles: the important mechanisms

Actual product prices, real estate prices, and share prices can differ from medium-term or long-term fundamental values. At the root of such a divergence are expectations of rising goods, basic materials, real estate, and share prices. These expectations are reinforced when the prices actually do increase (self-fulfilling expectations). If actual prices deviate more and more from a medium- or long-term fundamental value we speak of a speculative bubble. In this situation, self-fulfilling expectations move the price of a good away from the equilibrium level, which is determined by long-term fundamental factors.

Some preconditions for a bubble

There are several prerequisites for the appearance of a bubble. One is that the valuation of goods, real estate assets, and other financial assets can change abruptly; the price increase does not stimulate supply sufficiently to counteract the price rise. A second is that, apart from price information of the spot market, agents form expectations regarding the future rate of change of an asset price and take their expectations into consideration when pricing the asset. This implies that the current value of the asset is linked to its expected future value. A third condition is that expectations are temporarily reinforced. For instance, in an open economy the anticipation of a revaluation of the (domestic) currency implies the import of short-term portfolio capital, so that the currency is actually revalued. Or if an increase in land prices is expected, suppliers of land hold back their supply, and land prices actually rise. Thus, the expectation is (at least temporarily) confirmed. Finally, if there were a day of settlement in the future that was already known today, such a speculative bubble could not start because agents would rationally take the discounted value of the asset into account when deciding how to price the asset in the current period. Market participants would project the future equilibrium price backwards in a recursive process to the present day until the spot price would be somewhat in line with the long-run equilibrium. Such an intertemporal fix point[2] would control the expectations and link them to the real economy. Without such a fix point, it is advantageous and rational for every single individual to follow the herd. For instance, assume that a currency appreciates. It will keep on appreciating as long as all participants expect it to do so and keep on buying the currency.

Ignition

In order to start a bubble, there must be an stimulus in the initial situation that starts off the bubble. One such stimulus can be a change in expectations, for instance that oil prices will be rising owing to an increased actual scarcity or that additional gold will be found after the first nugget has been discovered. A specific stimulus may be an excessive expansion of the money supply. This may lead to an inflationary bubble in which the price level rises, eventually ending in a hyper-inflation. Alternatively, the excessive money supply may not affect the price index of traditional goods very much, but may show up predominantly in real estate and share prices and thus start a real estate and stock market bubble. Credit expansion is usually a mechanism going hand in hand with money expansion and feeding the price spiral, for instance in the real estate sector. This was the case in the 1994 Mexican crisis as well as in the 1997 crisis in Thailand.

When the bubble bursts

At some time during the process, the speculative bubble will reach a point when people realize that the process is not sustainable. Then the expectations change. The economic agents sell their shares, real estate, natural resources, inducing prices to fall and making other market participants adjust their portfolios as well. Banks are reluctant to renew short-term credits when expectations change. For instance, with problems in the real economy of South Korea in 1997, Japanese banks, under pressure themselves, were no longer prepared to renew credits to Korean firms.

Some reinforcing mechanisms

There are several mechanisms which reinforce the collapse of a bubble.

Balance sheet mechanics

As soon as asset prices are falling, the asset side of bank balance sheets is affected (Mishkin 1998). Bonds and stocks lose value, and the asset side shrinks;

Table 7.1 Balance sheet of a commercial bank

Assets	Liabilities
Cash reserves	Deposits by banks
Loans and advances to banks	Customer deposits
Loans and advances to customers	Securitized liabilities
Bonds	Equity
Stocks	

eventually loans and advances to other banks or to customers change their risk status (Table 7.1). Banks may not have enough coverage for their credits with the remaining value of their assets; deposits may be withdrawn, and banks lacking refinancing may have to start restraining credits. A credit crunch is the result. An example are the magic numbers for stock market indices. Thus, a Nikkei index of 15,000 was considered necessary to be surpassed at the end of March 1998 in order for the Japanese banking system not to get into trouble. The balance sheet mechanism means a ripple effect working its way through the banking system. It is aggravated when the majority of the banks are affected by the same phenomenon.

Balance sheet mechanics operate within a country when problems of one bank spillover to other banks. It is also relevant between countries. An example in 1998 were the credits given by Japanese banks to Korean firms. When Korean firms defaulted, the asset side of Japanese banks was affected. In addition, exchange rate changes play a major role, for instance when bonds or stocks in foreign currency lose value owing to a depreciation of the foreign currency.

Threshold values and changes in expectations

For a number of reasons, expectations can change. A case in point are the critical parameters in software programs for portfolio investment, the 'stop-loss' points. Another case is when threshold values are surpassed and market participants start to ask questions about sustainability.

7.5 A model to explain a bubble

In a speculative bubble, the actual price of an asset moves away from its fundamental price. Assume the asset price process is given by the following relationship:

$$s_t = x_t + \delta E(s_{t+1}) \tag{7.3}$$

where s_t is the asset price in period t under the assumption of rational expectations and δ is a discount factor. Iterating this process forward in time gives:

$$s_t = \sum_{i=1}^{\infty} \delta^i E_t(x_{t+i}) + \lim_{i \to \infty} \delta^i E_t(x_{t+i}) \tag{7.4}$$

This model can generate rational bubbles if $\lim_{i \to \infty} \delta^i E_t(x_{t+i}) \neq 0$. This means that the system has no intertemporal fix point, i.e. the so-called transversality condition does not hold. If such a fix point in the future would exist for an asset price, market participants could calculate a current value in a recursive process. In this case, rational speculative bubbles are compatible both with a macroeconomic equilibrium and rational expectations. To see this, denote the fundamental asset price by

$$s_{F,j} = \sum_{i=1}^{\infty} \delta^i E_t(x_{t+i})$$

A speculative bubble then implies:

$$s_t = s_{F,t} + b_t = x_t + \delta E_t(s_{F,t+1} + b_{t+1}) \tag{7.5}$$

such that the bubble term is given by:

$$E_t(b_{t+1}) = \delta^{-1} b_t \tag{7.6}$$

In the literature, three types of speculative bubbles are distinguished: the *never-ending* bubble with $b_{t+1} = \delta^{-1} b_t$. The *stochastic* bubble $b_{t+1} = \delta^{-1} b_t + \varepsilon$ where the stochastic term ε has an expected value of zero. Blanchard and Watson (1982) additionally analyze the case of a *bursting* bubble that has a certain probability to burst.

7.6 The impact of the bubble

A speculative bubble may be limited to the financial sector, but in most cases it has an impact on the real sphere of the economy as well. There are several mechanisms by which the real economy is affected.

Relative prices and relative demand change. Assume the real estate sector and the construction sector are over-expanding in a bubble. Too many factors of production are attracted to construction, leading to a distorted allocation of resources. When the real estate bubble bursts, the construction sector collapses. In other bubbles, too many resources may have been placed into specific sectors, for instance the oil industry. When prices fall and when demand weakens, the resource allocation is not sustainable. The misallocation has to be corrected after the speculative bubble has burst.

The negative wealth effect for households reduces consumption demand. Consumers lose wealth, and they will adjust their spending, albeit not in a one-to-one relationship because the lower valuation of financial assets and houses does not directly translate into lower household incomes.

The balance sheet effect forces firms to use their cash flows to pay back debt instead of spending it for investment. Moreover, firms experience a lower aggregate demand.

The change in asset values leads to a change in the balance sheet of banks who become more cautious in giving new credits; this leads to a credit crunch affecting the financing possibilities of firms.

Cost-cutting strategies of firms include the shedding of labor, which increases the economic uncertainty for households and makes them more than cautious in their spending. Taken together, these effects imply a lower growth rate with higher unemployment and lower tax revenues.

Individuals lose wealth; in addition they have to foot the bill of government intervention as taxpayers. Whereas the government will let the private sector take losses, it will have usually to step in helping the banking industry so that credits can flow again. The government usually collects the bad loans, organizes them in a separate asset management institution and capitalizes this institution (or directly the banks) with taxpayers' money.

Total costs depend on the type and the severity of the crisis. In the Great Depression, US GDP fell by 33 percent.

7.7 The Japanese bubble and its impact

The development of the Japanese stock and real estate markets between 1986 and 1990 is an example of a speculative bubble. In the second part of the 1980s Japan expanded the money supply strongly (Figure 7.2); the interest rate was reduced (Figure 7.3). This was in response to a strong political US pressure to play the demand locomotive for the world economy. Academics also asked Japan to expand aggregate demand. For instance, Bergsten wrote:

> Japan and Germany (and possibly the United Kingdom) need to adopt new expansionary measures on the order of 2–3 percent of their GNPs.
>
> (1986: 40)

and:

> [Japan and Germany] must keep their domestic demand growing rapidly for some time. They must cooperate to achieve and then maintain a set of equilibrium asset price s preferably through the adoption of target zones.
>
> (1988: 191)

Krugman plays a similar tune with respect to Germany:

> A ... problem is posed by the unwillingness of Germany to expand domestic demand.
>
> (1989: 104)

Using the devaluation of the US dollar as a means to get Japan and Germany to expand domestic demand was addressed by the late Rudi Dornbusch (1987):

> A falling dollar would do much good abroad. It would force on America's

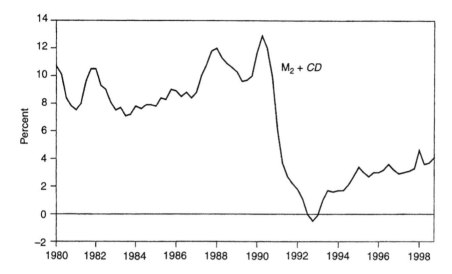

Figure 7.2 Money expansion in Japan[a] (source: OECD, *Economic Indicators*).

Note

a M2 + CD: quarterly data, seasonally adjusted; change over previous year for data.

reluctant trading partners the recognition that they must become the loco-
motives for the world economy or face deep recession themselves.

Owing to a strong revaluation of the yen, the strong expansion of the money
supply in Japan during the 1980s did not lead to an increase in the cost of living
(i.e. there was only a minor increase in the consumer price level, at least in the
case of the traditional goods). The additional liquidity, however, found its way
into the demand for shares and real estate, so that these prices rose. Then in
1989, the speculative bubble burst, the Nikkei stock index fell from almost
39,000 in December 1989 to 20,000 in January 1990 and moved further downward from then on. The prices for real estate went down dramatically as well
(Figure 7.4). The banks entered a state of crisis because of reduced asset values
in their balance sheets.

The Japanese economy was severely affected by the bursting of the bubble.
The immediate result of the burst bubble was that financial capital was lost. For
instance, cumulative capital losses in the period 1990–1996 since the 1989–1990
peak amounted to 967 trillion yen which corresponds to Japan's GDP of two
years (OECD 1998: Table 7.2).

The impact for the banking sector consisted of a serious amount of bad loans,
estimated to have stood at 11 percent of total loans (Uebe 1999). Banks had to
clean up their balance sheets before they could start to hand out new loans. This
is why they did not take advantage of the ample liquidity and the low short-term
interest rate provided by the Bank of Japan. De facto, this implied a credit
crunch. Non-financial corporations also took severe losses so that their balance

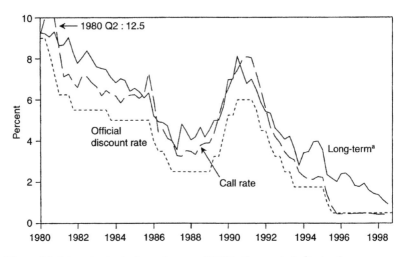

Figure 7.3 Interest rates in Japan (source: OECD, *Economic Indicators*).

Note

a Weighted average of government bond yields.

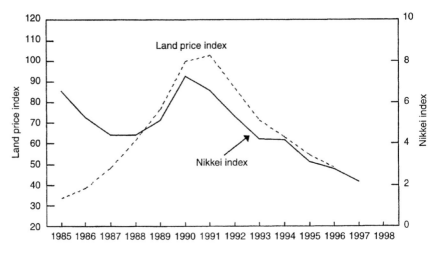

Figure 7.4 The Japanese bubble (source: Statistics Bureau, Management and Coordination Agency, Government of Japan, *Statistical Yearbook of Japan* 1993 and 1997).

sheets were in disarray as well. They had to clean them up as well, using profits (if they arrived) to write off the losses incurred instead of using them for investment. Households took more than 40 percent of the total losses. Together with the concern about rising unemployment they were reluctant to consume. All these factors implied that aggregate demand was weak and even declined. This

Table 7.2 Capital losses[a,b] in Japan, 1990–1996 (in trillion yen)

Non-financial corporations	334.7
Financial institutions	181.0
General government	98.5
Households	427.9
Total nation	967.3

Source: OECD (1998: Table 9).

Note
a Gross assets.
b Since the 1989–1990 peak.

process was self-reinforcing as soon as the price level fell since in a deflationary environment it pays to wait with spending.

The negative impact of the bubble showed up in increased unemployment and a poor growth performance. Since 1992 and until 2003, the Japanese economy has been nearly stagnant, (with the exception of 1996), the average annual GDP growth rate standing at 1.2 percent; it slid into a severe recession in 1998/1999 (Figure 7.5, Table 7.3). Japan's accumulated GDP loss for the period 1992–2004 amounts to US$13 trillion (in constant 2000 prices), if one assumes that Japan would have continued to expand at its average GDP growth rate of 3.94 percent from the 1980s for the period between 1992 and 2004. This constitutes 312 percent of Japan's 1990 GDP, i.e. three times the 1990 GDP. The 2004

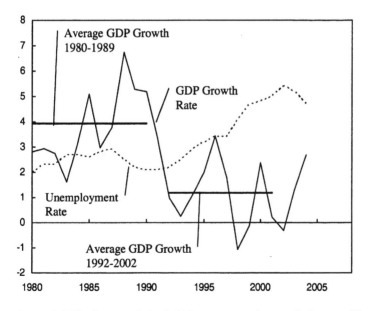

Figure 7.5 The impact of the bubble on economic growth (source: World Bank, *World Development Indicators* 2006).

Table 7.3 The performance of the Japanese economy since the bubble

Year	GDP growth rate	Unemployment rate	Inflation[a]	Short-term interest rate	Exchange rate[b]	Budget deficit[c]	Public debt[c]	Current account[c]
1990	5.2	2.1	2.4		144.8	2.0	68.6	1.5
1991	3.4	2.1	2.9	7.4	134.5	1.8	64.8	2.0
1992	1.0	2.2	1.6	4.5	126.7	0.8	68.6	3.0
1993	0.2	2.5	0.5	3.0	111.2	−2.4	74.7	3.0
1994	1.1	2.9	0.1	2.2	102.2	−3.8	79.7	2.7
1995	2.0	3.2	−0.6	1.2	94.1	−4.7	87.0	2.1
1996	3.4	3.4	−0.8	0.6	108.8	−5.1	93.8	1.4
1997	1.8	3.4	0.4	0.6	121.0	−3.8	100.3	2.3
1998	−1.0	4.1	−0.2	0.7	130.9	−5.5	112.1	3.0
1999	−0.1	4.7	−1.3	0.2	113.9	−7.2	125.7	2.6
2000	2.4	4.7	−1.5	0.2	107.8	−7.5	134.0	2.5
2001	0.2	5.0	−1.3	0.1	121.5	−6.1	142.3	2.1
2002	−0.3	5.4	−1.3	0.1	125.3	−7.9	149.4	2.8
2003	1.3	5.3	−1.4	0.0	115.9	−7.7	154.0	3.2
2004	2.7	4.7	−1.2	0.0	108.1	−6.5	156.3	3.7
2005[d]	2.4	4.4	−1.1	0.0	110.0	−6.5	158.9	3.4

Source: OECD, *Economic Outlook* 2005.

Notes
a GDP deflator.
b Yen per US dollar.
c Percent of GDP.
d Estimate.

GDP is about 46 percent lower than the potential GDP with the higher growth rate. If one assumes that Japan would have grown at just 60 percent of its 1980s average growth rate, Japan's loss would amount to a loss of 129 percent of its 1990 GDP. This is an incredible loss. If the profession wants to find an example for a serious error, the case of Japan will be high on the list.

Japan had severe difficulties to get out of the bubble. Expanding the money supply did not work, since the increase in the money supply was not accepted by the banks, even with a short-term interest rate close to zero. The banks did not need the liquidity offered since they did not give credits. Moreover, deflationary expectations kept consumers from spending; the GDP deflator was negative since 1996. Swelling government spending through government deficits of 5–8 percent of GDP since 1995 could not move the economy out of stagnation and deflation either. The Keynesian approach of stimulating the economy through government spending led to an increase in the public debt to GDP ratio from 68.8 percent in 1992 to 156.3 percent in 2004. Such a high level of public debt represents an extreme interest burden for the public budget in the future. Japan continuously had an export surplus in the 1990s, but this was not sufficient to pull the economy out of stagnation and deflation. In the period 1990-2005, then yen appreciated by 35 percent relative to the US dollar, with no contractionary effect on the export surplus. It then depreciated until 2004 (with temporary appreciations). It seems that excess monetary liquidity eventually showed up in a depreciated yen. Japan recognized rather late that it was necessary to atttack the problem at its root and recapitalize the banks by spending tax money. The Long-Term Credit Bank of Japan and the Nippon Credit Bank have been declared insolvent and the top fifteen banks were recapitalized in 1998.

7.8 Case study: financial exuberance in the US

Share prices in the US in the period from 1995 to 2001 developed similarly as in Japan in the period from 1985 to 1991. The S&P 500 rose from roughly 500 points to 1,400 in a similar way to the Nikkei index (Figure 7.6). Thus,

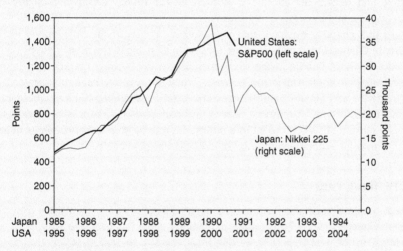

Figure 7.6 Share prices in Japan and in the US (source: OECD, *Economic Indicators*).

there is some similarity between the financial exuberance in the US (Shiller 2000) and the pre-bubble situation in Japan. There is also a similar increase in the share of investment of GDP during these two periods in the different countries. Nevertheless, there are differences. First, the US did not experience a construction boom. Second, the interest rate was not lowered as much as in Japan. Third, the US economy exhibits quite a flexibility in its production capacity. This is due to the fact that all the sectors of the economy are exposed to the competitive pressure of the market whereas in Japan some domestic sectors were protected by heavy regulation. Finally, the banking system is organized differently.

7.9 A new anatomy of the business cycle

The business cycle of an economy, i.e. the ups and downs of economic activity over time, is influenced by many factors. A most fascinating question is how it comes to a turning point from an upswing to a downswing. Many hypotheses have been put forward why an economy eventually runs out of steam. Besides negative external shocks such as an oil price increase, a first endogenous phenomenon is that labor becomes scarce with rising production so that labor costs rise. This may be amplified by trade unions pushing for higher wages and thus causing an internal negative supply shock to an economy. If costs increase, profits may be squeezed and investment is reduced. A second phenomenon is over-investment; too much capital is accumulated so that overcapacity squeezes profits. A third endogenous phenomenon is that the money supply is expanded excessively and that eventually the central bank will have to put its foot on the brake and reduce the excessive increase in the money supply by raising the interest rate and thus squeezing profits.

In this chapter, we have met yet another version of an endogenous cycle, namely financial exuberance. If the excessive increase in the money supply does feed a financial bubble in the stock market and the housing market, the bubble may burst at some time, for instance when the central bank no longer can provide the additional liquidity necessary to feed the bubble. Such a bubble goes hand in hand with over-investment in the real economy. In a way, it expands over-investment. When the bubble bursts, the rate of investment becomes negative. Financial exuberance thus aggravates the business cycle.

7.10 Bank runs

Bank runs are a specific form of a monetary-financial crisis. They arise from the mismanagement of a bank or an exogenous shock such as the loss of assets leading to an over-exposure of liabilities relative to assets. When the public audience gets to know the loss of assets, customers lose confidence in the reputation of a bank. When a bank panic occurs, customers tend to withdraw their deposits as quickly as possible in the attempt not to lose their funds. The reserves, in currency, in deposits in central banks, or in other liquid forms that a bank holds as a safety cushion against withdrawals may not be sufficient to provide currency to the customers. Reserves can dwindle quickly.

If only a single bank is affected, customers take their deposits to another bank. If the run spreads from one bank to others, customers shift from deposits into currency. Thus, the failure of a single bank can extend to other banks; it can lead to a systemic banking crisis affecting imprudent and prudent institutions alike.

Examples of bank runs and bank crises are the German banking crisis of 1931 and the US banking crisis in the Great Depression. In Germany, in May 1931, difficulties in an Austrian bank led to a loss of confidence in German banks and a withdrawal of foreign short-term money. Some banks had to be closed, the stock market was closed in July and a bank run occurred. In the Great Depression of the US, bank failures increased from 650 in 1929 to 4,024 in 1933. A four-day bank holiday had to be declared in March 1933 and non-solvent banks were suspended. Another crisis, the US bank crisis of 1907, led to the Federal Reserve System. In 2001, a bank run occurred in Argentina (see Chapter 8). Historically, English Goldsmiths issuing promissory notes suffered severe failures in the sixteenth century, due to bad harvests. Other examples are the 'Compagnie d'Occident Bubble' (1717–1719) and the 'Post Napoleonic Depression' (1815–1830).

The costs of a banking crisis affect the shareholders of a bank, depositors, the bank's creditors and borrowers and eventually the whole economy. Depositors lose their savings. Creditors of the bank may not get repaid. Shareholders experience a decline in the value of their equity holdings. Borrowers will be cut from funding. For the economy, households and firms may face a credit crunch so that consumption and investment will be restraint. If firms hold equity in banks, their balance sheets will get into disarray. This also applies to the insurance industry. Eventually, a public sector crisis resolution becomes inevitable. The taxpayer has to pick up the costs of the banking crisis. Costs of banking crisis, measured as cumulative output losses, are estimated at 15–20 percent of annual GDP (Hoggarth *et al.* 2002). Banking crises may go together with a financial crisis and a currency crisis. But they may arise independently from these types of crises.

Regulation attempts to prevent bank failures by requiring adequate capital and by other prudential standards. In most countries, some safety nets exist such as risk pools of savings and loans and of private banks. In case of a bank crisis, the central bank can serve as a lender of last resort by providing sufficient liquidity to keep the banking system from failing.

7.11 Deflation

Deflation is the opposite phenomenon to inflation. During a period of deflation, the price level of a country falls. Deflation is not to be confused with falling prices for some products while the prices of other products rise. In contrast to such changes in the price structure, which go together with structural change in the economy, for instance from the industrial sector to the service sector, deflation is a general fall in the price level. This is started by a severe uncertainty affecting an economy. An example is the aftermath of the Japanese bubble when the balance sheets of firms and banks were in disarray and prevented them from investing and extending credits. This turmoil in the balance sheets eroded public confidence.

If unchecked, deflation is a cumulative downward process in which the real value of money rises since the price level declines. For consumers, it is rational to postpone consumption and to wait until prices have fallen further. Similarly, investors have an incentive to wait when buying machines or constructing buildings when they expect prices to fall. Holding demand back implies that a country's production capacity is not fully utilized. The output of the economy shrinks, unemployment increases which, in turn, creates additional uncertainty reducing aggregate demand. The deflation turns into a recession and even a depression. This is why deflation has to be prevented.

Since consumers and investors hold back demand, they hoard money rather than spending it. The velocity of money falls. Even when the central bank supplies additional liquidity into the banking system at a low interest rate close to zero, as in Japan in the 1990s, banks are not interested in this additional liquidity since customers are not willing to take up credit. A customer drawing credit cannot enjoy tomorrow's lower prices. Thus, it is rational to postpone taking credit. Consequently, central banks have difficulty in leading a country out of a deflation by offering additional liquidity. Central banks can hardly implement a negative interest rate, offering a premium to banks if they accept additional liquidity. Increasing aggregate demand through government spending has the damaging effect of piling up public debt, and this burden for the future may further increase uncertainty for consumers and investors, fearing that they will face a higher tax load in the years to come. A way out is a depreciation of the currency which then stimulates export demand. Besides 'talking down' the value of the currency, an ample supply of money may eventually find its way into a lower external value of the currency.

8 Currency crises

What you will understand after reading this chapter

In an open economy, foreign currencies and capital flows enter the picture. Portfolio capital in particular is highly mobile internationally. Consequently, the optimal portfolio with foreign currencies can be a very delicate equilibrium (section 8.1). In open economies with mobile portfolio capital, the nature and the mechanisms of financial crises are different. The financial crisis is now mainly a currency crisis (section 8.2). A divergence between the nominal and the real exchange rate, occurring simultaneously with a widening current account deficit, can be a signal that the onset of a currency crisis is nearing (section 8.3). Some recent currency crises are surveyed in section 8.4. In the worst case, the currency has be rebased in a currency reform (section 8.5).

8.1 Currency crises – a disturbance of portfolios

Optimal portfolio with foreign currencies

When different currencies are taken into account, a portfolio equilibrium requires that the rates of return of assets denominated in different currencies are identical. To simplify the exposition, we abstract from the risks of different assets. Currency holdings can be treated like a stock, and exchange rate changes are variations in stock prices. An optimal portfolio requires a rate of return parity:

$$r = r* + \hat{e}^e \tag{8.1}$$

where r denotes the domestic rate of return, $r*$ the foreign rate of return and $\hat{e}^e$ the expected rate of change in the exchange rate. As we know from equation 5.4, the nominal exchange rate e is defined as the domestic currency in terms of one unit of the foreign currency, i.e. from the European point of view $e[€/\$]$. Consequently, $\hat{e}^e > 0$ means that more euros have to be spent for one unit of $\$$, i.e. a depreciation of the euro, and $\hat{e}^e < 0$ means an appreciation of the euro. Examples of the rate of return parity are equation 7.2 for shares and, of course, the interest rate parity (equation 5.12).

As in any portfolio equilibrium, expectations play a major role because expected depreciations and expected appreciations of a currency determine the rate of return parity. If expectations change, the given portfolio is no longer optimal: it cannot hold. Adjustment can be instantaneous because portfolio capital is highly mobile. Thus, if a currency is expected to depreciate, portfolio capital can exit immediately, implying that the exchange rate also changes instantaneously once expectations become different. A sudden massive outflow of portfolio capital, a sudden stop of capital inflows or a capital flow reversal are at the core of a currency crisis. Portfolio capital is said to have the memory of an elephant, the heart of a roe deer and the quick legs of an antelope. If a portfolio equilibrium is disturbed, capital flows will reverse.

As an example disturb a portfolio equilibrium in equation 8.1 with a domestic rate of return of 7 percent a foreign rate of return of 4 percent and an expected rate of depreciation of the domestic currency of 3 percent and disturb this equilibrium by a higher rate of expected depreciation of 10 percent (instead of 3 percent), then capital will leave the home country.

Besides sudden and abrupt changes, the exchange rate can also vary in the mid-term or in the long-run, deviating from a trend that is set by the fundamentals of an economy, for instance by an increase in competitiveness. Then appreciation or depreciation expectations are defined for a longer time period. As in sudden changes, these expectations may be corrected at a certain moment of time.

The costs of a currency crisis

Currency crises are a major economic shock. Their costs may be significant since they have an impact on the real side of the economy.

The country's central bank loses international reserves because reserves have to be used to defend the exchange rate when a capital flow reversal is imminent. Prior to the crisis, the central bank spends foreign reserves to buy up domestic currency in order to stabilize exchange rate expectations in the foreign exchange market. If the outbreak of a crisis can be prevented by central bank interventions, holding foreign reserves have been an insurance; the cost of holdings these reserves represents an insurance premium.

If the crisis is not prevented, international debt of the country, denominated in foreign currency, will become harder to service, because the country has to export more in order to earn foreign currency. If the country's international debt and bank loans are denominated in domestic currency, foreign debt-holders and creditors take the loss, since the real value of their bonds and credits is reduced. They will also lose, of course, if the country defaults on its debt in foreign currency. In the future, they may be less inclined to provide credit. In consequence, the country's access to credit markets is impaired.

On the domestic level, a major effect of a currency crisis is the increase in uncertainty and the loss of confidence in expectations, having an impact on domestic consumption, savings, investment, and production. The devaluation leads to an increase in the price level. The wealth accumulated by households melts down, and as a consequence consumption declines. Firms are thus less inclined to produce and their incentive to invest is lowered. Moreover, the combination of declining sales, raising interest rates, and inflation wipes out the firm's capital and disarrays their balance sheet. Firms are forced to use profits (when they rise again) to clean up their balance sheets rather than to invest into new projects.

The balance sheets of banks are also affected by a meltdown of the asset side and the withdrawal of deposits from households and firms. This implies a credit crunch for firms. In addition, the central bank has to raise the interest rate until uncertainty recedes in order to dampen the price level effect of the depreciation.

Some economies have lost up to 20 percent of their GDP and even more in currency crises during the twentieth century (Gordon 2005). Argentina lost 20 percent in three years in its 2001–2002 crisis (IMF 2003). According to Griffith-Jones *et al.* (2004) the accumulated output loss of the emerging market countries Argentina, Brazil, Indonesia, Korea, Malaysia, Mexico, Thailand, and Turkey which was due to the currency crises in the second half of the 1990s and early this century amounted up to a total of US$1,250 billion (in 2002 constant dollars).

Problems in estimating the losses arise with respect to the question which baseline of a growth path is chosen from which the loss is measured. This is a counterfactual question. Usually it is assumed that a given growth path can be projected into the future. This procedure is not justified as a currency crisis has its roots in some distortion of the economy, including an overheating, that is not sustainable. Moreover, a currency crisis often is intertwined with a banking crisis. It is nearly impossible to isolate the GDP loss associated with these two types of crises.

8.2 Mechanisms and origins of a currency crisis

In Chapter 7, we have discussed some mechanisms that lead to a financial bubble or reinforce it. When currencies are included in the analysis, additional mechanisms have to be considered.

The sustainability of the balance-of-payments position

A bubble will burst when it becomes apparent that a situation is not sustainable. An important restraint is the balance of payments, more specifically the current account. A bubble in a country will normally be associated with an inflow of short-term capital. This means that a current account deficit is financed by capital imports. The nominal exchange rate is supported by capital imports. Apparently, it is difficult to separate the formation of a bubble from a healthy situation in which capital inflows finance the accumulation of a capital stock. Then, a current account deficit is sustainable because capital accumulation will augment the production potential; this allows the repayment of debt and serving the interests in the future.

As soon as expectations change and investors fear the making of a bubble, financial markets will no longer be willing to finance the current account deficit of a country. Capital inflows will dry up and portfolio capital will leave.

Running out of foreign currency reserves

As long as foreign currency reserves are sufficiently large to credibly defend a currency, market participants will not attack the currency. As soon as reserves are exhausted, the value of a currency will fall very quickly. Moreover, when markets become aware of an increased risk that reserves will be depleted, they start to react. Shrinking reserves indicates that it becomes more difficult to finance a current account deficit. Consequently, the exchange rate has to give in and the currency depreciates.

Contagion

A change in expectations can be contagious in several different ways. International investors face restraint of their investment portfolios, as market risks increase in one of the countries of investment, thus affecting the risk exposure for their total investment. If assets in one of those countries become more risky, the overall risks of the portfolio of an international investor changes and a readjustment of the overall portfolio may be required, taking place in another country than the problem country. In addition, strategic thresholds in the investment program of investors may trigger portfolio adjustment in other countries and thus affect investment behavior abroad. There is also a psychological link. A problem showing up in one country leads to the question whether similar problems may develop elsewhere. This reasoning raises uncertainty, and makes investors and creditors more cautious to provide capital through portfolio investment. Once a general mood has spread and once the herd is running, other countries are affected and volumes of investment decrease on an international level. Finally, national breakdowns of currencies may affect other economies via changes in trade flows. The depreciation of a currency makes exports of other countries, for instance of a neighbor, relatively more expensive and thus less competitive.

Types of currency crises

Changes in the conditions that influence the optimal portfolio stand at the origin of currency crises. These changes affect portfolio flows which in turn impinge on the exchange rate. Different origins play a role, giving rise to different types of currency crises.[1]

A first type of a currency crisis is due to an over-expansion of the money supply of the central bank and an increase in credits provided by the banking system as in the traditional Latin American currency crisis. Time and again, the extension of the money supply was accompanied by a rising public debt which was monetized by the central bank. Eventually, these financial excesses in combination with populist policies of overspending showed up in high inflation rates including hyper-inflations.

A second type of currency crisis arises from an overheated economy. Credit expansion due to an insufficient regulation of the banking sector, for instance liberalization of capital account without adequate prudent regulation of the banking industry, can lead to a bubble in the real of the real side of the economy. Compare the real estate sector in Thailand which eventually had to burst when the over-investment became apparent and the distortion in the real economy had to be corrected.

A third type of a currency crisis is caused by the contagion effect from another country. A currency crises in one country can infect other economies through several mechanisms (see above). A precondition for contagion is the fragility of the infected economy. Another precondition is that some links exist, for instance in trade to the problem country or in the investment programs of international investors.

A fourth type can be due to a current account deterioration, for instance in the case of a loss of competitiveness of the export sector or a negative supply shock that increases the import bill of a country. The country is unable to perform the real depreciation necessary to regain competitiveness; for instance prices of non-tradables or of inputs for the export sector cannot be reduced due to political opposition.

A fifth type (related to the fourth type) arises in a severe case of policy inconsistency when major policies contradict each other, for instance inflation is used to hide the unemployment problem and nominal depreciation is not strong enough to cover the differential. Sweden before 1992 is a case in point. Other reasons may be relevant as well, for instance a level of social absorption and the implicit debt defined by it are unsustainable. Financial markets do not believe the politicians' declarations that they will tighten domestic absorption or solve structural issues.

A sixth type of crisis arises in an unsustainable situation with respect to public debt. A country is indebted to such an extent that it becomes unable to service its debt and repay it, for instance when prices for its export products in the world economy fall. This is especially severe if debt is foreign debt denominated in foreign currency.

A seventh type of currency crises arises when asymmetric real shocks occur that enforce a real depreciation while the exchange rate is fixed. Thus, German unification required an appreciation of the deutsche mark in the European Exchange Rate Mechanism. This was not acceptable for the other members so that eventually the financial markets enforced a nominal depreciation of the Italian lira and the British pound (see Chapter 6).

An eight type of currency arises from a bank run which then translates into a currency crisis (see Chapter 7).

In the real world, all these phenomena may play a role, in the worst case simultaneously.

Institutional conditions

Institutional arrangements may also play an important role in the making of a currency crisis. Deregulation of financial markets makes it easier for a bubble to arise. If a country's capital account is liberalized and if its domestic banking system lacks the appropriate regulation, banks may enjoy a too-easy access to foreign liquidity that then can be fed into overheated sectors of the economy, for instance, into the real estate sector. This was the trigger of the financial crisis in Thailand in 1997. A similar phenomenon of inadequate regulation of the banking sector could be observed in the Swedish crisis of 1992 (Lindbeck *et al.* 1994). The lesson of these two crises is that there is an optimal mix of institutional reforms. A specific measure like liberalizing the capital account may not be first-best if it is not accompanied by appropriate other institutional changes such as reforms of the domestic banking sector (complementarity of institutional reforms).

In a federal economy with a central government and federal states with some autonomy, another relevant factor is whether rules exist which regulate the ability of states to incur debt. In most countries, states are only allowed to go into debt if the credits are used for investment. Moreover, there may limitations on foreign debt. How relevant this is can be seen in the collapse of Argentina's currency board where the provinces were allowed to borrow internationally and increased their international debt. The phenomenon also played a role in the 1999 Brazilian crisis which was ignited when the governor of Minhas Gerais declared that his province would not service its debts. Note that the European Monetary Union restraints the debt of its members in the Stability Pact. EMU faces a Minhas Gerais problem.

8.3 Indicators for an impending crisis

When a situation is not sustainable, a crisis may break out. A major warning sign is that internal and external equilibrium are no longer given.

The divergence between the nominal and the real exchange rate

A potential clue that a currency crisis is in the making can be seen in the strong divergence of the nominal and the real exchange rate.

- A negative current account balance is a warning signal if capital imports are used for consumption purposes or for non-investive government spending (such as social policies).
- A negative current account is a warning signal if it is associated with a large budget deficit of the government.
- A negative current account is a warning signal if it is associated with an excessive increase in the domestic money supply and an excessive domestic credit expansion.

- A negative current account is a warning signal if it is associated with a diverging development of the nominal and the real exchange rate where the currency experiences a real appreciation but depreciates not enough in nominal terms to offset the inflation differential.

The real exchange rate

If the real exchange rate develops under a considerable divergence to the nominal exchange rate, while at the same time the imbalance in the current account increases, the deviation of the two exchange rates can be an indication that a fundamental disequilibrium is developing, even if the foreign currency market temporarily clears.

The idea behind the real exchange rate is to ask the question: how does the exchange rate move in real terms? Thus, the effects on trade flows of a nominal devaluation of a currency may be neutralized if the price level in the devaluing country rises correspondingly. Therefore, a country that devalues its currency in nominal terms has to make sure that increases in its price level (relative to inflation abroad) do not contradict the effect of nominal devaluation. This fact implies that monetary policy has to restrain potential price increases. It also implies that a nominal depreciation does not have to be completely neutralized by wage increases. The following discussion focuses on the concept of real appreciation. Therefore we need to clearly understand what a real appreciation means before we move on in our discussion of currency crises.

A real appreciation ($\hat{e}_R < 0$) of a currency (with $e_R = (peso/\$)xP^\$/P^{peso}$), i.e. the currency of an emerging economy like the peso) can mean two different things and describe either a negative or a positive event. The interpretation of a real appreciation also depends on the question whether we look at the trade or the capital account.

Let us first look at the exchange of goods. A real appreciation can occur if the price level in the domestic country increases by more than that in the foreign country – because of rising labor costs or because of a failure of stabilization policy – and if the nominal exchange rate does not change accordingly. In this situation, the currency is overvalued in real terms (an event which has happened quite often in developing countries). If this is the case, price competitiveness is lost, the current account situation will worsen, i.e. a deficit increases (in Figure 6.3 we move to the left on the e_R–axis). This type of real appreciation has to be regarded as a negative event and indicates a need for structural adjustments. A real appreciation can also signal that an economy has improved its competitive position in the exchange of goods. Owing to a more competitive supply in the home country, for instance technological progress, or a higher demand in the foreign country, the price level at home increases by less than the price level abroad when the nominal exchange rate is unchanged. Then, the terms of trade improve; the real appreciation roots in the greater competitiveness of a country's products. In that case, the curve in Figure 6.3 shifts to the left allowing a balance in the current account with a currency that has appreciated in real terms. The real appreciation then may be correlated with the reduction of an export deficit.[2] This type of real appreciation is positive for a country.[3] Apparently, we have to distinguish carefully between the two different processes which are described above when we talk about a real appreciation.

A real appreciation also means two different things, depending on the question whether we look at capital flows or the capital account. The inflow of capital can be used to finance private consumption or government expenditure for consumption or social programs. The resulting nominal appreciation that is due to the capital inflow leads to a (temporary or artificial) real appreciation (which means an overvaluation of the currency). A current account deficit that is accompanied by an overvaluation may not be sustainable. This process is a negative phenomenon. In perfect financial markets with rational expectations this phenomenon could not occur, as rational actors would not overvalue the currency. The picture changes when capital inflows are used for investment purposes. Then, the real appreciation can indicate a strengthened competitiveness (attractiveness of a location) for real capital. With the additional investment, the competitiveness for goods can be improved in the future. The curve in Figure 6.3 will shift to the left (in the future) as soon as the new capital becomes productive, allowing a balanced current account with a currency that has appreciated in real terms. This is positive phenomenon. Again, rational expectations and an intertemporal fix point play a substantial role since an overheating of an economy and an investment bubble can represent an unsustainable situation.

As for any real price, the real exchange rate has to be judged against the background of an equilibrium or a disequilibrium in the economy, both with respect to an internal macroeconomic equilibrium and with respect to a balance or an imbalance of the current account.

If the real exchange rate appreciates and if the nominal exchange rate appreciates much less, remains more or less stable and if at the same time a current account deficit develops, the risk arises that the nominal exchange rate will have to give in.

8.4 Some recent currency crises

A 'normal' currency crisis: the Czech devaluation

A divergence between the nominal and the real exchange rate developed in the case of the Czech crown (koruna). Czechoslovakia and (since 1993) the Czech Republic de facto pegged the crown to a basket of currencies (65 percent DM, 35 percent US$ since May 1993). Until 1996, the Czech National Bank was able to defend the nominal exchange rate. In real terms, the currency appreciated (Figure 8.1). This went along with an increasing current account deficit which was financed by capital inflows. The real appreciation hurt the competitiveness of the Czech economy. Eventually, a situation developed in which the nominal exchange rate could no longer be defended. The crown had to devalue between December 1996 and December 1997 by more than 10 percent. Looking at the

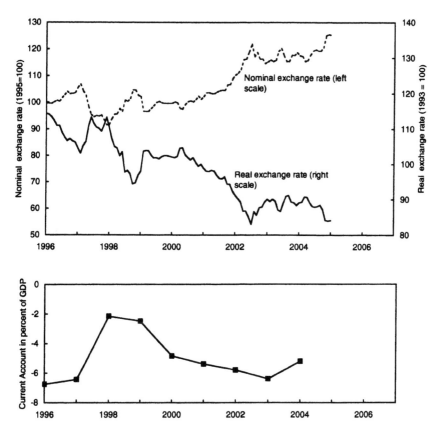

Figure 8.1 Czech Republic: nominal[a] and real[b] exchange rate and current account[c] (source: IMF, *International Financial Statistics*, Online Database, December 2005).

Notes
a 2000 = 100.
b 2000 = 100.
c In percent of GDP.

nominal and the real exchange rate since 1998, the divergence surprisingly increases again, and the current account deficit became larger until 2002. However, with the anticipated entry into the EU in 2004, the current account deficit was partly financed by longer term capital inflows. In 1996 the peg was effectively eliminated through a substantial widening of the fluctuation band. Today the Czech economy operates in the so-called managed floating regime, i.e. the exchange rate is floating, but the Czech central bank emphasizes its readiness for interventions 'should there be any extreme fluctuations.'

The typical Latin American calamity: the Mexican crisis

The Mexican peso more or less followed a crawling peg to the US dollar in the early 1990s. The rate of devaluation of the peso was lower than the inflation differential between the two countries, i.e. $\hat{e} < \hat{p} - \hat{p}^*$ where p is the Mexican and $\hat{p}^*$ the US price level. With prices and nominal wages rising at a higher speed than in the US, Mexico did not succeed in effectively using the exchange rate as a nominal anchor. The Pacto agreement between the government, the employers' associations and the trade unions to limit wage and price increases did not work out. The slow nominal depreciation and the higher inflation differential implied a real appreciation of the peso which began in the late 1980s (Figure 8.2). Monetary policy was expansionary (see Chapter 10). Together with a real appreciation of the peso, a current account deficit developed that was financed

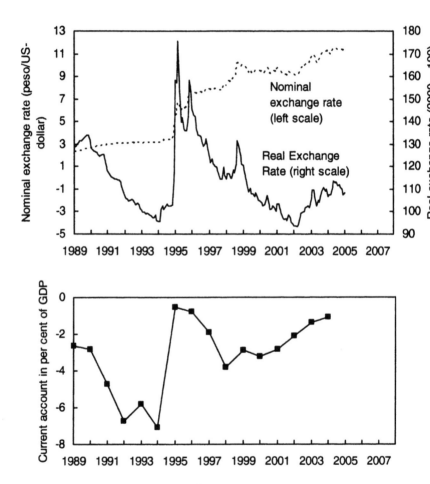

Figure 8.2 Mexico: nominal[a] and real[b] exchange rate and current account[c] (source: IMF, *International Financial Statistics* December, 2005).

Notes
a 2000 = 100.
b 1990 = 100.
c In percent of GDP.

by short-term capital inflow, attracted by high real interest rates and a booming stock market. Eventually, investors lost confidence, capital flows reversed, and Mexico lost US$122 billion in foreign currency reserves in 1994. The peso had to devalue and the current account deficit was almost eliminated afterwards.

Meanwhile, the nominal and real rates have diverged again. Since 1998, however, the balance-of-payments deficit reclined. The real appreciation did not lead to a balance-of-payments deficit. This may be owing to Mexico having joined NAFTA. Since 2001, the nominal and the real exchange rate move in line. Yet, whether the expansion of the money supply is under control remains unclear. On the one hand, government consumption remained stable at a rate of 11 to 12 percent of GDP from 1999 to 2004 and the current account deficit decreased from approximately -2.9 percent of GDP in 1999 to -1.8 percent in 2004. On the other hand, the Mexican consumer price index rose by 33 percent at the same time (1999–2004).

Brazil

In January 1999, Brazil had to widen its exchange rate band in the crawling peg and then to float the real which was devalued until March by about 40 percent. There was quite a divergence between the nominal and the real exchange rate (Figure 8.3). Brazil used a high real interest rate of 30 percent to defend the nominal exchange rate; this, however, proved not to be sustainable. The current account became more and more negative in the 1990s; at the same time, the budget deficit was 7 percent of GDP in 2003. The Brazilian crisis is thus more in line with the typical Latin American pattern of a currency crisis.

Brazil was able to weather the negative impact of the 2001 Argentinean crisis. About 11 percent of Brazil's exports went to Argentina (2000). Brazil's exports were severely affected when Argentina devalued the peso by more than 40 percent at the beginning of 2002. Moreover, Argentina in March 2001 unilaterally changed the common external import tariffs on capital goods agreed under Mercosur to zero while at the same time increasing duties on consumer goods in order to combat the ongoing recession. As a consequence, Brazil's exports to Argentina declined by 63 percent between 2000 and 2002. In 2002, only 4 percent of Brazil's exports went to Argentina. Furthermore, foreign direct investment in Brazil halved between 2001 to 2002 to US$10 billion.

The breakdown of the Argentinean currency board

Yet another experience is the financial crisis of Argentina in 2001/2002. With the currency board, the nominal exchange rate was fixed to the US dollar and remained constant. But at the same time, there was a considerable real appreciation of the peso vis-à-vis the currencies of Argentina's trading partners. The entry into the currency board was associated with an immense nominal and real revaluation. Compared to the situation in 1999 before the currency board, a size-

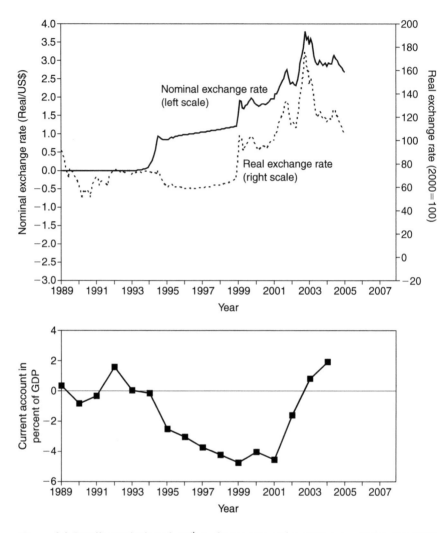

Figure 8.3 Brazil: nominal[a] and real[b] exchange rate and current account[c] (source: IMF, *International Financial Statistics* December 2005).

Notes
a 2000 = 100.
b 1990 = 100.
c In percent of GDP.

able real appreciation took place. In addition there was a real appreciation from 1991 to 1994. This made life more difficult for Argentinean exporters; imports became cheaper. From 1995, the current account situation worsened until 1998 while a real depreciation occurred. In spite of an improvement in (the still negative) current account, the real depreciation was not sufficient to prevent the crisis.

When expectations changed, especially after problems became apparent in the aftermath of the Asian currency crisis of 1997/1998 and elsewhere in the world and as a negative spillover of the Brazilian devaluation in 1999 on Argentine trade, the current account deficit was no longer sustainable.

The main structural deficits of the Argentine economy included an excessive public debt, a low share of exports in GDP with a high concentration on some export goods, a growing dependence on foreign investment, as well as the lack of labor market flexibility that limited the adjustment of real wages. Since the nominal exchange rate remained fixed due to the peg to dollar (which appreciated), competitiveness could not be restored through a real depreciation, i.e. a

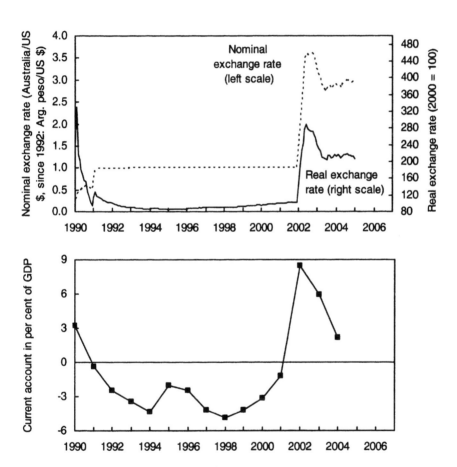

Figure 8.4 Argentina: nominal[a] and real[b] exchange rate and current account[c] (source: IMF, *International Financial Statistics* December 2005).

Notes
a 2000 = 100.
b 1990 = 100.
c In percent of GDP.

fall in the price of non-tradables. Consequently, Argentina could not export itself out of the crisis. This fact caused serious economic problems since the high external debt to GDP ratio of 59.2 percent in 2001 required high export earnings to be directed towards debt service (see Table 10.3)

Clear signs of the following breakdown were already visible in July 2001 when spreads between peso-dollar and US-dollar-denominated interest rates had reached 1,500–2,000 basis points and when large-scale withdrawals of deposits from Argentine banks took place (IMF 2003). In the last quarter of 2001, economic activity collapsed with industrial production falling by 18 percent (year-on-year), construction by 36 percent, and imports by more than 50 percent. At this time, the federal government ran an overall deficit of 4.5 percent of GDP (2001) and the provincial deficit widened to 2 percent of GDP. In addition, federal transfers to the provinces included one billion peso-dollars in form of federal guarantees or treasury bills, while the provincial governments issued about 1.6 billion peso-dollars in provincial bills to pay wages and suppliers, some of which could be used in lieu of tax payments to the federal government. When financial markets believed that this situation was unsustainable, the crisis broke out and a bank run began (see case study below). It was the largest sovereign default as of this stage. In June 2004 a preliminary offer to pay Argentine debt amounted to a 75 percent reduction of the net present value of Argentina's liabilities. This arrangement was replaced in 2005 by a final 65 percent cut of debt.

The Asian 'tigers' in financial crisis

In 1997, the Asian financial crisis broke out. Some of the Asian tigers, in the past greeted with the enthusiasm of international investors because of their high real growth rates, got into trouble in spite of sound macroeconomic fundamentals in the traditional interpretation: growth rates as well as savings and investment ratios were high, inflation was low, budget deficits did not give rise to concern, and export performance was more or less strong. Large current account deficits were excused because of the booming economies.

With hindsight, the countries were vulnerable to some extent for different reasons. In Thailand, for instance, where the crisis started, the relatively high capital inflows, i.e. the current account deficit, went hand in hand with a construction boom. Once the construction boom was no longer sustainable or was expected not to be sustainable, capital flows reversed. The liberalization of the domestic financial sector implied that prudential standards were not being implemented. This meant that a bubble could develop owing to credit expansion. Pegging the national currency to the US dollar contributed to an appreciation of the real exchange rate relative to the nominal exchange rate, which made it more difficult to reach a sustainable equilibrium even if the divergence was not too large. Finally, the Asian crisis showed that it is not sufficient to look just at budget deficits and public debt. A high indebtedness of the private sector, as in the case of South Korea, increased vulnerability.

South Korea

When the Asian crisis erupted, it was not expected that South Korea – number eleven in the world economy in terms of GDP prior to the financial crisis – could become part of the problem. The real exchange rate had only slightly moved away from the nominal exchange rate (Figure 8.5). The large current account deficit of 5 percent of GDP could be explained by the liberalization of current and capital account transactions in anticipation of South Korea's accession to the OECD. However, the deficit in the current account had increased in 1996, albeit not to high levels in comparison to Latin American countries. Moreover, the private sector had accumulated high debt, including foreign debt in

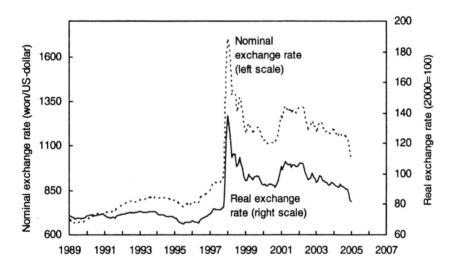

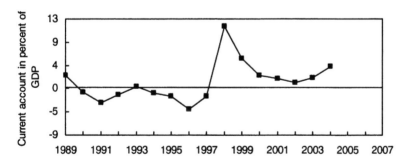

Figure 8.5 South Korea: nominal[a] and real[b] exchange rate and current account[c] (source: IMF, *International Financial Statistics* December 2005).

Notes
a 2000 = 100.
b 1990 = 100.
c In percent of GDP.

foreign currencies. This represented a liability for the country as a whole. The crisis erupted when it was reported that large conglomerates (*chaebols*) faced insolvency. From 1998 on, the nominal and the real rate move in the same direction and the current account is positive.

Thailand and Indonesia

The Asian crisis started when the peg of the Thai baht to the US dollar was abandoned on 2 July 1997. Within two weeks, the baht lost 15 percent of its external value. On 12 July, the intervention band for the Philippine peso was widened. On 14 July, Malaysia could no longer defend the exchange rate of the ringgit; the Indonesian rupiah lost about 10 percent of its value in the second half of July. By the end of October, these currencies had lost between 25 percent (Malaysia, Philippines) and 35 percent (Indonesia, Thailand) of their values. At the peak of the currency crisis, the currencies had devalued to one-fourth or one-

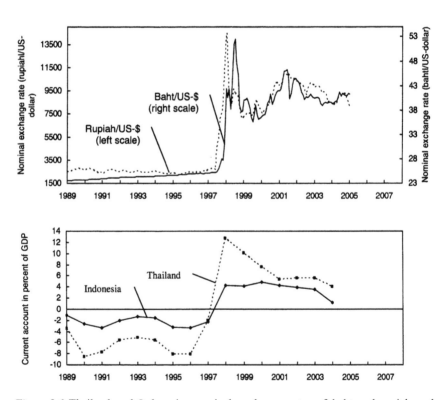

Figure 8.6 Thailand and Indonesia: nominal exchange rates of baht and rupiah and current account[a] (source: IMF, *International Financial Statistics* December 2005).

Notes
a In percent of GDP.

third of their pre-crisis values (Figure 8.6). The current accounts reacted and turned positive. In the year of the crisis, Thailand lost US$9.9 billion.

Some currency crises in Europe and Russia

Besides the 1997 Czech crisis, other currency crises occurred in Europe. In 1992, the European Exchange Rate Mechanism exploded (see Chapter 6). In the same year, Sweden experienced a financial crisis. Sweden had liberalized the capital account without having introduced sufficient prudent supervision of the banking sector (on the Swedish crisis see also Chapter 4). From 1984 to 1990 the debt-to-GDP ratio for private sector debt moved up from 85 to 127 percent. The credit boom coincided with an increase of share prices by a total of over 130 percent. Sizeable current-account deficits were associated with a growing stock of private sector short-term debt in foreign currency. Relatively high inflation rates in the late 1980s had weakened exports and required depreciations that were inconsistent with Sweden's membership in the European Exchange Rate Mechanism, resulting in relatively high nominal interest rates.

In 1990, share prices began to fall and the GDP growth rate became negative in 1991 and 1992. In the two years, unemployment nearly quadrupled and the public sector deficit rose to 12 percent of GDP. A wave of bankruptcies burdened the banking sector. In 1992, Swedish banks finally had to make provisions for loan losses totalling the equivalent of 12 percent of annual GDP. The crisis reached its peak at the time of the European currency unrest in the fall of 1992. On November 19, Sweden had to abandon its ECU peg, after it had suffered US$26 billion of reserve losses (more than 10 percent of Swedish GNP) in the preceding six days (Eichengreen 2001). Today, Sweden as a non-euro-country operates with a floating exchange rate and inflation targets.

In the Russian currency crisis of 1998, the rouble devalued by some 60 percent. On January 1, 1998, new roubles were introduced, one bill being equal to 1,000 old rubles. Old bills continued to circulate (with three zeros dropped) and were exchanged for new ones.

The financial crisis in Turkey

The Turkish currency crisis of 2001, after another currency crisis in 1993, exhibits some of the typical Latin American crisis patterns. We observe a real appreciation of the Turkish lira and at the same time an increasing current account deficit; we also have a widening gap between the nominal rate and the real exchange rate. While the real exchange appreciated, the nominal exchange rate depreciated throughout the late 1990s, but it never fully reflected the chronic inflation in Turkey that resulted in an inflation differential of 50 to 90 percent (annual inflation) relative to the US. Eventually, the discrepancy was too strong, and the Turkish lira had to devalue by more than 70 percent in the spring of 2001 (Figure 8.7). Meanwhile, both rates diverge again with a huge current account deficit of over 5 percent in GDP building up. According to our

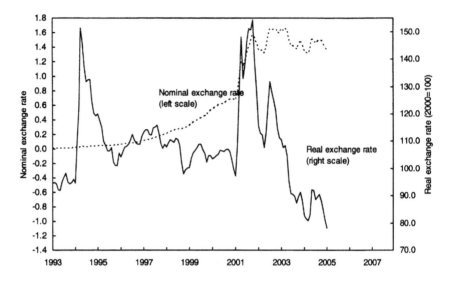

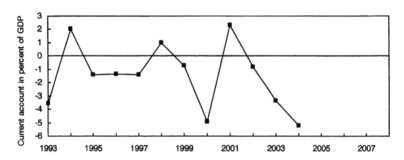

Figure 8.7 Turkey: nominal[a] and real[b] exchange rate and current account[c] (source: IMF, *International Financial Statistics* December 2005).

Notes
a 2000 = 100.
b 1990 = 100.
c In percent of GDP.

approach, this would mean that another currency crisis of Turkey is in the making.

8.5 Currency reform

The ultimate consequence of a monetary, financial or a currency crisis is a currency reform in which the value of the currency is rebased.

Before a currency crisis erupts, it pre-announces itself in that the official currency is repudiated. Substitutes for the currency appear. The free market only accepts easily tradable goods as a currency unit, for instance tobacco, cigarettes, and stockings (in the pre-currency reform situation prior to 1948 in Germany). The government may introduce a rationing system with ration cards. Under different conditions, international hard currencies may drive out the weak money (dollarization).

Case study: some measures in the Argentinean bank run

The Argentinean currency crisis is a telling story of how the government can intervene with the private life of individuals in order to stop a bank run. When the crisis unfolded, the bank run quickly culminated in a withdrawal of 3.6 billion peso-dollars (Argentinean pesos) in the last three days of November 2001. In December 2001 restrictions on travel and transfers abroad were set up. Banks were prohibited from granting loans in pesos. A weekly limit on withdrawals from individual bank accounts of 250 peso-dollars was introduced. After riots and protests, in which more than twenty demonstrators died, President de La Rua was forced to step down on December 20. The new president Sáa declared on December 23 the intention to default on government debt. Argentina owed more than US$100 billion to domestic and foreign bond-holders (Hornbeck 2004). The debt moratorium was confirmed by his successor, President Duhalde, who ended the convertibility regime. In January 2002, the US dollar-peso convertibility regime was replaced by a dual exchange rate of 1.4 peso-dollars per US dollar for the public sector and most trade related transactions whereas other transactions were supposed to take place at prevailing market rates. At the same time, the monthly limit of 1,000 pesos was raised to 1,500 pesos, coupled with a freezing of term-deposits. US dollar deposits were frozen until 2003. In order to reduce inflationary pressure, bills of privatized utilities such as water, gas, electricity and telephones were frozen indefinitely.

Rebasing a currency can be done in several ways. A soft reform is to simply drop zeros from the notes, eventually printing new notes and introducing new coins. Thus, France dropped two zeros when it introduced the 'franc nouveau' in 1960. Turkey slashed six zeros in January 2005. This approach only changes the digits of the price level. It has the psychological effect that people do not have to calculate with thousands and millions in their everyday life which tends to tell them that their currency does not have a high value. If the government does not succeed in suppressing inflationary expectations, the inflationary process will quickly pick up, and nothing is changed.

In other currency reforms, the currency is completely rebased, usually also by introducing a new name that hopefully has more credibility than the old one, bringing down inflationary expectation, changing the behavior of market participants, trade unions and the government. Thus, in the German hyperinflation of

1923, the new 'Rentenmark' took the place of the mark at the unbelievable conversion rate of one rentenbank for one billion previous marks. The rentenmark was based on mortgaging the productive farm land of Germany. In order to determine the value of the mortgage, a pre-war capital levy to finance military expenditures was used as a basis. In 1924, the rentenmark was exchanged into the reichsmark. In the (western) German currency reform of June 1948, the old currency (reichsmark) was exchanged against the new currency (deutschemark) at the fixed rate of 10:1, with an exception for the first 60 reichsmark of currency per capita. In 1993, Brazil introduced the cruzeiro which was replaced in 1994 by the real. After World War II currency reforms took place in various other countries reaching from the Albanian transformation of the lek into the new leck in 1965 over the South Korean transformation of the hwan into the won in 1962, or the replacement of the cordoba through the cordoba oro in Nicaragua in 1990/1991 to the monetary reforms in Zaire in 1967 which replaced the congo franc by the zaire (Mas 1995).

In all these currency reforms, accumulated savings, i.e. wealth, are melted down relative to real estate and shares. The value of savings, bonds, credits, and mortgages must be redefined, often at politically determined conversion rates. These rates may different. The government intervenes in many ways in the life of people and the citizen experiences what arbitrary decisions mean for him. This is the time of the interventionist, the bureaucrat, the politician, the lawyers, the courts who all can take many decisions that under normal conditions are not needed and are taken through market decisions. Following Kindleberger (1993) it is 'one of the great feats of social engineering.'

9 How to prevent a monetary–financial crisis

What you will understand after reading this chapter

Monetary–financial crises cause severe damage. Therefore, the goal of countries and international institutions must be to prevent such crises. A stable money requires a set of conditions including the independence of a central bank (section 9.1). The solidity of the banking system is an important condition for financial stability (section 9.2). When a financial crisis arises, it is the role of the IMF to prevent it from spreading into a systemic crisis of the global economy and to provide fresh capital to the country in trouble (section 9.3). The IMF cannot be the world's lender of last resort (section 9.4). Some propose to impede and control international capital flows in order to reduce exchange rate volatility, but this wipes out the gains from the international division of labor (section 9.5).

9.1 Providing a stable money

The experience of the burst Japanese bubble with a GDP loss of three times its 1990 GDP in the period 1992–2004, relative to its potential, and the currency crises in the 1990s and the first part of this decade (Sweden in 1992, Mexico in 1994, Thailand, South Korea, Indonesia, and other Asian countries in 1997, The Czech Republic in 1997, Brazil in 1999, Turkey in 2001, Argentina in 2001/2002) with GDP losses of 20 percent suggest that monetary and financial stability is an important goal. In addition there are former financial crises such as Great Depression in the 1930s with a loss of US gross national income of 33 percent, the hyperinflation in Germany in the 1920s and the Latin American hyper-inflations. The common element of all these disturbances is that they are the result of processes that have their own dynamics and that, once started such as a bank run or a currency run, are difficult to be contained.

The institutional arrangement of the international monetary system should prevent such monetary and financial disturbances, namely inflation, deflation, bank runs, financial bubbles (asset price inflation), and currency crises. In a crude definition of neutrality, money should be neutral; then we may speak of an efficient international monetary system. In addition to arrangements for exchange rate systems (discussed in Chapter 6), we therefore have to develop institutional set-ups that prevent such monetary–financial disturbances from arising and from spreading.

Inflation and hyper-inflation can be prevented by correct institutional arrangements for the central bank and the banking system and an adequate monetary policy. The independence of the central bank is of utmost importance. A basic rule is that public budget deficits must not be financed by printing money. This condition has been repeatedly violated in Latin American countries in the past. In industrial countries, the interrelations between politics and the central bank are more intricate. The position of the central bank must be strong enough to resist political pressure for an easy money policy. Governments with high debt will push for low interest rates to reduce their debt burden. A central bank giving in to this pressure jeopardizes price level stability. It loses credibility that is crucial preconditions for a stable money. Moreover, an excessive credit expansion endangers monetary stability.

Sound fundamentals

Another important prerequisite is that a country has sound fundamentals. Solid fundamentals are needed because without them inflationary expectations and expectations of a depreciation start to develop. In extreme cases, capital flow reversals will occur leading to a currency crises. Solidity relates to three different aspects.

First, the balance-of-payments situation has to be sustainable. Problems are likely to arise when absorption surpasses production. Economic policy should be oriented towards sustainability. Social security systems should not shift the burden of financing to future generations. If structural issues are not solved and if populism and short-termism dominate, the fundamentals are not in order.

Second, it is necessary that the government has a sustainable budget position. An exploding level of public debt, i.e. non-stationarity of debt, must be prevented. Constitutional constraints for policy-makers should ensure that long-run opportunity costs of budget deficits are not disregarded. In federal states, it is not sufficient to have restraints for the federal level only; there must be limits for the states as well. A country should be cautious not to move from a monetary policy dominated system to a fiscal policy dominated system (see Chapter 6) in which the only adjustment available is an increase in the price level since the country cannot generate sufficiently high primary surpluses in the current account. Thus, a country needs rules by which excessive public deficits are prevented.

Third, high private debt can make a country vulnerable if an external shock (Korea in 1997) or an internal shock occurs. Mechanisms must be developed that a too high private debt exposure is prevented.

To sum up, it is wise for a country to make sure that it is not vulnerable and that it is robust enough to withstand a blow from the outside and a less friendly international environment, including reduced credit access to the international capital markets.

Monetary strategies

With respect to monetary strategies, a rule-based monetary policy such as targeting the money supply (Deutsche Bundesbank) or inflation targeting (Bank of England) may be followed. Also a mixture of monetary targeting and inflation indicators may be used in a two-pillar strategy as in the case of the European Central Bank. Alternatively, monetary policy may be more or less discretionary, as under Fed chairman Alan Greenspan. A money supply target keeps the increase of the money supply in line with an economy's growth of the production potential. Inflation targeting aims at directly influencing the price level. Preventing asset price inflation is a new issue for monetary policy; this may be more difficult to achieve with targeting the consumer price level and easier to do with money supply targeting.

Price-level stability as an anchor

Usually, monetary policy is oriented towards a stable price level. In accordance with purchasing power parity, changes of the exchange rate are simply determined by the inflation difference to the foreign country. Thus, an appreciation of the domestic currency takes place when the price level of the domestic country rises less than that of the foreign country. In this way, a country is able to uncouple itself from the inflation of the foreign country.

Exchange rate policy

Countries can only use the exchange rate as a nominal anchor if their governments are strong enough to stick to a strict stabilization policy or, to put it differently, if they succeed in controlling their budget situation and if trade unions effectively subscribe to price-level stability. If these conditions are not satisfied (as, for instance, in the Pacto agreement in Mexico prior to the 1994 currency crisis), pegging the exchange rate will fail. Even a crawling peg cannot help if the inflation difference is larger than the rate of depreciation in the peg. The experience is that a country must have some room for maneuver with respect to real depreciation. Note that pegging exchange rates was one reason for the Asian crisis. A pegged exchange rate or a currency board will also come under pressure if there are no institutional constraints for provincial governments to engage in foreign-currency denominated debt (as in Argentina).

9.2 A solid banking system

The financial system of a country has to be constrained such that a crisis is unlikely to start or to be reinforced. This involves setting standards for commercial banks and other financial institutions including investment banks. The correct expression of risks in risk premia, accounting, and auditing are relevant issues. The financial sector needs to be robust so that an economy is not easily affected by shocks. This is the lesson that we can draw from the currency crises in the Asian countries.

Prudent supervision is an important aspect of preventing bank failures and financial crises. Regulation of the financial market includes a broad spectrum of policy instruments, ranging from capital adequacy requirements, margin requirements, and bank reserve requirements to restrictions on financial products, price controls, and governmental fees. Rules may intend to improve information for the investor and to assure the stability of the system over time. Regulation thus can generate benefits, but it also involves costs for banks and ultimately for the customer, for instance in increasing the costs for banks, often to raise government revenue.

Regulators compete with each other since financial institutions and investors can avoid a regulatory regime by doing their transactions in another country. In this case, regulation may drive out the financial industry or a financial product out of a country. Regulation should make use of the self-interest of market participants to monitor and control the performance of financial firms, for instance through credit ratings and specialized media. This approach of market supervision relies on the self-interest of market participants who want to prevent potential losses through improved information. This approach may help to control offshore markets that are less regulated; regulatory competition is complicated by the phenomenon that financial institutions move to offshore markets.

The 1988 Basel I Accord of the Basel Committee on Core Principles for Effective Banking Supervision has established a capital adequacy framework for individual financial institutions. Internationally active banks have to back their claims on the non-bank private sector by an 8 percent capital endowment (in terms of shareholders' equity or retained earnings). The Basel II Accord attempts a more risk-sensitive framework in which different types of risks of claims are distinguished. Not all claims receive the same weight. The overall limit of 8 percent continues to hold. External ratings and standardized internal control mechanisms can be used to assess credit risks.

Some standards should also be applied to hedge funds. One approach is to require them to register in a country; if they then go offshore, this signals to the customer that a higher risk is involved and that these funds are less likely to be bailed out. Credits given to hedge funds and derivatives should be adequately reflected in the risk evaluation of banks.

It has now been accepted that there is a sequencing problem in liberalizing the banking sector and the capital account (see section on capital flows below). If the capital account is liberalized and if, at the same time, the banking sector is not adequately regulated with respect to prudential standards, an over-expansion of credit may result. Sweden with its crisis in 1992 and Thailand in 1997 are two examples. Due to the complementarity in institutional reforms, the liberalization of the capital account should be accompanied or best be preceded by an appropriate regulation of the banking sector.

9.3 The role of the IMF

The purpose of the IMF, as specified in Article I of the IMF statutes, is 'to shorten the duration and lessen the degree of disequilibrium in the balances of payments' (section vi), to 'facilitate the expansion and balanced growth of international trade' (section ii) and to 'promote exchange stability' (section iii). In the post-Bretton-Woods system, the main objective of the institution is to help prevent currency crises from arising and from spreading; it also helps countries to get out of a crisis.

The institutional set-up of the IMF

Today the IMF comprises a membership of 184 countries. Members' rights and obligations are based on individual country quotas that reflect the country's relative size as compared to the world economy. The quota itself serves four distinct functions. It primarily determines a country's IMF subscription, it sets its voting rights, it limits a country's access to IMF financing and it is proportional to the allocation of Special Drawing Rights (SDR). Country quotas are denominated in SDRs. The United States currently has a quota of SDR37.1 billion, which roughly equals US$53.5 billion (IMF 2006). Quotas are usually reviewed every five years.

The IMF's decisions are made by the board of governors, which usually convenes once a year. Each member country appoints one governor, whose vote is weighted according to a quota based formula. Thus each country receives 250 basic votes plus one additional vote for each SDR100,000 of its quota. The United States – the IMF's most potent member – commands 371,743 votes, which equals 17.1 percent of all votes. Japan has voting rights of 6.1 percent, the countries of the European Union 31.5 (EMU-12: 22.9) and Asia (excluding Japan 9 percent). The allocation of voting rights no longer corresponds to the share of these countries and regions in total world exports.

The day to day running of the IMF operation is incumbent on the Executive Board based at the IMF's Washington headquarters and comprising twenty-four directors. The USA, Japan, Germany, Britain, and France each appoint one director; the remaining nineteen directors are elected within country groups. The weight of a director's vote reflects the sum of the quotas of the respective country group.

The IMF's financial operations are denominated primarily in Special Drawing Rights. SDRs were created as a third reserve asset in 1969 to balance the relative shortage of the two existing reserve assets at the time – gold and the US Dollar. The collapse of the Bretton Woods system in the early 1970s and the change to a floating exchange rate system lessened the need for another reserve asset.

The present day function of SDRs is limited primarily to the unit of accounting of the IMF. Countries can purchase and voluntarily exchange SDRs on the international financial market. Alternatively the IMF can mandate a country with a strong external position to exchange SDRs with a country that is in a weak external position. As part of their membership each country receives an allocation of SDRs proportional to its quota. In a limited sense SDR can thus be thought of as a form of international liquidity.

The IMF facilities

Countries with balance-of-payments problems can use the IMF-reserve tranche which does not constitute a credit. In addition to this support, the IMF has several credit facilities. The credits are usually deposited in the country's central bank and are freely available for use.

The initially created Standby Arrangements serve to alleviate temporary balance-of-payments disequilibria and allow members to draw up to 100 percent of their quota during a prescribed period (usually twelve to eighteen months, but up to three years) and up to 300 percent of the quota accumulative conditional on the borrower meeting specified performance requirements. The credit has to be repaid within three and one-quarter years to five years.

The Extended Fund Facility, created in 1974, is aimed at structural deficits, i.e. at balance-of-payments difficulties requiring a longer period of adjustment. It involves larger amounts of financing than under Stand-by Arrangements. Repayment is within four and a half to ten years.

The Supplemental Reserve Facility was established in 1997, aiming at a large short-run financing need and at exceptional balance-of-payments difficulties as they arose in the Mexican and Asian crises. It extends to a period of up to one year. This is in response to 'a sudden and disruptive loss of market confidence reflected in pressure on the capital account and the Members' reserves.' Repayment is expected within one to one and a half years; the interest rate starts 3 percentage points above the IMF lending rates; the rate increases over time. This facility was created in response to the new type of currency crisis, a currency run with a capital flow reversal.

The Contingent Credit Line was introduced in 1999 and ended in 2003. It was supposed to shield member countries with solid economic policy against contagion. However, this facility was not accepted by the countries; as a matter of fact, it was not used by a single country. The main problem with it was that a country signing up for this facility would signal to the markets that problems are around the corner.

In the Poverty Reduction and Growth Facility, established in 1999, the IMF provides low-interest to low-income countries and supplies grants under the Initiative for the Heavily Indebted Poor Countries. IMF lending under this facility is based upon Poverty Reduction Strategy Papers, which are prepared by the national governments in consultation with domestic stakeholders, the IMF and the World Bank. Economic policy advice is given under this facility; this can be understood as an informal form of conditionality.

Additionally, two facilities apply to special cases. The Emergency Assistance Facility aims to provide funds to countries that have suffered from natural disasters and catastrophes. Emergency Facility loans are subject to the IMF lending rate. Waivers for countries that qualify for the Poverty Reduction and Growth Facility exist. Repayment takes place within three and a half to five years. The Compensatory Financing Facility created in 1963 provides liquidity to countries that experience a sudden fall in export prices and a simultaneous increase in import prices due to fluctuations in world commodity prices. The terms of Standby Agreements apply.

The core function of the IMF

The IMF is a multilateral arrangement that has been established to deal with balance of payments problems and currency crisis. Poverty Reduction and Growth Facility, introduced in 1999 and a response to the NGOs critique of the IMF, has a different aim. It intends to help developing countries. It can be argued that this facility with advice and credits helps to make developing countries less vulnerable and it thus strengthens their balance-of-payments situation; and balance-of-payments is the domain of the IMF. However, giving credits to developing countries detracts from the core role of the IMF and this function overlaps with the World Bank and the regional development banks. It blurs delineating the responsibilities between the international organizations. To help developing countries may be a good product to sell to the international community, and the IMF itself may be enthusiastic about this new facility, hoping to boost its legitimacy in the eyes of the international audience. However, currency crises are here to stay. From the fact that the Asian currency crises are about ten years old, we can not conclude that the IMF's main role has become obsolete.

Short-term and long-term tasks

The IMF has a short-term and a long-term task. In the short-run, the IMF has to help a country to get out of a currency crisis, once it has broken out, and to prevent a currency crisis from spreading. In the long-run, the IMF has to prevent currency crises from arising.

To define the short-term role of restoring a balance-of-payments equilibrium and the long-term role of exchange rate stability was relatively easy during the time of the Bretton Woods system when the main objective of the IMF was to bridge foreign currency shortages in a world of relatively stable exchange rates and when trade in goods and services was the major driving force of balance-of-payments situations. Under these conditions, the IMF received its legitimacy from situations when financing was needed because of a temporary negative external shock that would eventually go away. In the days of Bretton Woods, this was the traditional balance-of-payments crisis that arose from a widening trade deficit, due, for instance, to temporarily unfavorable terms of trade. Of course, the issue was how to distinguish short-term from long-term, structural changes that caused balance-of-payments deficits.

Today, with flexible exchange rates and with portfolio capital being the main determinant of short-term exchange rate movements, the task of the IMF is to deal with currency crises triggered by a sudden capital flow reversal, reflecting some fundamental disequilibrium in the economy, i.e. a situation that is not sustainable. In today's world, the short-term and long-term roles of the IMF are more intertwined. In a world with high portfolio capital mobility, the capital flow view of the balance-of-payments and of the determination of currencies dominates the trade view. In this world, currency runs are the dominating problem. Unfortunately, currency runs, which are a short-run phenomenon when they take place, have long-run causes.

Note that the likelihood of currency runs varies with the type of capital mobility. FDI is less likely to participate in a currency run (if FDI is greenfield investment), and equity capital is more likely to stay than portfolio capital. Thus there is a pecking order of capital flows.

The two roles of the IMF are potentially conflicting. The short-run approach requires the IMF to bridge-finance a liquidity gap by providing liquidity. In this interpretation, the IMF is a fire brigade stopping a potential currency run from arising from a (short-run) liquidity problem. This is the IMF's role ex post. The more long-run approach is to prevent a currency run from developing and from spreading into systemic risk for the world economy; in this interpretation, the IMF undertakes a precautionary policy. This is its role ex ante.

A bankruptcy procedure

One view to understand the role of the IMF is to look at a situation when a currency crisis erupts. In this case the IMF has a similar role to a bankruptcy court judge (Sachs 1994, 1997; Minton-Beddoes 1995): working capital has to be arranged, a moratorium has to be declared and existing debt has to be restructured. Fresh working capital must have priority over obligations to previous creditors.

There are, however, no procedural rules for a bankruptcy procedure for sovereign debtors. Thus, the moratorium is declared unilaterally by the country in financial trouble. In contrast, a new system of international sovereign bankruptcy rules similar to Chapter 11 of the US bankruptcy code could be envisaged. In this case, the IMF would declare the moratorium; the IMF would also have a say in determining to what extent existing debt including bank credits would be rolled over into the future without interest payments or to what extent they would default. During such an instance, capital flight has to be prevented so that capital controls have to be put in place; such controls, however, are difficult to administer and deter fresh capital.

The moral hazard problem

By lending to national governments, the issue arises as to what extent the IMF sets the wrong incentives, so that governments and private lenders tend to rely on future IMF help and become negligent in their own efforts to prevent vulnerability. This problem of wrong incentives, also discussed under the heading of moral hazard, is a complex issue (Hayek 1973). Thus, wrong incentives and moral hazard do not necessarily mean an explicit calculus to take advantage of IMF support in the future in the form of opportunistic behavior. However, with crises often being homemade and being the result of a national institutional or a policy failure, potential IMF support may be in the minds of economic agents. More formally, with IMF support a side condition of decision-making changes, thus influencing behavior more or less implicitly.

Countries or creditors may feel protected against low-probability/high-damage risk in the tails of the probability distribution. The impact of institutional arrangements on incentives and the real economy is difficult to prove, especially econometrically, because the effects show up in a long-run process, very often without much short-run movement in the data. In addition, there is the counterfactual question what would have happened under different institutional arrangements ('Lucas critique'; see Lucas 1981). Nevertheless, there is no doubt that institutions matter and have an impact on economic behavior and processes.

The sums that the IMF has used in order to prevent financial crises have increased considerably since the 1960s and 1970s. During this time, credits amounted to roughly US$1 billion. In the early 1980s, the credit level reached US$3.5 billion. In the 1990s, IMF credits were in the US$15–20 billion range. In relation to the recipient country's GDP, IMF credits increased from below 2 percent to a range of 6–8 percent (Figure 9.1). Note that countries in crisis do

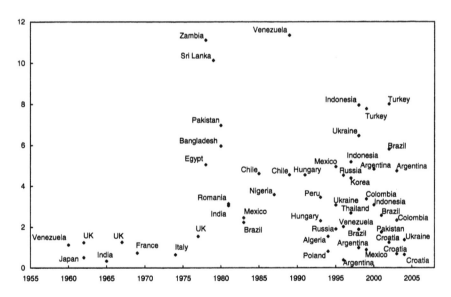

Figure 9.1 Approved IMF credits[a] in percent of recipient country's GDP (source: IMF homepage, www.imf.org, *Financial Data by Country*; for GDP data: World Bank, *World Development Indicators* March 2005; own calculations).

Note
a Year of approval or extension.

Table 9.1 Official creditors' long-term debt, outstanding and disbursed in countries in crisis (in billion US$)

		IMF	World Bank	Regional development banks[a]	Bilateral credits	Total
Mexico	1995	15.8	13.8	4.8	20.4	54.8
Indonesia	1997	3.0	10.7	5.0	26.7	45.4
South Korea	1997	11.1	4.6	2.3	1.9	29.9
Thailand	1997	2.4	1.8	1.8	11.8	17.8
Brazil	1998	4.8	6.3	10.1	14.6	35.8
Russia	1998	19.3	6.3	0.2	62.1	87.9
Turkey	2001	14.1	4.7	1.4	6.7	26.9
Argentina	2001	14.0	8.5	9.4	4.6	36.5

Source: World Bank, *Global Development Finance* 2005.

Note
a Includes loans from other multilateral and intergovernmental agencies, except the World Bank and IMF.

not only receive IMF credits, but that other institutions such as the World Bank and Regional Development Banks provide credits as well (Table 9.1). In 2003–2005, the volume of credits has declined considerably. But this can change quickly.

The size of operation of the IMF has come under scrutiny. The larger the size of operation, the more money the IMF takes in its hands, the weaker will be the willingness of private creditors (banks) to take over credit risk in the case of a crisis and the weaker is the incentive for governments to prevent the instances that lead to a stability problem.

The IMF must be aware of the two conflicting roles between the ex post function as a fire brigade and the ex ante role of setting incentives for solid monetary and financial stability. In its ex post role, the IMF also has an ex ante impact by forming expectations and influencing the behavior of sovereign debtors and private creditors. The line must be to improve the incentives for a stable banking and financial system and to make these systems robust (now not from the point of view of national policy but in order to prevent a systemic crisis affecting more than one country). Apparently, this requires voluntary commitments by the nation states. In any case, the IMF must be concerned with the announcement effect of its ex post behavior. A clear ex post rule will be helpful to reduce systemic risk ex ante.

A lender to troubled governments?

In a down-to-earth interpretation, the IMF lends to troubled governments. Unfortunately, in the real world a crisis may very well be homemade, i.e. it may be the result of a domestic institutional failure or of a national policy failure. As a matter of fact, all the financial crises of the 1990s and the first half of the new decade in the twenty-first century have domestic causes with homemade failures or weaknesses becoming apparent under changing international conditions. Even more unfortunate, the shock may prove to be permanent instead of transitory. Thus, the IMF is very close to national policy failure. It should be careful not to become a funding agency for countries suffering from self-inflicted problems, i.e. the troubled countries' global bank. Since the IMF itself is subject to political pressure, there is the risk of becoming an international correction agency for national government failure.

The IMF should not make up for national political mistakes and national institutional deficiencies. If it did, and sometimes it does, it would honor economic policy mistakes and it would thus be likely to induce additional ones in the future, generating a *perpetuum mobile* in which the causes for the next crisis are laid down. The IMF's role in Russia may be considered as a case in point; the IMF failed to implement conditionality for a long time, trying to iron out internal problems without being able to change the fundamental economic situation. Admittedly, the counter argument can be made that a country in transformation is a special case.

Preventing a crisis

The IMF should be more aware of what can be done to prevent a crisis from developing. A currency crisis arises when market participants lose confidence in a currency, i.e. in the money of a country relative to other monies, and when they move out of it. An economic situation and the exchange rate are judged to be unsustainable; and what is unsustainable is vulnerable. The root of this evaluation is that a fundamental disequilibrium or an imbalance exists that has to be corrected. Possible causes for this are that:

- the money supply has expanded excessively so that there is an oversupply of the national money and devaluation is unavoidable;
- financing a current account deficit for private or government consumption has driven up foreign debt, so that the intertemporal mechanics mandate some adjustment;
- financing long-term private investment by short-term foreign capital eventually runs into problems, especially if overcapacity and external shocks increase the risks of capital already invested.

In these and other cases, the currency crisis is rooted in a policy failure, especially in a deficiency of the institutional arrangements of the economy. This includes the misuse of monetary policy to finance public deficits, lacking independence of the central bank, unsustainable exchange rate binding, non-existent rules to prevent public deficits and the accumulation of public debt. Insufficient strength of the financial sector owing to ineffective regulation that does not prevent an excessive short-term financing of private long-term investment is another aspect.

Indefensible exchange rates

A pegged exchange rate that is in contradiction to economic fundamentals should not be defended at all costs. When the real exchange rate appreciates due to an inflation differential and if simultaneously the current account deficit increases, it does not make sense to defend an unsustainable exchange rate. Nominal depreciation early on must be seen as an instrument to prevent a currency crisis. Therefore, the IMF should change its policy and not implicitly defend a pegged exchange rate (Rubin 1999). It should be a specific rule that the IMF does not intervene and defend a pegged exchange rate when the money supply has increased excessively and when the nominal and the real exchange rate have been drifting apart markedly for some time (a year or more) while the current account deficit has been worsening. On the contrary, this should be a signal for an early warning.

An improved early warning system

It is advisable to use an explicit early warning system and to continue to improve it. More and more explicit information with clear wording should be provided to the markets so that market supervision will require higher risk premia from countries with a poor economic performance. The IMF should not be a silent supervisor who deliberates behind closed doors with the country in which a problem is developing. This involves the risk that not enough is done to prevent the crisis. Meanwhile, the country reports are published. It is better to blow the whistle before the train crashes. It is also better to allow a small crisis if, in this way, you can prevent a large one. Of course, signaling more actively to the markets that a problem is developing is a very delicate task, and the IMF should not play a part in spreading panic. At the same time, the IMF should not hold back information so that people are misdirected from protecting their interests.

The Asian crisis has shown that more information on the financial status of countries is needed, including more accurate data on foreign exchange reserves (are they swapped? Are they used as capital endowments for state banks?). In addition to macroeconomic data, more information on short-term private debt is required, especially on short-term debt of the private enterprise sector. Data must include the maturity structure of debt and its composition in terms of different currencies. Information should also cover the financial sector, for instance in the form of the consolidated balance sheet of the financial sector as a whole and of the major financial institutions (x percent of the market volume). Moreover, a measure of reserves' adequacy for the banking sector should be developed, indicating the necessary reserves in relation to total short-term debt. The problem with the attempt to define capital adequacy is, of course, that in a crisis assets melt away quickly. An important aspect of transparency is to what extent international banking rules, including prudent standards, have been adopted.

Data should be provided in a standardized form; they should get a stamp of approval from the IMF or other specialized international organizations like the Bank for International Settlements. This secures comparability of the data, and it enhances credibility of the data. If countries are reluctant to provide the necessary data, there should be definite costs of non-compliance, for instance by making non-compliance public or by requiring compliance as a precondition for IMF support in case of a crisis.

Ex post conditionality versus ex ante rules

So far, the IMF has relied on ex post conditionality to influence the stability policy of countries as of the moment support was given. This is an attempt to enforce restraints on a country's government and thus to change its economic policy. This approach raises the question of whether the basis of the IMF's legitimacy is to be a disciplinarian or taskmaster of national economic policy. To put it more bluntly: can a small team of country experts specify important aspects of national politics, as was done in the IMF's program for Korea (Feldstein 1998; Sachs 1997), when false conditionality was imposed? [1] In defining the role of the IMF, a line must be drawn somewhere preventing the IMF from becoming the chief controller of national economic policy.

Ex ante conditionality has been more or less neglected. An important result of the current discussion about the deficient incentive system induced by the role of the IMF and the moral hazard behavior generated by it is that more ex ante conditionality should be imposed by the IMF. In any case, taking over an ex post role has an ex ante impact, in that it forms expectations and influences creditor and debtor behavior.

Countries that diverge from financial stability pose a risk to the international financial system. One therefore can conclude that they should bear the burden of their behavior and should bear the costs of their unsound economic policies and of the externalities of instability they cause for other countries as well as for the international community. In analogy to the 'polluter-pays principle' of environmental economics, a 'troublemaker-pays principle' then would be a line of orientation. Such an approach attempts to internalize the social costs caused by countries behaving in a manner that generates instability and adds to the risk of a systemic crisis. The obligation to provide stability is assigned to the individual country. It should make sure that stability prevails at home and that the economic situation is sustainable. The alternative would be the 'victim-pays principle' which implies that the international community has to compensate the potential troublemaker for not causing trouble.

Admittedly, the "troublemaker-pays principle" is in conflict with the IMF's role to help out in the case of a crisis and prevent a systemic crisis from unfolding. However, the IMF should be more conscious of the incentive and moral hazard aspects of its support policy. It should define more credibly its line of operation in the case of a crisis. It should move away from the discretionary decisions of its case-by-case approach favored by US pragmatism and bind itself by rules (favored by the Europeans). Pre-announcing ex post rules and sanctions serving to deal with a crisis would reduce systemic risk ex ante. This would also protect the IMF against implicit or explicit political influence, including the criticism that IMF lending is dominated by US foreign policy interests.

Credible rules for sovereign debtors

The IMF takes over an ex post role, but this ex post role has an ex ante impact by forming expectations and influencing the behavior of sovereign debtors. The announcement effect of a clear ex post rule will be to reduce systemic risk ex ante, for instance by an improved early warning system. Countries should bear the costs of their unsound economic policies and of lingering problems early on. The IMF should apply a sliding scale of the costs of a credit, for instance in terms of interest rates rising over time or with the size of the credit. The costs should not jump upward in a discontinuous way (or to infinity) if a problem develops. An alternative would be a penalty rate for credits beyond a threshold (Meltzer 1998). By this, the country would have an incentive to avoid getting into a situation of illiquidity. Such a sliding scale should be pre-announced together with the modalities of the early warning system when IMF credits have not yet been provided. This would be an important signal to markets.

The IMF should specify the sanctions to be levied when standards are not respected. For instance, if standards relating to the banking system are ignored, countries should not have access to IMF loans (Calomiris 1998; Calomiris and Meltzer 1998). This can mean that an individual country would go without IMF support. The alternative is that non-qualifying countries would have to pay a higher interest rate on the IMF loans.

Letting private lenders take the risk

An important means of internalizing the social costs of instability is to involve the private sector in the case of a crisis. 'Bailing-in' the private sector requires an arrangement on how to handle private credits when private debtors and sovereign countries get into trouble. For equity capital, private creditors are bailed in automatically when stock prices fall. This holds irrespective of whether equity ownership is widely spread or concentrated on a few equity holders. For bonds and bank credits, sharing clauses, rules on collective representation and on majorities, required for the modifications of the terms of credit represent an institutional mechanism by which creditors could assume some of the risks (Eichengreen 1999a; IMF 1999). These rules would help to internalize the credit risks to the creditors, inducing them to be more cautious in giving credits. In contrast to the mostly used American-style bonds, British-style trustee deed bonds are more appropriate as they include such provisions. These provisions would also be instrumental in reducing aggressive litigation by dissident creditors. The clauses should not require a discretionary decision of the IMF to become active. Additionally, private creditors should develop their own international insurance schemes.

Note, however, that this type of bonds and these arrangements mean that foreign capital would become more costly for the debtor countries because it would increase the risk for creditors, so that they would be more cautious in buying bonds and giving credits. The IMF should credibly pre-announce rules on the involvement of private lenders that the IMF wants to be respected if it is supposed to intervene. It can specify such rules as a precondition for lending support in the case of a crisis. Thus, the IMF could trigger standards written into international agreements that have to be respected by sovereign states and private lenders when a liquidity crisis develops.

Reform proposals for the institutional set-up

Reform proposals refer to three different interrelated aspects: how should the IMF adjust to the change in the world economy? What should be the goals of the IMF? And how should the management adjust (Calomiris 2000; IFIAC 2000, Meltzer Report; IMF 2006)?

The Bretton Woods formula determining the allocation of capital shares and voting rights should follow the changed conditions in the world economy. The countries' shares in world trade should be a decisive criteria. Asia now has a larger share in world trade than its voting rights. It is not advisable to use the size of population. GDP as an indicator for a country's relevance is not as good as the share in world trade. GDP in purchasing power parity is a distorted indicator, since it represents an overvaluation of the sector of non-tradables, which are not relevant for trade and currency crises.

With respects to the goals, currency crises are the focus of the IMF. This means that solving these crises and preventing them through surveillance and ex ante rules remains the main task. Development aid should be left to the World Bank and the regional development banks or agencies. Surveillance should be strengthened, providing explicit information to the financial markets. This would require a stronger authority of the IMF. The IMF's biannual meetings with central bankers and finance ministers represent an occasion to exchange views, representing a sort of barometric coordination. However, the IMF is not in a position to be the disciplinarian on national governments' macroeconomic policy.

Management of the IMF is another issue. A new allocation of quotas will mean a different institutional arrangement for its twenty-four country representatives and its Executive Board. The King proposal from spring 2006 of strengthening the managing director's position competes with the idea to have decisions taken by a smaller committee with the managing director as chairman of the board and five deputies from Europe, North America, Latin America, Africa, and Asia (Eichengreen 2006). However, as the experience of the softened Stability Pact of the European Monetary Union shows, national governments are reluctant to cede sovereignty in this area.

9.4 A lender of last resort for the world economy

The IMF cannot credibly play the role of a lender of last resort. This holds for a potential role as a lender of last liquidity and as a lender of last financial means (picking up the costs of a crisis). There are three major differences between the IMF and the national lender of last resort. First, the national lender of last resort provides liquidity and/or financial resources to financial institutions, while the IMF lends to national governments when they run into trouble or threaten to default. Second, in the international context an insurance mechanism between banks, such as national insurance schemes in the case of bank failures, does not exist. Third, the national lender of last resort (of last liquidity) can print money and can thus credibly stop a crisis by providing liquidity. For the IMF, this is not possible. The IMF also cannot take recourse to tax money in order to alleviate a financial crisis. On the contrary, the IMF has only a limited amount of resources. The usable IMF resources of about US$173 billion (March 2006)[2] would be a trickle if an extended crisis developed, for instance, if Japan or the euro area needed financial assistance or if a group of countries that are more important than the past problem countries became involved in a financial crisis. In addition, weak currencies are not usable for lending. Therefore, the IMF could even accentuate a currency problem if it ran out of funds. This would be a destabilizing function because of 'bets' of financial markets on IMF budget constraints.

If a systemic crisis for the world economy develops, the central banks will have to play the role of a lender of last resort (last liquidity). It must be a concerted action of the Fed, the ECB, and the Bank of Japan. The institutional arrangement for such a scenario, however, cannot be put into writing. It has to be left open, whether and under what conditions central banks will step in and provide liquidity as they did on September 11, 2001. If the conditions were specified ex ante and if they became known, an uncontrollable moral hazard problem would develop where market participants and governments would play strategically against the central banks.

It seems that the IMF is only involved in the pre-battleground of the lender of last resort, somewhat easing the task of the true lender of last resort, the central banks. Borrowing an expression from chess, in the lender-of-last-resort game the IMF is the pawn, the central banker is the king.

9.5 Throwing sand into the wheels of capital flows

Instead of participating in the international division of labor, a country may opt to restrain trade and capital flows. This then reduces demand for and supply of currencies, and at the limit the volatility of the exchange rate disappears completely. The country then renounces on gains from trade and from capital flows in order to avoid the volatility of exchange rates. This is a high price to pay. Nevertheless, trade and capital flows have been restrained in economic history. We analyze the trade aspect of such restraints in Chapter 14.

The sequencing of liberalization

In liberalizing capital flows, a country has to consider three different policy instruments: first, it can liberalize the exchange rate, moving from a pegged currency to a free float. Second, it can liberalize the capital account, i.e. do away with all sorts of capital controls. Third, it can use the instrument of prudent regulation of the banking sector and the financial market.

The experience we now have from currency and financial crises suggests that these steps cannot be taken arbitrarily but must be put in a meaningful sequence. One could speak of two laws: first, liberalizing the capital account should not precede moving to a flexible exchange rate. If this rule is not respected, capital flows put pressure on the pegged exchange rate which then cannot be sustained, if conditions for a stable money are not satisfied. Second, liberalizing the capital account should not be done when a satisfactory prudent regulation of the banking sector is not yet in place. If this rule is not respected, capital inflows can initiate an excessive credit expansion which then leads to a bubble.

However, it is one thing to liberalize the capital account, it is another thing to undo a liberalization that has already been introduced. In the latter case, reputation is lost. Liberalization should be undertaken only when a country is strong enough to maintain it. Once liberalization has been introduced, care must be taken that it is not reversed.

The pecking order of capital flows

In discussing the relevance of capital flows for exchange rate volatility, it is important to distinguish different types of capital flows, namely foreign direct investment, equity capital, bonds and bank loans. Foreign direct investment tends to be a more long-run oriented form of capital flows. Equity capital is generally also intended for the longer run, but shares can be sold instantly. Bonds may have a longer duration, they also can be sold instantly. Bank loans may be for the medium- or the short-run. There is a pecking order of capital flows in the sense that some forms of capital flows have advantages relative to others. Thus, foreign direct investment is an appropriate form for developing countries, the main reason being that this type of capital flows usually brings a long-run involvement of investors to a country. The other forms of capital flows are less adequate for developing countries.

Since exchange rate volatility and financial crises are linked to the mobility of portfolio capital, it has been proposed that the free movement of portfolio capital be limited in order to prevent financial crises. This discussion runs counter to the view which has been prevailing until the Asian crisis broke out, namely that the gains from the international division of labor are seriously reduced if countries restrict the convertibility of their currencies. This impedes both the exchange of goods and the efficient allocation of capital. Therefore, the condition of the convertibility of currencies seemed to be generally accepted. Especially due to the experience of disintegration of the world economy in the

1930s, there has been much effort to establish convertibility and to liberalize capital flows in the period after World War II.

Forms of capital controls

Capital controls can have different objectives, for instance preventing foreign ownership of domestic firms and assets, reducing capital outflows, making monetary policy easier or simply generating tax revenue. Controls can come in a whole array of different forms (Neely 1999). We can distinguish national instruments such as a dual exchange rate or multilateral approaches such as the Tobin tax. Instruments may be used to influence the type of inflow, for instance favoring FDI relative to portfolio capital, controls may discourage the outflow in the case of a currency crisis or regulate repatriation of FDI. There may be price controls on transactions (taxes) including mandatory reserve requirements as applied by Chile or a surcharge on the purchase of assets as used by the US (Interest Equalization Tax 1963–1974). Moreover, quantity restrictions may be applied, putting ceilings on transactions. Administrative measures may be practiced banning certain transactions, as in the case of Thailand, or requiring transactions to be done at registered institutions that have to follow given rules (as in China).

Foreign exchange controls

There is a broad spectrum of foreign exchange controls, for instance requiring a license to obtain foreign currency, restraining convertibility, or using other administrative controls. This includes making capital exports illegal.

Multiple exchange rates

Another instrument is the privileged access to favorable exchange rates, for instance by splitting the exchange rates between different transactions, e.g. between goods considered to be important and less important or between trade of goods and capital movements as practiced in the system of import licenses and the exchange rate protectionism that was pursued in Latin America until the mid-1980s. Such an approach de facto implies multiple exchange rates. This approach, however, presupposes that capital flows can be clearly delineated from the exchange of goods and services. Experience shows that administrative capital controls can be circumvented in many ways, for instance by over-invoicing or under-invoicing of exports and imports

Non-residents' and residents' convertibility

Constraining the convertibility is another way of reducing the international mobility of portfolio capital. This relates to restricting a currency's convertibility for foreigners (non-residents' convertibility) and for residents (residents' convertibility). In order to attract capital, countries usually first introduce the convertibility of their currency for foreigners. This implies that foreign investors have the right to repatriate their profits and also their investment. Without this right, they will not provide capital. Convertibility for residents is often introduced at a later stage in the process of liberalization.

Limiting capital flight

Countries are very interested in attracting capital, but at the same time they want to reduce capital outflows, more specifically to prevent capital flight. It is difficult to define policy instruments that apply to one aspect of capital flows only. Policy instruments that may limit the outflow of capital such as capital export restraints simultaneously reduce the incentive to invest in a country. Capital outflow restraints always have an impact on the expectations of potential foreign investors. Even controls that limit the outflow of portfolio capital affect expectations on the freedom to take foreign direct investment out of the country. Limiting exit always reduces the incentives for entry.

Reserve requirements for portfolio capital

In order to make incoming capital less volatile, a non-remunerated reserve requirement has been proposed as a deposit for incoming capital so that no interest is paid during a certain time period, for instance a year. Chile has used this approach in the 1990s, requiring initially a non-interest-bearing 30 percent deposit for the first year for portfolio capital. This approach was given up in 1998 when Chile faced severe problems in attracting foreign capital. Such a deposit limits the inflow of capital (including short-run capital) but it does not prevent capital from leaving quickly at a given moment once it has been invested in a country. Malaysia imposed controls during the Asian crisis on September 1 1998, banning transfers between domestic and foreign accounts and between foreign accounts, temporarily preventing the repatriation of investment and fixing the exchange rate. The evaluation of Malaysia's approach is mixed. Such controls postpone and avoid structural change with adjustment costs in the future (Neely 1999).

An international Tobin tax

In contrast to national policy instruments, the Tobin tax on the movement of capital represents a multilateral approach to reduce the mobility of capital and the volatility of the exchange rate (Tobin 1978). The intention is to raise the costs of short-term capital movements. This is supposed to reduce the amount of short-run capital flows. The argument is that if less capital is moved, the exchange rate will be less volatile.

Consider a tax z per unit of a currency transaction and neglect changes in the exchange rate. Then, without a tax, interest parity is $i = i^*$. With a tax on capital flowing in and flowing out, i.e. a tax levied in the sending as well as in the receiving country, and neglecting the tax on interest earned, interest parity for an amount x is:

$$x(1 + it) = x\,(1 + it^*) - 2zx, \text{ i.e.}$$

$$it = it^* - 2z$$

where t is the time period of portfolio investment like a day or a week as a fraction of the year, i.e. 30/365 for a monthly investment. This can be written as:

$$i = i^* - 2z/t \qquad\qquad\qquad (9.1)$$

where the second term on the righthand side indicates that portfolio investment becomes less attractive the shorter the time period. Assume the interest rate in the home country is 5 percent. Then with a Tobin tax of 1 percent, the foreign country would require an interest rate of 7 percent for portfolio capital to remain there for a year $(5 = 7 - 2 \cdot 1)$ For half a year, the interest rate would have to be 9 percent $(5 = 9 - 2 \cdot 2)$ for a month (1/12) 24 percent and for a day 735 percent $(5 = 735 - 2 \cdot 365)$

There are quite a few serious arguments against a Tobin tax. First, exports and imports are financed by short-term credits; a Tobin tax would thus make trade more expensive and would prevent countries from reaping the benefits from trade. It would thus hurt developing countries. Second, foreign direct investment and equity flows are linked to portfolio capital. A Tobin tax would prevent countries from enjoying the benefits of attracting capital (often including technology) as a factor of production. Third, not all capital flows are speculative, quite a large part even of portfolio flows are related to hedging and using arbitrage gains. Arbitrage increases efficiency. Again, the international division of labor would be restrained with negative impacts. Fourth, in the real world, it would be impossible to put the Tobin tax solely on the 'bad' or unwanted portfolio flows and to exempt the good flows, for instance to finance trade or foreign direct investment. Fifth, while a Tobin tax may reduce the inflow of capital somewhat, it does not prevent a massive outflow of capital accumulated in a country when a crisis breaks out. Such a sudden outflow, however, is at the root of a currency crisis. Thus, the Tobin tax will not prevent currency crises. Sixth, the Tobin tax requires an international agreement with a uniform tax rate for all countries. It is unrealistic that such an agreement can be reached. It is also open whether the tax is applied to outflowing or inflowing capital and which country receives the tax revenue. If the Tobin tax is applied unilaterally by one country, the tax will negatively affect the necessary real inflow of capital as the case of Chile in 1999 shows. Finally, the Tobin tax would necessitate an immense amount of controls. In the real world, it is extremely difficult to delineate trade flows from portfolio flows. Market participants will find many ways around these regulations. A more promising approach is to assign the correct risk premia. This includes an effective banking regulation and an efficient supervision of the financial sector.

The cons against capital controls

The costs of capital controls consist of limiting or even preventing the benefits of capital flows (Chapter 4). The benefits are many: a quicker accumulation of a capital stock and higher growth for the capital importer, a higher capital income of the capital exporter, consumption smoothing for both, technology transfer, and risk spreading. Moreover, capital controls cover up policy mistakes by avoiding a depreciation. Since inconsistencies of policies tend to increase over time, inefficiencies will rise and distortions will intensify. Reforms are postponed.

Exit controls represent entry barriers since exit barriers are anticipated. If a country wants to have the long-term benefit of capital inflows, it must establish a reputation so that capital is attracted and so that capital has no incentive to leave the country. This requires that a stability-oriented policy be followed that is convincing for the international financial markets. Controlling portfolio capital is likely to limit the attractiveness for real capital that countries need for their development. Therefore, countries hurt themselves by introducing capital controls.

Part III

Regional dimensions of the world economy

Apart from a global view of economic structures and processes, economic phenomena within regions of the world economy are of interest. This is especially true for the integration of developing countries into the international division of labor. The overwhelming number of these countries have successfully managed to adapt to the global economy, but some countries still remain in poverty (Chapter 10). China has had an outstandingly high growth rate for more than two decades (Chapter 11). The emergence of regional integration schemes in the world economy is an interesting trend (Chapter 12), with the European Union being the most advanced form of integration (Chapter 13).

10 Developing countries

What you will understand after reading this chapter

Nearly two-fifths of the world's population live in low-income countries. A little less than half live in middle-income countries, while only a little more than one-tenth belong to the high-income group. Different countries have reached different stages in their development process (section 10.1). Least developed countries are frequently considered to be caught in a poverty trap from which they cannot escape (section 10.2). Several factors are at the root of low levels of development and a sluggish development process (section 10.3). Newly industrializing countries represent a specific group of countries, displaying strong dynamics, while newly industrialized countries have already joined the club of developed countries (section 10.4). Nearly all developing countries have improved in absolute terms over the last thirty-five years; many, among them China and India, have reduced their relative distance to the US (section 10.5). The core elements of a growth strategy consist in the accumulation of capital, both physical and human, and of acquiring technological knowledge developed elsewhere in the world (section 10.6). Different trade strategies, including import substitution and export diversification, have been adopted (section 10.7). Multilateral cooperation can support the effort of the individual countries (section 10.8). Whether growth and equity are complementary or conflicting objectives remains an important issue in development strategies (section 10.9). A high external debt burden exposes countries to higher risks of external shocks and impairs development in the long-run and can cause disruptions (section 10.10). Macroeconomic instability poses a further severe economic impediment (section 10.11). Finally, the role of the real exchange rate and of expenditure reduction and expenditure switching as stabilization policies are discussed (section 10.12).

10.1 Countries in different stages of development

Looking at the world economy, we find countries at different stages of their development process. A group of so-called least developed countries are trapped in a situation with a low and more or less stagnant GDP per capita or at best very small increases. Any GDP growth is almost immediately absorbed by a population increase. Malnutrition, poor health (expressed for instance by the under-five child mortality rate), a low literacy rate, and inadequate secondary school enrollment are typical characteristics to be found in these countries.

In developing countries, an increase in GDP per capita is taking place, based on a growth process that is under way. Quite a few of these developing countries have already experienced a stark sector change away from agriculture towards industry with a strong build-up of competitiveness in the export sector. These countries are referred to as newly industrializing countries or the threshold economies. Some of the former developing countries, the newly industrialized countries, now rank alongside the developed countries, i.e. the traditional industrialized countries. Newly industrialized countries have reached a stage of development similar to most industrial economies, having often leap-frogged to new technological sectors such as IT and also exhibiting a strong service sector. These countries which are now at par with the traditional industrial economies were the NIEs, the newly industrializing economies of the 1980s. To sum up: what used to be called developing countries some forty years, now exhibits a broad spectrum of countries at different stages of development.

The available classifications of countries into different development stages are not uniform since different authors and different international organizations use a variety of varying criteria. Accordingly the term 'developing countries' is often applied in a broader sense (than described here) to also include least developed countries. International organizations use different definitions and income levels for their classification. The United Nations distinguishes least developed, developing, and developed countries and applies, apart from the income criterion, a human asset index (including characteristics of nutrition, health, literacy, and school enrollment) to identify the least developed countries. The WTO uses the same classification. UNCTAD, the OECD, and the World Bank apply different income thresholds. The levels applied change over time. Using the World Bank classification, we distinguish low-income (with a GNI per capita of US$825 or less in 2004), medium-income countries (between US$826 and US$10,065) and high-income countries (with a GNI per capita of US$10,066 or more). All low-income countries in the World Bank classification are least developed economies. The OECD distinguishes LDCs and other low-income countries as categories.

Using the World Bank approach, more than one-third of the world's population (36.8 percent, 2.3 billion out of 6.4 billion people) live in fifty-nine low-income countries (2004). These are countries with an annual gross national per capita income of US$825 or less. Actually, the average income per capita is US$510. All the low-income countries taken as one group together produce 3 percent of world GDP. About three billion people, 47.4 percent of the world's population, belong to ninety-four middle-income countries, with an annual per capita income of US$825–10,065. Their average income per capita stands at US$2,190, their share in world production measures 17 percent. In the middle-income group, the average is US$1,580 for the lower middle-income countries and US$4,770 for the upper middle-income countries. About one billion, 15.8 percent of the world's population, live in fifty-six high-income countries, with an annual per capita income of US$10,066 and above. Their average income per head is US$32,040; all high-income countries together produce 80 percent of the world's GDP. Information on which country belongs to which category can be found in the appendix to the World Development Report 2006 (World Bank 2005d: Tables 1–5, 291).

10.2 Characteristics of the least developed countries

The least developed countries are characterized by very low income levels and poverty (Table 10.1). Indicators are malnutrition, diseases, high infant mortality, low life expectancy, and an inefficient supply of public goods in, for example, the public health sector, schools, and universities. Further characteristics include illiteracy, few opportunities to earn a sufficient income, and inadequate living and housing conditions. In some of these countries, people live on US$1 per day, calculated at nominal exchange rates and market prices, and on two to three US dollars in purchasing power parity.

On the production side of gross national product, a low-income country is often characterized by a primary sector (agriculture, exploitation of natural

Table 10.1 The ten poorest countries in the world, 2004

Countries	Gross national income, $ per capita	
	At nominal exchange rates	At purchasing power parity
Burundi	90	660
Ethiopia	110	810
Congo, Dem. Rep.	120	680
Malawi	170	620
Eritrea	180	1,050
Sierra Leone	200	790
Rwanda	220	1,300
Niger	230	830
Mozambique	250	1,160
Chad	260	1,420
For comparison:		
Portugal	14,350	19,250
Germany	30,120	27,950
United States	41,400	39,710
Switzerland	48,230	35,370
Japan	37,180	30,040
Singapore	24,220	26,590

Source: World Bank, *World Development Report* 2006: Table 1, p. 292.

resources) contributing a relatively high proportion to total national income and of employment. Agriculture has a relatively low productivity and is often economically discriminated against in favor of other sectors, namely manufacturing. Frequently, agricultural production is concentrated on just a few products (single-crop farming). Far too often, the natural resource sector represents an export enclave, i.e. it is not intensively linked to the rest of the economy, and therefore does not exert noticeable economic spillover effects. The high value-added stages in the chain of vertical production are missing. In other cases where industry accounts for half or more of GDP (as in the Democratic Republic of Congo with 56 percent, Angola with 65 percent, and Nigeria with 49 percent, all with a low per capita income of less than US$1,030 or where manufactured exports make up the overwhelming part of merchandise exports (as in Bangladesh with 89 percent), industry or manufactured exports do not generate a high national income or strong enough prices on the world market to move the country to higher income levels. Often the high share of industry is based on some processing activities of the primary sector (i.e. oil refinery) which in a dual economy does not have a spillover effect on the rest of the economy. In the least developed countries, the tertiary sector, especially domestic commerce and public services, binds many employees.

As in developing countries in general, real income is unevenly distributed in the least developed countries. This means that the Lorenz curve of income distribution deviates significantly from the 45° line. Most of the population is characterized by a low income per capita. No middle class exists, causing a wide gap to open between the rich and the poor. This implies that an important condition for political stability is absent from the system. However, the relationship between the level of development and an uneven income distribution is not altogether clear. For similar development levels, sub-Saharan African and Latin American countries display higher degrees of inequality than most Asian economies. Any analysis is made difficult by statistical problems, since measuring the distribution of personal income remains one of the most unreliable fields in development economics. There is hidden income and hidden unemployment, the latter being marked by many employees having a marginal productivity close to zero. Their work could be abandoned without a noticeable reduction of production.

The expenditures of the majority of the population are directed towards the necessities of life. Too often poor countries remain subsistence economies. Due to low incomes, it is alleged that savings are nearly impossible; this, however, is not correct since quite a few low-income countries have high savings rates. Groups with a high income exhibit a traditionally high propensity to consume and a low savings rate. They spend their income on conspicuous durable consumer goods without productive capacity. If there are savings at all, they frequently flow into capital exports. Very often the desire to be an entrepreneur is missing due to a mixture of adverse and volatile conditions for the private sector. Institutional aspects play a significant role in explaining the development performance of the least developed countries (see below).

10.3 Reasons for slow development or underdevelopment

Several factors have to be considered as possible reasons for slow development or for underdevelopment. Some of these factors do not only apply to low-income countries but to countries that are developing.

Excessive population growth

Even if the gross national product increases significantly, the growth of per capita income can be low or even negative, due to rapid population growth. This is shown in Figure 10.1 (Nelson 1956). Assume that there is a positive growth rate of gross domestic product ($\hat{Y}$), induced by savings and capital formation, that becomes possible once a threshold level per capita income is surpassed. Simultaneously, the expansion rate of the population ($\hat{B}$) increases with rising per capita income; it later stays constant (or even decreases in 'mature' economies). Above the income level y_0, the mortality rate falls quickly and the population expands rapidly, due to a higher life expectancy at birth and especially a far lower infant mortality as a result of better medical conditions. Eventually, with a higher income per capita the birth rate falls, inducing the population to be stable (or even to shrink). Below an income per capita y_0, the population decreases.

From the definition of income per capita, $y = Y/B$, the rate of change of income per capita can be derived as $\hat{y} = \hat{Y} - \hat{B}$. As long as the population is growing more rapidly than domestic product, income per head decreases ($\hat{Y} < \hat{B}$, i.e. $\hat{y} < 0$). Only when gross domestic product increases more than the population ($\hat{Y} > \hat{B}$, i.e. $\hat{y} > 0$), will income per capita rise. The income per capita at y_0 constitutes a low level steady-state equilibrium. To see this consider income levels below y_0; there income per capita tends to rise, since national income growth

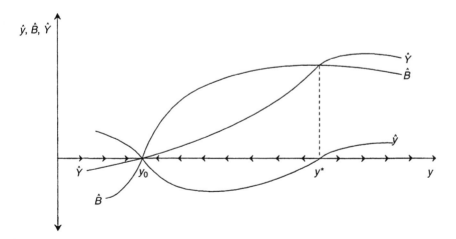

Figure 10.1 The development trap.

exceeds population growth. The economy moves to the point y_0. Above y_0, at first the population grows more than domestic product. This is the reason why the economy tends to go back to the point y_0. Only when the level y^* is exceeded does income per capita rise, because then national product rises more than the population. Between y_0 and y^* the economy is always drawn back to y_0. The country remains on a low level and is captured in a trap of underdevelopment. It requires a push, either through strong internal efforts with a change in the incentive structure or a positive external shock, to get out of this situation. The economy has to move beyond the threshold y^*.

Missing institutions

In many developing countries, there are no institutions that ensure that necessary long-term concerns, i.e. long-term opportunity costs, are taken into consideration. As a result, politicians are very often satisfied with short-term and populist solutions that impose damaging long-term costs for the country. A typical example is the lack of adequate rules preventing budget deficits. Due to the lack of an efficient tax system and too small a tax base, some states finance themselves partly through the central bank monetizing part of the public debt.

Corruption

In some countries corruption takes the place of markets or rule-based decisions. This means that incumbents and the status quo play a large role, that power is vested in groups that influence economic decisions, that new solutions are less likely to be found, and that higher transaction costs arise. This causes inefficiency. Conditions typical for developing countries such as a narrow tax base, a weak tax administration, and lack of accountability of policy-makers facilitate corruption. Yet, as high corruption strongly correlates with low per capita income, the causality is difficult to identify. Are countries corrupt because they are poor or are they poor because of high corruption? As high corruption always coincides with bad public governance, the same causality issue arises for the relationship between poverty and governance.

Internal wars

In sub-Saharan Africa, some countries are involved in internal civil wars, tribal conflicts, and religious clashes. In such an environment, uncertainty and the short-run prevail, negatively affecting economic decisions. An important prerequisite for economic development, confidence in the future, is missing. All economic decisions, among them consumption, investment, human capital formation, and entrepreneurship are taken on the wrong basis of uncertainty.

Lack of capital formation

Low savings result in a small capital stock which implies that production remains low. Usually, new physical capital embodies new technological knowledge. Thus, weak capital formation results in hardly any new technological knowledge being realized. Little capital formation, i.e. only little abstinence from consumption, also means that human capital formation does not sufficiently take place, for example, by training on the job. Impediments to capital formation are also due to a low income per head. If a government tries to finance its expenses through an inflation tax, the high inflation will work against savings, since people escape into unproductive inflation-proof uses of their income.

No entrepreneurship

Developing countries often lack entrepreneurship, for several reasons. One is that the role of the entrepreneur is not highly valued in society and that value orientation does not assign a special importance to achievement. Another reason is that the country has no entrepreneurial tradition, for instance because of its educational system.

National debt

Some developing countries, especially in Latin America, have accumulated a high foreign debt (V) on the international financial markets for several reasons, but mainly because of high budget fiscal deficits. This requires high interest payments (rV) and leads to a negative balance of services. Ignoring other positions of the balance of services and transfer payments, the financing restriction for an open economy is given by:

$$S - I + (T - G) = Z^H - rV - \dot{V} \tag{10.1}$$

where Z^H is the trade balance and $-\dot{V}$ is the reduction of foreign debt or the increase in foreign assets. For highly indebted countries, the trade balance minus the interest payments is negative, with low domestic savings and an often prevalent budget deficit of the government. This means that indebtedness rises $(\dot{V} > 0)$. It is hard for such an economy to reduce consumption in order to balance the public budget, to achieve positive net financial investment and a positive trade balance in the end.

Vicious circle

A multitude of factors can keep developing countries on a low-income level. Strong growth of the population, a low savings rate, a small stock of real capital (including infrastructure capital) and of human capital lead to a small output, which itself does not allow a sufficient formation of capital (Figure 10.2). High inflation rates and high foreign debt accelerate this vicious circle, which has to be broken through for economic development to take off. Instead of 'vicious circle' or 'cumulating effects,' this phenomenon is also called a 'low-level equilibrium.' Such a low-level equilibrium can be characterized as hysteresis. It is path-dependent in the sense that once such a situation is reached it is extremely difficult to escape from it. Similar considerations define the so-called economics of thresholds ('*économie des seuils*') which has to be overcome before economic development can take place.

Different endowment conditions

Yet another aspect is that the countries of the world are characterized by different conditions for economic growth. Some of these conditions are determined by nature, like access to the oceans (coastal country versus landlocked country, tropical conditions, etc.), others are synthetic (acquired comparative advantage). These conditions can lead to different growth rates.

10.4 The newly industrializing and the newly industrialized countries

The picture of developing countries described above corresponds to those countries where the developing process has not yet really started (least developed countries) or where it is slow. A number of African economies south of the

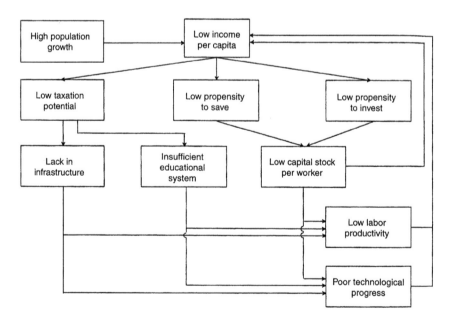

Figure 10.2 Vicious circle of underdevelopment.

Sahara and very few South Asian countries (like Bangladesh) belong to this category. It would however be wrong to place all countries that are typically labeled 'developing countries' in this category.

Within the broad group of developing countries a distinct group of newly industrializing countries have displayed strong growth processes, e.g. most Asian economies. Capital formation in these newly industrializing countries with a low GNI per capita is surprisingly high with investment and savings shares amounting to more than 30 percent of GDP, in some countries even 40 percent – an observation that disputes the widespread belief that poor countries cannot save. Industry accounts for half or nearly half of economic activity, as in China, Malaysia, or Thailand. Manufactured exports amount to three-quarters or more of merchandise exports, and some countries, in particular China, have a share of technology exports in manufactured exports that compares with technology-oriented developed countries such as Finland. In the case of Malaysia this share is even higher (Table 10.2). Surprisingly, Turkey appears in this category, although its share of industry is as low as that of India. To put Turkey into this category is also justified by the relatively higher GNI per capita and by the growth prospect that is due to the neighbor effect to the EU.

India, though having a high proportion of its merchandise exports as manufactured exports (77 percent), does not yet belong to this category. Industry accounts for only 26 percent of its economy, and income per capita in purchasing power parity is as low as US$3,100. In Vietnam a strong industrialization process is under way.

Indonesia, although at a higher income per capita level in current prices and in purchasing power than India, does not yet belong to the category of newly industrializing countries. The proportion of manufactured exports ranks as low as 52 percent, and that of high technology exports is similar to that of India. The Philippines too belongs to this intermediate category with a low proportion of the industrial sector. A potential explanation for the position of these two countries may be found in the country's size and its strong natural resource base (Indonesia) and a strong sector of non-tradables (the Philippines), although China suggests that size is not necessarily a hindrance for a strong export position. Alternative reasons may be seen in high transaction costs of island economies, bad governance, and in lack of economic momentum.

Most Latin American countries belong to the upper range of the middle-income group. One cannot say that a strong industrialization process such as in many East Asian economies is under way. Instead, most Latin American economies appear to be already industrialized, albeit not under open market conditions. In recent years, they have to face both increasing competition from East Asian manufacturers and price trends in favor of natural resource extraction due to strong Asian demand. Except for Argentina, industry therefore accounts for a relatively low percentage of GDP. Some countries such as Chile are traditional exporters of resources or resource-based products (agriculture).

Finally, for some economies the term 'newly industrialized countries' is becoming accepted. Cases in point are Korea, Hong Kong, Singapore, and

Taiwan. These states have succeeded in a broad increase of their industrial exports, and manufactured goods constitute a considerable part of their exports. Most of the economic policy problems to be discussed below have already been solved by these countries. For example, Korea's GNI in purchasing power parity is at US$20,610, industry accounts for 62 percent of GDP and high-technology exports are strong (32 percent). The country has joined the OECD (as has Mexico). Hong Kong and Singapore as city-states have taken a position as traders.

10.5 Which countries failed, which succeeded?

It is heavily debated by non-governmental organizations (NGOs) whether developing countries have benefited from the international division of labor. A number of

Table 10.2 Categories of industrializing countries, 2004

Countries	Gross national income per head in US dollars		Share of [a]		
	At current nominal exchange rates	In purchasing power parity	Industry in GDP	Manufacturing exports in merchandise exports	High technology exports in manufacturing exports
Newly industrializing countries with low income per capita					
India	620	3,100	26	77	5
Vietnam	550	2,700	40	50	2
Indonesia	1,140	3,460	44	52	5
Philippines	1,170	4,890	32	90	74
Newly industrializing countries					
China	1,290	7,170	51	91	27
Malaysia	4,650	9,630	48	77	58
Thailand	2,540	8,020	44	75	30
Turkey	2,630	7,310	28	84	2
Traditional industrialized countries in the upper range of the middle-income group (all in Latin America)					
Argentina	3,720	12,460	65	27	9
Brazil	3,090	8,020	32	52	12
Chile	4,910	10,500	34	16	3
Mexico	6,770	9,590	25	81	21
Industrialized countries					
Hong Kong	20,610	31,510	12	93[b]	13
Korea	13,940	20400	62	93	32
Singapore	24,220	26,590	35	85[b]	59
World	6,280	8,760	–	77	18

Source: World Bank, *World Development Indicators* March 2005.

Notes
a 2003.
b Includes re-exports.

NGOs advocate the view that the economic situation has worsened for the developing world. In order to shed some light on this question, two different criteria can be used. First, whether real GDP or GNI per capita have increased in absolute terms and, second, whether their position relative to the US has improved.

There are several methodological problems with this approach: in order to make a comparison in time and between countries, a common measurement standard has to be applied. This may be constant US dollars where, for international comparisons, market exchange rates are used. Alternatively, constant purchasing power parity rates can be applied. Purchasing power parity (PPP) means that at a point in time one international dollar has the same purchasing power over domestic GDP than the US dollar has over US GDP. Both datasets are provided by the World Bank. We here use purchasing power parity data in constant 2000 US dollar since it is more appropriate for comparisons of standards of living. PPP income comparisons always put poor countries in a better situation than exchange rate income comparison because of the non-tradable sector in which domestic and international prices are widely decoupled from each other.

Looking at the period 1975–2004, nearly all countries have improved their situation in absolute constant purchasing power terms. The exception is sub-Saharan Africa with the Democratic Republic of Congo being a particularly severe case (Figures 10.3a and b). Other countries, for instance Burundi and Niger, also have lost in GDP in absolute terms but not quite so extremely. Countries like Bangladesh, Cameroon, Ghana, and the Sudan are among those who have improved their situation.

An improvement in the relative position to the US is a strong indicator of a successful development process whereas a relative decline does not necessarily imply that the country has lost relative to its initial situation. Depicting the average annual rate of increase of the absolute GDP level per capita on the vertical axis and the change of the relative position to the US in terms of percentage points on the horizontal axis for the period between 1975 and 2004, the countries can be arranged in three quadrants with the winners on both accounts in the upper right quadrant and the losers in relative and absolute terms in the lower left quadrant (Figure 10.4).

China, India, Indonesia, Egypt, Botswana, Pakistan, Sri Lanka, and Chile have reduced their relative distance to the US (Figure 10.4, upper right-hand quadrant). Argentina, Brazil (the point is close to Mexcio's), Mexico, Cameroon, and Ghana have lost in their position relative to the US. Argentina has even lost half of its relative position to the US, declining from 54 percent in 1975 to 32 percent in 2004. It should be noted that Argentina was hit by a deep financial crisis in 2001 when the currency board collapsed and people's financial assets depreciated heavily. Most sub-Saharan countries are located in the lower left-hand quadrant, indicating a loss both in absolute and relative terms. Internal turmoil and civil war are the primary causes for this pronounced decline in economic activity. The per capita income of Singapore and Hong Kong, not shown in Figure 10.4, has increased by 4.5 percent annually, allowing them to close in on the US position by 1.3 percent per year.

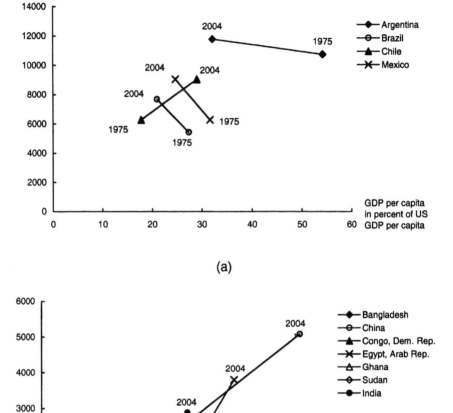

Figure 10.3 GDP per capita[a] of (a) Latin American countries and (b) Asian and African
countries, in absolute terms and relative to the US, 1975 and 2004 (source:
World Bank, *World Development Indicators* 2005).

Notes
a Constant purchasing power parity.

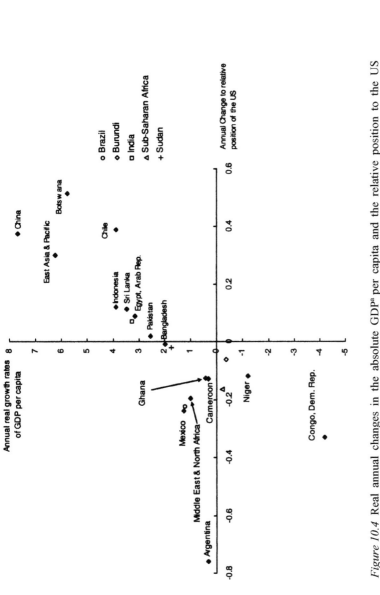

Figure 10.4 Real annual changes in the absolute GDP[a] per capita and the relative position to the US between 1975 and 2004[b] (source: World Bank, *World Development Indicators* 2005).

Notes

a Constant purchasing power parity.

b In terms of percentage points.

10.6 Core elements of a growth strategy

Growth and development mean different things, depending on the development stage that countries are in. Consequently, the core elements of a development strategy differ. In the least developed countries, the immediate goal is to improve the living conditions for people, the eradication of poverty and its impact is at the center. In the developing countries, in which poverty has been reduced, the goal is to start a self-sustained growth process and to keep it going. Of course, this distinction is somewhat artificial, since a self-sustained growth process is also the means to eradicate poverty.

The Millennium Development Goals

In the Millennium Development Goals, the UN has set development objectives for the least developed countries. The aim is to improve the living conditions for millions of people. This overall goal comprises eight individual targets: halving extreme poverty and doing away with hunger, achieving universal primary education, promoting gender equality, reducing child mortality, combating HIV/AIDs, malaria, and other diseases, ensure environmental sustainability, and develop a global partnership for development. The target date for reaching these goals is 2015. Table 2 in the appendix of the annual World Development Report informs on most of these goals.

The Millennium Development Goals are part of a multilateral approach to development (see below), and they establish a global yardstick for what should be achieved in a multilateral context. At the same time, these goals serve as frame of reference for national economic policy. They represent a benchmark for the individual country, for its politicians, its elite, and all the groups of society. Stating the goals does not specify how they goals can be reached; the goals by themselves do not define the necessary policy instruments.

A self-sustained growth process

A central goal of development policy is to initiate a self-sustained process of economic growth and to keep it going. The core change usually consists in an institutional modification or a revolution that newly defines the incentives for the economic agents. This serves as a decisive stimulus. The incentives must be directed towards production, exporting, investment, innovation, human capital formation, and sectoral change. This institutional change may be done abruptly by implementing a new system of governance as was the case in the post-communist transformation countries when they introduced the market economy. Or it may be done smoothly as in China where the rules of production and investment were gradually altered.

The goal of such a change is an expansion of the production potential, being brought about by the accumulation of stocks that represent the decisive factors of growth, namely physical and human capital as well as technological knowledge (see Chapter 4). Larger accumulated stocks in these growth determinants allow higher output. Public spending should be redirected towards education, infrastructure investment, and health; tax laws should provide sufficient incentives for investment, both in physical and human capital, and for innovations. Given these conditions, economic agents are needed to organize the production process and combine the growth factors, i.e. the entrepreneurs.

Sectoral change from agriculture to industry and then to services and a knowledge economy is an important aspect of the growth process. Trade provides a crucial stimulus as it forces firms and sectors to adjust to the relative product prices determined on the world market. To have an open economy also defines the relevant incentives for other market participants, including households and workers. An essential decision of development policy therefore is the commitment to an open economy, i.e. to the fundamental decision to let the world market play. This means that all forms of protectionism are to be banned, including quantitative restrictions and subsidies. Openness to foreign investment can help finance the accumulation of capital. In order to attract foreign investment, taxation policy must be credible; taxation rules are not to be changed ad hoc during the game.

Related to an open economy is the acceptance of competition. Institutional arrangements should prevent populist political approaches that will only serve the short-run. The institutional set-up should accept the market mechanism and should give priority to competition as the dominant form of organizing the economy. State enterprises should be privatized. Markets should be deregulated where regulations impede entry or restrict competition. Exempted are those regulations that are justified on safety, environmental, and consumer protection grounds and prudential oversight of financial institutions. Institutional arrangements play an essential role. If they are reliable, they provide confidence for market participants. Many decentralized decisions of market participants with a longer time horizon require a stable institutional framework, for instance decisions to save, to start up businesses, to invest, to innovate, and to build up human capital. Processes that will destroy the economic equilibrium in the long-run should be ruled. Institutional arrangements should prevent populist approaches with short-run benefits and long-term damages. The right of ownership, i.e. the acceptance of private property rights, has to be respected. Another crucial prerequisite is a stable tax system preferably with a broad tax base that prevents taxes from being changed frequently and irregularly thus minimizing uncertainty for private investors.

Of utmost relevance is a stable money. Above all, it has to be guaranteed that the state will not balance the budget by printing money, i.e. by obliging the central bank to increase monetary expansion and by channeling the increased money supply to the government, for instance by buying government bonds with central bank money. Monetization of the budget deficit is only possible because in many countries the central bank is not independent from political influence. For that reason, another important aspect is the independence of the central bank and the explicitly formulated prohibition of financing budget deficits through monetary policy. Increasing public debt, when used to finance consumption, is not sustainable once a certain threshold is surpassed. It has a negative impact on monetary stability. If these conditions are not satisfied, currency crises with negative repercussions on the real side of the economy are certain to occur. It is therefore necessary to make the country robust against financial crises, especially contagion that may come from abroad, even if the fundamentals of a country may not be a sufficient reason for a crisis to break out.

A key aspect is to guarantee economic freedom, in order that individuals can rely on the fact that decisions are not annihilated by actions of the government. It remains an open question whether economic freedom is sufficient for growth or whether in the long-term political freedom must be established as well (see the chapter on China).

All these approaches rely on the individual country undertaking the decisive steps. Each country has to initiate the growth process and keep it going. Many of these recommendations, except for institution building and income distribution, were included in the recipes for Latin American countries to stabilize their economies and to recover from the crises of the 1980s. These recipes were labeled the Washington Consensus (Willamson 2000). The political left has discredited them as 'neoclassical.' Unfortunately, labeling them in this way spawns a whole battery of negative associations. Like it or not, an economy has to respect restraints and it will follow incentives.

10.7 Trade strategies for development

Concerning trade strategies for economic development, we have to distinguish between import substitution and export diversification. These are opposite strategies that have been used by Latin American and Asian countries.

Import substitution

During the four decades from 1950 to 1990 the development policy of nearly all Latin American countries was characterized by a lack of confidence in the international division of labor as an important source of economic growth. Latin American development policy followed the strategy of import substitution. The starting point of this strategy was the hypothesis of deteriorating terms of trade, which was developed by Prebisch (1950) and Singer (1950). This policy was directed at replacing imports by domestically produced goods. The domestic sectors were supported in their development and shielded against foreign suppliers. An industrial basis was supposed to be built up by the protection of young industries (infant industry argument). In this respect it was significant that traditional trade relations had been interrupted by World War II. Unlike the European countries, Latin America did not place its hope on a closer integration of the world economy.

Typical instruments of such a policy were protectionist measures like import licenses or import duties, which increased with the vertical level of processing and thus protected the domestic producers of finished goods. This development strategy, which was predominant in the 1950s and 1960s, at first seemed to be successful in Latin America, but from the mid-1960s onwards, the problems became visible. Above all, the industrial sector developed very poorly. One reason was that the policy of import substitution was associated with considerable distortions. Domestically produced goods used as intermediate inputs became more expensive because of import protection, and this in turn reduced the competitiveness of the export sector which needed these goods as inputs. Import protection is thus equivalent to a tax on exports. The price structure was distorted in favor of the domestic import substitutes so that this sector expanded too much and attracted too many resources. Due to the protection from international competition, domestic producers did not feel the necessary pressure to cut costs and innovate. In the long-run, they lost their competitiveness and the system of import licenses opened the doors for political deal-making and corruption. To compensate for this distortion, domestic producers have often asked for export subsidies which the national budgets could not finance without resorting to the inflation tax. In the end, the strategy of import substitution caused serious misallocation and created more market failure – and also political failure – than had existed initially.

Export diversification

While the strategy of import substitution is rather inwardly oriented, the strategy of export diversification, which was pursued by most Asian countries, can be seen as an outwardly oriented development strategy. The objective was, and still is, to expose the export sectors to international competition and not to distort the allocation between the export sector and the domestic sector of import substitutes. To compensate for this distortion, domestic producers have often asked for export subsidies which the national budgets could not finance without resorting to the inflation tax. At first, detrimental effects of import protection for exports were compensated by special export promotions. Owing to high domestic savings this was not harmful to a balanced budget for the state. In short, the Asian approach tried to enhance domestic production, investment, and innovation by allowing intensive competition from the world market and by using this pressure to develop a sustainable economic basis. The predominant philosophy was that the world markets would offer interesting opportunities to the domestic producers. The exchange rate policy could prevent massive overvaluations. There is no proof for undervalued currencies over a longer period of time, with the possible exception of China (see Chapter 11). The real exchange rate was mainly left to the markets and could be stabilized, at least till the mid-1990s before the outbreak of the Asian crisis. There have been almost no bureaucratic restrictions for currency-related questions in the commercial area.

10.8 Multilateral strategies for development

Poverty reduction

Poverty reduction can be interpreted as an obligation of the international community. Development aid corresponds to a Kantian imperative and the Rawlsian principle: those in a poor position receive help in form of income transfers in order to advance their situation, i.e. alleviate poverty and improve the conditions for growth. Development aid can be spent to build schools and hospitals, pay teachers and doctors, upgrade water quality, and improve the infrastructure. For the least developed countries foreign aid can represent a high percentage of their GDP. For instance, in 2003 Eritrea and Sierra Leone saw aid account for 37 percent of their GNI. The industrial countries have pledged to support the developing world with at least 0.7 percent of the individual countries' GNI. Despite this pledge, the average for the countries that are members of the Development Assistance Committee, the OECD department responsible for development issues, was only 0.25 percent of GNI in 2004. The US and Italy are the laggards on this count, with 0.16 and 0.15 percent of their individual GNIs devoted to development aid. EU aid was only 0.36 percent of the union-wide GNI (World Bank 2005d: Table 10.1).

Even if the developed countries were to provide the financing that they have pledged to, there is no guarantee that the intended development goals would be achieved. Unfortunately, good intentions are not sufficient to achieve the intended goals. First, income transfers may be siphoned off by corrupt politicians and bureaucrats so that development aid may be ineffective. Whereas an empirical observation says that 1 percent of GDP in development aid reduces poverty and infant mortality by 1 percent, when good institutions and policies prevail (World Bank 2005d), funds may actually leak like water in the sand of a desert, having no stimulating effect at all. Aid then remains ineffective. For instance, there may be no increase in social spending despite a country receiving aid. It is puzzling that bilateral aid has often been giving over-proportionally to countries with undemocratic and poorly managed governments rather than to countries with sound institutions and a good governance record. This reflects selfish motives of the donors such as to secure access to natural resources. The record for multilateral aid is somewhat better with respect to the governance quality of the recipients than that of bilateral donors. Second, governments may use the funds for politically visible 'white elephant projects' that might impress the population, but end up having a zero effect on productivity. Third, the country may be less keen to use its own efforts to improve its economic situation, feeling secure in the knowledge that help is forthcoming Fourth, there is an economic mechanism: the income received from abroad may be spend on non-tradables, thus raising their price and making it less attractive to produce for exports. This is reminiscent of the often observed 'Dutch disease' – a phenomenon first observed in the Netherlands when the discovery of natural gas deposits led to a shift in demand in favor of non-tradables, to real appreciation and deindustrialization. This experience is not unrealistic. For instance, Bhutan and Tanzania received annual aid averaging 20 percent of their GDP in the 1980s, and in both countries the tradable sector contracted by 15 percentage points of GDP (IMF 2002: 2).

A more important aspect than aid is trade (aid through trade). This requires developed countries to open up their markets for the exports from low-income countries. Unfortunately, developed countries still protect some of their markets with tariffs, anti-dumping measures, quantitative restrictions, and subsidies. This applies in particular to the agricultural sector and to sensitive labor-intensive industrial sectors. For instance, the European Union spends about three euros per day on subsidizing a cow (in milk production) whereas people in some low-income countries live on one euro per day. The US heavily subsidizes its cotton production, to the detriment of cotton producers in Brazil and countries in sub-Saharan Africa. The effect of these subsidies is not only that the industrial countries' markets are de facto closed. The subsidies lead to excessive production, and the rich countries dump the excessive output on the world market, lowering prices artificially and reducing the production incentive for low-income countries. It is amazing that in the policies of the high-income country, the equity target – often at the root of trade barriers and subsidies – is only interpreted within a purely national (or EU) context.

A heavily debated question is whether intellectual property rights such as patents can be used as a policy instrument in a multilateral approach or whether they simply contribute to draw resources out of a developing economy. This would mean to allow low-income countries to produce certain products without respecting the property right. This is an issue that has been heavily discussed with respect to medicines, for instance against AIDS. The principal position on this issue is that property rights have to be respected. If the international community wants to grant the production rights to some countries, it should be prepared to pay a royalty to the companies that own the patent. Otherwise the incentive to discover new technological knowledge is reduced.

The role of the World Bank

The World Bank, founded in 1944 as the 'International Bank for Reconstruction and Development' during the Bretton Woods Conference, at first had the task to provide financial support in the reconstruction of the regions destroyed by World War II. Today its role is to promote economic development in the least developed countries through the financing of key investment projects. In 1956 the International Finance Corporation (IFC) and in 1960 the International Development Association (IDA) were founded. Together these three organizations constitute what is known as the World Bank Group. The IDA primary role is to administer loans to least developed countries. Loans are typically interest free and have longer amortization periods than IBRD loans. The IFC is the private sector arm of the World Bank Group. It encourages private sector investment and assists private enterprise to finance projects in developing countries.

In addition to its financing role the World Bank coordinates the work of international organizations, donor countries, and development agencies in developing countries. In this capacity the World Bank also advises developing countries on questions of economic policy, use of technology, and organizational and administrative issues. In recent years the World Bank has increasingly worked with the governments of developing countries to create an environment that encourages and sustains foreign investment.

10.9 Growth and equity – complementary or conflicting?

The issue of equity is interlinked with development in two ways. One is the line that developing countries have a low per capita income, i.e. that income distribution is uneven between countries. We have looked into this aspect already. The other is that in each country equity is an issue. Thus, in low-income countries a larger proportion of the population lives below US$1 (purchasing parity power) per day, for instance 70.8 percent in Nigeria, 72.3 percent in Mali, and 35.3 percent in India. The question is how growth and equity are interrelated.

In a historic perspective, economic growth has been the vehicle through which the economic situation of the overwhelming majority of groups in society has improved in the development process of the industrial countries over the last 200 years. Real income rose, working time was reduced considerably, living conditions improved, healthcare was introduced and enhanced, access to education (including university education) was opened up, and the vertical mobility of people in an open society helped to dissipate the benefits of growth to a wide part of the population. Governmental schemes such as social security, initiated for instance in Continental Europe in the last quarter of the nineteenth century, significantly reduced unprotected risks in particular in the cases of illness and old age, later on extended to unemployment. Redistribution through taxation and government spending was included later on. Growth came first, equity corrections followed later. In this direction, growth and equity were complementary. Groups and generations had to offer sacrifice so that their children could have a better life. Or they had to offer a sacrifice in the first stages of their lives to have a better life at old age. The Pareto criterion, according to which a situation represents an improvement if people are better off and no-one is worse off, unknown in the nineteenth century, was not an orientation for growth policy. Even in the reconstruction of Germany after World War II, the target of economic growth came first, '*Wohlstand für alle*' (Prosperity for all) was an implication of growth. Economic expansion was the means through which the lives of people improved.

The nineteenth century proposition of Marx to abolish private ownership and to expropriate the capital owners – an attempt for a political answer to the issue of poverty and deprivation – failed. Eventually, the communist countries were not able to adequately provide their citizens with goods. In the developing world of the 1960s and 1970s, where communist ideas were attractive to the intellectuals, where they provided a guiding philosophy for economic policy as in India and where they represented the ideological power base of dictators as in Africa, the ideas of communism eventually lost appeal when it became apparent that the implementation of communist concepts did not perform in the Soviet Union and the COMECON countries. In the industrial countries, the process of growth was fostered by democracy, which as an institution helped to open up society and to respond with institutional changes. New entrants included minorities such as immigrants to the US and redefined the position of the group of incumbents (land owners, capital owners relative to workers in Europe). In this interpretation, the approach was successful. Admittedly, these institutions were unable to prevent two World Wars, Nazism in Germany, and – more closely related to economics – the Great Depression in the early 1930s and – at the actual rim – the excessive welfare state with its shockingly high unemployment rate.

In spite of these political failures, growth continues to be the way out of poverty and low income. However, today more explicit requirements on the growth process are put forward. Equality of starting conditions in a person's life or the principle of equal opportunity is such a widely accepted obligation. It demands that a person's economic, social, or political success should not be predetermined by the conditions of birth, race, or gender, but should reflect his or her efforts and talents (World Bank 2006b: 18). Access to healthcare and education, the quality of the services available and most generally, the openness of institutions and the vertical social and income mobility in a society are seen as major factors in determining to what extent equal opportunity exists. The principle of equal opportunity helps to make optimal use of all the talents in society and to bring into play all the potential effort that is available. It therefore should have a positive impact on economic growth. It is more explicit than asking for an open society with vertical income and social mobility. Admittedly, inequality traps exist. Often, discretionary decisions controlled by groups regarding the access to services, for instance to university education, are at the root of inequality traps. In contrast, markets with an anonymous allocation decisions as a rule allow free entry.

Equality of starting conditions does not mean equality of outcome. The goal of equality of outcome for each individual, irrespective of talent and effort, would induce the wrong incentives into the economic system. People would rely on others to provide effort and to improve the general outcome so that they can benefit, without making a proportional effort themselves. Nevertheless, societies may opt to exclude outcomes that they do not want, even if they give all individuals or groups their fair chance according to the equal opportunity principle. The World Bank (2005b: 19) calls this the avoidance of absolute deprivation. With respect to this principle, the relationship to growth is less clear. It can be argued that absolute deprivation is inhuman, it can be argued that the protection of the neediest is an expression of the Rawlsian principle of inequality aversion, and it can be argued that a society without some minimal form of social protection is politically unstable. At the same time, the principle is open to interpretation.

A core question in the context of equity and growth is to what extent some groups have to lose in order to encourage growth. In an intergenerational context, the parent generation may be willing to accept sacrifices in order to allow a better life for the generation of their children. The institutional change necessary for growth often does not satisfy the Pareto criterion that no person (or no group) loses. For instance, in the change from communism to a free society, the old power elite had to go. The civil rights movement in the US had to tear down privileges of others. Overthrowing apartheid in Africa meant that groups had to give up their positions as incumbents.

Markets are often segmented, especially capital and labor markets. Even informal markets are segmented, the reasons being social and cultural origins, clan or tribal membership, and economic factors such as a lack of risk evaluation through infant financial markets. Consequently, groups are excluded from market processes. Human resources are not used. Privileged positions of incumbents gives rise to political risks of governments being overthrown instead of a due accepted democratic process. This increases uncertainty and reduces capital formation. Privileges mean a privileged access to life resources such as water. This hampers the health of people and lowers the growth potential. For all these reasons it is important that market segmentations be abolished.

10.10 High external debt burden

A high level of foreign debt represents a hefty burden for a country. It includes an obligation to pay interest and to repay the debt. Export receipts cannot be used to finance the import of investment and consumption goods. It thus reduces a country's maneuvering space. Besides, indebted countries have to pay a risk premium on their loans. Moreover, a country with high debt is vulnerable. Usually, external debt of developing countries is denominated in foreign currency (the so-called 'original sin' problem). If the foreign currency appreciates and if the interest rate in international market rises, for instance because of a shift in monetary policy, the debt burden increases. Finally, external debt can lead to a currency crisis. If financial markets lose confidence in the performance of a country, capital inflows may stop and capital flows may even reverse, forcing the domestic currency to devalue abruptly and markedly. This has severe repercussions on the real side of the economy.

Latin American countries experienced a severe debt crisis in the 1980s. For example, the volume of foreign debt in Argentina reached 61 percent of its gross domestic income in 1985; Brazil was at 49.1 percent (Figure 10.5). Net foreign debt in relation to exports of the seventeen most indebted countries was at 384 percent, in comparison to the 200 percent which is considered to be acceptable by some analysts (Cline 1995). Interest payments are one important reason for a negative current account. New credits have to be raised so that countries are able to pay interest. The new credits are used to finance the budget deficits of the state rather than to create a new capital stock. They are used for consumptive purposes and not for investment.

Once the financial markets realize that a country is not able to service its

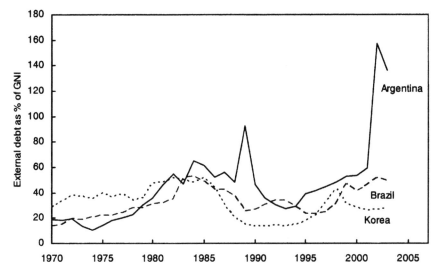

Figure 10.5 Debt of Argentina, Brazil, and South Korea, 1970–2003 (in percent of GNI) (source: World Bank, *World Development Indicators* CD-ROM 2005).

interest and repayment commitments, then the markets lose the willingness to provide the country with credits, i.e. capital. A minor disturbance can cause the financial markets to no longer provide fresh capital. With the expectation of a devaluation, capital flight sets in. The prices of bonds of highly indebted countries fall. Normally, bank syndicates and international organizations have to provide a fresh starting position for new capital. Creditors lose a considerable amount of their claims by accepting a write-off on their debt (Brady Plan).

The debt crisis of the 1980s is no longer in the spotlight, if it is interpreted as a crisis of insolvency (rather than lack of liquidity) of the middle-income countries. But debt is still a major issue for the indebted Latin American countries. In 2001, Argentina defaulted on its US$100 billion foreign debt. Argentina has reached nearly double the level of foreign debt in GNI (with 136 percent of GNI in 2003) in the aftermath of its currency board crisis. Its debt is 576 percent of its export revenue and it uses 38 percent of its export revenues to pay the interest on its net foreign debts and repay the principal. At the current rate, Argentina needs fifteen years until its debt is repaid. For Brazil, the debt level with 54 percent of GNI is higher in 2004 than in the mid-1980s. It has to use 64 percent of its export revenues to for pay for interest. Both countries are in a fragile position if the Fed's increase in the short-term rates transmits into a rise of long-term interest rates.

The Asian countries Korea, Malaysia, Thailand, and Indonesia experienced the damaging effects of debt exposure during the Asian Crisis. This crisis differed from Latin American crises in so far as Asia debtors and lenders were both private agents whereas in Latin America debtors were mostly states or para-states. This did not only bring new causes for the crisis to the agenda, such as private over-investment and imprudent lending of local banks. It also raised new problems when coping with the crisis such as implicit bail out expectations and moral hazard behavior of the private financial sector. Asian countries had similarly high debt levels in percent to GNI as the Latin American countries in 1985 (Korea 51.7, Malaysia 68.8, Thailand 45.8, and Indonesia 44.4). However, they were not affected by such debt crises in the 1980s as the Latin American countries. But in 1996, before the Asian crisis broke out, vulnerability was looming with the debt levels of 63.5 in Thailand and 58.3 in Indonesia. Even Korea and Malaysia were affected with only 22.3 and 41.3 percent of GNI, respectively. Then in the aftermath of the Asian debt crisis, in 1998 the debt levels rose to 167.9 percent in Indonesia, 97.2 percent in Thailand, and 43 percent in Korea. Meanwhile, by 2003 the Asian countries have managed to nearly halve their debt levels to 36.9 percent in Thailand, 67.5 percent in Indonesia, and 28 percent in Korea (Figures 10.5 and 10.6). This is in stark contrast to the Latin American countries. But still Indonesia is at a debt relative to GDP higher than those of the Latin American countries during the debt crisis. Note that the transformation countries in Central and Eastern Europe are approaching the 60 percent mark of the euro zone (Czech Republic 40, Hungary 58, Poland 46).

It is an open question how high debt should allowed to be. The euro area has set a limit for public debt of 60 percent to GDP. The concept is to prevent a situation where the debt situation becomes non-stationary so that a spiraling upward of public debt is unavoidable. The euro criterion applies to internal and external debt, but in the euro area most of the debt is internal debt. Taking this mark as a

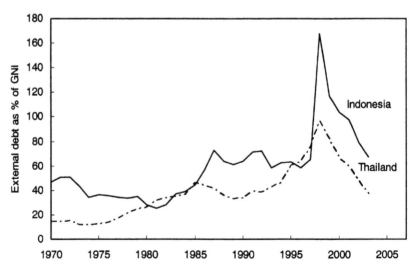

Figure 10.6 Debt of Indonesia and Thailand, 1970–2003 (in percent of GNI) (source: World Bank, *World Development Indicators* CD-ROM 2005).

Table 10.3 Foreign debt of selected countries, 2003

Countries	External debt in percent of		Debt service in percent of exports
	GNI[a]	Exports[b]	
Argentina	115	576	38
Bolivia	37	149	21
Brazil	54	296	64
Chile	67	169	30
Mexico	25	88	21
Korea	28	70[c]	12.5
Malaysia	56	43	8
Indonesia	71	185	26
Philippines	81	172	22
Thailand	41	54	16

Source: GNI: World Bank, *World Development Report* 2006, Table 4; Debt service: World Bank, *Development Indicators*.

Notes
a Present value of external debt.
b Calculated as debt/ (export share × GDP).
c Total debt in percent of exports.

reference value, the limit for external debt should be lower, especially for developing countries, say around 40 percent. Even this limit will not represent a protection in an environment when contagion is likely as in the 1997 Asian financial crisis and when the current account becomes negative, as in the case of Korea.

10.11 Case study: macroeconomic instability in Latin American countries

Macroeconomic instability has been a special problem for the newly industrializing countries in Latin America, for example with exorbitantly high inflation rates of 3,006 percent in 1990 for Argentina or 2,954 percent in the same year for Brazil. Such high inflation rates are correlated with an unusually high expansion of the money supply, for instance of 4,169 percent in the case of Argentina. The devaluation of the currency was similarly high, with 4,736 percent. The second half of the 1980s was characterized by high inflation rates (Table 10.4). Besides the high inflation rate another major problem is the volatility of the inflation rate, i.e. massive shifts in the rate. Most of the time, high public deficits and current account deficits occur simultaneously. This can be explained by insufficient institutional conditions for macroeconomic stability.

Table 10.4 Macroeconomic instability in selected countries, 1985–2004

	Expansion of the money supply[a]	Inflation rate[a]	State budget[b]	Current account balance[b]
Argentina				
1985–1990	181.1	192.9	−2.1	−1.2
1991–1995	19.5	9.9	−0.5	−2.5
1996–2000	1.0	−0.2	−2.0	−3.9
2001–2004	42.0	13.3	−0.5	3.8
Brazil				
1985–1990	201.5	204.5	−12.7	−0.3
1991–1995	219.9	214.7	−4.9	−0.3
1996–2000	14.3	5.2	−4.9	−4.0
2001–2004	15.2	9.4	−3.9[c]	−0.9
Mexico				
1985–1990	52.3	52.8	−8.5	−0.7
1991–1995	8.4	15.1	1.4	−5.0
1996–2000	20.4	14.6	−1.1	−3.1
2001–2004	55.1	461	−1.2	−1.8

Source: IMF, *International Financial Statistics* September 2005.

Notes
a Expansion of the money supply and inflation rate in percent.
b Budget deficit and current account balance in percent of GDP.
c Budget deficits for 2003 and 2004 Central Bank of Brazil.

Money expansion and inflation

The correlation between the expansion of the money supply and inflation can clearly be seen for Argentina (see Figure 5.1) and Brazil (Figure 10.7). Argentina managed to get the expansion of the money supply under control and stabilize the price level with the introduction of the currency board in the 1990s and to keep the price level stable. Yet, dollarization always remained high in Argentina even during the first half of the 1990s when the currency board was not yet under pressure thanks to a positive development of fiscal revenues after privatization. However, the currency board, having been started in April 1991, had to be given up in December 2001 after the fiscal position had massively deteriorated.

Usually, inflation has an effect on the exchange rate, although the impact might be delayed temporarily. This results from the purchasing power parity $e = \hat{P} - \hat{P}*$. For instance, the peak of the inflation rate in Argentina in 1989 and 1990 is related to a visible devaluation of the peso (Figure 5.4 in Chapter 5).

Brazil has seen several bouts of currency devaluation. At the beginning

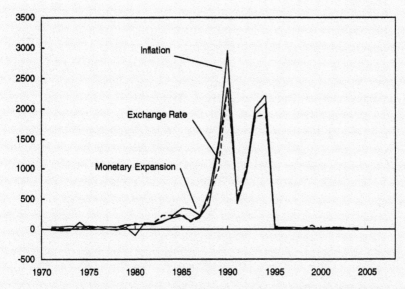

Figure 10.7 Money expansion, inflation, and the exchange rate change (in percent), Brazil, 1970–2003 (source: IMF, *International Financial Statistics* September 2005; IMF, *Country Report Brazil* 2003; Annual Report by the Central Bank of Brazil 2005).

of the 1980s a strong devaluation took place. The money supply continued to expand and the price level kept rising. This was the time when the debt crisis began. The other phases of devaluation were marked by currency reforms. In the mid-1980s the cruzeiro was replaced by the cruzado. Its exchange rate was regularly devalued in the framework of a crawling peg. The cause of the monetary reform was an internal imbalance with a budget deficit of 11 percent of GDP in 1985, financed by the Central Bank of Brazil. In 1990, the cruzeiro was introduced once again and was devalued by floating. Now, the cause was an external imbalance accompanied by a drop of foreign capital inflows. Finally, with a new monetary reform in 1993 the real was introduced. The Brazilian financial crisis of 1999, in which the real was devalued by 64 percent, shows up in Figure 10.7 with a tiny peak only because this devaluation of the real was low relative to the Brazilian long-run experience.

In Mexico (Figure 10.8) the connection between the expansion of the money supply and the inflation rate is also evident. Thus, during the debt crisis in the beginning of the 1980s, the increase in the inflation rate was high while at the same time – as in the case of Brazil – a strong devaluation took place. A drop in the inflow of foreign capital was visible in the mid-1980s and in connection with the peso crisis at the end of 1994. Unlike Brazil, the strong expansion of the money supply in the early 1990s surprisingly had at first neither an effect on the price level nor on the exchange rate. This might be the temporary result of the policy of an active crawling peg, attempting to stabilize the expectations on the foreign exchange markets. But if for a period of time the rate of change of the price index is higher than in the reference country (i.e. the US) as in 1983 and 1984 and in the period from 1988 to 1994, there has to be a realignment of the nominal exchange rate (compare also with Figure 8.4). In 1994, the peso crisis occurred and the peso devalued drastically (by 47 percent). After 1995, money expansion was much lower, the inflation rate

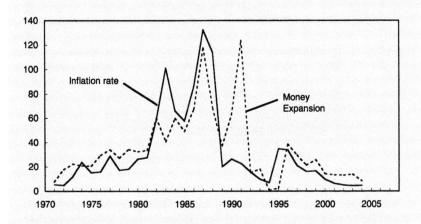

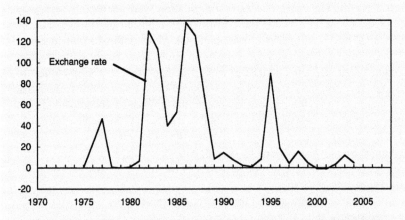

Figure 10.8 Money expansion, inflation, and the exchange rate change (in percent), Mexico, 1970–2004 (source: IMF, *International Financial Statistics* September 2005).

declined and the exchange rate remained more or less stable, except for 2003.

Chile pursued different exchange rate policies. During 1980–1981, a policy of fixed exchange rates was followed. This was combined with a real revaluation. This approach could no longer be sustained after the outbreak of the debt crisis. After a period of flexible exchange rates, Chile moved on to a passive crawling peg with an exchange rate band, in which since 1989 real economic realignments were regarded as more important than the fight against inflation. The parity of the peso was regularly adjusted to a basket of currencies. In between interventions were used to keep the exchange rate within a band. In comparison to a constant exchange rate, a crawling peg has the advantage of preventing abrupt adjustments if it is applied correctly. In 1999, Chile gave up its policy of an exchange rate band and committed itself to a 2–4 percent inflation target.

10.12 Real depreciation: a hard-to-use policy instrument

The nominal exchange rate can be used as an anchor for monetary stability, while the real exchange can establish internal as well as external equilibrium. Developing countries are often in a situation in which real depreciation is needed, for instance in order to reduce a current account deficit. However, the real exchange rate is a hard-to-use instrument. A nominal depreciation can imply a real depreciation, if inflationary effects and second round effects of rising wages can be prevented. If the exchange rate is pegged and if the peg cannot be given up, the price of non-tradables must fall in order to stimulate the production of tradables. This also implies that the price of immobile factors, including wages, cannot rise as in the past or even have to decline. This often is not acceptable politically.

Budget deficits and the real exchange rate

The experience of the Latin American countries shows that a stabilization policy with the exchange rate as a nominal anchor could rarely be sustained, if public budget deficits are not avoided and if inflation expectations cannot be broken due to unkept promises and inconsistent policies in the past. As a result confidence in the stability of a currency plummets. For instance, there was a remarkable public budget deficit in Mexico in the 1980s (Figure 10.9). Combined with an expansion of the money supply, this was the cause for the rise of the price level and the subsequent devaluation of the peso. Although the budget deficit had been reduced by the early 1990s, the current account deficit increased after huge short-term inflows of portfolio investment and a massive real appreciation. The collapse occurred in December of 1994, when the capital flow reversed and

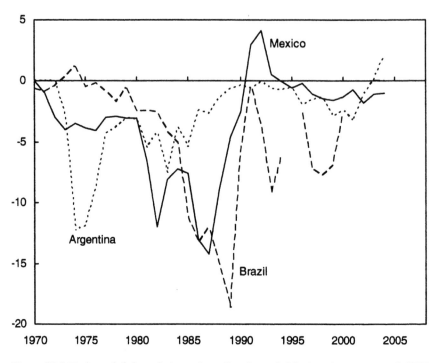

Figure 10.9 Budget deficits of Argentina, Brazil, and Mexico, in percent of GDP
(source: IMF, *International Financial Statistics* 2005).

the peso had to be devalued. At the same time, an international support program became necessary. During the 1980s, Brazil also had a significant budget deficit with up to 20 percent of its GDP. Similarly, an increase of the budget deficit became visible in Argentina particularly in the first half of the 1980s. Such budget deficits signal that credible stabilization policies were not carried out. Thus, monetary policy is not the only reason that the nominal exchange rate as an anchor did not function. The nominal anchor will also be affected when populist economic policies prevail, dominated by income distribution considerations and consumptive spending of the government. A lack of flexibility in the labor market as well as wages that do not correspond to labor productivity, also make a stabilization policy more difficult in the long-run.

Instability and the real exchange rate

Fixing the nominal exchange rate does not imply a constant real exchange rate. The real exchange rate differs from the nominal exchange rate in that the nominal exchange rate is weighted by a ratio of goods prices Very often the domestic inflation rate is higher than the foreign one. Then, a real appreciation takes place. P rises stronger than P^*. The real exchange rate $e_R = eP^*/P$ falls. This is also valid for a crawling peg if the devaluation rate does not fully compensate the difference between the internal and the external inflation rate. A real appreciation can turn out to be even stronger if high net capital inflows occur. As we have seen in the discussion on currency crises, a stark deviation of the nominal and the real exchange rate will eventually require a correction. Then, a real depreciation has to take place. Normally this means a nominal devaluation and very often a currency crisis in which the peg is given up

Although the Latin American countries have been successful in establishing macroeconomic stability for some time now, the question is whether this stability will last or whether a new crisis will occur, thus making new stabilization efforts necessary. Debt is high in some countries; budget deficits in the early 1990s are low with the exception of Brazil. Because of political constraints, too often there are deviations from the stabilization programs. This happens because institutional changes are insufficient to keep the expansion of the money supply at a low level in order to assure a constant money value. The volatility of the price level and of the exchange rate will remain the Damocles sword of Latin America.

Expenditure reduction and expenditure switching

The real exchange rate is an important variable that influences both the equilibrium of the balance of payments and the internal equilibrium of the goods market. As a relative price, it determines absorption, i.e. consumption and investment, production, exports, and imports. If the ratio refers to the prices of foreign and domestic goods, the real exchange rate, i.e. $e_R = eP^*/P$, provides information on the production incentives for domestic goods relative to foreign goods. If the real exchange rate is defined alternatively and if the ratio refers to the prices of tradable and of non-tradable products, i.e. $e_R = eP_T^*/P_{NT}$, the information signal is on incentives for the production of tradables relative to non-tradables.

A case in point are developing countries with a current account deficit, which they have to reduce. Such a situation can be seen in Figure 10.10. The real relative price $eP_T^*/P_{NT,}$ i.e. the real exchange rate (Q_{NT}/Q_T) is given by the tangent of the angle α. The country's production point is D and the consumption point is F. The country absorbs more than would be feasible according to its production conditions. There is a trade deficit between demand and supply of the tradable DF. If the deficit is to be reduced, there are two possible ways.

First, absorption can be reduced (expenditure reduction, movement from F to D). For instance, government demand can be reduced. Higher taxation can cut down private consumption (then, with given relative prices and a homothetic utility function, the point of consumption is on a line OF, not drawn in the figure).

Second, the country could carry out a real devaluation, i.e. the real exchange rate has to increase in order to reduce the deficit of the current account

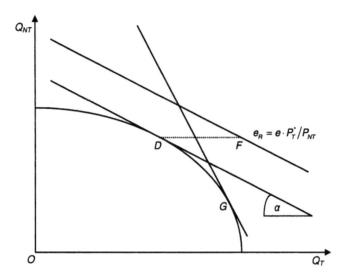

Figure 10.10 The real exchange rate.

(expenditure switching, movement from *D* to *G* along the transformation curve). This implies that the price of tradable goods denominated in national currency rises relative to non-tradable goods resulting in a change of the sector structure in favor of the tradable.

After a real depreciation, it is more profitable to expand the production of tradable goods, and the production of non-tradable goods decreases. Owing to the change of relative prices there is a reallocation of resources towards tradable goods (export goods and import substitutes). The trade account is balanced in point *G*. The production of non-tradable goods has decreased and the production of tradable goods has risen. A real devaluation can be brought about by a nominal devaluation; but it can also be induced when the price for the non-tradable goods falls in the home country while prices for tradables remain constant. A reduction of the current deficit can be brought about by a combination of the expenditure reduction and expenditure switching.

11 China – a new global economic player

What you will understand after reading this chapter

China has enjoyed high annual GDP growth rates of about 10 percent in the last twenty-five years. Exports and investment were the two driving forces (section 11.1). Developing property rights is an important aspect in transforming a communist society (section 11.2). Structural issues such as the state-owned firms and the loss-making of the banking industry have to be solved (section 11.3). Monetary policy is complicated by the accumulation of reserves; China pegs its renmimbi to a currency basket of its main trading partners (section 11.4). Major policy issues in the future include the institutional deficit, especially the rule of law and the lack of democracy (section 11.5). An economic crisis in China would have a severe impact on the world economy (section 11.6). India follows a different policy approach (section 11.7). In the context of the transformation experience of other ex-communist countries, China has not seen the valley of tears as the Central and Eastern European economies (sections 11.8 and 11. 9), including disintegration as of the Soviet Union (section 11.10).

11.1 Characteristics of the Chinese economy

China has enjoyed high average annual GDP growth rates of about 10 percent in the last twenty-five years. It increased its world market share of exports considerably and is now the fourth largest economy of the world.

High GDP growth

China has seen an astonishing development since the Deng Xao Ping reforms starting in 1978. In US dollars, it is now a 1.93 trillion economy with a GDP larger than the UK in 2004 (revised data). It accounts for 4.7 percent of world GDP, representing the world's fourth largest economy. Gross national income at current market prices (GNI) per capita in 2004 was at US$1,290 (non-revised data), somewhat lower than the average of the lower middle-income countries (US$1,580) and at 3 percent of the US level. According to this measure, China ranks at position 132 in the world economy. It is powerful in the aggregate, but still poor in the disaggregate. According to World Bank data, 16.6 percent of the population live below US$1 (PPP) per day (2004)

If instead of current market prices purchasing power parity is used, China's GNI amounts to US$7,170 (non-revised data), the US having a GNI of US$11,655. In this calculation, China's GNI is about 60 percent of that of the US. According to this measure, China accounts for 13 percent of the world's GNI, the US for 21 percent and the euro area for 21.8 percent. GNI per capita is estimated at US$5,530, i.e. at the average level of the lower middle-income countries, and at 14 percent of the US level, standing at US$39,100. Note that purchasing power parity is an indicator of welfare. It can be seen as denoting economic or even political power.

Looking at international statistics of Eastern European countries prior to the fall of the Iron Curtain in 1989, data on China may be subject to political influence. Local politicians do have an incentive to distort data. Moreover, the actual enthusiasm may be due to international hype. In any case, it is difficult to portray such a large economy in some statistical numbers. It is therefore open as to how reliable the data are (Holz 2006).

Analyzing the production side of GDP, industry generates 40.8 percent of GDP, services account for 40.7 percent and the primary sector including agriculture for 13.1 percent (2004, revised data). On the expenditure side, gross capital formation is the dominating component of GDP with 45 percent, household final consumption coming in second with 42 percent and general government final consumption accounting for 12 percent (2004, non-revised data). It is estimated that the share of investment is somewhat lower at 41 percent when the revised data are available for the expenditure side of GDP. The external balance of goods and services accounts for 1 percent of aggregate expenditure (see below).

The driving forces of growth

China has experienced unusually high annual real GDP growth rates of over 9 percent since it started its reform in the late 1970s. In the periods 1979–1990, 1990–2000 and 2000–2004, the growth rates were 9.1, 9.9, and 9.2 percent, respectively (Table 11.1). Real income of people has risen markedly. According to World Bank estimates, poverty was reduced for 400 million people in the past twenty-five years, using the criterion of US$1 per day income. The driving forces for growth were exports and investment.

Export-led growth

Exports represent an important stimulus to the Chinese economy. Looking at merchandise trade, i.e. at the goods that China provides to the world economy (excluding services), China has an unusually high export share in GDP of 36 percent (in 2004). Its merchandise trade balance (merchandise exports minus merchandise imports) is 1.9 percent of GDP. Its current account surplus amounts to US$45.9 billion (Ibid. Table 4), that is 2.8 percent of GDP (2004). As

Table 11.1 China: real growth rates of GDP, investment, FDI, and exports[a]

	1970–1979	1979–1990	1990–2000	2000–2004	1979–2004
GDP[b]	6.1	9.1	9.9	9.2	9.7
Gross capital formation	11.9	8.2	9.8	13.2	10.3
Exports[c]	n.a.	7.4	13.6	24.4	12.5
Memorandum item: Nominal growth rates for FDI[d]	n.a.	31.05	37.98	6.81	32.87

Sources: World Bank, *World Development Online Indicators* April 2006; World Bank, *China Quarterly Update* February 2006.

Notes
a Arithmetic average of annual growth rates (constant 2000 US$ prices).
b Based on revised data including 2005.
c Arithmetic average of growth rates with data from World Development Indicators.
d Based on nominal inward cash flows calculated in current US$.

mentioned above, the external balance of goods and services (exports of goods and services minus imports of goods and services) in the macroeconomic accounts is given with 1 percent of GDP (World Bank 2005d: Table 3).

The difference between these three balance concepts can be explained by several factors. First, the three concepts mean different things. The merchandise trade balance does not include services. Services in the trade and service balance of the expenditure approach in the macroeconomic accounts are measured differently from services in the balance of payments. Thus, the current account includes some services such as interest payments that are not included in the external balance. The current account also reflects unilateral remittances from abroad. Second, data are from different sources, from the World Development Report and from the country fact sheets. Both are produced by the World Bank, but these sources diverge.

China has a world market share of 6.5 percent, measured in terms of merchandise trade. Nearly all merchandise trade is produced in the manufacturing sector (91 percent). China is considered to be the manufacturing workshop of the world. Amazingly, its exports do not only consist of low technology products. One-quarter of its merchandise exports (27 percent) are high technology exports. According to the World Bank classification, China is playing in the same league as Finland (24 percent), Japan (24), Korea (32), the Netherlands (31), the United Kingdom (26), and the US (31).

Chinese exports, a strong driver for the economy, rose at a high real rate of 12.5 percent since 1979 while world exports expanded at 7 percent in same period. In calculating the increase in the volume of exports, the problem arises which price deflator should be used to correct the nominal export figures given in renmimbi. Usually, the trade deflator for goods published by the Customs

Administration is applied. In comparisons with other countries, the US GDP deflator is used.

This increase in the trade volume is not unprecedented. It is below the rates of increase of other newly industrializing economies (NIEs), for instance Japan, Korea, and the four tigers. Setting an export index in 1979 for China equal to 1 and comparing it to an export index also of 1 for Japan in 1955, China's real exports in the period 1979–2002 increased at a lower rate than the exports of Japan (Figure 11.1). A similar result holds, when Korea with the initial year 1965 and the four tigers (Hong Kong, Korea, Singapore, and Taiwan) with 1966 are considered (Prasad 2004: Figure 2.3).

China has used its entry into the WTO in 2001 and the required adjustment to the WTO standards as means to restructure its economy. WTO membership requires the dismantling of non-tariff barriers. Although this hurts certain sectors, trade liberalization helps the country in its structural adjustment. Thus, WTO membership improves China's export conditions and enables it to continue its export-led growth. Whereas implementing a WTO-consistent institutional arrangement in intellectual property rights, safeguards procedures and standards will hurt some of China's exports, WTO membership reinforces confidence for international investors and makes China a favorable destination for foreign investment.

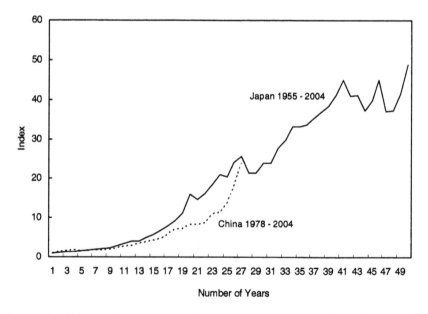

Figure 11.1 China and Japan: comparative export growth[a] (source: WTO, *WTO Online Statistical Database* April 2006; IMF *International Financial Statistics*, Online Database, April 2006; own calculations).

Notes

a Deflated by the US GDP-deflator and indexed, basis year = 1. Japan 1995, China 1978.

Investment – the other driving force

Gross capital formation is unusually high at over 40 percent of GDP (2004). Annual average growth rates of gross capital formation amounted to 10.3 percent in the period 1979–2004 (Table 11.1). It is through this new capital that the economy is restructured, that new firms are born, new technologies are embodied in new machines, and new products are introduced into the product set of the economy. New capital embodies more modern technology. Investment together with exports modernizes the economy through learning-by-doing processes. At the same time, labor productivity is raised. Capital accumulation and total factor productivity growth contribute about 4.5 percentage points each to the GDP growth rate of about 10 percent in the early 2000s, with about one percentage point coming from employment growth (IMF Country Report 2005: 12). Marginal capital productivity is at about 13 percent, after about 16 percent in the 1990s. Capital accumulation is one of the important vehicles for growth. Labor productivity in terms of GDP per worker has increased at an annual average of between 7 and 8 percent in the early 2000s, with productivity growth coming half from capital intensity and half from total factor productivity (Ibid).

The falling capital productivity can be regarded as a sign of inefficient investment. The incremental capital output ratio, i.e. the investment need per additional unit of output, has risen from three in the 1980s to 4.5 in the early 1990s. This indicates that more capital is needed to produce additional output. There are also signs of over-investment in several sectors, creating a distortion in the economy that will have to be corrected in the future with pain. When over-expansion is corrected, unemployment will rise. A reason behind overheating is the high money and credit growth.

China's economic growth process exhibits a stark sector change. Agriculture declined from a 32 percent share in GDP in 1984 to below 12.5 percent in 2005 (this is the figure for the total primary sector, revised data, World Bank 2005a, 2006a). Industry expanded from a share of 43.3 percent in GDP in 1984 to 47.8 percent in 1994 and to 52.9 percent in 2004, according to un-revised data. According to the revised data, industry is estimated at 40.8 in 2004; it has held that percentage more or less since 1993. The service sector expanded from 24.7 percent in 1984 to 31.9 percent in 2004 un-revised data; according to the new data, the service sector is given with 40.2 percent. In terms of employment, the primary sector declined from 68.7 percent of total employment in 1980 to 50 in 2002 (non revised data) whereas the secondary sector increased from 18.2 percent to 21.4 percent and the tertiary sector from 13.1 percent to 28.6 percent in the same period (Prasad 2004: 55).

Migration of growth clusters and labor

China has seen a north- and westward migration of its growth clusters. Starting in the coastal regions of the south, economic dynamics has spread to the other regions through backward linkages. These were the production of intermediate inputs and migratory workers. It is estimated that the number of rural labor migrants rose to around sixty million in 2000, ninety-four million in 2002, and 114 million in 2003 (Ping and Shaohua 2005). These workers migrated from the interior to the coastal growth poles. Regional disparity can be regarded as the key cause of labor flows. Eventually, the growth clusters themselves started to migrate to the West.

Entrepreneurship

An important condition for growth is the entrepreneurial spirit of the Chinese. They have been traders historically; they enjoy accumulating family wealth. These characteristics together with the traditional value orientation are a sturdy basis for entrepreneurship and represent powerful incentives for effort and growth. Entrepreneurship is the essential driving force for economic growth and development, as Schumpeter (1943) has stressed in his book *Capitalism, Socialism and Democracy*.

Resource inflows and the balance of payments

China has had a surplus in the current and the capital and financial account for many years. It accumulates reserves (Table 6.2). The capital and financial account includes foreign direct investment and portfolio flows. In 2004, capital inflows of US$54.9 billion were foreign direct investment (3.3 percent of GDP and about 7 percent of gross capital formation); in 2003, US$52.8 billion were foreign direct investment (again approximately the same percentage of GDP). FDI inwards in 2005 was US$60 billion. It is estimated that FDI in 2006 has the same magnitude. In addition to the ample supply of domestic capital due to the high savings rate, China succeeds in attracting foreign capital, and very often this also includes modern technology, management, and market access in foreign countries. Some economists question the need of such a high capital inflow. However, 7 percent of gross capital formation does not seem extraordinarily high.

In 2004, both the current account and the capital and financial account had a surplus of US$179.5 billion (10.6 percent of GDP). Taking into account errors and omissions, China accumulated US$206.1 billion of reserves in that year. In 2003, the current account and the capital and financial account together had a surplus of US$143.6 billion. If US$45 billion used for the recapitalization of the banking system are subtracted, the surplus is reduced to US$ 98.6 billion.

China's open door policy for foreign direct investment used joint ventures between foreign investors, i.e. multinationals, and state-owned enterprises in its early stage. Now whole ownership by foreign investors is allowed. Foreign owners can buy out their Chinese partners. Meanwhile, China's new strategy now also includes foreign direct investment abroad. Its outward FDI in 2005 amounted to US$6 billion; it is used to acquire foreign enterprises and build-up Chinese multinationals.

Table 11.2 China's current and capital account balances

	Current balance	Capital and account financial account balance	Errors and omissions[a]	Increase in gross official reserves
Annual average				
1990–2004	+15.2	+18.0	−10.6	+22.6
2003[b]	+45.9	+52.8[b]	+18.0	+116.7
2004	+68.6	+110.7	+26.8	+206.1
2005[c]	+129	+138 [d]	−	+204

Sources: IMF, *International Financial Statistics,* Online Database, January 2006; own calculation; World Bank, *China Quarterly Update* February 2006.

Notes
a Includes counterpart transaction to valuation changes.
b 2003 figure includes the counterpart transaction to the US$ 45 billion of foreign exchange reserves used for bank recapitalization. With this figure, the capital and financial balance would show a surplus of US$ 162 billion.
c Estimate.
d Including errors and omissions.

11. 2 Property rights

Changes in property rights are crucial in transforming a communist society into a market economy. China has developed its property rights in a step by step fashion. Property rights are far from their interpretation in market economies.

First, China introduced land use rights for peasants (outside the collective) in the Deng Xao Ping reforms. With these reforms and freeing prices for some crops, agricultural output rose considerably. Land use rights are leases on the use of land. They are granted for thirty years. According to the Land Management Law of 1998, a contract between the collective land owner and the private farm household defines the rights and duties of both parties (Article 14). A secondary market for land use rights exists; it has been constitutionalized in 1988 (de Lisle 2004). Peasants can rent out the land, although having to pay a fee to the village administration. Permission is needed. Extension of the land use may be possible.

However, land use rights do not comprise full ownership. Land cannot be sold, it cannot be mortgaged. Although land readjustments are restricted (Article 14), peasants are not protected when the land is allocated to expanding firms or is needed for residential construction. Compensation, if any, is low; for rural land it is at about one-tenth of the market value. De facto local bureaucrats have ultimate control and ownership of rural land. Since peasants cannot negotiate directly with locating firms and developers, they cannot use the proceeds from selling land for investment in firms and for moving to the city. Not allowing the marketization of rural land impedes the reduction of rural poverty and hinders structural change. Apparently, there are ideological constraints in creating property rights. Establishing a rural land-owning class would undo the Mao reforms in which rural land owners were expropriated; quite a few of them were executed.

Second, municipalities were allowed to open up firms (township and village enterprises). Under conditions controlled by the party, land can be used for industrial purposes. Nevertheless, township and village enterprises, representing collectives, remain under the control of local officials and several supervisory bodies. China knows a variety of ownerships for firms, including local collective ownership, private-public partnerships and private ownership. Foreigners, including multinationals, can own enterprises. Enterprise ownership is linked to the ownership of land and thus hinges on the permission of the party officials. Private ownership depends on the sector of the economy and on provinces and localities. If an entrepreneur has good connections with the local government, land use rights may not be limited in time. When there is a change in leadership, the contract may be void. The relationship of the former leader and the current leader is crucial. However, the local government has the right to take over your property whenever they like; there is no way to prevent this. Entrepreneurs have been expropriated if they do not have a land use title, even when the shares of their firm were already transacted in Wall Street.

Third, China allows the conversion of agricultural land into residential uses for individuals. In contrast to rural land, most of urban housing is now privately owned; residential leases run for seventy years (some for fifty or forty years). Property owners elect their landlord committees in order to protect their property against local party politicians.

All these property rights can be bequeathed (within the limited period they are granted). Property rights may be extended.

Property rights are far from being clearly defined; neither are they strong. The characteristics of property rights have simply followed what is needed for high growth. A crucial constraint is that the new rights established do not jeopardize the position of the party.

Property rights are rarely respected when an expanding firm needs new location space, when a private investor puts up new residential structures, and when the government pursues an infrastructure project. A pay compensation requirement with respect to real estate was to be written into the constitution (planned in 2004). Implementation of the property rights system and of individual claims is, however, far from being established. Compensation is controlled by the state. Corruption is prevalent, the court system is in development, legal advise is scarce. The rule of law is one of China's institutional deficits. A clear bankruptcy law that would sort out property claims in the case of economic failure also does not exit.

A property right seems to exist as long as it justified by economic success. This form of adjustable property right may be appropriate to the Chinese situation where everything is in flux. Apparently, these adaptable property rights create enough certainty for people to invest in the initial periods of transformation of China when expected yields are high. They are likely not to be sufficient later on when yields become somewhat lower; lower yields require more certainty. The approach to property rights is also the result of a process of transforming a communist society in which property rights are not supposed to exist. Witness President Jiang Zemin's doctrine of the 'Three Represents' according to which the entrepreneurial class – usually the class with private property – is to be included into the communist party.

With its entry to the WTO, China has taken over the obligation to respect intellectual property. Its laws and regulation must be amended so that they are in conformity with the 'Agreement on Trade-Related Aspects of Intellectual Property' (TRIPs). This applies to patents, trademarks, and copyrights including production technologies, fashion and audio, and video products. It requires that the Chinese government forcefully fights product pirates.

11.3 Structural issues

State-owned enterprises

State-owned enterprises account for less than one-third of GDP (in 2005, *The Economist* 2006).They do not include municipal firms that are counted as private. Another source quotes 38 percent of GDP for the state-owned firms (Pei 2006). The bulk of the non-state sector are municipal enterprises. There are only forty private firms among the 1,520 companies listed on domestic and foreign exchanges (Ibid). The state is the monopolist or the dominant player in the most important sectors, namely in steel, automobiles, energy, transportation, and in the service sectors of banking and telecommunication.

State-owned enterprises make losses and are over indebted; they have to be restructured or given up. This means unemployment and a lacking insurance coverage for the unemployed in the case of illness and during old age, representing a potential area of severe future conflict.

In the past, China's policy has been to circumvent the restructuring of state-owned firms simply by letting new activities develop. In this way, the relative importance of state-owned firms declined. Due to the new firms, the J-curve effect with a valley of tears and a decline of GDP, experienced by the post-communist countries of Central and Eastern Europe, was prevented (see below). The losses of the state-owned firms are covered by credits from state-owned banks which are under pressure from local politicians to provide financial support to them. Eventually, the loans will become non-performing.

The banking sector

Banks are state-owned, for instance the four big commercial banks. Foreign ownership is limited to 25 percent. Loans of the state-owned banks are given to state-owned firms and thus lead to unproductive use. Moreover, banks are under pressure from local politicians to provide credits to municipal and state-owned firms. Fully functioning bond and equity markets are not yet developed. More than half of investment is self-financed.

The Chinese banking system is fragile. Liquidity is high, banks hold excessive reserves and inter-bank interest rates are low. The stock of the banking system's non-performing loans is estimated to have amounted to about 40 percent of GDP in 2004 (Blanchard and Giavazzi 2005). Other sources estimate the percentage of total bad loans in GDP at 21 and – with a higher legacy – to 56 percent (Roubini and Setser 2005: Tables 1 and 2). According to the IMF, the proportion of non-performing loans to GDP has fallen in 2005. Recapitalizing the banks while assuming a recovery rate of 20 percent would add 30 percentage points to the debt GDP ratio, bringing it up to 55 points (Blanchard and Giavazzi 2005).

Banking deposits are the main form of saving. Apparently, the Chinese saver has confidence in the banks, in spite of their fragile situation. Recapitalizing the state-owned financials institutions from time to time adds credibility to the financial system. It cannot be ruled out that this credibility will be lost instantaneously at some time in the future and a bank run follows.

Even if banks were advised by the central government to learn to make money, the local party leader would pressure the banker to provide credit to the state-owned and municipal enterprises. Consequently, the banking system represents a risk factor in development. A bank failure and a bank run have to be prevented. From time to time, the government has to recapitalize the state banks with sizable amounts. In 1998, the government spent US$32.6 billion (about 3.5 percent of GDP) in order to safeguard the four existing wholly state-owned commercial banks (Prasad 2004). In 1999–2000 the government injected about US$169.1 billion (RMB1.4 trillion) or 14 percent of GDP via state-owned asset management companies into the financial sector in order to clear the balance sheet of the state-owned commercial banks (Ibid); bad loans in the order of US$ 168 billion were taken off the banking system's books in 1999 and given to four asset management companies (Roubini and Setser 2005). In 2003, US$45 billion – about 4 percent of GDP – were used for the same purpose. The People's Bank of China transferred the amount to a holding company in order to recapitalize two of the four state-owned banks (China Construction Bank and the Bank of China). The banks will not convert these assets into renmimbi and instead retain them as international reserves. This means that the risks in the central bank's balance sheet increase. In 2005, an amount of US$15 billion was given to the Industrial and Commercial Bank of China. Problems with non-performing loans also exist in rural credit cooperatives and smaller city commercial banks.

Thus, China uses its international reserves to clean up the balance sheets of its banks. It is amazing that China's reserves relative to GDP amount to a similar proportion as the non-performing loans of the state banks. Viewed this way, its international reserves represent an insurance against a failure of the banking system. Following this view, it is less justified to condemn China's accumulation of international currency reserves.

After 2006, China will have to admit foreign banks according to its WTO commitment. Then Chinese banks must be competitive, at least a major part of them. Whereas this means that China will have to open its banking industry, it does not imply that the capital account will be fully liberalized (see below).

One option to continuing the piecemeal approach of cleaning up the banks' balance sheets from time to time would consist in an explicit policy of improving the risk management of banks, thus strengthening the banking system's balance sheet. This would mean getting old non-performing loans out of the system and preventing new ones from arising. This policy would conflict with the still important role of loss-making state-owned enterprises and the party's pressure at the local level. Another alternative is to follow a good bank–bad bank policy as Japan did in its crisis in the 1990s and put all the losses into one or several institutions (which the government would have to recapitalize from time to time). The good banks could then become competitive banks, striving even for competitiveness internationally. This option can go together with separating deposit taking and lending institutionally, for instance turning the existing banks with non-performing loans into closed mutual funds, holding assets of state-owned firms. The government would have to take over some of the write-offs of the assets; still the assets may be risky for the public audience. Finally, capital markets with reliance on equity capital have to be developed in order to reduce the role of the banking system.

Regional imbalances

It is not surprising that such the strong economic growth was not uniform in China's regions. Strong growth tends to be unbalanced. A strong dynamic prevails in the urban centers, especially those of the coastal regions, whereas the west and the north are not growing as strongly. There is a stark divide between the urban centers and the countryside. Migration of rural workers and the movement of the growth centers inwardly alleviate this structural problem over time.

Unemployment

Unemployment is high, given the high GDP growth rate. The urban unemployment rate is estimated at about 5 percent (Prasad 2004: 52). Surplus labor in the rural areas amounts to about 150 million. 60 percent of the population lives in the rural areas.

A distorted economy

Imbalances can be seen as a vehicle to achieving high growth. But at the same time, they imply serious adjustment costs and the risk of a crisis. The strong expansion of the export sector requires sector readjustment later on, the investment boom may have to be corrected at high costs, the real estate boom may end in a bubble that bursts and a banking crisis may have a serious impact on the real side of the economy. Major distortions arise from falsely set prices due to institutional conditions: prices for credit, land, energy, and the environment – some also argue for the renmimbi – are too low, leading to a distorted allocation (Roubini and Setser 2005). For instance, cheap credits favor capital relative to labor and lead to substituting labor through capital; they imply an investment and a real estate boom.

11.4 Monetary, fiscal, and exchange rate policy

Money supply and inflation

The money supply (broad money according to the IMF definition) has been growing in the range of 13.1 percent to 19.6 percent in the period 2000–2005 (IMF 2005c: Table 4; World Bank 2006a: Table 1). Domestic credit has been expanding at a similar annual average rate (16 percent for 2000–2004), the rates fluctuating between 9.2 (in 2004) and 29.3 percent (in 2002). Consumer price inflation, being mainly driven by food prices, was between 0.26 percent (in 2000) and 3.99 percent (in 2004). These recent inflation rates are much lower on average and are far less volatile compared to the previous decade and a half for which data are available. Whereas the inflation rate stood at 18.3 percent in 1989, only one year later it had fallen to a comparably low 3.1 percent, then reaching its maximum of 24.2 percent in 1994. Inflation pressures may arise in the future, for instance when wage demands of workers surface, when environmental costs are felt, and when energy becomes more expansive and other constraints materialize.

The high current account surpluses and large capital and portfolio inflows make an independent monetary policy difficult. These surpluses increase outside money. The Chinese Central Bank, the Peoples Bank of China, purchases foreign exchange and builds up reserves. In the period 1993–2005 the annual average build-up of reserves amounted to US$61 billion; in the years 2001 to 2005 it was US$131 billion. And from 2003 to 2005 the yearly build-up actually exceeded the value of US$200 billion. The bank's international reserves stood at US$819 billion in December 2005 (a little less than Japan), accounting for 40 percent of GDP (in 2004). The accumulation of reserves can be seen as swapping Chinese export goods for US Treasuries and other papers; these papers are under the risk of losing value with an appreciation of the renmimbi.

Since there is the need to sterilize monetary expansion, the Bank of China sells sterilization bonds to the state-owned banks. From 2003 to 2004 the stock of sterilization papers increased by about 265 percent, from 2004 to 2005 it increased by about 88 percent or by a value of US$117 billion – reaching a value of US$250 billion for the overall stock of bonds (other data in Roubini and Setser 2005). However, this vast increase covers only slightly more than half of the increase in reserves. Not all of the outside money can be sterilized; thus there is an increase in liquidity showing up in low inter-bank interest rates and the strong increase in credits.

Capital flows are controlled. Whereas current account convertibility exists since 1996, the capital account has not been liberalized. In April 2006, the permission for domestic institutional investors to complete transactions outside China was introduced; private citizens can buy foreign currency up to

US$20,000 instead of US$6,000. Only authorized institutions are allowed to perform transactions in foreign currency. China follows a cautious and gradual approach to capital account liberalization. Given the fragility of the banking system, this approach is appropriate. The Asian crisis and other currency disruptions, for instance in Sweden in 1992, have shown that it is risky to liberalize the capital account when the banking sector is not sufficiently regulated and when foreign exchange rates are rigid and financial markets underdeveloped, for instance when an equity market is lacking. It is therefore reasonable to first regulate the banking sector and make it robust. Moreover, the foreign exchange rate can be made flexible prior to capital account liberalization. It would also be risky to introduce resident's convertibility immediately and fully. Market participants would then place their money abroad looking for higher rates of return and for a diversified risk. That is why the option to introduce mutual funds that can absorb the savings of Chinese households, including entrepreneurs, is discussed (see above).

China uses a peg for the renmimbi. Since June 21, 2005 the renmimbi is no longer tied to the US dollar only, but to a basket consisting of the US dollar, the euro, the yen, and the Korean won. In addition, the Singapore dollar, the British pound, the Malaysian ringgit, the Australian dollar, the Russian rouble, the Thai baht, and the Canadian dollar are taken into consideration. The weights of the currencies in the basket are not disclosed by the Chinese central bank; they are supposed to reflect the importance of China's trading partners. Disclosure of the weights would allow speculators to guess where the renmimbi might be in the future and when the central bank is likely to intervene.

China's medium-term strategy seems to achieve a greater mix and a better return for its high international currency reserves. Such a reorientation would benefit the euro and would put the US dollar under pressure.

The nominal and the real effective exchange rate of the renmimbi depreciated sharply through the 1980s and the early 1990s. The nominal rate (renmimbi to the US dollar) depreciated from 1.5 in 1980 to 8.62 in 1994 (Figure 11.2). The real effective exchange rate index (which is the index of the inverse of the IMF's real exchange rate index) rose from thirty-three in January 1980 to 150 in June 1993, with 2000 set equal to 100 (in contrast to the index used by the IMF an increase in this index means a depreciation). This development is consistent with China's transition to a market economy and its opening up for trade, including the sizable reduction in import tariffs. Since 1994, the renmimbi appreciated relative to the US dollar until 1998, i.e. the renmimbi/dollar rate fell, and then was kept steady at 8.28 until 2004. In 2005, the renmimbi appreciated by 2.6 percent to a rate of 8.07. This looks like a soft crawling peg to the US dollar. In real terms, the renmimbi appreciated from 1993 until 2001, then depreciated, and appreciated again in 2005. The revision of the macroeconomic data from December 2005 indicate that real appreciation was ten percentage points higher than previously estimated (World Bank 2006a: 21).

During the Asian financial crisis in 1997, China kept the nominal rate to the US dollar steady, whereas the real exchange rate appreciated. This was due to

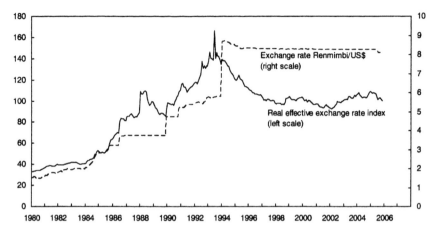

Figure 11.2 Renmimbi: the nominal and real exchange rate[a] (source: IMF, *International Financial Statistics* March 2006; own calculation).

Note
[a] Monthly values.

the fact that the other Asian currencies depreciated heavily relative to US dollar and consequently also to the renmimbi.

There is no reason why the renmimbi should not be more flexible. In the presence of large current account surpluses and capital inflows, exchange rate flexibility would help to pursue an independent monetary policy. However, it is unclear in which direction a flexible renmimbi would go. This question is related to the heavily debated issue of whether the renmimbi is undervalued.

In this debate, an undervaluation of the renmimbi is seen as having the advantage to stimulate exports and to be a strong impulse for investment and growth and at the same time a vehicle for structural change. The disadvantage would lie in a higher inflation rate since inflation is imported with an undervalued currency. Moreover, an undervaluation means higher renmimbi prices for agricultural products since these products are quoted in US dollars, and China is a price taker. This in turn implies a lower real income of industrial workers. Furthermore, the sector structure would be distorted in favor of the export industry. Adjustment costs could arise in having to correct this distorted allocation later on. Finally, a future depreciation of the reserve currency, especially the US dollar, would mean that the value of accumulated international reserves would be partially lost. Moreover, the renmimbi value of the state's bank capital (denominated in US dollars) falls; the banks' capital to asset ratio is reduced (Roubini and Setser 2005). Of course an undervalued currency would have negative effects on China's immediate competitors, among them Pakistan, Egypt, and the Maghreb states.

Economic forces pull the exchange rate in different directions (Table 11.3). Some forces clearly work in favor of an appreciation. Following the trade flow view, an increase in labor productivity and improved access to foreign markets generates pressures for appreciation. Moreover, the trade account surplus is seen to suggest an appreciation. Often, the bilateral current account surplus with the US is used as an argument. However, as already discussed in Chapter 6, China's 2004 bilateral trade deficit with the US only amounts to US$80 billion (and US$111 billion including Hong Kong); the figure is not too different from the bilateral surpluses of the EU, Japan, and the oil-exporting countries. This suggests that a unilateral appreciation of the renmimbi by China would not solve the US problem. Reducing regulations that impede imports works in favor of a depreciation.

Following the capital flow view, labor productivity growth and improved market access would also operate in favor of an apppreciation, making China more attractive for foreign capital. This would also hold if a more reliable rule of law would be introduced. Other factors would work in favor of a depreciation, among them a too-high inflation rate (representing a real appreciation but requiring a depreciation) and a liberalization of the capital account. Thus, residents' convertibility with a future outflow of domestic savings would increase demand for US dollars (and euro) and would imply an increased supply of the renmimbi, dragging its value down. Thus, the existing capital controls for residents imply an overvalued renmimbi. In terms of macroeconomic equilibrium, lacking full employment can be interpreted to indicate that internal equilibrium is not fully established, indicating the need to depreciate.

Economic models run into difficulties in accommodating all these and other factors, including expectations. Applying the approach used by Wang (2004) for determining the medium-term path of the real exchange rate (see Chapter 6), one may conclude that the renmimbi is not substantially undervalued (Wang 2004: 25).[1] Existing studies come up with a wide range of estimates of under valuation, ranging from 0 to nearly 50 percent (Dunaway and Li 2005). Different methods used, diverse explanatory variables included, and instability in the empirical underlying economic functions in a rapidly growing development country are reasons for the difference in estimates.

Table 11.3 Factors influencing the renmimbi exchange rate

	Appreciation	*Depreciation*
Trade flow view	Productivity growth of the export sector	Inflation
	Access to foreign markets	Unemployment
	Trade surplus	
Capital flow view	Labor productivity growth in the export sector (larger capital inflows)	Resident's convertibility
	More certainty in the rule of law, respect of property rights	Political uncertainty

Fiscal policy

The public budget deficit has been in the range of 1–3 percent of GDP in the period 1999–2005, for instance 1.1 percent in 2006 (forecast). Fiscal policy was slightly expansionary. Subsidies to state-owned enterprises make up 1 percent of GDP. Public debt stands at about 24 percent of GDP (2004). Although this is low compared to other economies, implicit liabilities of the state are high if a system of social insurance with health payments and pensions would be developed, if the rural-urban divide would mandate additional expenditures of the government to keep social unrest from exploding, and when eventually environmental degradation will have to be amended. Explicit and implicit debt are estimated at 49 percent (IMF Staff Report China 2005: 42). Moreover, center-local fiscal relations are crucial. The central government provides transfers to local governments. Local authorities borrow through public enterprises, thus circumventing the formal ban on direct borrowing. Clearly, implicit liabilities arising in this way have to be limited.

11.5 Chinese policy issues in the future

The crucial issue for the future is whether the growth process of the last twenty-five years is sustainable. The high savings rate, entrepreneurship, the migration of the growth clusters to the west, surplus labor, the expansion of the real estate and construction sector, and exports will all be drivers of growth. Moreover, China seeks to move out of its position of low-cost producer by pushing into high-value lines of production by improving its research and human capital formation. As opposing forces, structural issues and bottlenecks will represent constraints for the growth process. The structural problems already discussed such as the inefficiencies and capital losses of the state-owned firms and the fragility of the banking sector will continue. Other weaknesses will come to the fore, such as the bottlenecks in infrastructure, environmental degradation, and a stronger demand for energy. Yet another major area is inadequate social security. Finally, the weak institutional fundamentals can affect growth dynamics. The institutional deficits are likely to be more relevant for the sustainability of the growth process than the economic bottlenecks.

Infrastructure

Congestion in infrastructure is likely to arise. In order to keep congestion costs from increasing excessively, more funds will have to be invested into infrastructure projects which tend to have a lower capital productivity than investment in the private sector.

Safety and environmental constraints

China will have to pay more attention to accidents at the workplace and in industrial production, for instance in the chemical industry. Moreover, environmental constraints will make themselves felt more and more. Toxic industrial dumping in the countryside has to be halted; toxic dumps have to be amended. Air and water pollution and the deterioration of the soil become less and less acceptable with rising income. They cause social costs in terms of serious health damages. All these factors will increase the costs of production. Moreover, China as an international player will eventually want to be part of multilateral solutions to global environmental problems such as reducing CO_2 emissions.

Energy

Energy intensity has to be reduced. Retail gasoline prices are still lower than those in the US. The cheap energy helps to keep inflation in check, but it distorts energy use. China's appetite for energy and raw materials will drive up world market prices and this will increase energy and resource costs for China itself. China's oil demand is projected by the Energy Information Administration to more than double and reach 14.2 million barrels per day by 2025, with net imports of 10.9 million barrels per day. Furthermore, China is both the largest consumer and producer of coal in the world. It should be mentioned that China faces major energy-related environmental problems. According to the World Health Organization, seven out of the ten most polluted cities in the world are in China.

Labor

Registered unemployment in urban centers and townships has increased due to the restructuring of state-owned firms. The excess of rural workers is estimated at 150 million. About ten million new workers are joining the work force each year. Eventually labor will become more scarce.

Social policy

Protection against health hazards and old-age pension insurance is inadequate. With the decline of the old state-owned enterprises, which provided such an insurance, a mixed system has developed where, for instance, part of the health costs are covered by firms, but a large part is self-paid. In 1988, 44.1 percent of health costs in the cities were estimated to be self-paid. In the countryside the percentage is much higher at 87.4 percent (Blanchard and Giavazzi 2005: Table 10). The inadequate insurance arrangements for health and old-age are one of the reasons for high savings. The private savings needed as a substitute for insurance are inferior in terms of efficiency to an insurance solution. Health insurance, for instance, can be provided more efficiently, if a large quantity of people with different health risks are insured. Apparently, China has different options other than following the European social model. However, contingent liabilities of the state-owned firms from healthcare and from pensions may add to public debt. The need to develop a social insurance system will put a burden on the public budget, increase debt, and require higher taxes.

The growing inequality in income distribution and the rural–urban divide represents a severe risk for the power of the communist party. Discontent among peasants for reasons of relative low income, high costs of healthcare, insufficient pensions in old age, and arbitrary decisions of bureaucrats with respect to land use rights including arbitrary local levies may lead to social unrest in the countryside that traditionally has played an important role in political changes in China. Massive lay-offs in the rust belt, toxic industrial dumping affecting farming, fishing, and water, and industrial accidents add to the unrest. Social upheaval can threaten the ruling party. That is why rulers fear the Latin-Americanization of the country.

Another growth paradigm

It can be argued that the unbalanced growth in China (exports and investment instead of consumption, foreign direct investment instead of financing from domestic savings, credit expansion in favor of production, production and investment instead of social protection, pollution in favor of production, stimulation of urban centers relative to rural areas) cannot be sustained and that another growth strategy with less distortions is required (Roubini and Setser 2005). In any case, too-low scarcity prices for land, capital, energy, and the environment have to be corrected through institutional changes.

Demographic challenge

The aging of the population will aggravate these social policy issues in the future. Public health insurance and old age insurance will be more difficult to organize when the median age of the population increases. The systems are harder to finance and the economy is likely to become less dynamic with an older population.

Corruption

When rules and institutional frameworks for economic decisions are lacking and when bureaucratic decisions take their place, decisions become arbitrary. Informal relationships, family networks, or networks of friends take the place of rules. Those who have the power to decide can hand out favors, usually against some compensation. Corruption is the unavoidable outcome.

Rule of law

An efficient economic system requires a reliable institutional frame of reference. Many decisions of economic agents need a long-run orientation with reliable rules. Arbitrary decisions by bureaucrats, party officials, or government counter this requirement. The rule of law therefore is a necessary requirement for a sustained growth process. An important aspect of the rule of law is that rights are given to private firms and households and that the holders of these rights can enforce them. This calls for corruption to be pushed back. In addition, the communist party has to withdraw from intervening in administrative and court decisions. Rules must be stable in order to be credible.

The demand for a stable institutional set-up is not a sufficient condition for strong growth; economic freedom for the individual to decide his or her affairs is another necessary stipulation. This mandates that the party defines a decision space for the private sector, guaranteeing economic freedom. To respect the dignity of man goes beyond the demand for economic freedom. All of these requirements can limit the power of the party.

Democratic challenge

The actual Chinese system of governance has been described as neo-Leninist state, blending a one-party rule and state control of key sectors of the economy with market mechanism and an open economy (Pei 2006). Patronage secures support from key constituents, including the bureaucracy, the military, and the business community.

It is an open question to what extent economic freedom will start a process in which citizens will eventually demand political freedom. A major aspect is that economic agents will insist on the right to elect those who make the laws governing economic freedom. Whether this demand will be forcefully articulated in China in the future cannot be answered at this stage.

One answer is that the Chinese derive an immense happiness from being and becoming rich and will be satisfied (for a long time) with a situation in which the political party just lets them get rich. Then economic freedom is all there is. In this scenario, the government is more or less authoritarian. The disintegration of the Soviet Union is seen as a negative example by the Chinese party.

Another answer is that the communist party will introduce some cautious steps towards decentralized democratic procedures, for instance letting mayors be elected on a decentralized level. Among the political leaders there is fear that the communist party will fall apart and that the country will break up. Again, the disintegration of the Soviet Union serves as negative example. The result may be a cautious attempt of controlled capitalism, which then may serve as a prototype for other countries, for instance the Arab oil countries and some developing countries. The least likely case is the third answer, a full move towards democracy, Western style.

Apparently, economic fundamentals may impact on the political system and vice versa. Thus, in generating Chinese multinationals, the issue arises how China's products are viewed outside China and whether their image includes the characteristics of freedom. Social inequality may lead to political unrest. Lower growth rates may put the political system into question. And political turmoil may jeopardize the economic growth dynamics of the past.

An unstable China, for instance with a growing unrest of the rural population, will represent a threat to the world. Political rulers may then be tempted to play with nationalist sentiment to bolster legitimacy.

Taiwan

Taiwan may be a bone of contention in international relations in the future, especially when China is becoming more powerful economically and will be challenging the leading economic and political position of the US.

Hard or soft landing

It is likely that constraints, such as the increased energy demand, environmental degradation, the need to introduce some social insurance, and the potential necessity to take equity into consideration, will affect the growth rate. They clearly represent risk factors. From a political management point of view, all these constraints may be seen as issues that can be solved in a technocratic way if political leaders have sufficient wisdom. But more constraints mean less growth. This would mean a lower growth rate of say 6 percent annually in the next twenty years. The movement of workers from the low-paid regions in the west to the urban centers in the east may continue for some while, raising labor productivity. However, capital moving from the east to the west may find lower profitability there. Besides the constraints, the growth prospects depend on whether China can keep up, or even raise, the increase in total factor productivity by a continuous stream of original innovations.

A scenario for the next twenty-five years could be as follows. China grows at a rate of 6 percent per year, the US at 2.5 percent. The world grows at 3.5. Using the revised GDP data, putting China at 4.7 percent of world GDP (in 2004) and the US at 28.4 percent (in 2005), China would be at 8.5 percent of world GDP, the US at 22.1, using market prices. Thus, in twenty-five years China would represent 38 percent of the US GDP, compared to 16.6 percent in 2005. The economic core of the world economy is slowly, but steadily, moving towards China. Of course, such calculations are highly questionable. Economic growth knows booms and busts, i.e. a constant growth rate is unlikely, even in a stable political environment.

A hard landing in form of crisis cannot be excluded. Such a crisis may come from the banking system, when non-performing loans can no longer be covered by accumulated reserves. It may arise from the real side of the economy, if over-investment and a distorted capital stock force major readjustment. It may also appear if the world economy moves into a slump and if Chinese exports have to compete with other countries in a situation of oversupply. This then could feed into a capital flow reversal with FDI no longer flowing in; eventually a financial crisis may arise. Furthermore, a crisis could emerge from an energy price shock, for instance if an oil price shock that would cut China off its needed energy inputs. Last not least, a political crisis could spillover to the economy.

11.6 China's impact

As the world's fourth largest economy, China will have its impact in Asia and on the world economy. Together with Japan, it is already the economic hub of

Asia. More than half of its imports come from Asia (52.8 percent in 2003), of which 18.0 percent from Japan (Rumbaugh and Blancher 2004: Table 2.2). It accounts for an import share of 6 percent of the world's total imports (2004). A reduced growth in China would affect growth elsewhere, especially in Asia. A one-time decline in China's imports by ten percentage points, being consistent with an initial fall in GDP growth by 2.9 percentage points and in investment growth by 5.5 percentage points in real terms, is expected to reduce GDP growth in Asia by 0.4 percentage points (0.5 percentage points in Japan, 0.6 in the Asian newly industrializing economies, IMF 2004: 10). An economic crisis in China, for instance zero growth for two years, would have severe repercussions.

China's import penetration is strongest in Asia. Chinese exports to Japan make up 18.5 percent of total Japanese imports (in 2003, Rumbaugh and Blancher 2004: Table 2.1). The corresponding figure is 12.5 percent for the US and 8.9 percent for the EU-15. Historically, Japan had reached a higher import penetration rate of the US market, peaking at 22 percent in 1986.

Of China's trade surplus of US$25 billion in 2003, China's bilateral trade surplus with the US (US$55 billion), the EU (US$18 billion), and Hong Kong (US$61 billion) was largely offset by bilateral deficits with the Asian countries (US$109 billion).

11.7 India – growing out of poverty with the market approach

India with a population of 1.1 billion people generated a GDP of US$689 billion in 2004 (in the following most data are taken from the World Bank Fact Sheet, August 2005), about 40 percent of that of China. Gross national income per head is US$620 in current at nominal exchange rates; it amounts to US$3,100 in purchasing power parity. GDP growth has been at a rate of 5.4 percent in the period 1984–1994 and at 5.8 percent in1994–2004. Population growth is at 2 percent annually. Gross domestic investment is at 25 percent of GDP (2004). According to World Bank data, 35.3 percent of the population lives below one US PPP dollar per day (2004).

India has a large service sector (51.8 percent in 2004), while industry produces 27 percent of GDP and agriculture continues to play an important role with 21.2 percent. Exports account for 16 percent of GDP; 77 percent of exports are from manufacturing, but only 5 percent are high technology exports. The current account is in balance. India uses a managed exchange rate with a crawling peg of 3 to 5 percent per year relative to a basket consisting of six currencies. The band is not pre-announced. The overall government deficit is high, amounting to 10.6 percent in 2004. FDI inflows of US$4.6 billion were registered in 2003, representing 0.8 percent of the GDP. Like in China, a growing middle class drives domestic consumption and economic growth, although growth is likewise unevenly distributed across the country.

In 1947, two years before China turned into a centralized communist country, India gained its independence from the United Kingdom, becoming a federal republic in 1950. In its early postcolonial period, economic independence was focused by the government introducing trade restrictions and suppressing the private sector, installing a complex licensing system to force entrepreneurs into the government's development strategies. The 1980s and 1990s saw a liberalization of the Indian economy, the licensing system was abandoned, governmental monopolies were reduced, the financial sector was liberalized, and international trade supported. India became a member of the WTO in 1995. From the 1980s on, the Indian government started to emphasize tertiary education. Consequently India specialized in skill-intense services.

Compared to China, India has a democratic structure. Due to social conflicts in its heterogeneous society over the last fifty years, it has developed the ability to politically manage conflicts.

11.8 Different philosophies for transforming a centrally-planned economy

Three areas of reform

China's success in transforming its centrally planned system into a market economy is best understood when contrasted to the experience in the post-communist countries in Central and Eastern Europe and to the tasks that had to be solved in their transformation process.

In restructuring a centrally planned economy, three main areas of reform have to be distinguished: the creation of a new institutional framework, macroeconomic stabilization, and the real adjustment of the firms and sectors on the microeconomic level. In the institutional framework, the rules and incentives of the centrally planned economy have to be replaced by institutional arrangements that allow market transactions, that let firms decide on their production and their investments autonomously and let households determine their consumption, savings, and labor supply on their own. A reliable legal framework is imperative, particularly the law of contract and the law of enterprises. Property rights are needed for long-term effects to be taken into account in economic calculations. They are crucial for the incentives of individuals to do business and for decentralizing economic decisions. Above all, property rights establish an area of decision-making in which the individuals can move without being influenced by government. Thus, one essential element of the framework of a market economy is from which responsibilities the government withdraws, leaving them to the private sector. Finally, a two-tier banking system, in which the responsibilities of monetary policy and intermediation are separated, can be regarded as an important aspect of the institutional framework.

In the macro-economy, monetary instabilities have to be prevented. One typical problem encountered in the Central and Eastern European countries was the existing excess supply of money. Usually, the excess supply of money was done away with by letting the price level increase. The high inflation rate implied a devaluation of the currency. As a result, there were negative effects on the real sphere of the economy during the transformation process. In order to keep these disturbances smaller, a currency reform was needed, in which a massive currency cut was carried out. Moreover, the newly independent successor states of the Soviet Union and Yugoslavia had to introduce their own new currencies. All these currency reforms remained unsuccessful unless an institutional design for the monetary sector was introduced, in which it was prohibited, in particular, that the central bank finances government budget deficits with its monetary policy. Another important step was to guarantee the independence of the central bank.

At the core, the transformation had to take place on the microeconomic level, inside the existing enterprises or in creating new firms. After the state-owned enterprises had been converted into separate legal entities (commercialization) and had been privatized, the real adjustment process then had to take place inside the privatized firms.

Different transformation philosophies

In Central and Eastern Europe the discussion was on the 'big bang' versus gradual adjustment. Psychological aspects and political economy arguments spoke well in favor of the 'big bang' approach. After the collapse of a centrally planned economy, people were prepared to try a new approach and to make sacrifices for it. For example, real wages (we use producer wages for lack of data on consumer wages) in Poland (1990) and in the Czech Republic (1991) fell by more than 30 percent within one year. The mood was that the quicker the necessary and painful steps of adjustment are carried out, the quicker the country gets out of the 'valley of tears'. The Poles have expressed this philosophy with the motto: 'You cannot cross a gorge with two leaps.' When the countries of Central and Eastern Europe introduced the new economic system, they simultaneously changed their political system and introduced democracy. This is another important argument in favor of the 'big bang' approach: there is a narrow time window for reform. If the fundamental social consensus for reform loses momentum, the government can be replaced; then, the reform approach may stall or fail.

As an alternative, a gradual approach was discussed in the early literature on the transformation. The argument in favor of the gradual approach was that the transformation process would turn out to be less hard if the steps of reform were stretched over a longer period of time. But this requires a deep breath for the transformation, particularly a prolonged willingness of people to stand the necessary reform steps. If the willingness to reform is lost in the course of time, the transformation process can come to a halt. The same may hold if the government changes.

The Chinese philosophy of 'crossing the river by feeling the stones under the feet' was a cautious approach to transformation. As the other reforms mentioned above, China had to solve the same three areas of reform. However, it proceeded gradually by first opening some coastal provinces in southern China to the free market and eventually extending the liberalization to the costal regions in the north and then to the whole country. It did not introduce democracy.

11.9 The valley of tears in Central and Eastern Europe

The transformation of the centrally planned economies in Central and Eastern Europe involved a collapse of national output, the so-called J-curve of transformation. A crucial reason for this breakdown was that the capital stock of the transformation country, adapted to the old conditions of a centrally planned economy, had become obsolete to a large extent due to the new scarcity relations. Therefore the reform countries had to rebuild their capital stock. This process took time and, moreover, involved adjustment costs. Additionally, the existing human capital had to be integrated into the new factor allocation. Another aspect of the economic breakdown was the institutional vacuum at the beginning of the transformation process, which implied uncertainty over the rules for a longer time.

All the countries in Central and Eastern Europe, Poland, Hungary, the then still united Czech and Slovak Republics, where the reforms started around 1989, had to face a breakdown of roughly 20 percent of their GDP. In Russia where the reforms started around 1991 rather than 1989, it was even more than 40 percent (Figure 11.3). The decrease in Lithuania was still stronger. While the

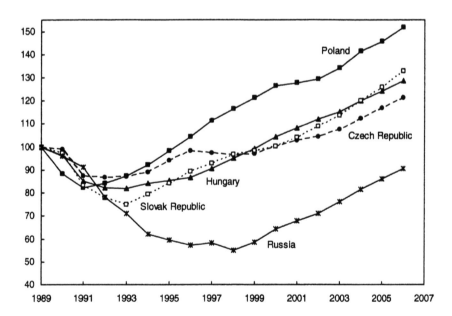

Figure 11.3 The J-curves in Central and Eastern Europe (GDP in real terms)[a] (source: EBRD, *Transition Report* 2000; IMF, *World Economic Outlook* 2005).

Note
a 1989 = 100.

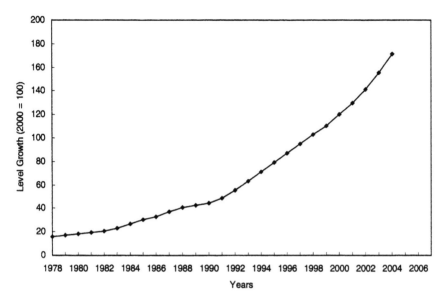

Figure 11.4 Growth of real GDP in China[a] (source: World Bank, *World Development Indicators*, Online Database, January 2006).

Note
a 2000 = 100.

breakdown took place at a similar pace, the Czech Republic, Hungary, and the Slovak Republic needed more time to recover than Poland.

East Germany experienced a massive breakdown, with industrial production falling to one-third of the former level. In contrast, China did not see a J-curve of transformation (Figure 11.4). GDP has continuously risen with real growth rates of approximately 9 percent per year since the beginning of the reforms at the end of the 1970s. Some reasons have been given for this development already: one was the gradual cautious approach with a long breath. Another factor is that China, still being a developing country at the beginning of the reforms, had only a relatively small capital stock and a weakly developed industrial sector. Therefore it was possible to realize substantial efficiency gains by introducing property rights for land in the rural areas, even though valid for only thirty years and unsound. Moreover, liberalization was taken step by step from the coastal regions in the south to the whole country. Last but not least, as already mentioned, nearly all the countries in Central and Eastern Europe introduced democracy quickly and the voter influenced the transformation process.

Case study: the transformation of East Germany

East Germany is a special case in the transformation process. Two of the three big reform steps in the transformation process – the creation of an institutional infrastructure, macroeconomic stabilization, and the economic adjustment in real terms – were realized practically overnight: by joining the Federal Republic, the constitution and all other legal arrangements of West Germany were taken over. At the same time, the currency union guaranteed monetary stability. The real economic adaptation was therefore at the core of the transformation process in East Germany.

The hypothesis of a special case is also justified for East Germany because transformation overlaps with integration, i.e. German reunification. Owing to this, the exchange rate was not available as a buffer in the transformation process. The enterprises had not only been forced to cope with the inefficiency of the centrally planned economy, but they also had to survive a strong appreciation of the East German mark (by approximately 400 percent). The population quickly pressed for similar living conditions and a rapid wage alignment. In this way, a wide gap opened up between wages and productivity. This involved high unemployment and, moreover, hampered investment. East Germany is also a special case in the sense that, quite differently from the usual transformation process, significant transfers were made. Initially, they amounted to 5 percent of

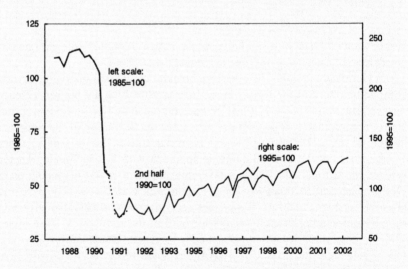

Figure 11.5 The J-curve in East Germany, industrial production 1988–2003[a]
   (source: Statistisches Bundesamt, *Produzierendes Gewerbe*, various
   issues; Statistisches Amt der DDR, *Statistisches Jahrbuch*).

Note
a Quarterly data; since 1997 new classification of economic branches (WZ93).

the gross domestic product of Germany as a whole, per year ('big bang with a big brother').

East Germany experienced a dramatic collapse of production. Gross industrial production, with all reservations regarding the comparability of data, fell to less than one-third of its former level (Figure 11.5); prior to 1990, gross production (including intermediate inputs and depreciation) is used. Moreover, East German 'industrial production' included huge amounts of additional contributions such as fringe benefits, which are no longer counted. Gross domestic product fell to approximately two-thirds. Employment decreased from ten million to almost five million if the political measures concerning the labor market (for example, up to two million short-time workers at times) are not considered (Siebert 1995).

East Germany (including West Berlin) reached approximately 67 percent of the West German GDP per capita of the population, after approximately 30 percent in the new Länder (without West Berlin) in 1991. Relative to the German level, it is 72 percent; this is not too different from regional percentages in other countries. If the results concerning catching-up processes are analogously applied, we have to conclude that a complete alignment is unlikely (see Chapter 4).

11.10 The disintegration of the Soviet Union

The transformation crisis became particularly apparent in most of the successor states of the Soviet Union. The former Soviet Union, a union of fifteen 'republics,' dissolved at the end of 1991 (Gros and Steinherr 1995). It dissolved into a number of now autonomous states, as the communist party lost its power. The political center was not accepted any longer; it disappeared. The individual states declared themselves independent and pushed through their own laws instead of the rules of the Soviet Union that were in place at that time. But this presupposed that each country created its own new institutional set-up. This held especially true for tax revenue and public spending, but new social security systems and a separate currency also had to be created.

The rouble zone dissolved in 1992 when the countries began to introduce their own currencies, starting with the Estonian crown. The collapse of the Soviet Union and of the rouble zone also involved an almost total collapse of the system of payments between the successor states, and thus the trade relations suffered significantly. As the successor states showed particular patterns of specialization within the former Soviet Union but maintained only minor trade relations with the rest of the world, they were severely hit by the breakdown of trade flows among themselves. The necessity to adapt their production structure to the changed scarcity conditions and to divert their trade to the world markets is therefore even bigger for the successor states of the Soviet Union than for other transformation countries.

12 Regional integration in the world economy

What you will understand after reading this chapter

With regional integration countries aim at intensifying the international division of labor, albeit within regional borders. We first report the experience with different forms of regional integration (section 12.1). An important aspect is the impact of regional integration on regional and world welfare, i.e. whether regional integration is trade-creating or trade-diverting (section 12.2). A fundamental question is whether regional integration facilitates or impedes the development of a multilateral order (section 12.3).

12.1 Regional integration

Types of regional integration

Regional integration is characterized by a lowering of transaction costs between member states relative to non-members. In fact, it is a mutual preferential treatment between countries in international trade. Thus, regional integration deviates from the WTO principle of non-discrimination because of different rules being in force with regard to non-members. The WTO rule of non-discrimination has a waiver for regional integrations (see Chapter 17). Depending on the extent of economic integration, different types of regional integration have to be distinguished.

Preferential trade agreements (PTAs) are the least strict form of regional integration. For certain goods tariffs are reduced among the members of a preferential area (sometimes even unilaterally). There is no equal treatment of non-members according to the most-favored-nation clause. Within preferential areas there is neither a general reduction of internal tariffs nor a common external tariff. Examples of this type of economic integration are the ACP treaty (seventy-seven participating countries in Africa, the Caribbean, and the Pacific areas – originally known as the Lomé Convention which expired in 2000 and has been replaced by the Cotounu Agreement) with the European Union as well as the preferential system of the Commonwealth.

Free-trade areas (FTAs) abolish internal tariffs, but there is no common external tariff. Each member maintains its own external tariff against non-FTA members. To prevent opportunities of arbitrage in conflict with the FTA agreements, rules of origin and strict controls of the origin of goods are of great importance. Examples are EFTA (European Free Trade Association, founded in 1960 by Austria, Denmark, Norway, Portugal, Sweden, Switzerland, and the United Kingdom, with Finland becoming a member in 1961; still in existence with Iceland, Liechtenstein, Norway, and Switzerland as members), NAFTA (North American Free Trade Agreement) and CEFTA (Central European Free Trade Area) of countries in Central and Eastern Europe.

Customs unions abolish internal tariffs like free-trade areas, but additionally there is a common external tariff as well as a common external trade policy with respect to third countries. Examples are the European Economic Community, founded in 1957, which changed into the European Community (EC, from 1967) and then the European Union (EU, from 1993).

Common economic areas, as established by the EU-12 and by five EFTA countries (Austria, Finland, Iceland, Norway, and Sweden) in 1994, are characterized by the use of common rules and common technical standards. The European Economic Area (EEA) now consists of all twenty-five member countries of the EU as well as three of the four current EFTA countries, namely Iceland, Norway, and Liechtenstein; in 1992, Switzerland, the fourth EFTA country, decided by plebiscite not to participate in the European Economic Area.

A common market is characterized by the complete abolition of all barriers, not only with respect to the free trade of goods, but also the free exchange of services and the free movement of capital and labor. Additionally, it is aimed at a common competition (or antitrust) policy and common rules for procurement as well as a subsidy code. The EEA agreement entered into force in 2004.

A monetary union performs a common monetary policy, having a joint monetary authority. A common policy also applies to exchange rates.

An economic union strives for harmonization of other elements of economic policy including the institutional framework of the market economies, for instance in common competition policy and subsidy control. Table 12.1 displays the features of various types of regional integration.

Table 12.1 Different forms of regional integrations

Type	Free trade among members	Common external tariffs	Free movement of factors of production	Harmonization of major economic policies
Free trade area	✓			
Customs union	✓	✓		
Common market	✓	✓	✓	
Economic union	✓	✓	✓	✓

Finally, in a *political union* common institutional mechanisms (constitution) are created in the area of political decision-making (i.e. the right to vote, a common parliament) with some political power being allocated to a central level, especially the power to tax.

Existing groups of regional integration

Since the establishment of the GATT in 1948 up to September 2005 334 regional trade agreements have been notified by GATT/WTO. Of these agreements, around 183 are currently in force.

Europe

The European Union (EU) with its twenty-five member states (in 2006) has developed from the European Economic Community, which was founded in 1957 by Belgium, France, Germany, Italy, Luxembourg, and the Netherlands. The realization of the four freedoms allows the free movement of goods and services, of capital and residents, including labor. With the northern enlargement, Denmark, Ireland, and the United Kingdom joined in 1973. With the southern enlargement in the 1980s, Greece (1981), Portugal, and Spain (1986) became members. With another enlargement the neutral states Austria, Sweden, and Finland joined in 1995. Finally, eastern enlargement by the new market economies of Central and Eastern Europe took place in 2004, increasing the number of members of from fifteen to twenty-five. Bulgaria and Romania will join in 2007. The European Monetary Union started in 1999. The EU has opened official negotiations with Croatia and Turkey. It now has an extended sphere of economic influence through associations, bilateral trade agreements, and preferential agreements, including most countries of the Mediterranean (for instance Turkey and Israel), but extending also to Latin America (trade association with Chile, bilateral free trade agreement with Mexico) and Africa (free trade agreement with South Africa) and preferential agreements with many developing countries (see below).

The European Free Trade Association (EFTA) was founded in 1960 by Austria, Denmark, Norway, Portugal, Sweden, Switzerland, and the United Kingdom in order to secure free trade in industrial goods. Since then Denmark and the United Kingdom (1973), Portugal (1986), and Austria, Finland, and Sweden (1995) have left the EFTA, which now consists of Iceland, Liechtenstein, Norway, and Switzerland.

The Europe Agreements between the European Union and the potential accessions countries were concluded individually in the years 1989–1991 with different post-communist states; they were intended to allow prospective EU members to adjust their economies in order to be able to join the European Union later on.

The Central European Free Trade Area (CEFTA) between the Czech and Slovak Republics, Hungary and Poland, the so-called Visegrad states, came into force in 1993. They were joined by Slovenia in 1996 and by Romania in 1997. The aim was to reduce tariffs and barriers to trade and to increase intra-regional trade which collapsed with the breakdown of the COMECON in 1990. At the same time, CEFTA was a waiting room for EU membership. Meanwhile, all members of CEFTA are EU members.

The Americas

The North American Free Trade Agreement (NAFTA) between the US, Canada, and Mexico started in 1994. Its aim is to remove tariffs and substantially reduce non-tariff barriers over a period of ten to fifteen years. By liberalizing the trade of goods and services, facilitating foreign investment, and establishing an effective dispute settlement mechanism, NAFTA is expected to become an important area of regional integration in the world. Additional agreements have been concluded upon environmental standards, intellectual property, and labor standards.

In contrast to the European Union, NAFTA is not a customs union with a common external tariff; it is a free-trade area. NAFTA does not intend to introduce a common market with the free movement of people. Moreover, NAFTA does not have an executive arm; the NAFTA commission plays only a mediating role in resolving conflicts. Finally, there is no transfer of resources.

At the moment there is a discussion about widening NAFTA by the accession of new members in Central and South America as well as plans for further free trade agreements with African and Asian countries. In January 2004, a US-Chilean free trade agreement started. Under its umbrella, all tariffs and quotas on industrial products shall be removed until 2014. The NAFTA countries are members of APEC (see below).

DR-CAFTA, the Dominican Republic and Central American Free Trade Agreement, represents a comprehensive trade accord between Costa Rica, the Dominican Republic, El Salvador, Guatemala, Honduras, Nicaragua, and the US. It has been adopted by the US in 2005.

In 1960, Mexico and most of the South American countries formed a free trade area called the Latin American Free Trade Association (LAFTA). As a result of the reduction of tariffs and non-tariff barriers, intra-trade between the LAFTA countries was growing until the end of the 1970s. But, as the barriers to trade with the outside world remained in place, the competitiveness of their economies diminished. In 1980, eleven of its members changed the LAFTA into the Latin American Integration Association (LAIA), which has so far not been successful in liberalizing trade. In 1991, Argentina, Brazil, Paraguay, and Uruguay created the MERCOSUR (Mercádo Común del Sur), which is a customs union, additionally linked with Chile and Bolivia by a free trade agreement. Within this free trade area, internal tariffs have been abolished, but Chile has a lower external tariff with respect to third countries than do the members of MERCOSUR.

The Caribbean Community (CARICOM, comprising Antigua and Barbuda, Bahamas, Barbados, Belize, Dominica, Grenada, Guyana, Jamaica, Montserrat,

St. Christopher and Nevis, St. Lucia, St. Vincent and the Grenadines, and Trinidad and Tobago) is a free trade area and has mostly succeeded in eliminating all barriers to intra-regional trade.

In the long-run, the creation of a so-called Free Trade Area of the Americas (FTAA), which would require an integration of both NAFTA and MERCOSUR and other Latin American countries, is aimed at reducing barriers to trade in the western hemisphere. Negotiations for an FTAA are stalling due to opposition from Venezuela (2006).

A Trans-Atlantic Free Trade Area (TAFTA) is proposed to integrate the European Union and NAFTA (Siebert 2005c). But instead of a free trade area it may be attempted to first create a common economic area, in which production standards representing non-tariff barriers would lose their significance, e.g. by mutual recognition of standards. In a Trans-Atlantic Free Trade Area, the development of basic elements of a common competition policy seems to be necessary; moreover, the agricultural sector should be included.

Asia

Regional integration was not particularly important in Asia in the past, the reason being that the economies have been open to the world market anyhow. With more regional integrations coming into existence, attempting a separate approach from the WTO, this trend may change.

The Association for South-East Asian Nations (ASEAN), consisting now of the ten South- East Asian countries Brunei Darussalam, Cambodia, Indonesia, Malaysia, Myanmar, Laos, the Philippines, Singapore, Thailand, and Vietnam, was founded in 1967 with the intent to establish an Asian Free Trade Association (AFTA). ASEAN is oriented towards economic cooperation. AFTA was launched in 1992. Recently, ASEAN heads of state have set a more ambitious post-AFTA goal and agreed to establish an ASEAN Economic Community (AEC), taking European integration as a model (Plummer 2004, 2005; Plummer and Jones 2005). This includes reducing obstacles of investment and creating a more uniform institutional frame of reference. The Asian Europe Meeting (ASEM) has similar objectives as TAFTA, i.e. defining common standards and reducing obstacles of trade.

Moreover, plans are being discussed to establish a wider Asian Free Trade Area. In the future, one can envision a regional integration with China and India as the main members and other Asian countries joining.

In 1989, the Asia–Pacific Economic Cooperation (APEC) was founded in 1989 in order to encourage free trade among its member states, now comprising twenty-one members including Japan, China, Australia, New Zealand, South Korea, and Taiwan as well as ten fast-growing economies of South-East Asia (ASEAN), the NAFTA members, Russia, Chile, and Peru. In accordance with the WTO principles, APEC wants to reduce barriers to the trade of goods and services, but there is no desire to establish a common external tariff (open regionalism).

Between Australia and New Zealand, the Australia New Zealand Closer Economic Relations Trade Agreement (ANZCERTA or CER for short) came into force in 1983, and induced the unrestricted free trade of goods. Additionally, both states strive for a liberalization of the trade in services as well as a harmonization of regulations and business law.

12.2   Elementary theory of integration

Usually, static and dynamic effects of regional integration are distinguished. In a static (or comparative-static) framework, it is analyzed how the allocation of resources, of production, of sectoral structure, and of welfare change when some countries form a customs union and others remain outside. Dynamic effects arise when the impact of integration on economic growth is considered.

Trade-creating and trade-diverting effects

According to Viner (1950), the static effects can be trade creation and trade diversion. Assume country A forms a customs union with country B, excluding country C. We analyze both effects first from the point of view of country A (the home country), then from the point of view of countries A and B together, and finally from the point of view of all countries (the world). We will use the partial analysis of a market diagram rather than a general equilibrium analysis.

When analyzing trade creation (and trade diversion), we have to specify for which country trade is created (and for which it is diverted). From the point of view of the home country, a simple case of trade creation is realized when, despite import tariffs, the home country A had obtained imports from country B before the customs union came into being. By abolishing internal tariffs trade is created. This is shown in Figure 12.1a, depicting the curves of demand (DD) and supply (SS) of the home country. Before the customs union was established, the home country had imported quantity MQ, afterwards it imports $M'Q'$. Supposing that the total revenue (c) generated by tariffs prior to the trade union was transferred to the households, the households of the home country will have a net gain from the customs union equal to the amount of the triangles a and b.

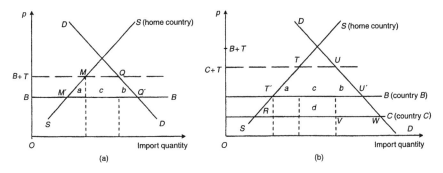

Figure 12.1 Trade-creating and trade-diverting effects of a customs union.

The case is different when a third country with a horizontal supply curve C is more favorable for the home country than that of country B, i.e. $B > C$. Prior to the customs union, country C is competitive even though the home country imposes a tariff, whereas country B is not competitive when a tariff (T) is introduced. $B + T$ lies above $C + T$. It should be noticed that the initial import tariff in Figure 12.1b is supposed to be higher than in Figure 12.1a. In the initial situation, the home country imports TU from country C. After the formation of the customs union country C still has to pay the tariff (in this case the initial tariff), but for country B the tariff has been abolished. As a result of the customs union, country B now supplies the imports $T'U'$, whereas country C loses its price competitiveness.

What is the effect on the welfare of the home country? On the one hand, there is additional trade with country B which induces a gain in consumer surplus of $a + b$. The previous revenue from tariffs c has become a consumer surplus for the households. On the other hand, the country now loses revenue from tariffs d of the previous imports that have been transferred – as assumed above – by the government to the households. If the area d exceeds $a + b$, the net welfare effect for the home country is negative. The negative effect of trade diversion exceeds the positive effect of trade creation. Then the home country loses. Consequently, in a partial analysis, the result of integration can be a loss of welfare for a member country of a customs union. It is important to notice that in this partial analysis the home country would experience even stronger gains from introducing free trade globally instead of joining a regionally restricted customs union. In comparison with a customs union, the additional gain from global free trade would consist of additional consumer surplus as indicated by the area $RT'U'W$.

In order to find out whether the total effects of a customs union are positive for the union members as a whole, it would be necessary to calculate the trade-creating and trade-diverting effects for all member states and net them out.

A third country loses when the revenues generated by its exports, induced by a shrinking demand in the members of the customs union, are smaller after the formation of the customs union. Its terms of trade deteriorate and the consumer surplus shrinks. Remember that welfare is measured in terms of consumer surplus, which means that other criteria, e.g. the change in unemployment, are not relevant in this respect.

Finally, it is necessary to consider whether the welfare of the world as a whole – all the member states of the customs union and the third country – has been increased by the formation of the customs union. To assess the total effect for the world as a whole, the trade-creating and trade-diverting effects for the customs union as well as for the third country have to be calculated and netted out.

Dynamic effects

Apart from a comparative-static change of trade flows of a customs union in the partial equilibrium models, there are additional effects in a richer analysis.

These impacts are in fact equal to the advantages of foreign trade (see Chapter 14). These effects are, inter alia, the exploitation of economies of scale and increased specialization, intensified intra-industry trade and – in a more general sense – a higher mobility of both capital and labor. In addition there are dynamic effects stemming from an improved competitiveness of firms, from innovation, from the accumulation of capital and from higher growth. These gains in efficiency also have positive effects on third countries because a higher GDP implies an increased import demand. For regional integrations of developing countries enhancing industrialization has been given as an argument. Empirical studies have emphasized the relative importance of dynamic effects in comparison with comparative-static effects.

12.3 Block formation as a step towards a multilateral order?

Regional integrations may eventually lead to a multilateral order and may thus be a way to reach a maximum of welfare in the world economy in the long-run. Or they may lead to separation and thus reduce the chances of increasing welfare. This is a central issue for trade policy. Clearly, regional integrations violate the WTO rule of non-discrimination (and the most-favored-nation principle); they represent a kind of discrimination against non-members. Nevertheless, there is a waiver for regional integrations.

Consider the three largest trading blocs in the world, the European Union, NAFTA, and Japan, which had a combined share in world merchandise trade of about 63 percent in 2004 (Table 12.2). Note that these data do not net out intra-EU and intra-NAFTA trade. When intra-regional trade is excluded, the share in world trade is 33 percent. In Europe, an internal market is clearly established; eastern enlargement is in the making. In America, politicians aim at strengthening NAFTA by integrating the countries of Latin America. In Asia, it remains to

Table 12.2 EU, NAFTA, and Japan, 2004

	EU(25)	*NAFTA*	*Japan*
Population (million)	491.3[a]	433	127.9
GDP (billion US$)	12,865	13,403	4,671
GDP per capita (US$)	28,077	30,948	36,596
Share of intra-exports to total exports	67.6	56	–
Share in world total merchandise exports[b]	41.6	14.8	6.2
Share in world total merchandise exports[c]	18.1	8.5	6.2
Trade to GDP ratio	25	24.9	23.5

Sources: IMF, *International Financial Statistics*, *World Economic Outlook* September 2005; WTO, *International Trade Statistics* 2006; own calculation.

Notes
a 2005.
b Including intra-regional exports.
c Excluding intra-regional exports.

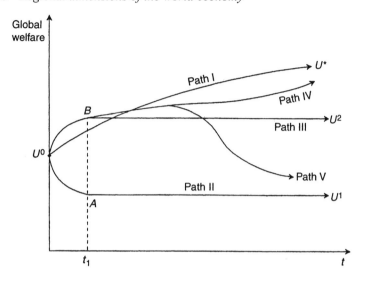

Figure 12.2 Regional integration and free trade.

be seen whether the Pacific area with Japan (and China?) might develop into a region similar to an internal market, with low barriers to trade.

Figure 12.2 illustrates some possible time paths depicting the development of welfare in respect of multilateral trade liberalization and regional integration (Bhagwati 1992). In the initial position, a utility level U^0 is given. Different paths are portrayed.

Path I characterizes the development of welfare in a scenario of multilateral rounds of liberalization. At the end of this process, a situation of free trade providing a utility level U^* is realized. Paths II and III show the effect of regional integration having both a trade-diverting and a trade-creating effect. When the trade-diverting effect prevails, then utility is falling to a level U^1 (point A) and remains at this level (path II). When the trade-creating effect is stronger, then welfare is rising to U^2 (point B). If only short-term effects had to be taken into account, then the world economy would stay on this level (path III). But there are also dynamic effects which raise welfare. Especially when regional blocs open up to new members and expand liberalization according to the most-favored-nation principle to third countries, and, vice versa, when third countries themselves grant such 'concessions,' then regional integration is moving towards the utility level of free trade (path IV).

Does a multilateral approach to liberalization represent a faster and more secure track towards free trade than a regional approach (Bhagwati 1992; Frankel 1997)? The advantage of the regional approach is that barriers to trade are more or less totally abolished within a partial area of the world. In addition, the member states are enabled to conclude an agreement much more easily. For that reason, regional integration might be realized faster. Further barriers can be dismantled in the long-run, when the regional integration opens itself to additional members. This is especially the case when regional integration can be extended multilaterally by the use of the most-favored-nation rule.

The advantage of the multilateral approach consists in creating a set of rules that are legally binding nearly all over the world. GATT Article XXIV, which departs from the most-favored-nation principle by explicitly allowing free trade areas and customs unions, in principle gives rise to the risk of destroying the multilateral order by the formation of regional trading blocs. Regionalism might be combined with protectionism which would impede utility from rising to U^*, the level of free trade. Then the path could lead away from U^*; and even a level below U^2 might not be reached in the case of retaliation against third countries (path V). Thus, the risk of disintegration of the world economy exists. For instance, the world economy could be subdivided into the triad Europe, North America, and China plus Japan.

These theoretical considerations apart, the empirical evidence suggests that bilateralism and regionalism is a threat to the multilateral order. Countries use these agreements to circumvent the WTO rules. It is astonishing that the WTO most-favored tariffs of the European Union only apply to nine countries of the world, admittedly among them the US and Japan. Preferential tariffs apply to all other countries (WTO 2004b). The rule system corresponds to a spaghetti bowl (Bhagwati). The preferential tariffs of the some 300 free trade arrangements in force undermine the WTO multilateral tariffs.

It is true that so far attempts towards regional integration in Latin America have not proved to be powerful, with the exception of MERCOSUR. In East Asia, APEC has the goal of market integration with no tendency towards protectionism. European integration has proved to be open to new members, and despite some protectionist measures trade-diverting effects unfavorable to the rest of the world have been, judging with a grain of salt, over-compensated by its growth. The European Union has been open to the accession of new members in the northern, southern, and neutral enlargements. The internal coherence of NAFTA is different from that of the European Union. The importance of intra-regional trade has been rising steadily during the last forty years (Table 12.3).

However, both Europe and the US use regional integrations to develop their own hub-and-spoke system. Thus, the European Union has the European Economic Space around it and many agreements with neighborhood countries, for instance a free trade arrangement with Turkey, and association agreements with Israel and the Maghreb states. Eventually, some agreement will be reached with the Ukraine and Russia. The EU has reached a free trade agreement with Mexico and an association agreement with Chile, and also is actively searching for a free trade agreement with MERCOSUR, so to say being active in the US's backyard. Moreover, it has granted duty free or preferential access to its markets for most of the imports from developing countries and economies in transition under its General System of Preferences. It has a free trade agreement with South Africa and is negotiating a free trade arrangement with members of the Gulf Cooperation Council. Finally, the EU has a new trade strategy with respect to seventy-seven ACP countries (Africa, Caribbean, Pacific). The US concluded a Free

Table 12.3 Share of intra-regional trade (exports plus imports) as percentage of each region's total trade, 1948–2003

	1948	1958	1968	1979	1993	1999	2003
Western Europe[a]	42	53	63	66	70	68	67.7
North America[b]	27	32	37	30	33	32 (46)[d]	40.5[d]
Asia	39	41	37	41	50	51	50
World[c]	33	41	47	46	50	51	50.5

Sources: WTO, *Annual Report* 1995, 1997; WTO, *International Trade Statistics*, 2006.

Notes
a Share of intra-European trade in total Western European trade.
b Canada and the USA.
c Weighted average.
d Including Mexico.

Trade Agreement with Chile taking effect in 2004 after the creation of NAFTA in 1994. Moreover, the US is pursuing the idea of a Free Trade Area of the Americas (FTAA) and also is a member of APEC, the Asia- Pacific Economic Cooperation, and has a free trade agreement with Singapore since 2003. China is actively negotiating twenty-seven bilateral free trade agreements (Siebert 2006b). Such an integration a la carte for specific regions of the world gives rise to the risk of destroying the multilateral order through the formation of regional trading blocks which then engage in strategic behavior, attempting to gain benefits from the international division of labor at the expense of the other regions. In such a scenario, regionalism can appear as the prolonged arm of unilateralism. The multilateral rules erode. Therefore, it is necessary to find mechanisms which allow a multilateralization of regional integrations.

13 The European Union

What you will understand after reading this chapter

In the European Union, nation states have given up sovereignty in a number of policy areas and subjected themselves to joint decision-making with other nations. The core of European integration is the single market and its four freedoms (section 13.1). With respect to the role of government, fiscal federalism is at the heart of European integration (section 13.2). The institutional arrangement for decision-making in the EU-25 is quite complex (section 13.3). The future of the constitution-like set-up is uncertain. Monetary union is a major step in the process of European integration (section 13.5). The rigidity of the national labor markets, especially in the larger continental countries, contrasts with the requirement of more flexibility in the monetary union (section 13.6).

13.1 The four freedoms and policy areas in the single market

As an economic union, the European Union aims at establishing a common market by abolishing market segmentations in the institutional framework of the national economies. But European integration goes beyond establishing a common market in the strict sense. A set of economic policy areas is no longer in the hands of the nation states but is either shifted to the European level or requires some type of joint decision-making of national governments. Joint decisions go together with different decision procedures (Commission, Council) and may require different majorities.

The EU began with the Community of Six in 1957 (Treaty of Rome) and the alternative concept of the EFTA. It continued with northern enlargement in 1973 (Denmark, Ireland, and the UK), southern enlargement in the 1980s (Greece 1981, Spain and Portugal in 1986) and the addition of the neutral states in 1995 (Austria, Finland, and Sweden). In 2004, the European Union of fifteen has been enlarged to a Union of twenty-five, including eight Middle and Eastern European nations. Bulgaria and Romania will join in 2007.

The four freedoms

Free movement of goods

The common market requires the dismantling of all obstacles to the free movement of goods. (Articles 23, 28, and 29 of the Treaty establishing the European Community – hereafter EC Treaty).[1] Barriers to trade include not only tariffs and quantitative restrictions but also national regulations. It has proved to be impossible to harmonize all legal rules of the different countries. Therefore, in the Cassis-de-Dijon case of 1979, the country-of-origin principle was established by the European Court of Justice. The Cassis-de-Dijon, a fruit liqueur, was widely in use in France. It was not allowed, however, to be marketed in Germany. The German regulation, the monopoly law on spirits (Branntwein-monopolgesetz) of 1922 required fruit liqueurs to have an alcohol content of at least 32 percent; thus the alcohol content of 17 percent in the Cassis-de-Dijon was 'verboten.' The sense of such a law is a different question. The European Court of Justice ruled that a product legally brought to the market in one country of the European Union also has to be accepted by other countries. This verdict then allowed the export of beer from Belgium to Germany, even if it was not brewed in accordance with the German beer purity regulations of 1516, and it allowed pasta to be exported that was not made from Italian buckwheat. According to this principle, the different regulations are de facto mutually recognized and coexist. This principle has proven to be a can opener for national regulations. Only in the cases when products are hazardous and damaging to health, to safety, or to the environment does the principle not apply (article 30 of the EC Treaty).

Free movement of persons

Workers have the right to work anywhere in the European Union (right of free movement according to article 39 of the EC Treaty). Individuals have the right to assume dependent employment in any of the member states, irrespective of their actual place of residence, under the same conditions as those applicable to the nationals of that state. Individiuals also have the right to establish businesses everywhere in the European Union (right of establishment). Discrimination based on nationality is to be abolished.

Free movement of services

Services offered in one member country can also be supplied in the other member countries. Thus, the Cassis-de-Dijon verdict of the European Court of Justice not only holds for goods, but also applies to services, for instance to banking and to insurance. The country-of-origin rules for services are mutually recognized. The free movement of services is especially linked to the right of establishment.

Free movement of capital

Until the late 1980s, capital flows were still controlled in some countries. With monetary union in the making, national controls of capital movements could no longer be justified. Consequently, they had to be given up.

Free movements of workers after enlargement

After the 2004 enlargement, individual member states were given the right to limit the free movement of workers from the new members for a seven year period. With the exception of the United Kingdom, Sweden, and Ireland, the EU-15 members exercised this right and chose to liberalize their labor markets gradually. Their action was prompted by the fear of a mass influx of workers from the new member countries, where real incomes are lower than in the old member countries. Poland reached 43 percent of the EU per capita level of GDP when purchasing power parity is used (data for 2003, EU 2005). For Hungary the relative level was at 55, for the Czech Republic at 61, and for Slovenia at 72 percent. In contrast, Romania reached only 27 percent and Bulgaria 29 percent of the EU-15 level. When GDP per capita is compared in current prices and nominal exchange rates, the Czech Republic was at 33 percent, Hungary at 31, and Poland at 21 percent of the EU average.

It is, however, not actual income differences and actual differences in unemployment rates that drive migration but expected income and employment gaps. Some regions in some of the new member countries meanwhile reach income levels that are not too far off from the EU average or are even higher. Thus, the region of Prague is at 153 percent of the EU-25 level, Bratislava at 120 percent and the region Közep Magyarorszag in Hungary at 96 percent (EU 2005). For people in these areas, on average, out-migration is unlikely to pay. In migration decisions the future stream of income is compared to the costs; the present value of the additional income in future periods net of migration costs must be positive. Therefore expectations on future income play an important role. If people expect that the income gap will be leveling off over time they tend to stay at home. In a model with uncertainty, for instance with a Brownian motion on future income, the option value of waiting is a relevant variable. If the option value of waiting is positive, people will stay at home. We know from many empirical studies that convergence takes a long time; nevertheless the expectation of convergence implies a positive option value. Looking at these analytical considerations and the empirical experience of past migration in the case of previous enlargements, the tentative conclusion is that we will not see a major wave of migration from the new EU-members when the seven year interim period expires (Siebert 2006b).

Migration from the very low-income countries like Romania and Bulgaria will be more important. Moreover, commuters in the border regions of Austria and Eastern Germany may reach sizable numbers. Migration from Turkey, if Turkey were to join, would be a different story.

However, even if workers are not allowed to migrate, the free movement of services for which the presence of service personnel in another EU country is necessary (for instance repairing an elevator) may substitute for the free movement of workers. The EU-principle of the free movement of services is to accept the country of origin-rule for services. This means that a new member country would be able to provide services in another member country according to the country-of-origin rule. In the past, national governments have used bureaucratic measures in order to keep off services from other member countries, for instance not accepting the qualification of employees or requiring notification of the work (for supervisory purposes). In 2006, the EU parliament did not accept the country of origin principle for services requiring the presence of personnel. Services of that type have to be performed according to the country-of-destination principle, i.e. according to the regulations (and wages) in use in the country where the service is provided. This is a severe hindrance for the freedom of services.

Policy areas in the single market

Trade policy

Since the European Union is also a customs union, it has a common external tariff which now is at 2.7 percent for all trade in industrial products. Other trade policy instruments are applied uniformly. The EU has a Common Commercial Policy vis-à-vis non-members, for instance the US or in the WTO.

Competition policy

In a single market, competition policy (antitrust policy) has to apply to the market as a whole. Competition policy has to prevent cartels and to ensure that dominant positions within the common market do not arise. Thus, the abuse of market power in the EU and the creation of new dominating positions (monopolies) by mergers have to be controlled on the European level, where the Commission has taken a lead position.

Subsidy control

Competition in the single market should not be distorted by national subsidies. The Commission controls national subsidies and has established a respected power in this domain.

Agricultural policy

Agriculture receives special treatment. It is shielded from the market by Common Agricultural Policy (CAP) which defines reference prices. Agricultural prices in the EU are protected against the world market by variable import tariffs. Moreover, export subsidies are paid; they are to be abolished by 2013 according to the WTO agreement in the Doha Round. Inside the European Union, agricultural prices are guaranteed by market interventions. Agricultural policy is undertaken on the European level and absorbs nearly two-fifths of the EU budget. In recent years, direct subsidies have been substituted by income transfers. Such transfers could also be handled by the member states; it is therefore debated that agricultural policy can be nationalized.

Indirect taxation

Different rates for indirect taxes including value-added taxes may create unnecessary distortions in the common market. For this reason, article 93 of the EC Treaty stipulates that the Council should adopt provisions for the harmonization of legislation pertaining to indirect taxation. Though VAT rates are ultimately under the jurisdiction of the individual member states, the member states have agreed to a minimum VAT rate of 15 percent.

Monetary policy

With monetary union, monetary policy has been centralized for the EU-12 countries (EU-15 with the exception of the United Kingdom, Sweden, and Denmark (see section 13.5)).

EU finances

The EU budget for 2006 was set at €121.2 billion, equivalent to 1.24 percent of the member states' GNIs. This upper ceiling to the EU's finances was adopted in 1999. It is financed by contributions of the member states and 'traditional own resources,' since the EU does not have the right to tax or incur debt. Contributions by member states consist partly of the harmonized value-added tax (VAT) resource and partly of the gross national income (GNI) resource. The resource based on VAT is a uniform percentage rate (0.31 percent) that is applied to each member state's VAT assessment base. The GNI-based resource, calculated as a uniform percentage rate (0.73 percent) of each country's GNI, currently, and will continue to, represent the largest source of revenue. 'Traditional own resources' consist of customs duties imposed on products coming from a non-EU state, agricultural duties, and sugar levies. In 2006, 14 percent of revenues came from the VAT-based resource, 72 percent from the GNI-based resource, and 13 percent from EU-levied duties. The remaining 1 percent came from unspent funds from previous years and from contributions from EU staff.

For the next seven-year planning period (2007–2013), the EU-27's level of expenditure is reduced to 1.5 percent of GNI in payment appropriations, expected to amount to €864.4 billion over the entire period. The most remarkable feature of the new seven-year budget is that the funds reserved for common agricultural policy are decreasing, in line with the EU's declared commitment to increase the competitiveness of its agricultural sector.

EU expenditures

EU expenditures total €121 billion in 2006. Of this, 36 percent is spent on agricultural policy, 39 percent on structural, regional funds, and new member national funds, and 11 percent on rural and development funds.

Degree of centralization

The short survey in Table 13.1 indicates the most important areas of centralization and of decentralization. Centralization does not imply unanimity.

13.2 Fiscal federalism and the subsidiarity principle

The economist's answer to the issue of the optimal degree of decentralization or centralization in a system of political units is the subsidiarity principle. According to this concept, an economic activity should be assigned to the lowest organizational level that can efficiently deal with that activity. The reasoning behind this principle is that a more decentralized unit has better information on preferences and on the structure of problems. Higher levels of an organization tend to have less information; distortions in collecting information are likely. The lower level can deal better with local or regional issues, it can respond more flexibly.

For the organizational set-up of states and other political units, fiscal federalism can be interpreted as an expression of the subsidiarity principle. According to the approach of fiscal federalism, the central governmental level should be in charge of public goods with a spatial dimension extending over the whole political area. Lower levels should be responsible for those public goods that are

Table 13.1 Degree of centralization

Centralization	Trade policy
	Competition policy
	Control of state subsidies
	Monetary policy
	Single Market
Shared responsibility between the EU and nation states	Environment
	Consumer protection
	Cross-border movement of labor
	Energy
	Transport
Decentralization	Fiscal policy
	Taxation
	Wage and income policy
	Social security systems
	Health
	Education

spatially less extended. Note that the spatial dimension of public goods is also discussed under the heading of the spatial extent of technological externalities or spillover effects. Assigning public goods of different spatial dimensions to different levels of governments implies that the revenue side has to follow the expenditure side (fiscal equivalence, Olson 1969).

For the EU, this means that economic problems of a European dimension such as trade policy should be dealt with at the European level, problems with a national dimension should be decided at the national level, and regional problems should be under the responsibility of the regional authorities.

13.3 Institutional arrangements for decision making in the European Union

Giving up some national sovereignty

The European Union is not a confederation with an intra-state pattern of rules and it also is not an association of completely sovereign nation states. European integration relies on the method of intergovernmental cooperation where most of the decisions are taken in the European Council by reaching agreements between the heads of state or between the ministers of specific portfolios (Siebert 2002a).

Its basis is the European Treaty as a multilateral arrangement by which sovereign nation states give up some sovereignty in favor of joint decision making on the European level. The European Treaty has developed in different stages from the Treaty of Rome (1956), to the Single Market Act (1981), and the Treaties of Maastricht (1992), Amsterdam (1997), and Nice (2000). With the coming into force of the European Treaty, member states have agreed to respect the decisions of the European Council and abide by them. This holds for decisions with simple and qualified majority. In other areas where unanimity is required each member state has a veto. In addition, a vital interest procedure has been practiced in the past when a qualified majority applied. Whenever a national government declared an issue as one of vital national interest, the member state was not out-voted.

The Community has been empowered by the individual member states through the treaty. The Community's power is to establish secondary laws. New laws can only be created in the context of the treaty, if they are in accordance with the stipulations of the treaty. The treaty can only be changed in the same way that it was originally concluded, namely by negotiation and ratification by the individual member states. Thus, the member states are the masters of the treaty.

The European Treaty is not a constitution. If the EU had a constitution, the fundamental decisions would not be made by the Council but by the sovereign, that is, by the people or by a parliament representing the people. Lacking one of the decisive elements of a constitution, namely the European people as a sovereign, the EU cannot be considered a state.

Institutions

The system of governance of the European Union is a multi-level system. Decisions are taken by a complex web of decision-making bodies.

Council of the European Union

The Council of the European Union is the central decision-making body. It is made up of the member states and meets in more than twenty different forms, for instance, as heads of states (the Council) or as ministers for a specific portfolio (Council of Ministers, e.g. Foreign Affairs, Economy and Finance, Agriculture, Transport, etc.).

The European Commission

The Commission is the administrative arm of the European Union. Its main function is to implement policies, to launch initiatives, and to be the arbiter between member states as the guardian of the treaty. The Commission has the right to propose new laws; it can create derived or secondary law according to article 308 (EC Treaty). The Commission has a legislative monopoly. A set of decisions of the European Council presupposes recommendations by the Commission. Changes of the treaty require approval by national parliaments. The Commission also represents the Union in international negotiations.

The European Parliament

The European Parliament participates in the different forms of approval, joint decision, and hearing. The approval of parliament is needed in declarations of fundamental violations of the treaty. The proceedings of joint decisions according to article 251 of the EC Treaty apply to proposals of the Commission to which parliament submits a statement. On the basis of this statement, the proposals of the commission become enacted by the Council. If the European Parliament alters the Commissions' proposals in joint decisions, rules specify how to proceed. The Parliament does not have the right of initiative.

The European Court of Justice

The European Court of Justice is concerned with the interpretation of EC law. The Court also provides the judicial safeguards necessary to ensure that the law is respected. The types of actions include actions brought before the court by a member state against a member state and by the Commission against a member state.

Types of legal rules

Community law, adopted by the Council – or in the case of co-decision procedure by Parliament and Council used in forty-three areas – can only be established in those areas which have been defined for joint decisions. Where unanimity is required, the power to legislate still rests with the individual member state. Article 308 of the EC Treaty is a general clause for the Commission to become active; however, this does not imply that the Community has the right to go beyond the creation of secondary law.

Community law may take different forms. Regulations are directly applied; there is no need for national measures to implement them. Directives bind member states with respect to the objectives to be achieved. It is up to the national authorities to choose the appropriate means to implement the directives. Decisions are addressed to any or all member states and are binding. Moreover, informal procedures and rules of the game play an important role in the decision making of the European Union.

Different types of majorities

For decisions of the Council, article 205 of the EC Treaty stipulates three different types of majorities required for the Council to reach a decision: simple majority, qualified voting and unanimity:

- If not stated otherwise, the majority of votes of the member states is needed. This is fourteen out of twenty-seven in the enlarged Union.
- In the EU-27, a qualified majority consists of 258 votes (74.79 percent out of the overall 345) and the majority of the member states. This holds for decisions which are taken by the European Council with respect to proposals of the European Commission. In all other cases, it is additionally required that the 258 votes represent two-thirds of all member countries. The blocking minority is eighty-eight votes, cast by at least four different members. Further, in cases when adopting a decision by a qualified majority, a member of the Council may request verification that the member states constituting the qualified majority represent at least 62 percent of the EU total population. If this condition is not met, the decision in question will not be adopted. Whenever a vital interest of a member state is involved, a consensus has arisen among member states not to take a vote, but instead to continue negotiating.
- Unanimity is required in the most important policy areas.

Policy areas and majorities

It is very seldom that a simple majority is required. It is applied, for example, to the Governing Council of the European Central Bank, although the Council does not take formal votes. Qualified majority is required in areas pertaining to the functioning of the internal market, economic affairs, and foreign trade. In the enlarged Union, it has become the most commonly used voting method. With the ratification of the Treaty of Nice, those policy areas that require qualified majority are now subject to co-decision, a procedure used for most EU-law making. A piece of legislation put forward by the Commission to the Council and the European Parliament becomes law only with their joint enactment. Qualified majority is required in such areas as agriculture and trade policy in a narrow sense (on the operative level).

Basic decisions require unanimity. The most important areas where unanimity is required are: admitting new members (article 49 EU Treaty), indirect taxation (article 93 EC Treaty), direct taxation (article 190 EC Treaty), the budget of the European Union (article 269 EC Treaty), foreign policy and defense (article 23 EU Treaty), police and judicial co-operation in criminal matters (article 34 EU Treaty), and fundamental rules (articles 94, 95 EC Treaty). Unanimity is also required in international treaties in trade policy (article 133 EC Treaty), cultural policy (article 151 EC Treaty), industrial policy (article 157 EC Treaty), social cohesion policy (article 161 EC Treaty), research and development policy (article 166 EC Treaty), and environmental protection (article 175 EC Treaty). Asylum policy while respecting international agreements is under national authority and has required unanimity so far. As of 2004, the procedure of co-decision with qualified majority will apply if agreed upon unanimously by the heads of state. Of course, the unanimity principle in the area of taxation is at the heart of the question of national sovereignty and political union. Table 13.2

Table 13.2 Required majorities

Policy Area	Required majority
European Central Bank Council	*Simple majority*
Agriculture	Qualified majority
Internal market	
Environment	
Transport	
Trade policy in the narrow sense	
Harmonizing the legal framework	Unanimity
Foreign policy and defense	
Police and judicial cooperation in judicial	
Asylum	
Indirect taxation	
Direct taxation	
Regional and social funds	
Admittance of new members	
Entering into international agreements including trade policy	
In the wider sense	
Culture	
Environmental protection	

exhibits some policy areas and the required majority in a very simplified presentation.

Allocation of votes

The allocation of votes has changed through the Nice treaty (Table 13.3).

Table 13.3 Allocation of votes in the EU-27

	Population[a] *(in million)*	*Votes*
Germany (DE)	82.5	29
France (FR)	62.4	29
United Kingdom (UK)	60.1	29
Italy (IT)	58.5	29
Spain (ES)	43.0	27
Poland (PL)	38.2	27
Romania (RO)	22.2	14
The Netherlands (NL)	16.3	13
Greece (GR)	11.1	12
Czech Republic (CZ)	10.2	12
Belgium (BE)	10.4	12
Portugal (PT)	10.6	12
Hungary (HU)	10.1	12
Sweden (SE)	9.0	10
Austria (AT)	8.2	10
Bulgaria (BG)	7.8	10
Slovakia (SK)	5.4	7
Denmark (DK)	5.4	7
Finland (FI)	5.2	7
Ireland (IE)	4.1	7
Lithuania (LI)	3.4	7
Latvia (LV)	2.3	4
Slovenia (SI)	2.0	4
Estonia (EE)	1.3	4
Cyprus (CY)	0.8	4
Luxembourg (LU)	0.5	4
Malta (MT)	0.4	3
Total votes	491.3	345

Source: Council Decision of January 23, 2006, *Official Journal of the European Union*; Declaration No. 20, Treaty of Nice.

Note
a 2005.

13.4 The future of decision-making and a constitution-like arrangement

Voting according to the Nice Treaty

Enlargement to a European Union of twenty-five in 2004 and twenty-seven in 2007 implies that it will become more difficult to make decisions. In an enlarged European Union, the veto power that each country has due to the principle of unanimity becomes a powerful hindrance, eventually meaning that no decision can be taken at all.[2]

For a qualified majority, things will also get more complicated. The votes have not been allocated proportional to the population (Figure 13.1). The medium-sized countries (from Slovenia to Romania) have received an over proportionally larger share of the votes relative to the larger countries. Germany with 82.5 million people has only marginally more votes than Spain and Poland with half the population size. In the case of Germany, there is also a distortion relative to the three other larger countries, France, the UK, and Italy.

In search of a constitution-like arrangement

Besides this practical view of reaching decisions, there is a fundamental issue: the EU has a democratic deficit. Many decisions are taken at the European level, by the Commission and by the Council, that directly affect the lives of people. But people only have a very indirect and remote way of expressing their preferences and influencing these decisions. They do not have the option to vote

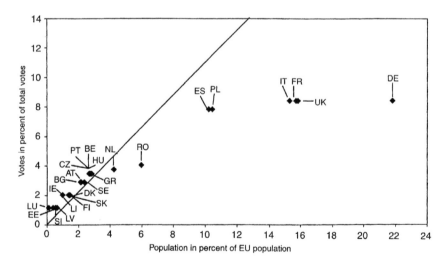

Figure 13.1 EU: population shares and shares of votes in the council after the Treaty of Nice[a] (source: see Table 13.3).

Note
a Population 2000. Abbreviations, see Table 13.3.

someone out of government if they dislike a specific policy. After all, their national governments will put the blame on other countries if the public does not accept decisions. Thus, the argument of the German Constitutional Court that the European Union takes its democratic legitimacy from the people of the member states by having the decisions of the organs of the European Union coupled to the national parliaments may be practical, but it is rather weak. Europe lacks the democratic responsibility of those who take decisions; it lacks democratic legitimacy.

The proposal of the Convention was an attempt to get out of that impasse. Whereas fourteen member states have ratified the constitutional treaty by March 2006, the French and the Dutch said 'no' in their referendums. Other member states such as the UK have postponed a decision on the treaty. Nevertheless, parts of the constitutional proposal may be agreed upon by the European Council. In any case, the proposal shapes the discussion on this issue in the future. It is therefore appropriate to analyze some of the stipulations.

According to the Convention proposal, some decisions are to be moved from unanimity to qualified majority. For instance, it is envisioned to increase the powers of the Union in areas such as asylum and immigration, energy, and space research. Member states would retain, however, the right to set national entry levels for third-country nationals (in spite of qualified majority voting in immigration policy). The co-decision process, whereby the European Parliament has to agree on measures shaping policy, is to become the general rule between Parliament and Council; it is now only used in limited areas. By and large, not too many areas are designed to be moved to qualified majority. As a rule of thumb, about 65 percent of the decisions will be done under qualified majority instead of 60 percent. The core decisions remain under the heading of unanimity. This means that the constitution would represent only a small change towards a more intensified form of integration. In any case, moving unanimity items to qualified majority will in no case reduce the democratic deficit because it would only increase the power of the Council.

The main point in the original convention proposal that failed to find consensus among the heads of state was a new decision rule for qualified majority. In this dual majority proposal the majority of the member states, and the majority of the people, defined as 60 percent of the population, were required. This 50–60 voting rule was intended to substitute the voting procedure as defined by the Treaty of Nice where votes have been assigned to the member states (see Table 13.2). This proposed procedure was not accepted. The compromise proposal consisted of a new definition of qualified majority, consisting of 55 percent of the member states, at least fifteen of them, and 65 percent of the population (article I-25). In this way, a majority of the large countries was intended to be made more difficult. In addition, a new type of qualified majority was intended when the Council would not act on a proposal from the Commission or from the Union Minister Council of Foreign Affairs. Then a majority of 72 percent of the member states, representing at least 65 percent of the population of the Union, would be required.

Other planned changes involved organizational matters. A more permanent presidency of the European Council of two and a half years was to replace the current six-month member state rotating system. A post of Foreign Minister was to be established to represent the EU on external matters. The Commission was designed to consist of fifteen voting commissioners and fifteen non-voting and rotating commissioners (from 2009); the alternative proposal was that each member has one commissioner. The position of the Commission president is strengthened. He draws the guide lines for the commissioners; upon his request, commissioners have to step down.

For the European Central Bank, the Convention proposal originally contained a major change, namely that the target of 'non- inflationary growth,' a description of price level stability, would be no longer have been mentioned as one of the economic policy goals of the European Union and the member states that was laid down in article 2 of the EU Treaty and in the articles 2 and 4 of the EC Treaty. Price stability would only have been mentioned as a task of the European Central Bank in article I-30 of the Convention proposal so that formally this target would have been given up by the union. This clearly could be interpreted as giving a stable money less weight. The change would have affected the independence of the ECB. In contrast to this original plan, the target of price stability kept its constitutional rank in the final convention proposal (article I-3, para 3); it is also an explicit target with priority for the ECB. The ECB continues to be an institution *sui generis* (article I-30, para 3).

A major drawback for the ECB is that the European Council can change the institutional arrangement of the ECB in Part III Title III without calling a governmental conference. Whereas such a decision continues to require unanimity and ratification by the member states, such a procedure removes the decision from the public's attention.

The Convention proposals lay out the basic goals of the European Union, putting some weight on social coherence. It seems that Europe partly finds its identity in the idea of reducing differences in income and endowment with public goods. Although only a minor part of GDP is actually spent for these purposes, one can have the impression when reading the proposal that it can be interpreted in the sense of distributive federalism, where integration is seen as bringing people together by the vehicle of redistribution. In that sense, one can say that the Convention proposal is a welfare state and social-democratic document, not a liberal one in the European sense. It does not cultivate the spirit of competitive federalism. Looking ahead, the interpretation of social cohesion by the European Court of Justice Europe may rely more on the equity element than on the competition element in the future. In any case, the Convention can be seen as moving the center of gravity away from the market mechanism.

A vision for the distant future

Looking into the very distant future, one can envision how far away the European Union is from an intensive form of integration if one studies a scenario with an improved democratic legitimacy of the European level as follows: more decision power is given to the European parliament. This implies that national parliaments cede some of their competencies. The European parliament itself can be conceived as a two-chamber system. Members of the two chambers are elected, for instance by a majority rule for each election district. The electoral districts for the election of the members of the first chamber should be delineated such that each district represents a similar percentage of the population. The second chamber should represent the member states, ideally by electing the representatives of the member states directly (as in the US Senate). The Commission represents the European government. A constitution-like system of rules would define the competencies of the European parliament, of its two chambers, the Commission, the member states, and the regional level in the member states.

Describing the future road in this way exposes all the problems that an enlarged Europe faces. From historical experience we know that the principle 'no taxation without representation' is the basis of democracy. It seems realistic that the European population is not prepared to cede national sovereignty shifting the power to tax, the power to spend, and the power of the budget to the European level. This would mean that a European institution such as the European parliament would be authorized to decide the type of tax, the tax base, and the tax rate for the individual taxpayer; it would also be able to decide that a tax collected in country A can be spent in country B, either explicitly or implicitly.

Variable geometry

The European Treaty allows member states to form special clubs that intensify their cooperation in specific areas such as border controls (Schengen countries) or monetary union. Countries may move at different speeds of integration. According to this approach, the dynamics of integration is provided by a subset of the member countries.

Different speeds and variable geometry cannot relate to the essentials of a union. They must refer to additional steps that one may consider as desirable but not strictly necessary. A variable geometry also cannot solve the core issue of a democratic void; it is simply not conceivable that a European club as a subset of member countries develops a separated constitutional arrangement diverging from the other members, including for instance parliamentary voting and taxation. Thus, the strategy of multiple speeds can only be applied in the context of intergovernmental decision-making. It is not suitable for a more intense form of integration. Variable geometry, or separate speed, can only be an intermediate step of integration.

Another aspect is opting out, an option granted to the member countries by the constitutional proposal. Opting out, that is granting an exception, may prove to be a dangerous strategy for a union because it leads to a greater heterogeneity in the institutional arrangements. It can be used as a threat to have one's way for a greater heterogeneity in the institutional arrangements. An opting out clause can be granted only in most unusual circumstances when otherwise the union can not be held together. The EU is a single undertaking, and the net benefits come in a package.

The borders of the European Union

It is an open question for the future of the European Union where Europe defines its borders. This issue is discussed particularly with respect to Turkey. It also applies to the successor states of Yugoslavia, and in addition it relates to the Ukraine, possibly Russia, Israel, Lebanon, and the Maghreb countries Morocco, Algeria, and Tunisia. If one follows the British concept of the EU as an enhanced free trade area, then the task of finding an answer to this question is easier. However, if one prefers a concept of a deepened European integration that has at its core the gradual evolution of a European citizen with a distinct European identity, then an answer is difficult to come by. A more intensive integration requires the aggregation of citizens' preferences coming from different member states. Such an aggregation becomes difficult if preferences and cultural characteristics diverge greatly. Immobilism in the decision-making process can be the outcome. Moreover, it is questionable whether the EU's population will ever support such an extensive enlargement.

Furthermore, the recent eastern enlargement has shown that the freedom of movement of persons, one of the great achievements of the European Union, is being retrenched in the intended services directive. Finally, it is unclear whether the geopolitical advantages of a common European foreign policy, expected from a major enlargement, will materialize. Foreign policy would have to take into consideration the then neighbor states of the EU – the Caucasus, Syria, Iraq, and Iran. Unquestionably, the European Union must find forms of cooperation with Turkey. A privileged partnership is such a concept.

13.5 Monetary union

The introduction of the euro in 1999 has been a project of historical importance. As a common currency, the euro is intended to bring the peoples of Europe closer together. From this point of view, monetary union was politically motivated. In addition, monetary union abolishes the cost of exchanging currencies. The transaction costs for the trade of goods, the exchange of services, the movement of people, and the flow of capital – for the four freedoms – are reduced; the single market is completed from the monetary side.

Institutional design

Monetary union means that monetary policy will be shifted to the European level. The institutional set-up can be explained as follows. In the European System of Central Banks, decisions on monetary policy are made by the European Central Bank (ECB). The decision-making bodies of the ECB are the Governing Council, the Executive Board, and the General Council (Figure 13.2).

The Governing Council comprises all the governors of the national central banks of the member states of the monetary union and the six members of the Executive Board. Each member of the Governing Board has one vote, giving the

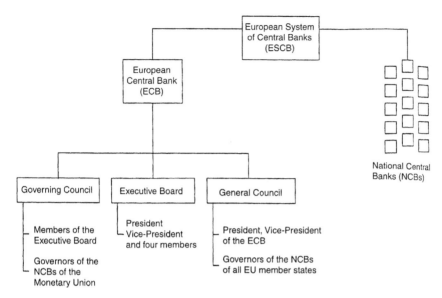

Figure 13.2 Set-up of the ECB.

governor of a central bank of a small country the same weight as that of a large country. The governors of the National Central Banks are appointed by the national governments for a minimum of five years; the appointment is renewable. The main task of the Governing Council is to formulate monetary policy and take decisions on the strategy as well on the monetary policy instruments such as the key interest rates.

The Executive Board comprises the President, the Vice-President, and four other members. They are appointed by a common accord, i.e. by unanimity, of the governments of the member states at the level of the heads of state or government, on a recommendation from the European Commission after it has consulted the European Parliament and the Governing Council of the ECB. The members of the Executive Board are appointed for a non-renewable term of eight years. This gives them personal autonomy. The main responsibility of the Executive Board is to implement monetary policy in accordance with the guidelines laid down by the Governing Council of the ECB.

The General Council comprises the President, the Vice-President, and the governors of all the National Central Banks of the European Union, including those EU countries which are not members of monetary union. Its task is to deal with issues related to the preparation of countries for EMU membership. Formally, the ECB is part of the European System of Central Banks which also consists of the EU National Central Banks. The National Central Banks of those countries which do not participate in the euro area nevertheless are members of the European System of Central Banks, albeit, with a special status. They do not vote on issues of the monetary union.

The institutional set-up gives a large weight to the twelve votes of national central bankers (in 2006) relative to the six votes of the members of the Executive Council. This weight will tilt even more to the favor of national central banks if new members are admitted. Then a new procedure has to be found, for instance by rotating the membership for some countries. This formal structure points to the fact that the position of the ECB in the European system is different from the Bundesbank's Central Council in the German system where the state central banks had only nine votes relative to the eight votes of the directorate. In the Open Market Committee of the Fed (Federal Reserve Board), only five governors of regional reserve banks are represented relative to seven Washington-based members.

The European Central Bank is independent from other institutions in the EU (article 108). Neither the ECB nor any member of its decision-making body may take instructions from national governments or the EU. The statute of the ECB can only be changed by a new treaty which would require unanimity (see above). The Constitution proposal provides that the President, Vice-President, and other members of the ECB's Executive Board will be appointed by the European Council, acting by qualified majority (article III-382).

The task of the ECB

Article 105 of the EC Treaty defines the main objective of the European System of Central Banks (ESCB): 'The primary objective of the ESCB shall be to maintain price level stability'. Other targets such as supporting employment are only secondary and conditional with respect to the target of price level stability. 'Without prejudice to the objective of price level stability, the ESCB shall support the general economic policies in the Community with a view to contributing to the achievement of the objectives of the community as laid down in Article 2' (article 105). Article 2 of the EC Treaty defines the task of the Community in general, namely 'to promote ... a harmonious and balanced development of economic activities, sustainable and non-inflationary growth respecting the environment, a high degree of convergence of economic performance, a high level of employment and of social protection, the raising of the standard of living and quality of life, and economic and social cohesion and solidarity among Member States.'

The role of the ECB is to define monetary policy, i.e. to develop a strategy and to implement this strategy. The ECB has set the target of price level stability as a change of the price level below 2 percent. It applies a two-pillar strategy with the first pillar referring to a reference value for the expansion of the money supply (monetary targeting) and the second pillar relating to the price level including the future price level. In addition to defining and implementing monetary policy, the ECB will also conduct foreign exchange rate operations, manage the official reserves, support the authorities supervising financial institutions, and ensure the smooth operation of payment systems. It has legislative power; its regulations are binding.

Instruments

The ECB conducts monetary policy by making use of three tools: temporary open market operations, standing facilities, and minimum reserve requirements. Open market operations represent the most important instrument and take the form of reverse transactions (repo). Under a repo agreement, the ECB buys assets or grants a loan against assets given as collateral. This type of activity in the money market allows the ECB to provide liquidity to the eurozone's financial system on a weekly basis and to signal the stance of monetary policy. Liquidity is allocated by standard tenders in which banks indicate the amount of liquidity they wish to have. Usually more liquidity is demanded than offered by the ECB so that the total quantity has to be allocated to the individual banks in proportion to their demand. To restrict the volatility of short-term overnight interest rates, the ECB offers two standing facilities: the marginal lending facility and the deposit facility. The rates on these two facilities, by setting a ceiling and a floor to the overnight rate, create a corridor within which the overnight rate can fluctuate. Finally, the ECB requires credit institutions to hold minimum reserves on accounts with the national central banks.

Since reverse transactions in the repo agreements are based on adequate collateral, the ECB defines acceptable assets in order to protect against the risk of the loss of the asset. This instrument gives the ECB a handle on the quality of government (and private) debt. So far, the ECB has not used this instrument to make a distinction in its financial market activities between government bonds for countries with low and high public sector debt. In 2006, the ECB has stated that all assets offered as collateral have to meet a set of criteria. The minimum credit rating threshold is at least A- from Standard and Poor's or Fitchs Ratings or A3 from Moodys (ECB 2006: 82). Even when the bonds of all EMU countries satisfied this requirement, this announcement may be seen as a signal for the financial markets that the ECB intends to use this requirement in the future. If the bonds of member countries threaten to reach the limit, the financial markets are likely to raise the country specific basis points. The ECB's signal can thus be seen as an attempt to use the financial markets as a controlling mechanism.

Enlargement

Since the launch of the euro in 1999, Denmark, Sweden, and the UK are the only EU members not to have joined the monetary union. Unlike the ten new member states, as well as Bulgaria and Romania, these three older members have no clear roadmap for adopting the single currency. The accession treaties of the new member states require them to enter the European Exchange Rate Mechanism (ERM II) and subsequently join the eurozone as soon as the convergence criteria are met. The four Maastricht criteria laid out in article 121, Para 1 of the EC Treaty have specific requirements regarding the inflation rate, government finances, the exchange rate, and the long-term interest rates (Table 13.4).

Table 13.4 The Maastricht criteria

Inflation rate	*No more than 1.5 percent higher than that of the three best-performing euro states*
Government finances	
Annual government deficit	Should not exceed 3 percent of GDP
Government debt	Should not exceed 60 percent of GDP
Exchange rate	Two-year membership of the ERMII without devaluation
Long-term interest rates	No more than 2 percent higher than the three best-performing euro states

Conflict between price level stability and employment

There can be a conflict between the objective of a stable money and other objectives of economic policy such as reducing unemployment. One should not have the illusion that the Phillips curve postulating a trade-off between the rate of inflation and unemployment can be a basis for monetary policy and that an excessive increase in the money supply can stimulate employment in the medium-run. People would anticipate the inflation rate and they would require higher nominal interest rates, the value of money would deteriorate, and the ECB would lose its reputation. Eventually, the ECB would be forced to put on the brakes, and a 'stabilization recession' would be the result. An excessive expansion of the money supply may also lead to an asset price inflation without affecting the consumer price index as happened in Japan in 1989. When the bubble bursts, the real sphere of the economy will be affected negatively.

Conflict with the European Council in exchange rate policy

The European Council, the central decision-making body of the EU (see above), has the right to conclude formal agreements on exchange rate systems with non-EU members (by unanimity) and it may (by qualified majority) formulate the general orientation for exchange rate policy (article 111 of the EC Treaty). As a rule, the European Council consists of the economics and finance ministers (ECOFIN). In the area of exchange rate policy, a conflict between the ECB and the Council can develop.

Exchange rate decisions or orientations of the European Council can be incompatible with an independent central bank. If the ECB were forced to maintain a predetermined exchange rate vis-à-vis other currencies, this would mean an exchange-rate-oriented monetary policy. In this case, the central bank would not be free to determine its monetary policy. The exchange rate would be the nominal anchor instead of price level stability. Hopefully, this conflict between policy-makers and the central bank is softened by the requirement of article 111 that exchange rate policy must be consistent with the objective of price level stability.

Some want to use the exchange rate of the euro against other currencies of the world – like the dollar or the Japanese yen – strategically in the interest of the European export industry by driving down its external value in order to stimulate European exports. This is a misleading idea. Disruptions and quarrels in the international division of labor, turmoil in the financial markets, and reactions of other players in the world economy would ensue. What is more important, a lower external value of a currency can only be brought about if this currency is supplied more generously than other currencies. That is, the expansion of the aggregate money supply has to exceed by far the growth of the production potential (plus the tolerated inflation rate and a correction factor for the velocity of money). This, consequently, causes the internal value of the currency to fall. External value and internal value of a currency are interrelated, so to say two sides of the same coin.

Shielding the Central Bank from political pressure

Central banks are always exposed to political pressure. Political pressure on the European Central Bank may originate from countries facing severe economic problems. This holds particularly true for countries with excessive deficits and high indebtedness. Countries with high government debt are interested in low interest rates, a rather lax monetary policy, and a slightly higher inflation rate than the one anticipated by financial markets, because all this would ease their budgetary situation, especially because debts would melt away in real terms. Such a policy becomes even more attractive when political maneuvering space in the future is restricted by a high interest burden. Political pressure on the European Central Bank will be further increased if the economy of a highly indebted state is taken by recession and if it faces severe financial difficulties or social unrest. The issue is not that a country will deliberately follow a policy of excessive deficits in order to eventually force the European Central Bank to step in as lender of last resort. The problem is that a long-run process of accumulating debt may occur as a result of political weakness so that eventually the European Central Bank has no other option than to monetize the public debt by a lax monetary policy. Consequently, the criterion of a sustainable public budget within the monetary union is well-suited to shielding the central bank from political pressure.

Control of unreliable fiscal policy with the Stability Pact

Sustainability of the governmental financial condition is therefore an important precondition for a monetary union (article 104 EC Treaty). The overriding target is that governments remain solvent. Usually, this condition is interpreted as requiring stationarity of public debt. This means that the debt/GDP ratio has to remain constant. In the EU Treaty, this limit for debt in relation to GDP has been set at 60 percent. This restraint for debt is consistent with a limit for an excessive deficit of 3 percent of GDP if real GDP growth is 3 percent and the inflation rate remains below 2 percent. The intention is to limit political pressure on the European Central Bank. Such a constraint on fiscal policy becomes especially necessary if countries have institutional arrangements which are not conducive to solid governmental finances. A case in point is a constitutional weakness with respect to limiting governmental expenditures as in Italy.

The general rule of the Stability Pact is that a budget deficit surpassing 3 percent of GDP is considered excessive. It triggers an excessive deficit procedure, which can culminate in financial sanctions on the country in the wrong. However, the changes to the Stability Pact adopted in March 2005 weakened this rule by introducing a myriad of exceptions to it. In the initial Stability Pact the country with a deficit exceeding 3 percent of GDP was able to avoid an excessive deficit procedure if it was in recession, defined as a 2 percent negative annual growth. After the adoption of the changes, the country can be spared the sanctions if it was exposed to an 'unusual event outside the control of the member state,' a 'negative growth rate' or a 'protracted period of very low growth relative to potential growth.' The leniency of the Pact is compounded by the incorporation of 'all other relevant factors' as possible exceptions from the 3 percent ceiling. These range from research and development expenditure to development aid and to pension reform.

The determination of an excessive budget deficit remains undecided if a member state, after being put into delay by a formal resolution, indeed takes appropriate measures. Whether measures taken are appropriate is also decided by the European Council. It should also be noted that initially only a non-interest-bearing deposit is required. This will be converted into a fine after two years if the budget deficit remains excessive. There is a conflict of roles since those who are responsible for the excessive budgetary deficit will also be the ones to define it and to vote on the fines. All these considerations, together with the extension of procedural deadlines and deadlines for correcting the excessive budget deficit increase skepticism about the Pact's effectiveness.

No-bail-out clause

According to article 103 of the EC Treaty, the EU is not liable for the financial difficulties of any member state with a budget deficit, nor are other member states liable for this state's difficulties. Nevertheless, the political pressure for transfers granted by the European Union or by member countries will become perceptible in the future. Thus, if transfers have to be made after all – in spite of liability being excluded – the donor of transfers, as well as the recipient, may develop an interest in keeping these transfers as low as possible, replacing them by a rather lax monetary policy.

Common monetary policy and national decision-making

Common monetary policy must be oriented towards price level stability in the monetary union as a whole. Consequently, it cannot take into consideration specific national conditions. In a monetary union, the monetary 'suit' is no longer custom-tailored for each nation, the one size must fit all. Thus, if nations are in a different position in the business cycle, one being in a boom and another in a recession, if countries experience an asymmetric shock and if they get stuck in a self-inflicted crisis, they must cope with the same monetary policy.

In this context, an increasing divergence in the growth performance of member countries of EMU is an issue. There are two different groups of countries. In one group are countries of the periphery, e g. Ireland, Portugal, and Spain, which have high inflation rates and as a consequence low real interest rates, high current account deficits, and high growth rates. This group will become larger when the new EU members join EMU. In the other group, the countries of the core such as Germany and France have low inflation rates, consequently a higher real interest rate than the periphery, current account surpluses, and a low growth rate. This growth divergence represents a puzzle. Economists like to explain these differences by the Balassa Samuelson effect and better investment opportunities in the periphery for mobile capital; nevertheless, the growth difference may give rise to political debates.

The crucial institutional characteristics of the European Monetary Union is that monetary policy is still judged in national political decision-making processes, since a political union did not come into existence simultaneously with a monetary union. From this, a potential for conflicts inevitably arises between a common monetary policy and national economic interests. Quite a bit of political discipline is required from a country in crisis to accept a monetary policy that is oriented towards European price level stability. If, however, the country in crisis could have its way in getting an easy monetary policy adopted, inflation in Europe would result.

By entrusting an independent European Central Bank with the authority to steer the money supply, i.e. to set the interest rates and determine other monetary policy instruments, the EU Treaty has taken monetary affairs out of the hands of politics altogether; it has depoliticized the process of money creation.

It is an imperative requirement for the monetary union to establish a long-lasting consensus on the very essence of the European Monetary Union, namely on the depoliticization of the common currency. Thus, policy-makers have to respect the decisions of the European Central Bank, above all, in situations where these decisions are unfavorable for a single country or its government – for instance, in times preceding an important governmental election or when a country is facing unfavorable economic conditions.

Currency unions haven fallen apart in the past, in most cases when political disintegration took place. The two most prominent examples are the breaking-up of the Austrian–Hungarian Empire after World War I and the disintegration of the Soviet Union after the fall of the Iron Curtain. In these cases, the currencies were no longer supported by the political conditions. A disintegration of the euro area would have a severe impact on European integration. It could only occur if the concept of European integration lost support in the member states.

On the issue of an optimal macroeconomic policy mix

On the macroeconomic level, the issue arises to what extent macroeconomic policies should be coordinated. This question is especially relevant since monetary policy now has been Europeanized whereas the other areas of macroeconomic policy such as fiscal policy are still at the national level. One approach is to limit negative spillovers between the different macroeconomic policy areas. Thus, the Stability Pact is intended to control excessive fiscal deficits and in this way to protect the ECB and the euro against free-rider behavior of individual nation states. It is coordination by restraint. A rule that real wage increases in the different countries should not exceed labor productivity growth in the member countries would help to prevent a negative spillover in the sense that national unemployment is not aggravated. Other attempts of coordination represent a form of atmospheric coordination including mutual information. This means that national policy-makers are informed on what is intended elsewhere and start from a common frame of reference. Partly, coordination will have to rely on moral persuasion for instance if a country with high growth rates benefits from the low interest rates of the ECB and is not willing to reduce its governmental absorption. Finally, most of the coordination philosophy is based on extremely simple and naive Keynesian ideas of controlling and fine-tuning aggregate demand over the cycle; inside and outside lags are neglected. In nearly all countries, the political process seems to be unable to smooth government expenditures over the cycle. While additional spending in a recession is grabbed wholeheartedly by the politicians, reducing demand in a boom is unlikely to take place.

13.6 Monetary union and the labor market

In a monetary union, exchange rates are no longer available as a mechanism of adjustment. This has implications for the labor market. There are two lines of argument which describe specific requirements for the labor market and for wage policy in the monetary union: one relates to diverging labor productivities, the other to the role of wages as a substitute for the exchange rate.

Diverging labor productivities

The differences in labor productivity per head of person employed in the current and future members of the European Union are quite impressive (Figure 13.3). Let us define labor productivity as the nominal GDP (in current market prices) in euros per person employed. The average of EU-25 is set equal to 100. The values for EU countries diverge remarkably. At the high end of the spectrum, there are the older members EU-15 members with an average labor productivity per person employed of 111 percent in 2005. Besides Luxembourg, which is a special case, the most notable performers are Ireland (154 percent), Denmark (140 percent), and Belgium (132 percent). Two larger continental countries, Italy (109 percent) and Germany (108 percent), are slightly below the EU-15

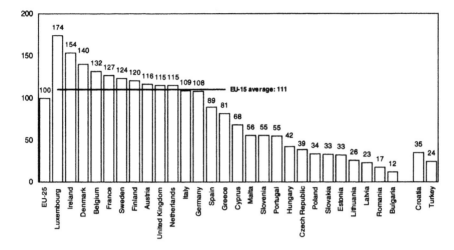

Figure 13.3 Labor productivities in the EU-27, 2005[a] (source: Eurostat Database, National Accounts Data, 2006).

Note

a Labor productivities calculated as ratios of GDP at current prices and total employment in respective countries.

average. Spain, Greece, and Portugal are the Western European economies whose labor productivity diverges markedly from the EU-15 average: 89, 81, and 55 percent, respectively. These data show that differences in labor productivity within the monetary union are still strong.

Out of the members that acceded in 2004, productivities range between 68 percent (Cyprus) and 23 (Latvia). The new members are at a far distance from the EU-25 average; Romania and Bulgaria reach only 17 and 12 percent, respectively. Croatia and Turkey stand at 35 and 24 percent, respectively. It is notable that while labor productivity has increased all across Europe, especially in the countries catching up, some countries like Italy and Germany exhibit stagnation.

Transaction costs are reduced and market segmentations disappear in a monetary union. As a stylized fact, Jevons's law of one price will prevail. This equilibrium condition for the goods market translates into an equilibrium condition of the labor market. Diverging national labor productivities in the currency union are consistent with full employment only if national labor productivities are not exceeded by national labor costs. This means that labor costs have to be differentiated in the monetary union in line with productivity differences.

Asymmetric shocks and the real exchange rate

In a monetary union, the real exchange rate has to take over the role of nominal exchange rate adjustments which can no longer be used as an equilibrating mechanism if economic development between countries diverges. An important case of diverging development is when a shock affects countries asymmetrically, that is when a member country is struck by a negative exogenous shock more intensively than other countries in the currency union. Prior to the monetary union, the country could have devalued its currency to regain competitiveness. Within a monetary union, a member country fully experiences the asymmetric shock: in the case of a negative disturbance, production falls, the utilization of the production potential decreases, and unemployment rises. The economy now has to adjust by using mechanisms other than the nominal exchange rate.

Moreover, the nominal exchange rate can no longer be used in other instances: when some countries have weaker growth than others, when the business cycle in the European Union is out of synchronization, when homemade problems evolve in some countries, when some countries respond more flexibly to a shock that is symmetric to the European Union as a whole and when the unemployment rates diverge strongly between countries.

Three substitution mechanisms for the exchange rate

A first mechanism of adjustment which can be taken into account as a substitute for a nominal depreciation of the currency is the migration of labor. If workers leave a country which has been struck by a crisis and move to more prospering countries, unemployment decreases in the crisis area. The per capita income of the country in question will rise again. However, this is a 'passive' cure. Moreover, under European conditions, one can assume that this form of adjustment will not be accepted by the countries from which people emigrate nor from countries to which workers would have to migrate. The willingness to absorb workers from abroad will generally be low. Moreover, language barriers and cultural diversity will limit the mobility of people. Even though the free movement of labor is one of the four freedoms of the single market, it seems realistic that labor migration will play a minor role as an equilibrating instrument in the divergent structural development in Europe. Unlike the US, where labor mobility is generally high and where migration between regions as a reaction to an economic shock plays a central role (Blanchard and Katz 1992), labor mobility in Europe cannot be expected to be a sufficient substitute for exchange rate changes.

If labor migration is ruled out as an alternative to exchange rate adjustment, relative prices will have to do the job. In the case of a negative shock, a real depreciation will bring about improved competitiveness. This means that the relative price of non-tradables must fall, in order to stimulate the production of tradables. In bringing about this change in relative prices, wages, i.e. the price of the immobile production factor, will have to bear most of the burden of adjustment. Under static conditions, a decline in national wages makes a country regain its competitiveness. Under conditions of a growing economy, which is a more realistic case, wages should not rise as much as before. The decline in wages or their reduced increase stimulate the economy in the same way a depreciation would. There is one difference, however: a devaluation re-establishes competitiveness for all goods, a fall in wages favors labor-intensive production and thus re-establishes the competitiveness of jobs.

If wages do not react flexibly, differences in unemployment between the countries of the currency union are likely to develop. Then transfers are the only remaining mechanism to help nations adjust to a crisis (see below).

Thus, a cascade of equilibrating mechanisms exists which can be used to replace an exchange rate adjustment. First, the migration of labor can take the place of a devaluation of the home currency. If this is not possible, prices of the immobile production factor, predominantly wages, can adjust. Alternatively, if this also is not possible, financial transfers have to take over the shock-absorbing role of a devaluation.

Implications for wage policy

Since labor productivities diverge considerably between the countries of the European Monetary Union and can be expected to diverge in the future, labor costs will have to be differentiated between the member states of the monetary union. The reason is that national labor costs must be borne by national productivities. Otherwise, unemployment will increase. Moreover, we know from empirical studies that convergence of productivities takes a long time.

Future wage policy in the individual countries should orient itself at the national labor productivities. Wage harmonization in the European Monetary Union should not be aimed at. People must understand that the level of national wages must reflect the differences in national labor productivities.

Institutionally, wage formation should not be Europeanized, even if people now compare their wage in a single currency and thus money illusion will no longer segment wage-bargaining behavior of unions. Political demands of 'the same wage for the same type of work' that are likely to be articulated are not well founded with diverging differences in labor productivity. Europeanizing wage formation would definitely increase the unemployment rate in the European countries. What is needed is a decentralization of wage formation, shifting wage formation from the economy-wide or sector level to the regional and to the firm's level. Wage formation, especially in the major countries of the continent, should follow more closely the market process.

Employment being a national responsibility, employment policy must be national as well. To organize employment policy on the European level and use national contributions to the EU budget or tax revenues for this purpose, would allow the governments of the member states to shift responsibility to the European level and to use the EU as scapegoat, thus hurting the European cause if unemployment actually rises. National contributions and tax revenues would be used in favor of the countries that perform poorly. Countries which reduce unemployment would pay the contributions. Such an approach would represent the wrong incentives.

Implications for social union

Labor costs also include the contributions to the social systems paid by the firms. These labor costs, too, have to be borne by national productivities. The divergence in labor productivities makes clear that the costs of social security systems in the different countries must also be different. This means that social security benefits cannot be harmonized. With such a divergence of national productivities, a social union cannot be realized and the Europeanization of social policy should be avoided. The territorial principle of social insurance in Europe, according to which benefits can only be obtained from the system to which contributions have been paid, is quite appropriate. But even if labor productivities were identical, the social security systems would have developed differently over time. What is more, countries have chosen different levels of public insurance relying for instance on a larger role of private insurance or accepting a lower level of social insurance than others. Differences in the systems do not preclude that the issue of portability of claims in order to allow the mobility of people is to be solved.

Monetary union and transfers

Large economic regional units are usually characterized by some type of transfer mechanism. Transfers replace the exchange-rate adjustment mechanism when labor is not sufficiently mobile and when wages are not sufficiently divergent and flexible between countries. Taking as an example the US – an area with a common currency – transfers are made between different regions via the allocation of revenue between federal and state authorities and via the social security system. Additionally, the assignment of competences for expenditure and taxation to the various regional administrative bodies – the different hierarchical levels of the state – plays an important role in regional adjustment processes. In principle, a political union will be accompanied by higher transfers. As a rule, competences for expenditure and taxation will be assigned in a way that financial transfers between the different regions only have to net out major discrepancies in revenue. One must therefore be aware that the monetary union will necessarily be associated with a strong political demand for an additional transfer mechanism and for more tax revenue competences at the central level unless labor markets become more flexible.

Part IV

National economic policy versus a world economic order

Again and again, conflicts arise between national interests and the welfare of the world as a whole, i.e. of all countries together, with regard to the international division of labor. National interests may be rather short-term or even be linked to the advantage of particular groups in one country only, opposed to long-term benefits for that country or advantages for the world as a whole. Thus, the conflict between protectionism and free trade comes to life again and again (Chapter 14). With locational competition between countries, the mobility of capital has opened up a new dimension of international interdependence where countries are competing for the mobile production factors of capital and technology (Chapter 15). The utilization of the environment, a subject that will attract more attention in the future, is another field where national interests and worldwide concerns also can collide (Chapter 16). To prevent strategic behavior of states, the countries have to commit themselves to a set of rules for the international division of labor that excludes non-cooperative behavior as far as possible. Such an international order includes rules for the exchange of goods, for factor migration and for utilizing the environment (Chapter 17).

14 National protectionism versus worldwide free trade

What you will understand after reading this chapter

For a variety of reasons, the international division of labor has been tampered with through trade policy measures. Historic periods of protectionism were followed by epochs of free trade and vice versa (section 14.1). The most important trade policy instruments are surveyed in section 14.2. A whole arsenal of arguments for taking trade policy measures have been put forward. A number of arguments have a defensive orientation (section 14.3), others are rather aggressive (section 14.4), and yet other arguments concern retaliation (section 14.5) and the demand for a level playing field in competition (section 14.6). These arguments are critically reviewed. The reasons for a free international division of labor are summarized (section 14.7). Finally, the most prominent globalization fears are discussed (section 14.8).

14.1 Periods of protectionism and free trade

In the international division of labor, periods of liberalization and of protectionism have alternated in economic history. The beginning of the nineteenth century, with the Napoleonic Continental Blockade against the United Kingdom, was protectionist. In 1815, the British Corn Laws took effect. Intensely discussed in the literature, these laws aimed at ensuring self-sufficiency in agricultural goods in case of another conflict. The remaining part of the first half of the century was then marked by the intention of reducing trade barriers. The Corn Laws were abolished in 1846, allowing for lower agricultural prices and an increase in real income for the working population in the industrial towns. A phase of liberalization began. Until World War I broke out in 1914, there was a time of free trade, especially in the exchange between Great Britain and its then colonies as well as its former ones; important capital flows went into the newly independent states. But the continental countries also reduced their trade barriers, e.g. in the German Tariff Union (1834). This phase of liberalization was accompanied by largely stable currency conditions in the framework of the gold standard.

With World War I, the phase of integration in the world economy came to an

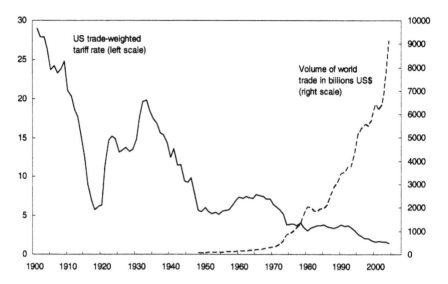

Figure 14.1 Tariffs and world trade in economic history (source: IMF, *International Financial Statistics*, 2005; US Department of the Treasury, Various annual reports; WTO, *World Trade Statistics* 2005).

end. The hyper-inflation that hit Germany and other European countries in 1923 and the Great Depression starting in 1929 seriously disrupted the world economy. Tariffs and other trade barriers increased; the 1930s saw devaluation races in which states tried to stimulate their exports by devaluing their currencies and thus improving their employment possibilities thereby hurting the other countries ('beggar-thy-neighbor policy').

After World War II, a framework for the world economy was created with the GATT (General Agreement on Tariffs and Trade) in 1948. Based on this framework, the international division of labor could develop beneficially, without trade barriers. Until 1971, the currency system of Bretton Woods succeeded in keeping exchange rates relatively stable. The World Bank and the International Monetary Fund, international organizations aiming at a stronger integration of all countries into the world economy, were created (see Chapter 17).

A snapshot of this development is given in Figure 14.1. From 1900 on, the US trade-weighted tariff rate declined until World War I, then it went up again until the 1930s. From then on, it was continuously reduced. World trade, measured as world merchandise trade, has risen continuously in the last fifty years.

14.2 Trade policy instruments

We briefly survey the most important policy instruments and their effects.

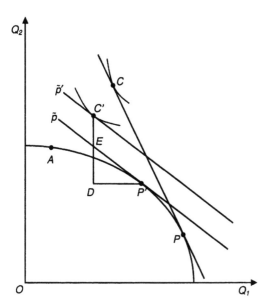

Figure 14.2 Effects of a tariff on imports.

Import duties

A tariff on the imported good 2 makes this good more expensive. The incentive to produce becomes stronger for the domestic producers, whereas, owing to the higher price, the domestic consumers demand less. The domestically produced quantity of the import substitute increases, the imported quantity declines. Let $\tilde{p}_2 = p_2(1 + t)$ denote the domestic price after the introduction of the tariff (where t is the tariff rate). With a tariff, the relative price $\tilde{p} = p_1/\tilde{p}_2 = p_1/[p_2(1 + t)]$ falls. The production point moves from P to P' (Figure 14.2). This price ratio also determines the consumption point, C'. We assume that the tariff revenues are redistributed to the households as a lump-sum payment, shifting the budget line to the right. On the world market, the home country (as a small country) continues trading at the world market price ratio, p. For giving away $P'D$ in exports, it receives DC' in imports. The domestic price ratio is DE/DP'. The tariff rate is EC'/DE where EC' is the government's tariff revenue in terms of good 2.

The tariff on imports protects the domestic import substitutes sector, but the opportunity costs are considerable:

- The export sector (producing good 1) shrinks as the import substitutes sector attracts production factors. Protecting one sector thus weakens the non-protected sector. In a dynamic economy, import protection hampers the development of export opportunities. For instance, by protecting agriculture and coal-mining, more modern sectors, like engineering or the semiconductor industry, are penalized. If we enlarge the model to comprise monetary effects as well, an import tariff leads to a tariff-induced revaluation of the domestic currency, as the protection against imports reduces the demand for foreign currency.

- If the production of import substitutes is concentrated in a particular region of a country, protection against imports hampers the development prospects of this region or of other regions in a number of ways. One example is that protected sectors tend to pay high wages, impairing the development of new enterprises and also of the export business in that region. Furthermore, the incentives to increase efficiency are weaker, and finally – leaving the allocation model aside – the protection against imports leads to a reduced demand for foreign money and thus to a revaluation of the domestic currency, causing a negative effect for the export business in other regions.
- Consumers reach a lower welfare level in the consumption point C' (instead of C). The trade triangle shrinks.

Subsidies

Besides a tariff on imports, the domestic (or import-substituting) sector can also be protected through a subsidy. If, as an example, a production subsidy (s) is paid for the (domestically produced) import substitute, the producers face a change in the price ratio, as the producer price ($\tilde{p}_2^P$) for the domestically produced import substitute rises. The domestic producers' incentive to produce becomes stronger. The relative price that producers face, $\tilde{p}^P = p_1/\tilde{p}_2 = p_1/[p_2(1+s)]$, declines. The production point moves from P to P' (Figure 14.3).

In contrast to a tariff on imports, consumers still face the world market price despite the subsidy: there is no market segmentation, and – if the country is small – they trade according to the world market price line that has to be drawn through point P', as it was in the case of a tariff. The difference, however, is that a subsidy for an import substitute leads to a split between the consumer price (DC'/DP') and the producer price (DE/DP') in the home country. The size of the trade triangle is determined by C', the point of tangency between the indifference curve and the world-market price line. Subsidizing the import substitute makes this trade triangle shrink, and the country incurs a welfare loss. The point of consumption, C', is situated on a lower indifference curve than C, and the trade triangle $P'C'D$ is smaller than that without the subsidy (not shown in Figure 14.1).

If we now take into consideration that the subsidy has to be financed, further effects arise; for instance, if sector one is taxed to finance the subsidy. With the taxation of sector one, the price ratio would yet again change in favor of sector two. The production point then wanders up the transformation curve, starting from P'. In production as well as in allocating factors, taxes may distort the allocation and cause efficiency losses. The production point moves into the interior of the transformation area (point S), and the country incurs further welfare

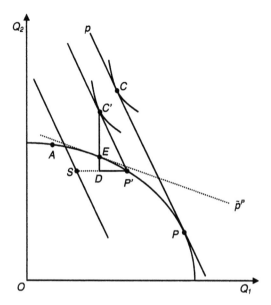

Figure 14.3 Subsidy for import substitutes.

losses. The difference between a subsidy and a tariff on imports is that a produc-tion point S would represent a less favorable economic situation compared to P'. The world market price line ($\tilde{p}$) then runs through point S.

Case study: Worldwide distortions through subsidies

Subsidies have sizable opportunity costs. They cause distortions. Whereas producers receive a producer's rent through higher producer prices and consumers enjoy a consumer's rent, the two rents together are lower than the subsidies paid by the government. Inevitably, there is a deadweight loss. The opportunity costs may arise at home, in other countries, in the future.

They arise at home when, for instance, non-tradables are subsidized. Thus, subsidizing the construction sector may lead to an excess capacity in real estate, requiring the over-expanded sector to shrink in the future with the consequence of unemployment. The country hurts itself. In the case of subsidizing tradables, a country causes damage to other countries. For instance, agricultural subsidies of the European Union and the US prevent other countries from developing their own agricultural production. Developed countries dump their surplus production on the world market and do not grant market access to developing countries. Such subsidies are trade-distorting. Opportunity costs may also arise in the future. For instance, subsidizing outdated sectors may mean to postpone adjustment and to make the economy less flexible towards shocks. Subsidies may then require more serious adjustments later on.

Some subsidies are even inconsistent (perverse subsidies). Think for instance of subsidizing coal and simultaneously charging a CO_2 fee for emissions or subsidizing tobacco farmers and financing anti-smoker campaigns or forbidding advertising for cigarettes for health reasons. Subsidizing the fishing industry leads to over-fishing and depletion.

Subsidies in the world economy are estimated at US$1 trillion (2.5 per cent of world GDP); agricultural subsidies in the OECD countries are estimated at US$300 billion. The Kiel Institute calculates Germany' subsidies in its subsidy inventory even at 6.6 percent of Germany's 2004 GDP (Boss and Rosenschon 2006).

An important new development in subsidies are the WTO rulings in dispute settlement in 2005 in the cotton case brought against the US by Brazil and in the sugar case brought against the EU by Brazil, Thailand, and Australia. In the cotton case, Brazil won a ruling that the US cotton subsidies (US$2.06 billion in 2001) caused a damage of US$600 million in the harvest season 2001–2002 to Brazil. The Appellate Dispute Settlement Body of the WTO came to the verdict that the US paid higher subsidies than the ones it had internationally agreed to. It has to change its cotton subsidy regime. A similar verdict applies to the EU's sugar policy. It can be expected that other countries will use the dispute settlement procedure to bring about a change in other agricultural subsidies, for instance for dairy and for rice (Oxfam 2005).

Subsidies are often motivated by social protection. For instance, agricultural subsidies are supposed to protect the small family farms. Amazingly, agricultural subsidies go overwhelmingly to large farmers and agribusiness. Think of the newspaper reports on the agricultural subsidies received by the Royal Family in the UK. Moreover, subsidies lead to rents that are captured by the inputs and assets used in the production process; for instance they cause land prices to rise. They also can be captured in the downstream activities, i.e. by agribusiness. Most importantly, however, they damage producers in developing countries. In an integrated world, equity can no longer be defined in purely national terms.

Quotas

The domestic sector can also be protected by the use of quotas. Assume that the import quantity should not exceed *DF*. In this case, the permitted trade triangle is limited to *PDF* (Figure 14.4). If we move this permitted trade triangle along the transformation curve, the curve *FF'F"* describes the trade points allowed. A quota can be chosen to yield just the same result as a particular tariff on imports,

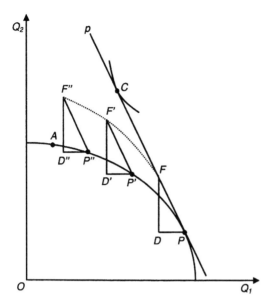

Figure 14.4 Quota.

and vice versa. Under certain conditions a tariff and a quota are thus equivalent. We might choose a tariff rate so that the import quantity DC' in Figure 14.2 corresponds to the quota DF in Figure 14.4. This equivalence of effects occurs only if the government sells the import quotas (import licenses) in an auction and redistributes the revenues (which correspond to the tariff revenues EC' in Figure 14.2) to the households.

If the quotas (licenses) are distributed in another way, other effects will occur. For instance, let DC' in Figure 14.2 represent the quota. If the import licenses are distributed according to the 'grandfather clause' (who imported in the past?), the households cannot reach the consumption point C'. This also holds if they are handed out in the first-come-first-served mode (who submits the application form first?) or due political relations, as happens from time to time in developing countries (who has a good friend?). These distribution modes make it impossible to redistribute the revenue from the licenses uniformly to the households, and the households' budget line does not move outward by EC' as in Figure 14.2.

Voluntary export restraints

With an agreement on restraints for exports, governments agree on a maximum import quantity (from the point of view of the importing country) or a maximum export quantity (seen from the exporting country). Exporting countries enter export restraints under the threat of facing even harder entry barriers for their exports. An importing country could basically auction a quota among the exporters of a foreign country; as a rule, however, the distribution of the allowed export quantity among the exporters is left to the exporting country. This means that the exporting country receives the rent of the agreed quota, leaving the home country with an additional welfare loss compared to a self-managed import quota. If the foreign government leaves these rents to its home companies, these have higher profits. As a rule, quotas cause foreign firms to export products of higher quality (upgrading). This can lead to further competitive distortions in the importing country. An example is the voluntary agreement on export limitations for cars between the European Union and Japan in effect until the end of 1999. This agreement was initially intended to protect firms in the lower product segment, but the upgrading of Japanese car exports brought increased competition in the upper segments of the European car market. According to new WTO rules, voluntary export restraints are no longer allowed.

Variable levy

This type of tariff lifts a low world market price to a guaranteed reference price at home. The lower the world market price, the higher is the levy. This system, for instance, was practiced in the framework of the European Union's agricultural policy until after the Uruguay Round variable levies have been transformed into import tariffs (except for cereals).

14.3 Arguments for trade policy interventions: protection of domestic production

Trade policy interventions are defended with a variety of arguments. The motives can either be defensive or aggressive. They can be geared to an economy as a whole (or an economic region) or to single sectors. They can refer to national instruments or to international rules. Often equity considerations play a role. We will first examine the arguments that deal with the protection of domestic production, especially of import substitutes.

Autarky

Under the label of 'autarky,' political and also military arguments have been put forward. During the second half of the nineteenth and the first half of the twentieth century for instance, this motive served to justify the protection of agriculture in Europe or the US as well as the special position of German hard coal and of the steel sector. Today, the autarky argument reappears in the somewhat refined form of supply risk, i.e. of being cut off from imports. However, in the modern world economy, the sources of supply for import goods are dispersed worldwide so that single-sided dependencies hardly exist. The risk of being cut off from deliveries is thus reduced. The globalization of the markets counteracts the dependency of countries vis-à-vis exclusive suppliers. Furthermore, a high-cost self-sufficiency has considerable disadvantages for those domestic export sectors that use these goods as inputs for their production. Suppose that a country isolates itself from the import of, say, semiconductor products, to protect its domestic semiconductor producers. This will hamper its own export sectors (like the machine-building industry) that use semiconductors intensively in their products. And finally: even if we assume for a moment that reducing the supply risk was a goal of economic policy, this does not necessarily imply the protection of domestic producers; this goal can be better attained by piling up stocks. Autarky thus entails considerable welfare losses.

Protection of established industries

Another assertion is that existing domestic sectors have to be protected against foreign suppliers. In general, the starting point is a loss in competitiveness for a domestic sector producing import substitutes; the relative prices for the domestic producers become less favorable. In this situation, policy-makers try to hold on to the production and employment of the domestic sector.

Stretching structural change

The argument of protecting certain sectors also appears in the form of stretching structural change. The assertion is that old industries like coal and steel should be helped to adapt to a new situation, but experience shows that subsidies tend to become irremovable over time.

Protecting infant industries

Some countries are not yet fully integrated into the international division of labor; they are still at the beginning of a development process. In these countries, the argument goes, import duties and other trade barriers should protect newly founded industries, so-called infant industries, until they become competitive. This process comprises making use of falling average costs by accumulating production know-how over time and by exploiting future economies of scale in production. Various measures can be applied: tariffs, quotas, or preferential access of the privileged sector to the domestic market for capital.

The basic intention of such policies is to temporarily protect the domestic sector against imports until it has reached a sufficiently strong position on the world markets. However, experience shows that such a protection tends to become entrenched in the course of time, contrary to its intended temporary character. This is confirmed by Latin America's experience in the four decades 1950–1990 with its import substitution policy that aimed at replacing imports with domestic production. As this policy neutralized competition, cost control and incentives to find new economic and technical solutions did not exist. The centrally planned economies also tried to make use of economies of scale by concentrating their production facilities at a small number of locations and isolating themselves from the international division of labor. They even tried to implement a division of labor from the top by making the specialization of the national economies a political decision. This method has proved a failure as well.

Social protection

Tariffs and subsidies in the developed countries are also motivated by equity considerations. Thus, agricultural subsidies are justified as protecting the small farmer or the coal miner having to work under extremely unfavorable conditions. These equity motivations do not hold if high-income farmers benefit from the instruments. Moreover, if equity considerations are used as arguments, the negative impact on low-income groups in other countries has to be taken into consideration. The issue is to what extent equity can be defined nationally or whether in a more intensely integrated world equity has a wider spatial dimension.

14.4 Arguments for political trade interventions: the maximization of profits from external trade

A different type of argument focuses on strategically maximizing a country's gains from trade. International trade causes gains; the idea is to redirect these gains into a specific country's pocket. In this case, the opportunity costs of the trade intervention do not arise in the country itself but elsewhere. Optimal tariffs and strategic trade policy belong to this category.

Optimal tariff

In contrast to a small country, a large country can influence the prices on the world market. As its market position is influential, it does not have to take prices as given by the world market.

Influence on the terms of trade

If a large country demands less of its import good (good 2) as a result of the tariff (making its offer curve shift to the left) there will be an excess supply at the previous price, and the price p_2 has to fall. The relative price $p = p_1/p_2$ rises, meaning that the terms of trade for the tariff-imposing country improve. With better terms of trade, domestic welfare improves, as the home country receives more import goods for its exports. The gradient of the straight line OS in Figure 14.5 represents the world market price ratio, p; the line runs steeper as p rises. Through its trade policy, the country shifts the equilibrium solution from point S to point S'.

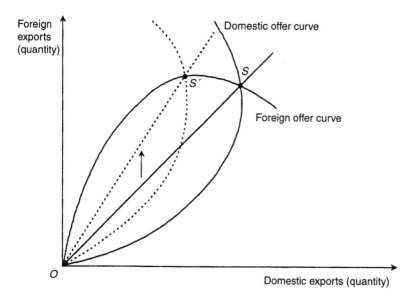

Figure 14.5 Tariff effects on the terms of trade.

Tariff rate and welfare

Figure 14.6 shows the effects of a tariff on national welfare, depending on the tariff rate. It is assumed that the foreign country does not react to an increase in the tariff. At a tariff rate of zero we have free trade, and the country reaches a real income *OF* that serves as a welfare indicator. A large country can increase its welfare by raising the tariff rate. *OC* is the optimal tariff, with a welfare level *OB*. To further raise the tariff lowers the welfare level because the quantity effect – the limitation of trade – now overcompensates the positive terms-of-trade effect on welfare. If the tariff is raised sufficiently (*OD*), we are back in the autarky results: the welfare level *OA* in this situation is lower than with free trade.

According to the assumptions, a positive terms-of-trade effect does not occur if the country is small. A rising tariff makes the trade triangle shrink; welfare decreases (along the *FA'* curve in Figure 14.6).

Tariff and opportunity costs: the large country case

At first sight, the argument concerning the optimal tariff appears striking. A country is able to increase its welfare by measures of trade intervention, but opportunity costs arise as well.

- First of all, a position of market influence for our large country has to be assumed. Monopolistic positions, however, are often not defensible in the long-run as processes of substitution take effect on the demand side. OPEC is a good example for this effect. Even if the short-term import demand for a product may be inelastic, the long-term demand will become more elastic. In particular, markets that are contestable in the long-run make it impossible for a country to pursue an optimal tariff strategy.

•   A tariff, whether on imports or exports, always entails long-run inefficiencies. What is optimal in a static model may prove absolutely wrong under the dynamic conditions of real life. The tariff-protected companies flag, and eventually their competitive advantage disappears. The rents, i.e. non-functional incomes, are no incentive for efficiency, and rent-seeking develops (see below).

•   The home country's welfare gains may prove elusive if the outside world reacts to the domestic tariff by imposing a tariff of its own: this makes the foreign trade curve shift as well, to the right. With such a retortion tariff, the former equilibrium situation *S* before tariffs (Figure 14.7) develops into the

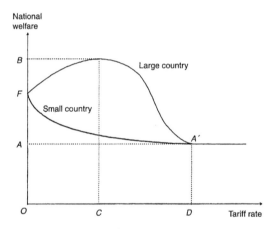

Figure 14.6 Tariff effects on a country's welfare.

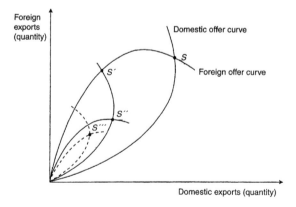

Figure 14.7 Tariff war.

new equilibrium S'' instead of S' (single-side tariff imposition by the home country). This non-cooperative behavior makes world trade shrink. The lens of potential trade gains becomes smaller (Figure 14.7). The form of the two countries' trade curves determines where this tariff war will finally end. In general, both countries lose.

Strategic trade policy

The basic model

In an approach similar to the argument concerning infant industries, strategic trade policy also has the goal of improving the domestic sector's position in foreign trade. This is based on the idea that the government can help a domestic company to reach a monopolistic position on the world market or a stronger position in an oligopoly. According to the models of strategic trade policy (Brander and Spencer 1985), this can be attained by paying export subsidies (or subsidies for research and development) to the domestic firm, giving it – at least in the model – an earlier start and helping it to reach a monopolistic position. The profits linked to this activity flow into the home country (rent creation). If another supplier is already present on the foreign market, the government may strengthen the domestic company's market position, e.g. by paying export subsidies. This gives the domestic firm the Stackelberg leadership in a duopoly, and profits are shifted from the foreign country into the home country (rent shifting).

Criticism

The approach described above is based on extremely simple models, like the one of Brander and Spencer (1985) where two duopolists from two different countries produce for the market of a third country, i.e. the world market. It has to be doubted whether models of such simplicity can yield sufficiently well-founded recommendations for economic policy.

- The simple model is not robust with regard to the modeling of competition in a duopoly. In a model with Cournot quantity competition, an export subsidy is recommended for economic policy. If, on the other hand, the duopoly is modeled as a Bertrand price competition, even the export sector has to be taxed to shift rents to the home country.
- Worldwide monopolies and worldwide oligopolies are rare. As a rule, markets are contestable; this contestability has been intensified by globalization. It is extremely difficult to find examples of oligopolistic structures on the world markets. The automobile industry is characterized by a worldwide dispersion, the market for semiconductors is competitive simply due to the short lifespan of its products. A duopolistic structure can be found in the market for large passenger airliners, with two suppliers (Airbus and Boeing).

- Similarly to the optimal tariff argument, the models of strategic trade policy assume that the foreign government does not react, but reality looks different (compare the disputes of the US vs. Japan and of the US vs. the European Union). When governments retaliate with subsidies for their own companies, strategic trade policy results in welfare losses for all countries.
- With respect to the concepts of 'rent creation' and 'rent shifting' we need to add the further concept of 'rent seeking.' Let us assume an environment where the government actively tries to shape the conditions for its export industries, according to each sector's specificities. In this context, companies invest a good deal of energy and considerable resources to get favorable conditions for their export sector. They will thus become active in the political arena instead of concentrating on the entrepreneurial task of pushing through new factor combinations and on creating new products. This binds resources, which cannot be used in production. A large share of the rent, or even the rent as a whole, is thus lost in the process of rent-seeking. An efficiency loss is inevitable.
- Most of the models are partial (and naive), as they finance the governmental subsidies 'out of nothing' (as a lump-sum tax taken from the households). The negative effects that arise from financing the subsidies through distorting taxes are not considered in this partial equilibrium framework.
- If the state wants to help companies to achieve a Stackelberg leadership position in the context of strategic trade policy models, it needs to know which products will thrive on the world markets of the future. Governmental offices and parliaments do not have this information. The information provided by industries about expected technological developments is biased by these industries' vested interests. Strategic trade policy thus lacks the necessary information base that is assumed in the models. Competition as a method of discovery in the sense of Hayek (1968) is given up.

14.5 Arguments for political interventions in trade: retortion as a necessary answer?

Anti-dumping

A frequently repeated argument is that a country cannot remain passive if another country's firms offer their products below production costs or below the domestic price on the world market but that instead it has to answer with anti-dumping measures such as quotas or import tariffs. It cannot be denied that an explicit dumping represents a distortion to the international division of labor; consequently, it is prohibited according to article VI of GATT. It is equally true, however, that in many anti-dumping cases, protectionist goals gain the upper hand. Anti-dumping then can easily develop into a protectionist division (Messerlin 1989).

Sliding into a non-cooperative trap

Unfortunately, retaliation entails the danger that a trade war develops. This would bring a less favorable welfare situation for both countries. It is therefore important to have rules for the international division of labor in the framework of the WTO that limit strategic behavior of particular economies. This also holds for anti-dumping measures, which must not be instruments of protectionism. Free trade is always advantageous for a country as a whole, as is shown in the following.

14.6 Arguments for interventions in trade: creating a level playing field

Industry and trade unions of the industrialized countries demand a worldwide equalization of conditions under which firms (and labor) compete (a level playing field), focusing often on equal social and environmental standards. As an example, demands are voiced that employees in newly industrializing countries should have the same social conditions as their counterparts in the industrialized countries.

As far as they are members of the International Labor Organization (ILO), the countries of the world have already laid down minimum standards for working conditions, like the ban on child labor. Most countries have also agreed to have free trade unions. To level out further social standards and to extend the industrialized countries' social standards to developing countries and newly industrializing countries would be amiss, however. Just as wages in China cannot be raised to the German level, a rich industrialized nation does not have the right to impose its social standards on a newly industrializing country. The decision as to how much social security a country wants to allow itself must be left to that country, as the purpose of the international division of labor is precisely to exploit the differences in factor endowment conditions. If everything were harmonized, there would be no need for an international division of labor. This reasoning holds analogously for environmental standards.

Case study: the free-trade-for-one theorem

Free trade is beneficial for a (small open) country even if the other country or the rest of the world behaves in a protectionist way (free-trade-for-one theorem). For example, the foreign country can put an import duty on its import good (good 1), i.e. the home country's export good. This decreases the foreign demand for good 1. The world market price p_1 of good 1 falls and the terms of trade $p = p_1/p_2$ of the home country deteriorate. This also hold if the foreign country puts an export duty on its export good (good 2) which would increase this good's price on the world market. As a small country, the home country has no possibility of reacting and the world

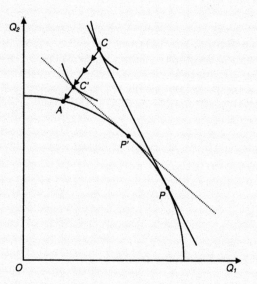

Figure 14.8 A country's advantage from free trade.

market price line is relevant. This line runs flatter and the home country shifts its production from point P to point P' (Figure 14.8). Owing to the protectionist policy of the foreign country – e.g. if the foreign country applies its optimal tariff – the home country suffers a welfare loss as the new consumption point C' represents a lower welfare level than point C of the free trade situation. But the home country is still left with an advantage from trade, as long as the consumption point C' is situated above the welfare level of the autarky point, A.

However, the theorem of the advantage of free-trade-for-one must not deceive the fact that a single-sided activity of a particular country influences the distribution of gains from trade between the countries. If a country is large, it can seek to influence the terms of trade on its own by imposing a tariff. This may cause conflicts that finally lead all countries into a prisoners' dilemma of trade policy that they cannot get out of on their own.

14.7 Arguments for a free international division of labor

The arguments in favor of a free international division of labor are not only arguments against protectionism. They are powerful arguments in favor of free trade in their own right.

Welfare gains for the world

The world as a whole gains from free international trade. This follows from the fact that free trade overcomes national restrictions: the more restrictions are overcome, the more leeway for economic decisions results, which in turn causes efficiency gains. If the production of one good remains constant, the possible production quantity of the other good rises. This argument can best be understood if we start from free trade and if then additional national restraints are introduced. This limits the choice set. Free trade takes away such restraints.

Figure 14.9 shows two situations: $A = A^*$ is characterized by trade-restricting measures (autarky), while E represents free trade. In the initial situation, A, the price lines p and p^* intersect, indicating unexploited arbitrage opportunities and efficiency gains. The condition $p < p^*$ means that Home can specialize in producing good 1 and Foreign in the production of good 2 if the trade barriers are lifted. In point E, the price ratios in the two countries are equal. The total worldwide production rises (shift from point O' to O'') and the production of at least one good is higher now.

Welfare gains for a particular country: allocation-driven gains

Regarding welfare gains for a particular country, we distinguish between allocation-driven gains (or static gains) and dynamic gains.

Increased utility

Imports allow consumption at a lower price than in autarky. External trade permits specialization in producing the good for which a country has a comparative

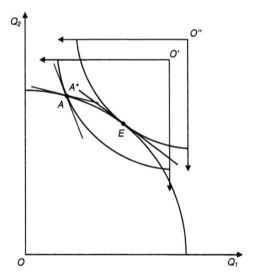

Figure 14.9 Welfare gains for the world.

advantage. By shifting its production from point *A* to point *P* (Figure 14.10), a country can reach a higher welfare level in point *C*, as the households have more goods at their disposal than they had before trade. External trade enlarges the consumption space: whereas the consumption space was limited by the transformation curve before trade was opened, it is now – with free trade – determined by the world market price line (budget line) running through point *P*. The production value, which is equivalent to the gross domestic product (measured in units of the import good) rises from *OD* to *OE*. An alternative representation with the simple market diagram of supply and demand shows that the households receive a higher consumer surplus by imports.

In detail, the welfare effect can be split into three effects. First, the quantity or volume effect represents the country's ability to buy more imports at given prices. The new price ratio on the world market is represented by a price line that would, other things being equal, run through point *A* (this line is not shown in Figure 14.10). Second, the price effect stems from lower opportunity costs and from terms of trade that are more favorable than those in autarky. Finally, we have a specialization effect. The combination of the quantity effect and the effect on the relative price can be called the 'trade effect'; its origin lies in the possibility of trading at a free trade price ratio that differs from the ratio in autarky. The specialization effect results from adjusting production to the new price ratio, i.e. by moving along the transformation curve.

The effect on factor incomes

Owing to the rise in the gross domestic product, the overall real income of the production factors increases. However, the real income of a particular factor

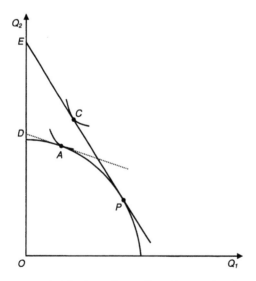

Figure 14.10 The welfare effect of external trade.

(here: low-skilled labor) may decrease if the country (partially) specializes in producing goods whose production is characterized by an intensive use of the other production factors capital, technology, and human capital.

The variety effect

If we consider preferences for different varieties of a product, external trade enlarges consumers' consumption possibilities. On the production side, the variety of inputs allows for higher efficiency owing to a more specialized utilization of intermediate imports.

The scale effect

When economies of scale characterize the production process, factor and resource input per unit of output decrease. Average costs fall with rising output

The profit effect

In models with imperfect competition – i.e. with a product price above marginal cost – a rise in output means that the value of the additional production exceeds its production costs. Firms have higher profits; national welfare rises. However, trade can make markets contestable; this reduces market segmentation.

Dynamic welfare gains

In the long-run, the dynamic effects of free trade can be considered to be more important than the ones that can be expected in a comparative-static context.

The competition effect

Free external trade ensures intensified competition between suppliers. The domestic producers have to face up to the foreign supply. This triggers a tendency to cut costs. Competition controls cost and ensures efficiency. It also forces economic actors to find new economic solutions and to discover new products. In the sense of Hayek (1968), competition is thus a method of discovery. External trade disposes of national monopolies; free trade is the best competition policy.

The innovation effect

External trade stimulates technological progress, as the strengthened international competition induces a search for cheaper production possibilities and for new products.

The accumulation effect

Trade is also an incentive for accumulating a larger factor stock (Baldwin *et al.* 1997). This accumulation effect holds for physical capital (including infrastructure capital) and human capital. For instance, the import of capital goods allows to hold a larger stock of capital. The innovation effect is another form of the accumulation effect because a larger stock of knowledge is accumulated, enabling producers to use the given production factors more effectively.

Whoever is still not convinced by these effects may take a look at the discouraging experience of those regions of the world that behaved to the contrary, i.e. those who isolated themselves from international competition over a long period: Latin America in the four decades until 1990 and the centrally planned economies until the end of the 1980s.

14.8 On the most prominent globalization fears

Globalization has given rise to many concerns and fears among important groups of societies. These concerns are forcefully and sometimes militantly expressed by the NGOs. In the following, we will look at some of these concerns in more detail.

An overriding concern is that welfare is not enhanced, but seriously impaired. One line of argument is that developing countries will lose by the international division of labor. In contrast to countries such as China and India that have gained in the absolute level of GDP per capita in purchasing power parity as well as in relative terms to the US (see Chapter 10). Most countries in Asia and to a lesser extent in Latin America have improved their economic position. They have succeeded in building up an industrial sector and exporting industrial products. The (non-oil-exporting) developing countries have nearly doubled their share in world exports from 17 percent in 1970 to 35 percent in 2004. The post-communist transformation economies in Central and Eastern Europe have gained as well.

However, it is true that for national welfare to increase certain conditions have to be satisfied, among them political stability and non-disruption of the private sector by government and internal turmoil. Furthermore, countries have to be able to adjust to permanent demand-and-supply shifts in the world economy. These conditions are not fulfilled in some of the sub-Saharan countries where a reliable institutional framework is lacking. Owing to path dependency, nations may be locked in their economic situation in vicious circles with no carryover from export enclaves in a dual economy.

Developing countries can also benefit from the inflow of foreign direct investment and foreign technology. Again, conditions must be met for these benefits to arise.

Some voice concern that industrial countries will lose in welfare. This is inconsistent with the fear that the developing countries will incur a loss; both the industrialized countries and the developing countries cannot lose simultaneously. On the contrary, all nations can gain through trade because trade is a positive-sum game. The developing countries experience an improvement in their terms of trade by specializing in the production of those commodities in which they have a comparative advantage. The industrialized countries have better terms of trade for their export products.

Another concern is that jobs will be destroyed in the industrialized countries. It is true that in our model of intersectoral trade real wages for low-skilled labor in the industrialized countries come under pressure when labor-rich countries enter the international division of labor. However, wages for human capital will rise in the industrial countries. Wages for low-skilled labor will rise because of the benefit from trade. Moreover, the model assumes that all countries produce with identical technology and that labor is homogenous. But labor is much more productive in the industrial countries owing to a higher stock of human capital and to being equipped with a better technology and with more physical capital. Finally, labor in the non-tradable sector is protected against international competition.

It is feared that countries face additional constraints through trade and lose maneuvering space. This is wrong because trade dispenses with the restraint that not more commodities can be used for final consumption than can be produced according to the production possibility frontier. In that sense, trade increases the choice set of an economy. However, this does not mean that with trade there are no restraints whatsoever. Each country has to respect its budget constraint, i.e. it cannot import more in terms of value than it exports in any given period unless it can pay its imports through accumulated currency reserves, by drawing on its accumulated assets or by going into debt. Thus, the balance of payments has to respected. Beside the budget restraint, countries must be prepared for competition. Their internal economic and political processes must be such that they can compete internationally.

Yet another aspect is the deterioration of environmental quality. If countries produce more for the international division of labor, they also produce more pollutants and harm their environment, the argument goes. This must not necessarily be the case. Scarcity prices for emissions can be introduced (see Chapters 16 and 17).

15 Locational competition

What you will understand after reading this chapter

Whereas the mobility of factors of production gives rise to benefits in the international division of labor, countries compete for the mobile factors of production on a global basis (section 15.1). The essential channel of locational competition is the mobility of capital (section 15.2). The economic instruments used are the supply of public goods and taxation (section 15.3). Locational competition has a major impact on the position of the immobile factor labor and restricts the maneuvering space of national economic policy (sections 15.4 and 15.5). Furthermore, it can be interpreted as institutional competition; that is, competition between different institutional set-ups (section 15.6). It is quite controversial, in how far locational competition will lead to a race to the bottom (section 15.7). Locational competition can also be interpreted as controlling excessive government power, the Leviathan (section 15.8). In particular, the smaller countries of the world economy are accustomed to locational competition (section 15.9).

15.1 On the concept of locational competition

Locational competition is geographic competition, competition between places, between cities, between metropolitan areas, between regions, and between countries. It takes place at three different levels. First, firms compete in the world product markets. Second, countries compete in the world market for capital, for technological knowledge, for high-skilled mobile labor, and to some extent (for instance in historical cases), for residents. Third, there is a complex and intricate system of interrelations between the immobile production factors of countries, especially labor, by which these immobile factors also compete on a worldwide scale (Figure 15.1).

Firms aim for higher profits by selling their products in markets of other countries. They enhance their competitiveness by producing goods in high demand, by developing new products or by providing goods at lower costs. Governments attempt to maximize the utility of their residents, i.e. the income of the immobile factors of production. In a scenario without factor mobility, national

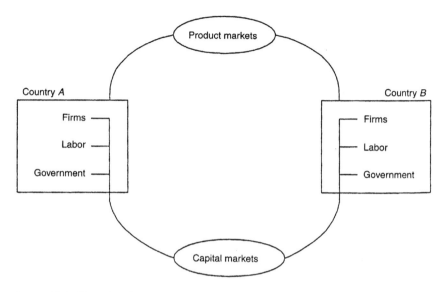

Figure 15.1 Channels of locational competition.

governments can induce an increase in the supply of factors of production such as:

1 capital through savings;
2 human capital through education, training, and learning-on-the-job and;
3 technological knowledge through invention and innovation.

In a scenario with factor mobility, countries can augment the income of the immobile factors of production by attracting mobile capital and mobile techno-logical knowledge as well as inducing mobile factors not to leave the country. This improves the factor endowment of the country, which in turn increases the productivity of the immobile factors. Besides firms and governments, workers strive to maximize their utility by searching for jobs with a higher income and with more secure employment. At first sight, they compete on the national labor markets. But the demand for labor is a derived demand, being linked to demand for the goods that workers produce. Thus, national labor markets are linked through global product markets, albeit through intricate mechanisms.

These three levels of international competition – firms, governments, and workers – are interdependent. Whether a firm is competitive or not depends, among other things, on the framework that is provided by the government. Whether it is worth investing in a country or not depends on all conditions that influence firms. Whether the reward of labor is high or low depends on the capital endowment of workers in a country. The higher the capital stock the higher the marginal productivity of labor. Additionally, the marginal productivity of labor is influenced by technological knowledge. Finally, because of the fact that the demand for labor is derived from the demand for goods, the position of workers depends on the competitiveness of their firms.

Our concept of locational competition is thus a broad concept combining each of the three interdependent levels of competition (for another view see Krugman 1994). The traditional theory of trade is more focused on analyzing just one element of that broad concept of locational competition, i.e. competition between firms on the world product market, including the implications of the Heckscher–Ohlin theorem for the income of factors of production (see Chapter 2). The traditional theory of capital flows stresses the benefits for the world economy, for capital-importing countries and for capital-exporting countries (see Chapter 3). In contrast to these traditional approaches, locational competition means that the immobile factors of production in a country compete for the mobile factors of production of the world (Siebert 2006a). The issue is to what extent countries are able to keep mobile factors of production at home or whether they can attract mobile factors of production from abroad. In such a Tiebout (1956) context, countries provide public goods and semi-public or meritorious goods, e.g. infrastructure capital, internal and external security, quality of the educational system, and cultural amenities, thereby attracting mobile factors of production such as high-quality labor, capital, and technology. These goods, however, have to be financed by taxes, fees, and prices. Countries have to find the optimum mix between the supply of public, semi-public, and meritorious goods and the opportunity costs of financing them. An ample supply of these goods may not be too desirable if it requires too high taxes. Conversely, very low taxes may not be attractive after all if the supply of public goods is extremely poor.

15.2 Channels of locational competition

Locational competition operates through different channels. In this paradigm, the main channel of interdependence between countries is the mobility of factors of production, especially the mobility of physical capital and of new technological knowledge. In addition, the exchange of commodities leads to locational competition. A special kind of interdependence results from the mobility of portfolio capital. In extreme situations, people start to migrate. Finally, communication processes can lead to international demonstration effects.

The mobility of physical capital

Mobile capital can be relocated if conditions for investment change. It is necessary to distinguish physical and portfolio capital. Physical capital is completely mobile ex ante when capital is not yet embodied in machines; thus the mobility of physical capital mainly refers to new capital, i.e. to investment (or to clay in a putty–clay model). But even physical capital in place can be turned into funds ex post when depreciation allowances for physical capital are earned in the market and not reinvested in the same machinery, but reallocated to other uses. Then sunk costs no longer play a role. Thus, even ex post, the movement of new capital is a powerful force of interdependence between countries. This also holds if it is taken into account that real capital movements only represent a mechanism netting out excess demand or supply of national capital markets with national investment and national savings being in equilibrium most of the time. Empirical studies suggest that the importance of the global capital markets is increasing and that the segmentation has been reduced (Chapter 3). Furthermore, capital movements of different periods are gaining weight if accumulated in the long-term. Finally, we know the importance of marginal changes in economics that are able to start new long-term processes. Therefore, there is no reason to neglect the importance of capital mobility.

Foreign direct investment accounts for about 10 percent of world gross investment. Whereas some countries have succeeded in financing an important part of their annual investment through foreign direct investment, for instance Hungary more than half of it in 1995, for other economies the export of capital plays a vital role. Thus, gross annual investment abroad of Germany's industry amounted to 34.8 percent of total investment in the period 1996–2001; the gross inflow made up only 8.8 percent of industry's annual gross investment. The larger European economies, Germany, France, Italy, and the United Kingdom, had a net outflow of foreign direct investment in the period 1991–2003 in most of the years.

The mobility of portfolio capital

Apart from physical capital, portfolio capital is another important channel of interdependence between countries. When financial markets lose confidence in the monetary and economic policy of a country, they reverse capital flows and induce a depreciation which signals to the voters the poor evaluation of national economic policy by the markets. As a result, financial markets and competition between currencies act as a controlling mechanism for the soundness of the economic policy of a country.

The exchange of commodities

It is not correct to relate locational competition to capital mobility alone. In principle, capital movements represent a similar mechanism to the movement of goods. In this sense the movement of factors and the movement of goods can create similar effects. Suppose capital and technological knowledge are totally immobile internationally. Locational competition will still take place through the exchange of goods. Consider a country that is making production less attractive, for instance, by a sharper regulation of business activities or by substantial increases of capital taxes. Consequently, the competitiveness of its exporting firms will deteriorate, absolute and comparative advantage will be reduced, exports will decrease, and in the long-run other countries in the same economic sector will gain a comparative advantage. As a result, the country with heavy regulation and high taxation will suffer from its own policies. In the long-run, it will be less attractive to accumulate capital in the exporting sectors and in the sector producing import substitutes (of course, it will also be less attractive to accumulate capital in the sector of non-tradables, but competitive pressure will be particularly strong in the tradables sector). The country will have a reduced capital stock that is not due to capital leaving the country but to a slackening capital accumulation, especially in the area of tradable goods since investment in this area has become less attractive. It is true, however, that the impact of changes in commodity flows is less noticeable than the impact of capital flows.

Migration

The importance of migration and its potential impact became obvious in the breakdown of central planning in Eastern Europe at the end of the 1980s. The mobility of people was an enormous factor in locational competition between the economic systems. The socialist planned economies were weakened politically when people started to exit, specifically when 600 East German tourists broke through the Hungarian border at Sopran on 19 August 1989 and Hungary did nothing to hold them back. It is therefore reasonable to relate the collapse of the communist systems to the exit of people. As already pointed out by Tiebout (1956), the exit option of people has a controlling function for national governments. Besides such an extraordinary case, the exit of highly qualified labor can represent a severe loss to a country.

The demonstration effect

Finally, another channel of locational competition is a demonstration effect, which must not be underestimated. By observing the performance and success of others, people are able to gain experience, or, as Mark Twain mentioned: 'There is nothing so annoying as a good example.' This demonstration effect was of crucial importance in the competition between East and West.

   As the global integration of economies further increases the mobility of physical capital and technological knowledge, locational competition is intensifying as well. The globalization of markets implies that the concept of locational competition becomes more important.

15.3 Competition in taxes and public goods

Instruments of locational competition

In the concept of locational competition, the comparative advantage of firms and sectors of an economy is not only an advantage owing to natural conditions, but it is also an acquired comparative advantage, which is influenced by political decisions. Whether a country is able to attract mobile factors or not, does not only depend on its natural resources, but also on the skills of its workers (the quality of human capital), the efficiency of its infrastructure and on its institutional set-up. All these factors can be influenced. At least in the long-run, i.e. over ten, twenty, or thirty years, these endowment conditions can be improved substantially by investment in education and training as well as in transport and communication systems and by changing the institutional arrangement (acquired comparative advantage).

Which are the instruments governments can use to attract mobile factors and induce them not to leave the country? On the one hand, a state can increase the attractiveness of a location by supplying public goods. On the other hand, any government activity has to be financed and raises the tax burden. In this respect, it is necessary to weigh up the advantages of the supply of public goods and the burden of financing them; a generous supply of infrastructure does not increase the attractiveness of a location unless taxes on mobile factors are kept at a reasonable level. But a country that levies very low or even no taxes on economic activity can also be unattractive for mobile factors if the infrastructure is not sufficiently developed. Obviously, there is a conflict of targets that can be solved by comparing costs and benefits.

Apart from competition in taxation and in the supply of public goods (competition in infrastructure), there is also competition between institutional arrangements of countries. Indeed, a large part of locational competition is institutional competition in the regulatory framework that determines the way things are carried out in a society. These institutional rules can be formal aspects, such as the constitution, the independence of the central bank, or the right to free collective bargaining, as well as informal aspects, such as non-codified, habitual behavior, e.g. to start collective bargaining in a pilot region and then to generalize it to the other regions and the economy as a whole (as in Germany).

The effects of taxes and infrastructure

Mobile capital has the option to leave a country when conditions become less favorable, e.g. in the case of a tax increase. Consider an investment decision of a firm that maximizes profits. A source-based tax, e.g. a corporate capital tax, is levied at a tax rate t per unit of capital. Profits[1] are maximized if the marginal productivity of capital (F_K) equals the sum of the real interest rate (r/p) and the tax (t/p) per unit of capital in real terms, i.e. $F_K = r/p + t/p$. In Figure 15.2, line RR is the real interest rate, given by the world capital market, which means that we are considering a small economy. Line PM is the marginal productivity of capital. OK is the country's capital stock that is built up before levying a tax. The rectangle $ORHK$ denotes capital income, whereas the area $OPHK$ denotes national output. The triangle RPH indicates the income of labor. A tax levied on capital reduces the marginal productivity of capital: the net productivity curve of capital is shifted downward ($P'M'$). In the new equilibrium I, less capital is employed in the country. Capital LK leaves the country. Interpreting the area

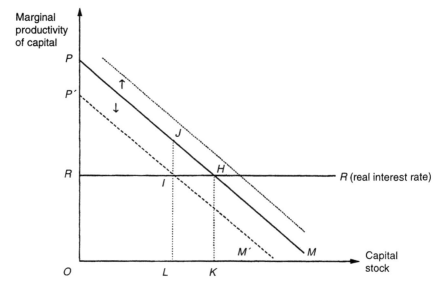

Figure 15.2 The impact of a source tax on capital.

under the capital productivity curve as national output, the country experiences a reduction of gross domestic product of *LJHK*. Gross national income additionally includes capital income *LIHK* from abroad. Gross national income is reduced by *IJH*.

Figure 15.2 depicts the isolated impact of taxation. Assume taxes are used to finance public goods such as infrastructure *G*. If an improved infrastructure raises the marginal productivity of capital, the productivity curve of capital is shifted upward, and there is a higher incentive to accumulate capital. Thus, there are two opposite effects: taxation reduces capital accumulation and induces capital to leave the country whereas infrastructure attracts capital. Obviously there is some kind of trade-off between the two effects.

The optimal supply of infrastructure

It is necessary to find out which level of infrastructure and taxation is optimal. Figure 15.3 depicts the marginal benefit curve (*MB*) and the marginal cost curve (*MC*) of a public good like infrastructure *G*, which is financed by taxes. The positive effect of infrastructure, the marginal benefit, decreases when the provision of infrastructure is increased. However, the more infrastructure is provided, the higher are its marginal costs. The optimal quantity of infrastructure (*OA*) is determined by the point where both curves intersect, i.e. where marginal social benefits and marginal social costs of infrastructure are equal. *OZ* is the price of using the optimal quantity of infrastructure, determined by the equality of marginal costs and marginal benefits.

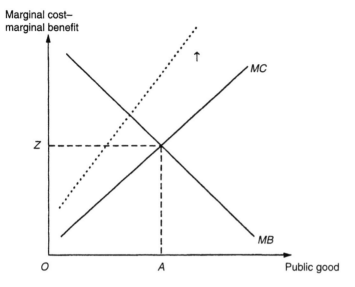

Figure 15.3 Marginal benefit and marginal cost of infrastructure.

When explicitly taking infrastructure into account in the production function, i.e. $Q = F(L, K, G)$, then, from the point of view of society, the supply of infrastructure is optimal if the marginal productivity of infrastructure F_G equals the marginal cost of infrastructure (in real terms) $C'(G)/p$:

$$F_G = C'(G)/p \qquad (15.1)$$

Firms follow a different optimality condition than society. They view marginal benefits of an input provided by government (or by someone else) as increasing their revenue, i.e. as marginal revenue; marginal costs of a unit of the input are given by the price firms have to pay for that input, for instance in the form of taxes. For firms, the optimal condition is that marginal profits are positive. In the case of benefit taxation, the beneficiaries of a public good and its payers are identical; there is no divergence between social and private costs and benefits.

Effects on the tax base

Consider now an open economy instead of a closed one, i.e. an economy with capital mobility instead of an economy without capital mobility. As a result, the marginal cost of supplying infrastructure also comprises the effect of capital leaving the country. Capital may leave a country if the price of infrastructure is more favorable in the foreign countries or if the price (taxes) to be paid for using the infrastructure in the home country does not correspond to the benefits for the firms. If capital leaves a country because of a tax,[2] e.g. a corporate capital tax, the tax base is reduced. This has to be taken into account in the equation of the optimal amount of infrastructure as a loss in the objective function.[3] It means that the marginal cost curve of a public good shifts upward in comparison with the closed economy, because the opportunity costs of capital leaving the country have to be considered as additional costs (Figure 15.3). Let t be the tax rate per unit of capital and $dK/dt < 0$ the outflow of capital due to a tax-financed infrastructure. Let $\eta_{Kt} = (dK/dt)/(t/K)$ be the elasticity of capital with respect to the tax rate. Then the condition for the optimal supply of infrastructure is given by:

$$F_G(G) = \frac{C'(G)}{p(1+\eta_{Kt})} \tag{15.2}$$

The marginal benefit (F_G) has to equal the revised marginal costs [$C'(G)/p(1 + \eta_{Kt})$]. If the capital stock declines with an increase in the tax rate, the revised marginal cost is *ceteris paribus* higher than in a closed economy (equation 15.1). If t is chosen too high, then $F_G(1+\eta_{Kt}) < C'(G)/p$ and the cost of supplying infrastructure is too high. This is as an incentive for capital to leave. Consequently, the exit option of capital can change the cost–benefit calculation of governments.

With the introduction of capital mobility, another reason for the outflow of capital could be a better provision of infrastructure abroad at lower marginal costs owing to differing natural conditions, such as the existence of natural waterways. In such a case of better endowment owing to natural conditions, capital movements induce a more efficient global allocation.

The empirical evidence seems to suggest that the effects of capital mobility that we derived analytically are relevant. Thus, in the European Union corporate taxes have been reduced in most countries in the last twenty years. Sweden has lowered taxes on mobile capital relative to immobile factors of production (Scandinavian tax model).

Other policy areas

The necessity of comparing benefits and costs is relevant, not only for infrastructure, but in a similar way it also holds for other government activities. If, for example, the government finances basic research, then the marginal productivity curve of capital in Figure 15.2 moves upward. But since technological knowledge does not fall from heaven, it has to be produced somehow and the state has to find a method of financing it, e.g. by taxation. As a result of taxation, the marginal productivity curve moves downward again. It is obvious that there are positive marginal benefits of basic knowledge as well as marginal costs of its supply (Figure 15.3). The efficient supply of new basic knowledge is reached at the point where its marginal benefit just equals its marginal cost.

Environmental policy is another example of a government activity influencing the marginal productivity of capital. Consider an environmental tax on production processes. There are two effects. First, the marginal productivity curve of capital shifts downward (Figure 15.2). Second, even if the improvement of environmental quality induced by such a tax is not necessarily an advantage for mobile capital in the strict sense, there may be an indirect advantage by increasing the attractiveness of a location for a firm, e.g. through improved living conditions (environmental quality) for its employees. This shifts up the marginal productivity curve of capital.

15.4 The impact of locational competition on labor

Another important matter is the question of how the distribution of income is affected by capital mobility. This can also be shown in Figure 15.2. In the initial position (*H*) national investment is financed by internal savings. With the outflow of capital, savers and capital owners receive the same income as before the introduction of the capital tax. But now they earn income *ORIL* at home and income *LIHK* abroad. The income of the factor capital does not change: capital is able to avoid the capital tax entirely.

Labor income falls from *RPH* to *RP'I*, which is a substantially smaller triangle.[4] With the outflow of capital, labor as a production factor loses, its real income declines.

This illustrates an important principle of taxation: mobile factors are able to avoid a tax put on them. In the long-run, such a tax always hits the immobile factor, which means that a tax on internationally mobile capital always affects labor.

The bargaining position of trade unions aiming at a high income for their members and at secure employment are affected by capital mobility. Assume they succeed in pushing for a wage increase above productivity growth. In an open economy with capital mobility, capital will leave the country, and labor productivity will be reduced. Either wage income falls or, with the previous wage remaining constant, more people will be unemployed. The opportunity costs for trade unions rise, and they must change their strategy except when social policies of the government accommodate the unemployed. Thus, the globalization of markets and increased capital mobility have altered the relative bargaining position of trade unions.

Locational competition may also have an implication for the institutional set-up of wage bargaining because the bargaining equilibrium between employers' associations and trade unions is affected by the increased mobility of capital. Firms have an exit option, and this may lead employers' associations not to resist wage increases too strongly. Then, delegating the wage formation process to the social partners (as in the German concept of *Tarifautonomie*) will no longer yield positive results for the economy as a whole with respect to employment. This implies that locational competition requires the redefinition of the checks and balances of wage bargaining.

It is thus quite conceivable that locational competition has affected – among other factors such as deindustrialization or the reorganization of the work process – the position of trade unions in Europe. For instance, the German Trade Union Federation (DGB) lost about 4.8 million members in the period between 1991 and 2004, leaving its membership at seven million at the end of 2004.

15.5 A change in opportunity costs for national politics

Locational competition changes the cost–benefit calculus of national politics.[5] The exit option of capital redefines the opportunity costs of economic policy measures in the usual cost–benefit analysis. It has an impact on the constraint set, the maneuvering space, of the government. Locational competition reduces governmental power. The best example is the emigration of people from the centrally planned states of Central and Eastern Europe. Emigration affected the maneuvering space of decision makers so much that the political systems either collapsed or were compelled to adapt themselves entirely to the new situation.

Another example for the impact of locational competition on the maneuvering space of national governments is the controlling function of capital markets in the case of portfolio capital which can be reallocated at will. Consider stabilization policy (monetary policy, fiscal policy) and assume that a country expands its money supply in excess of the growth of the supply side. Then, purchasing power parity indicates that the national currency will be devalued and market participants will anticipate the devaluation. Thus, purchasing power parity affects exchange rate expectations. A similar effect also holds if public debt is increased and if therefore exchange rate expectations are affected. This mechanism (an interplay of purchasing power parity forming exchange rate expectations and interest rate parity determining portfolio adjustments) represents a check on governments having a lax stability policy. This could be witnessed in 1983, when France had to reverse its economic policy, which had aimed at stimulating internal demand during the first two years of the Mitterrand presidency.

15.6 Institutional competition

Locational competition also takes place as institutional competition, i.e. competition over regulations such as mechanisms of licensing or other regulations (Siebert and Koop 1993). For historic reasons, each state has developed its own institutional design, e.g. its legal system. These institutional rules can induce different effects on economic events, including for instance a slowing down of growth or an impediment to employment. For that reason, it is necessary to compare internationally the way things are (to be) handled within a country. Some regulations will persist in this competition, others will have to be adapted.

The best example for institutional competition still is the Cassis-de-Dijon verdict of the European Court of Justice (Chapter 13). This verdict started the recognition of the country-of-origin principle, which automatically leads to institutional competition. Not only in Europe, but all over the world there is institutional competition taking place beyond the demonstration effect described above, in the sense that everybody poses the question of how others behave in a similar situation and whether others might accomplish the same tasks much more easily by doing things differently (benchmarking).

The alternative to the country-of-origin principle, according to which the country-of-origin rules are also applied to the importing country, is the country-of-destination principle. This means that the importing country defines the standard for an imported product. In the international exchange of goods, the country-of-destination principle would cause distinct impediments (Chapter 17). If every importing country were allowed to define its own product standards, this would represent numerous barriers to trade and especially a risk of protectionist abuse of product requirements. In order to prevent the rise of further barriers to trade, the WTO rules attempt to apply the country-of-origin principle.

15.7 Locational competition: a race to the bottom?

Some fear that locational competition leads to a race to the bottom in the supply of public goods, e.g. infrastructure, as capital mobility induces the marginal cost of the supply of public goods to rise. It is feared that individual countries might vie with each other in the creation of favorable conditions for private capital, e.g. by lowering taxes, which could cause the supply of public goods to fall to an inefficiently low level, possibly even to zero.

This is not true. First, if capital is leaving and if locational competition has an influence on the infrastructure that is supplied, the marginal benefit curve still defines a lower floor below which the supply of infrastructure cannot fall. This is due to the users of infrastructure, who – in spite of capital mobility – are willing to bear a higher tax rate in order to get the advantage of an improved infrastructure. It is therefore not correct to state that locational competition will lead to a zero supply of public goods.

Second, consider such goods as roads, ports, and airports. They can be financed quite often by user charges and market prices. In this case no tax on the capital invested is necessary, so that the opportunity costs of providing infrastructure are not influenced by an outflow of capital. Indeed, by assuming an equivalence of the supply of infrastructure and user prices, the government cannot require revenues to be higher than the funds which are used for the supply of infrastructure.[6] Thus, there are a number of possibilities of how to secure an efficient supply of infrastructure even in the case of international competition. For example, benefit taxation could be introduced, which means that someone who takes advantage of a certain good has to pay the corresponding tax according to the equivalence principle. Additionally, it is possible to privatize parts of the previously publicly supplied infrastructure in order to set scarcity prices for infrastructure. A further variant is the interpretation of infrastructure as a club-good, which leads to the concept of fiscal equivalence (Olson 1969). In this respect, it is quite realistic to consider public goods as having different spatial scopes. A theatre, for instance, is important only for the residents of a certain region. As a result – assume the costs of organization to be irrelevant – a specific form of organization is needed for each public good with a certain spatial spreading, which allows the supply of the public good as a club–good enabling the use of corresponding prices or user charges.

Even though there is only a weak correlation between taxes and the supply of public or merit goods in the sense of the equivalence principle, firms are still able to recognize positive effects from taxes as long as the advantages from the supply of a public good exceed the tax burden. For instance, this is true in the case of a good system of education. Firms are still willing to pay for public or merit goods such as social coherence or the cultural environment, which have no direct influence on the production function of a company. Therefore a race to the bottom does not necessarily take place.

15.8 Checking the Leviathan

Locational competition restricts the scope of action of the state: when the state is considered as an insurance against low incomes (Sinn 1997), possibly under the veil of ignorance concerning the individual's income (Rawls 1971), then the ability of the state to finance such an insurance by taxes on capital and companies is indeed limited by capital mobility. Accordingly, the social security contributions paid by the employers make labor more expensive, thus decreasing the return on capital. Since investors are able to elude payment by leaving the country, demand for labor diminishes and the revenues of the social insurance system are reduced. The opportunity costs of politics change.

But is this to be deplored? Locational competition – like competition on product markets – is a means to lower costs and to discover new solutions in the sense of Hayek (1968). Competition between states increases efficiency; rent-seeking of groups can be reduced (Lorz 1998). Locational competition can thus be seen as a device for taming the Hobbesian Leviathan (Sinn 1992b). This is especially relevant when people vote with their feet and leave their country as some residents of the centrally planned economies of Central and Eastern Europe did in the late 1980s. People in general leave their country only with the greatest reluctance, when they have lost all hope at their previous place of living. In this respect, the exit option controls governments. Thus, locational competition can be seen as an important political mechanism to promote freedom.

There are proposals to limit institutional competition, e.g. by international cooperation extending the right of a state to levy taxes on its citizens beyond national frontiers. This is quite understandable for fiscal reasons, and it may not be easy to draw the line where some tax coordination in a common market like the European Union may be justified. But on a worldwide scale, proposals of limiting tax competition must not eliminate the exit option of people, which is a central human right of freedom. Any form of cooperation destroying the exit option would be a cooperation in favor of totalitarian systems, a cooperation against freedom. This would be in complete contradiction to an open society in the spirit of Popper (1945).

The terrorist attacks of September 11, 2001 have added a new dimension to the topic of locational competition. Terrorism is a threat to security, and people are understandingly looking to the state to establish security. International terrorism requires international cooperation. This reminds us that locational competition between nation states finds its limit when global public goods are in question. We will study this issue of a global system of rules in more detail in Chapter 17.

15.9 Locational competition between the regions of the world

Locational competition is also competition between political systems and economic philosophies. The diverging experience of different regions of the world with respect to policy approaches is quite impressive. Regions of the world that have faced locational competition head-on have had economic success in the past; regions that have shied away from locational competition have often fallen back.

Eastern Europe had a division of labor imposed from above and built on managed trade where the exploitation of economies of scale was the leading doctrine. But in essence, Eastern Europe had not been exposed to competition from the world economy. Latin America was misled for nearly four decades up to the late 1980s by the economic doctrines of Prebisch (1950) and Singer (1950) and the policy of import substitution. This approach implied that the tradable sector of the economy was not exposed to world market prices. Eventually, Latin America lost its efficiency, but it changed its policy in the 1990s.

It is worth noting that these efficiency losses are long-run phenomena and that it takes some time for the erosion of efficiency and the slowdown of dynamics to eventually become apparent. This holds for Eastern Europe where the 1950s basically indicate a normal pattern of the catching-up process relative to the US, but where eventually the grinding force of paralysis and inefficiency took over. A similar story holds for Latin America where, with the passing of time, the restrictions imposed by the policy of import substitution eventually showed their fatal result.

The Pacific rim countries have followed the opposite route. They were outward oriented and they did not distort relative prices between export goods and import goods. Thus, their infant industries had to compete from the start with the world economy and find the markets for their products. This proved to be an incentive to make the national economy more efficient. A country or a region of the world not participating in this competitive process will eventually fall behind.

Some innovators in worldwide institutional competition are small countries like New Zealand and Chile. Owing to a high degree of openness, which is a distinct attribute of small economies, there is great pressure to adapt to institutional competition. New Zealand undertook a complete change of all aspects of economic policy in 1983. Incidentally, the reforms were induced by a Labor government. It seems as if New Zealand has solved many of the problems which arose in the past. Chile switched to a capital-funded national pension system during the 1980s. Two European examples of small economies that have been successful in locational competition are Ireland and the Netherlands.

But even the big regions of the global economy have to face locational competition. The US has always been an open economy, which means that the US always had to adapt to the needs arising from locational competition. Continental countries in Europe, though open in most of their product market, have been slow to adjust in some areas, especially in the labor market.

16 Using the national and global environment

What you will understand after reading this chapter

For the economist, the environment is a scarce good. Environmental systems have a spatial dimension. The environment can be a national or a global good (section 16.1). If the environmental endowment of countries differs, the traditional theories on the international division of labor hold (section 16.2). For global goods, new institutional solutions should be found, in order to avoid non-cooperative behavior (section 16.3).

16.1 The economic paradigm of the environment

The environment is the set of the natural conditions of the human biosphere; it includes the quality of air, of rivers, of lakes and the sea, of the soil, and the quality of the living environment (e.g. biodiversity). From the point of view of an economist, the environment is a scarce good, but a good with its own specific features.

The environment as a scarce good

The environment has two competing functions for the economic system (Siebert 2005a): it is a public consumption good (arrow 1 in Figure 16.1) and it absorbs waste from consumption and production (arrows 2 and 3). These two roles are in conflict. Emissions from consumption and production are transformed into pollutants ambient in the environment by natural processes (diffusion), which influence the quality of the environment (damage function, arrows 6 and 7). In addition, the environment supplies inputs for the production process (arrow 5). Competing uses are linked to externalities. Indeed, the arrows in Figure 16.1, representing waste absorption by the environment, the diffusion function, and the damage function, describe an externality in greater detail, by introducing the intervening variables, emissions and pollutants ambient in the environment.

In its role as environmental quality, the environment is a public good, that is, it is used to the same extent by all. Nobody can be excluded from the consumption of this good (non-excludability), and there is no rivalry in consumption

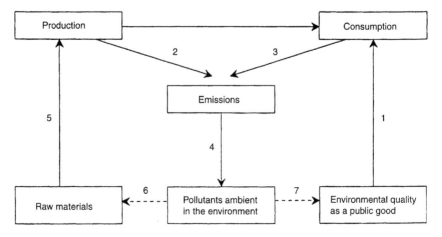

Figure 16.1 The economic system and the environment (source: Siebert 2005a).

(non-rivalry). In its role as an absorber of waste, the environment is not a public good, but a good for which exclusion rights can be defined (private good). With respect to environmental quality, the supply of a public good cannot be determined by the market system, because no institutional arrangement is available to aggregate the consumers' willingness to pay. Thus, the optimal supply of a public good must be determined in a political decision-making process. Once the desired quality of the environment is set, user rights can be defined for nature as an absorber of waste. With these user rights market processes can develop. In this way, prices can be put on emissions either by introducing transferable emission permits or by taxing the emissions. The public good should not be mixed up with a free good for which no price is charged. Historically, the environment was used as a free good in its capacity as an absorber of wastes; this implied a deterioration of environmental quality as a public good. Instead of the term 'free good', the term 'common property resource' ('the commons') is used for a situation in which no property rights are defined and free access prevails.

The spatial dimension of environmental goods

Environmental systems always have a spatial dimension. With respect to their dimension in space, environmental goods can be divided into three categories. The first comprises national environmental goods, i.e. those that fall completely within the borders of one nation such as a river system or the tributaries of a river. The second group is formed by cross-border environmental goods, which are shared by (at least two) countries like transfrontier pollution (e.g. acid rain). The third category consists of global environmental goods, i.e. goods that pertain to the Earth as a whole like the ozone layer. Of course, environmental problems are mostly related to several environmental systems, but the separation into these three groups is very helpful for the analytical solution of the problem.[1]

The environmental problem is characterized by an extensive casuistry: pollutants are bound in products, they are emitted from stationary or mobile sources (like cars), they accumulate over time and, finally, there is a difference between the use of non-renewable and renewable resources (Siebert 2005a). All these issues pose specific problems for the international division of labor. In the following, we will assume that emissions originate from production processes by stationary sources and are delivered into air and water.

16.2 Environmental abundance as a national factor endowment

As far as the environment is a national good, its scarcity can be different from country to country owing to the following reasons:

- The absorption capacity of the environment as a receptacle for emissions may vary between countries because the assimilation capacity can differ owing to natural conditions.
- The population of one country may have stronger preferences for environmental quality than that of another country, consequently assigning a higher value to the environment. Even if international preferences are equal, a higher income per head can lead to a stronger demand for environmental quality. Finally, institutional rules also influence the demand for environmental quality, as they affect political decisions by which the desired state of the environment is determined.
- The demand for environmental assimilation services may be different because of the level and structure of consumption and production, but also due to abatement and disposal technologies for emissions and waste.

The different abundance of the environment means that the goals for environmental quality, set by the political process, differ. Defining U as environmental quality, the domestic environmental quality U is different from the foreign U^*, and thus $U < U^*$ or $U > U^*$. Different abundance also means that the absorption capacity for emissions E is not equal in different regions of the world: $E > E^*$ or $E < E^*$. This holds even if environmental quality as a public good is identical.

Different environmental qualities have to be considered in the same way as differences in factor abundance. The Heckscher–Ohlin approach can thus be applied. Countries with a relative abundance in environmental quality will export commodities that use the environment intensively in their production. If the environmental endowment is not equal, prices will differ as well, owing to the differing scarcity. Through trade, prices will tend to become more equal over time, because the country with the relatively abundant environment specializes in the production of the good that uses the environment intensively, its price will rise, and therefore the demand for assimilation services of the environment will increase. In the country where environment is relatively scarce, the production of the good that uses the environment intensively will fall, and therefore the prices for emissions will do so as well. If capital is mobile, these effects will occur through capital movements from one country to the other.

In so far as the environment is a national good and its scarcity can be expressed by market prices, environmental endowment and environmental policy signaling the preferences of the citizens are no reasons for international regulation. The environment must then be treated like any other factor endowment. When we consider the large casuistry on environmental problems, environmental political instruments can work as trade barriers (Chapter 17).

16.3 Global environmental problems

Looking at global environmental problems, the environment appears as a public good that covers the whole world and that everyone uses to the same degree. Examples are the atmosphere and the ozone layer. One of the current hypotheses of physicists is that the global climate is warming up owing, among other factors, to the increased concentration of carbon dioxide. Another hypothesis is that the emission of chlorofluorocarbons (CFCs) damages the ozone layer. These effects do not occur overnight; instead, it is a process that takes several decades to develop.

Let us consider two economies. The environmental quality U^W is a global public good, so that $U = U^* = U^W$. As environmental quality is a public good, it cannot be assigned to a single nation. The total emissions of the world E^W are composed of the emissions of both countries, $E + E^* = E^W$. They have a negative influence on global environmental quality, so that $U^W = G(E^W)$.[2]

The decision problem for allocating global environmental goods consists of two interwoven questions:

- Which environmental quality of the global environmental goods should we aim at?
- How should the costs of reaching the desired global environmental quality be divided among the individual countries?

Analytically, the approach to determining the target level for public environmental goods is to derive the aggregate willingness of nations to pay. The problem is that sovereign nations can behave as free-riders. The corresponding institutional difficulties surface when it comes to determining the benefits that arise from the protection of global environmental goods for individual countries, say the (monetary) value of prevented environmental damage, and to assigning the costs for the attainment of the protection, say the prevention of waste. According to the polluter-pays principle, cost assignment would be fair in terms of pollution caused. However, this principle requires a sovereign authority that does not exist for the world as a whole.

For these reasons, nations have to find mechanisms by which they bind themselves in using global environmental goods. In the end, this is a question of a contractual rule governing the use of global environmental goods in the way the Coase theorem on environmental agreements has suggested (Siebert 1998b), with the additional difficulty that sovereign states are doing the bargaining. In this process, the interests of important polluters and the preferences of countries with higher environmental awareness will play an important role, as well as income per head and a variety of other variables. Consider China, for example, a country with large coal reserves that it will want to use for its development, without worrying too much about how this might influence the concentration of carbon dioxide in the world's atmosphere. As individual countries will behave strategically, it will be difficult to come to (and to implement) a self-restriction of sovereign states in using global environmental goods. Besides the problem of realizing multilateral solutions, another issue lies in the necessity that multilateral agreements should remain stable in the long-run. Once a multilateral agreement is signed, it should be made sure that sovereign states have no interest in reneging and walking away from the contract.

Looking at possible institutional solutions, an example would be an agreement on a worldwide certificate system for carbon dioxide emissions. In such an agreement, the total quantity of worldwide-allowed emissions is fixed. Difficulties arise when a consensus has to be reached on who will be entitled to these certificates, as they determine a user right, more precisely the right to use the global environment and indirectly the natural resources that generate carbon dioxide. Possibly, a proportional reduction rate for the given emissions is a starting point for industrial countries. This is the approach of the Kyoto Protocol or a follow –up multilateral solution in which the US and China will join. Developing countries will require that industrial countries reduce emissions at a higher rate since they have a higher per capita level of emissions. Unfortunately, such an approach does not take into account that the level of emissions increases with the economic growth of the newly industrializing countries. Another area for a multilateral approach are international agreements on safeguarding biodiversity.

17 An institutional order for the world economy

What you will understand after reading this chapter

After having discussed several areas where national interests and world interests can clash, like trade policy, locational competition, and environmental allocation, we now look at the institutional design for the world economy. The issue is how strategic and non-cooperative behavior of nation states can be channeled into a system of rules defining a global frame of reference. Countries can behave strategically in their national policies, in order to derive the greatest national benefit out of the international division of labor. In their trade policy, they can levy an optimal tariff or they can attempt to implement strategic trade policy in favor of certain sectors. Countries can also behave as free-riders towards global public goods. All these cases imply non-cooperative behavior of countries, which eventually leads to a welfare loss for the world as a whole and possibly even for the individual country. Consequently, an institutional order has to be created which prevents countries from falling into the trap of non-cooperative behavior. Furthermore, mechanisms should be established that enable countries to get out of a situation of non-cooperative behavior. Strategic behavior in trade policy is explained in section 17.1; other areas of non-cooperative behavior or of externalities are discussed in section 17.2. The world economy needs a system of rules (section 17.3). We then look at the history of the WTO and how it works (section 17.4). A number of new problems have to be addressed, e.g. free market access versus national regulation, competition policy and aggressive trade policy (section 17.5). Moreover, as an implication of the paradigm of, locational competition, rules for the mobility of production factors are receiving increasing attention in the discussion of economic policy (section 17.6). Social norms are a major matter of debate (section 17.7). The integration of the environment in the world trade order represents a specific problem (section 17.8). The mechanisms to stabilize and strengthen the world order are analyzed (section 17.9). The role of the IMF is briefly assessed (section 17.10). Finally, the main elements of the global economic order are summarized (section 17.11).

17.1 Strategic national behavior

States can behave strategically against other states. Trade policy is a major area where non-cooperative or strategic behavior of nation states can be observed. The goal is to maximize the gains from trade.

Cooperative and non-cooperative trade policy

Countries can improve their terms of trade if they are sufficiently large. When a large country implements such a strategic policy, the gains from the international division of labor dwindle for the other countries. For our analysis, we consider a two-country case and first introduce a situation of free trade as a reference point, in which both countries gain from international trade. As a simplification we assume that both countries are identical but are in different autarky positions before trade starts. This assumption is for simplifying purposes only. If the two countries indeed were identical and in the same autarky situation, they would have the same relative price initially and would not trade. In Figure 17.1 these autarky situations are depicted by points A and A*. Gains from trade, i.e. the gains in welfare in comparison to autarky, will then be equal for both countries. We assume that the trade benefits in a situation of free trade amount to (17,17*). In the following, the first number of such a set denotes the (additional) domestic trade benefits, the second number indicates the (additional) foreign trade benefits. Note that these numbers do not denote the level of utility, but the change in the level of utility in comparison to the autarky situation. In Figure 17.1, the free trade situation is characterized by the point F_I (17,17*), which is tangential to the indifference curves of both economies. In point F_I, the transformation curves of both economies are tangent to each other, and the straight line p denotes the equilibrium world price ratio.

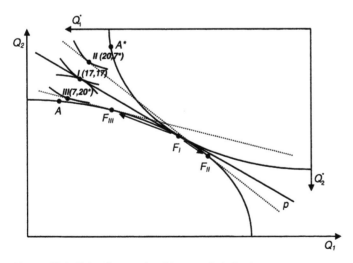

Figure 17.1 Gains from trade with strategic behavior.

When the domestic country behaves strategically by levying an import duty or intervenes in other ways, then the domestic gains from trade can be increased; the gains from trade of the foreign country decrease. The domestic country can achieve production point F_{II} by using an optimal tariff. Point II (20,7*) denotes the distribution of gains from trade. Note that the system of coordinates related to F_I of the foreign country is not valid any more.

Alternatively, the foreign country could raise an optimal tariff in order to increase its gains from trade, which causes the domestic gains from trade to decrease. Then the production point of the domestic country moves to F_{III} with bundle (7,20*). In this case again, the system of coordinates for the foreign country is rendered equally invalid.

Figure 17.2 depicts the trade benefits, that is the increase in benefits U, U* relative to the autarky situation. The points I, II and III correspond to the respective points F_I, F_{II}, F_{III} in Figure 17.1. The area within the curve through 0, II, I, III is the area of the possible gains from trade. Also, a situation IV (9,9*; not shown in Figure 17.1) can occur, in which both countries are implementing a tariff policy. Finally, in the extreme case in which both countries take protection to the limit and are in the autarky situation A and A*, the gains from trade are (0,0*). Assume both countries to be in the initial position in situation IV, with trade benefits amounting to (9,9*). Then the area between the curve and above point IV defines the possible trade benefits for both countries.

In the initial position IV, both countries can benefit from the transition to free trade. If they cooperate, they will proceed to situation I, where the two of them reach a welfare maximum, i.e. where the gains in total utility are maximized. Agreement is needed on how the total benefits are to be distributed. However, in the case of non-cooperative behavior, they will not reach the optimal situation I.

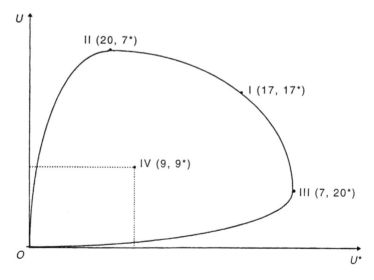

Figure 17.2 Trade benefits area.

Table 17.1 The prisoners' dilemma: welfare levels with free trade and tariff policy

Domestic country/foreign country	Free trade		Tariff policy	
Free trade	I	(17, 17*)	III	(7, 20*)
Tariff policy	II	(20, 7*)	IV	(9, 9*)

Both countries strive for the positions II and III, but instead they remain in situation IV or even move closer to the origin. This is a typical prisoner's dilemma. They cannot agree, because one country will always expect that it will have greater benefits in a situation different from situation I. The situation considered above corresponds to a game with four possible outcomes. In Table 17.1, the gains from trade are represented in a pay-off matrix for the players. In the case of free trade (situation I), both countries can benefit. Note that the game presented here is a single round game. In a repeated game with many periods, reputation of the two players comes into play, making a cooperative solution more likely.

Trade benefits due to liberalization

Some studies attempt to estimate the world gains resulting from lower tariffs. For example, Brown *et al.* (2003) calculate in an applied general equilibrium model that an assumed reduction in post-Uruguay tariffs on agricultural and industrial products and on services by 33 percent would increase world welfare by US$ 686 billion (Table 17.2). A complete removal of all tariffs and other barriers would increase world GNP by US$2.1 trillion, by boosting the GNP of all world economies, for instance the US (5.5 percent), Europe (6.3 percent), Japan (6.2 percent), China (7.75), and even 16.4 percent for the Philippines.

Table 17.2 Global welfare of free trade

Countries	33 percent reduction in tariffs		Global free trade (all barriers removed)	
	Percent of GNP	*Billion of US$*	*Percent of GNP*	*Billion of US$*
US	1.81	164.0	5.5	497.0
Japan	2.04	132.4	6.2	401.9
EU and EFTA	2.07	227.0	6.3	688.0
China	2.56	23.2	7.75	70.3
Philippines	5.42	4.8	16.4	14.5
Mexico	0.96	3.4	2.9	10.25
World	686.4	2,079.8		

Source: Brown *et al.* 2003.

Different concepts of trade policy

So far, we have outlined only two possible trade policies, i.e. free trade and tariff policy. However, in reality we can observe a great diversity of approaches to international trade policies. In Figure 17.3, these approaches are ordered on a continuum that spans from free trade to autarky. In the situation of a centrally planned division of labor from above, as practiced in the former COMECON until the late 1980s, the allocation of production factors and goods was executed along political lines. Moreover, the economic area remained more or less closed to the outside world. Protectionism, import substitution, and strategic trade policy intervene in different forms. Aggressive trade policy strives for the opening of foreign markets and is not afraid to use protectionist measures to achieve this goal. Regional integration approaches the free trade situation from a cooperative stand point.

17.2 Free-rider behavior, public goods, and externalities

Strategic behavior in trade policy is possible when a country is large enough to acquire a monopolistic position. Additionally, strategic behavior can occur when other interdependencies apart from trade exist, e.g in the case of global public goods, that is, those goods that are consumed in equal amounts by all. An example of a worldwide public good is global environmental media. Public goods are strongly related to technological externalities. These interdependences do not represent interdependences via markets, but via 'technological' systems. Thus, in the case of global warming the global atmosphere is such a system. Technological external effects are interdependencies in the output and input space of production and utility functions of economic agents.

If we consider strategic behavior towards public goods, then countries may behave as free-riders. They use a public good without contributing adequately to its production. A country could use the high quality of the global environmental good, but at the same time heavily burden this good through its emissions. In a similar way, a country could enjoy the stability of international trade rules, but break them at the same time, and in this way undermine the stability. Whenever global public goods are concerned, rules for the world economy have to be developed.

17.3 The world trade order as a system of rules

Nations autonomously pursue a trade policy in order to promote their welfare. Such an economic policy can get into conflict with a free international division

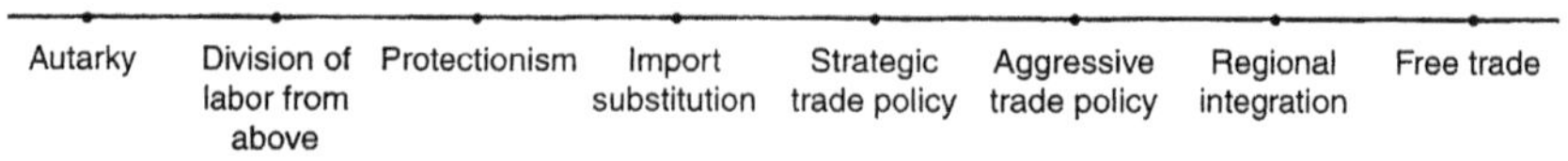

Autarky	Division of labor from above	Protectionism	Import substitution	Strategic trade policy	Aggressive trade policy	Regional integration	Free trade

Figure 17.3 Different concepts of trade policy.

of labor. Consequently, a rule system is needed to reduce transactions costs, most prominently to diminish uncertainty arising from the behavior of market participants or originating from the non-cooperative conduct of sovereign nation states. The basic idea of such a world economic order for the trading system is to provide an institutional framework that allows the participating economies to capture the potential welfare gains from the international division of labor.

A system of rules for the behavior of governments takes the place of ad hoc negotiations between governments. A central element of such a rule-based institutional framework for the world economy is that sovereign states voluntarily commit themselves to respecting rules which prevent strategic, i.e. non-cooperative, behavior by individual countries. The contractually binding commitments, entered freely by governments, are ratified through domestic legislative processes. Strategic behavior of national governments would destroy the international order as a public good, representing a negative externality for the rule system. The rules must prevent such strategic behavior. Self-commitment by states limits national governments' choice of actions in the future and in this sense represents a 'negative catalogue,' a restraint on government behavior. It protects the international division of labor against national governments (Tumlir 1983). The self-commitment of states is also a shelter from the power of protectionist groups within individual economies. Moreover, the rules must induce nation states to act cooperatively in certain areas (Haggard and Simmons 1987) and to develop the system further. The World Trade Organization (WTO) is not only about respecting rules but also about making rules. An international order thus provides a skeleton of an international economic constitution for sovereign nation states in the area of international exchange.

Despite the game-theoretic character of international negotiations on rules for the division of labor and the related possibility of strategic behavior, countries have succeeded in concluding a multilateral agreement for trade for a variety of reasons. First of all, there is the historic experience that the way out of the prisoners' dilemma induces welfare gains to all, and that a tariff war is by no means advantageous for any single country. Second, an agreement on rules is not a solitary event, but only part of a sequence of agreements on rules. In such a repeated game with an infinite time horizon, gains are divided again and again. From this point of view, cooperation can pay off, because countries will care about their reputation. Finally, the uncertainty over future gains from new negotiations can lead to a less aggressive, more cooperative behavior.

17.4 The WTO – how it works

How the rules are set

The WTO practices decision-making by consensus. Members are not outvoted. If consensus cannot be reached, the 'one country – one vote' principle is applied. Unanimity is required whenever the core rules (most favored nation clause, decision procedure) are changed (article X of the Agreement Establishing the World Trade Organization). A substantive change in the treaty must be approved by the national parliaments. Other changes of the multilateral treaty that affect the rights and obligations of member states require a two-third majority. The changes in the treaty bind only those who have agreed to the changes. Yet other changes that do not affect the rights and obligations of member states hold for all members when accepted by a three-quarter majority.

A little bit of history

The first attempt to establish an International Trade Organization (ITO) in 1947 failed. As a compromise, the GATT (General Agreement on Tariffs and Trade) was founded in 1948 by twenty-three countries. In 1995 it was followed by the World Trade Organization (WTO). At the time when the GATT was established, after the protectionist experiences of the 1930s, the goal was to create a stable framework for international trade in order to provide the preconditions for growth and an augmentation of prosperity. Membership increased continuously over time (Table 17.3). As of December 2005, the WTO has 150 members, and thirty states are applying for membership, among them Russia. China is a member since 2001.

Rounds of liberalization

GATT succeeded in the course of nine liberalization rounds in significantly cutting tariffs and reducing other barriers (Table 17.4). The Doha Round was not yet concluded when the manuscript for the book was closed. In the years before the Geneva Round of 1947, the tariffs of the industrialized countries were as high as about 40 percent of the import value (on average). After the Uruguay Round, they were brought down to about 4.3 percent. The first five GATT rounds were concentrated on tariff cuts. The last rounds, all of them lasting several years, embraced new themes. The Kennedy Round, for example, developed an anti-dumping code, although this was not ratified by the US. In the Tokyo Round, a proposal for a new anti-dumping code saw daylight, but an

Table 17.3 GATT/WTO membership,[a]
1948–2005

1947	23
1960	38
1970	78
1980	85
1990	100
2005	150

Source: Homepage   2006;   GATT,
International Trade (several issues).

Note
a End of year.

improved code on subsidies was left aside. Finally, the Uruguay Round extended the agenda with new rules on services, intellectual property, and property rights, and a dispute settlement procedure. The topics of the Doha Round were agricultural subsidies, market access for agricultural and industrial products of developing countries, some liberalization in services (like banking, telecommunication, IT, and water) and a less restricted access for industrial goods to developing countries (Siebert 2006c).

This tendency to liberalization was opposed by some developments that are rather protectionist. The US obtained a waiver for agriculture in 1955; this then became very important for European agricultural policy. In 1961, the Short Term Arrangement on Cotton Textiles was introduced during the Dillon Round. It included the right for countries to impose unilateral import quotas. It took more than four decades to dismantle this type of protection. Since January 1, 2005, all restrictions on textiles and clothing are terminated. This means that

Table 17.4 Liberalization rounds and protectionist counters

	Liberalization rounds	*Average tariff reduction for industrial goods in percent*	*Protectionist arrangements*	
1947	Geneva Round	19		
1949	Annecy Round	2		
1950–1951	Torquay Round	3		
1955–1956	Geneva Round	2	1955	The US attains an exceptional arrangement for agriculture (waiver)
1960–1961	Dillon Round, Geneva Round (all five rounds on tariff cuts)	7	1961	Quantitative restrictions on trade in textiles; terminated in 2005.
1963–1967	Kennedy Round, Geneva Round (anti-dumping-code)	35		
1973–1979	Tokyo Round (new anti-dumping code, subsidy-code)	34		
1986–1994	Uruguay Round (rules on services and intellectual property, dispute settlement)	40	1984 1994 1998	New trade policy instrument of the EU Trade Defense Instrument Omnibus Trade and Competitiveness Act of the US. Retaliation instrument
2000 2001	Seattle Round failed Doha Round started, not yet concluded in Mai 2006			

Source: GATT/WTO, Annual Reports.

trade in textile and clothing products is no longer subject to quotas under a special regime outside normal WTO/GATT rules but is now governed by the general rules and obligations embodied in the multilateral trading system. In 1988, the US introduced the 'Omnibus Trade and Competitiveness Act' (Super 301) and created the legal possibility of retaliating in the event of trade-restricting measures by other countries. The European Union developed its 'Trade Defense Instrument' in 1994 (see below).

Decision structure of the World Trade Organization

The WTO is an international organization based on a multilateral agreement. The ministerial conference, the central decision-making body, is responsible for general questions and meets at least once every two years (Figure 17.4). The General Council meets several times a year in the Geneva headquarters.

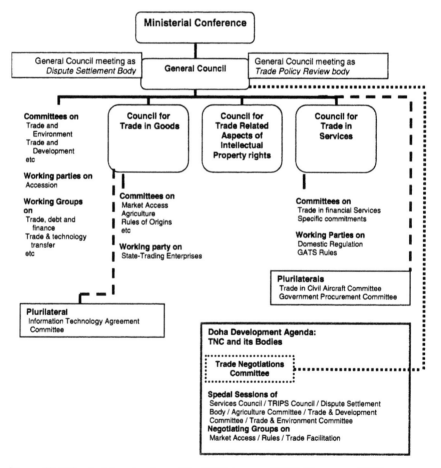

Figure 17.4 The decision structure of the WTO (source: WTO, Homepage 2006).

Additionally, the General Council meets as the Dispute Settlement Body and Trade Policy Review Body. At the next level, three councils are assigned to the issues of Trade in Goods, Trade Related Aspects of Intellectual Property Rights (TRIPS), and Trade in Services. Furthermore, various specialized committees, working groups and working parties operate in several areas such as environment, development, and regional trade agreements. The Trade Negotiation Committee, which works under the authority of the WTO Council, and its subsidiaries are in charge of the negotiations mandated by the Doha Declaration. In principle, all members can participate in all councils or committees. There are some exceptions, however, for example not all members signed the agreements within the activities of the Plurilateral Committee or the dispute Settlement Body.

The WTO is different from GATT in several respects. First, member states have formally ratified the WTO agreements, whereas GATT was simply signed by governments. GATT only dealt with trade in goods; in addition, the WTO covers services and intellectual property as well. Third, the dispute settlement mechanism is more effective. Note, however, that the GATT rules referring mainly to trade remain valid as an element of the WTO framework.

The basic principles

The world trade order is based on three main principles: the principle of liberalization, the principle of non-discrimination, and the principle of reciprocity. More specific principles support and specify those main principles.

Liberalization

The simple idea of GATT/WTO is to reduce trade barriers. This principle is a general point of reference. Nations have to abstain from raising existing tariffs or from levying new ones. In addition, quantitative restrictions or non-tariff barriers are forbidden. The nine liberalization rounds since the foundation of the GATT in 1948 are proof that the concept of liberalization works.

Non-discrimination

Trade policy measures should not discriminate against countries, all countries should be treated equally. In particular, there must be no discrimination between domestic and foreign products. This principle can be explained very well with Thailand's cigarette case, decided by GATT in 1990. Thailand had raised a tariff on imported cigarettes, referring to health policy reasons, but without taxing domestically manufactured cigarettes. In the Thailand cigarette case, it was ruled that it is consistent with the world trade order for a country to take measures for health reasons (article XX), but it must not make a difference between domestic and foreign products and it should not discriminate against imports.

Most-favored-nation

The most-favored-nation principle is an expression of the non-discrimination principle (favor one, favor all). The obligation towards a general, positive and unconditional most-favored treatment, which is included in article I of the GATT treaty, implies that a tariff reduction that is granted to one country has to be granted to all countries. In this way bilateral tariff reductions are multilateralized. While the non-discrimination principle is a negative mechanism banning discriminatory behavior, the most-favored-nation principle is a positive mechanism strengthening free trade.

Reciprocity

The principle of reciprocity requires that concessions have to be granted mutually. This means that a tariff cut in one country has to correspond to an equivalent cut in another country. This is practiced by a bilateral demand–supply system. For example, a country will offer a concession x when another country has offered a concession y. However, a country can only ask for a concession for a specific product if it is in the position of the principal supplier, which means that it provides the main part of the imports of the partner country (principal supplier rule).

Bound tariffs

When countries agree on reduced tariffs, they bind their commitments. Changing the bindings requires negotiating with the trading partners and compensation for a loss of trade. Thus, binding creates opportunity costs of non-compliance.
The concept of reciprocity of concessions is based on the mercantilist idea, according to which the reduction of trade barriers is a sacrifice. This contradicts the theory of the international division of labor, according to which a country can raise its welfare by unilaterally reducing its tariffs. The notion of concession stems from public opinion on international trade. It can possibly make the political realization of tariff cuts much easier.

Single undertaking

The single-undertaking nature of the WTO reflects the concept of packaging the benefits arising in different areas of the international division of labor. In the past, plurilateral agreements, introduced in the Tokyo Round, allowed a subset of GATT members to sign contracts for specific areas, for instance the Agreement on Civil Aircraft and the Agreement on Government Procurement. Such a procedure, though easing a contract among at least some GATT members, represents an *à la carte* approach and entails the risk of fragmentation of the multilateral trading system. In principle, it can be expected that the single-undertaking nature of WTO will strengthen the rule system because it forces countries to swallow less favorable rules in one area if they are compensated by rules allowing higher benefits in other areas. The approach of packaging is also helpful in focusing the bargaining process when a liberalization round is being concluded. However, the 'offsetting' between the advantages of suborders should not be carried too far. If in the course of time the advantages of countries shift asymmetrically in the individual suborders, a fragile structure of acceptance could collapse like a house of cards. To avoid domino effects, it makes sense that the suborders should basically legitimize themselves on their own and not be conditionally accepted.

The most important articles of the WTO

The most important stipulations are:

- *Preamble*: 'Recognizing that their relations in the field of trade and economic endeavor should be conducted with a view to raising standards of living, ensuring full employment and a large and steadily growing volume of real income and effective demand, developing the full use of the resources of the world and expanding the production and exchange of goods.'

  'Being desirous of contributing to these objectives by entering into reciprocal and mutually advantageous arrangements directed to the substantial reduction of tariffs and other barriers to trade and to the elimination of discriminatory treatment in international commerce.'
- *Article I*: 'any advantage, favor, privilege or immunity granted ... to any product originating in or destined for any other country shall be accorded immediately and unconditionally to the like product originating in or destined for the territories of all other contracting parties.'
- *Article III*: 'internal taxes and other internal charges, and laws, regulations and requirements affecting the internal sal ... should not be applied to imported or domestic products so as to afford protection to domestic production.'
- *Article VI*: 'dumping, by which products of one country are introduced into the commerce of another country at less than the normal value of the products, is to be condemned.'
- *Article XI*: 'No prohibitions or restrictions other than duties, taxes or other charges, whether made effective through quotas, import or export licenses or other measures, shall be instituted or maintained.'
- *Article XII*: 'Notwithstanding ... Article XI, any contracting party, in order to safeguard its external financial position and its balance of payments, may restrict the quantity or value of merchandise permitted.'
- *Article XIII*: 'No prohibition or restriction shall be applied ... on the importation of any product ... or on the exportation of any product ... unless the importation of the like product of all third countries or the exportation of the like product to all third countries is similarly prohibited or restricted.'

- *Article XX*: 'nothing in this Agreement shall be construed to prevent the adoption or enforcement by any contracting party of measures: ... necessary to protect human, animal or plant life or health.'
- *Article XXIV*: 'the provisions of this Agreement shall not prevent ... the formation of a customs union or of a free-trade area.'

Further rules of the WTO

Further rules relate to other aspects of trade barriers such as waivers, anti-dumping, and subsidies. Other aspects refer to national regulation. The general aim is to restrain trade-restricting or trade-distorting activities of nations by a set of rules.

Voluntary export restraints

All voluntary export restraints which were used to circumvent tariff liberalization have, in principle, been eliminated since 2000. No new forms of quantitative restrictions should be allowed.

Waivers

Within the framework of the international trade order there are a number of exceptions. A waiver from the non-discrimination principle and from the most-favored-nation clause holds for regional integrations according to article XXIV, although they discriminate against third countries. It is assumed that regional integrations inducing free trade within a spatially limited area will eventually lead to global free trade. This exception relates to customs unions, free trade areas, and preference zones.

Another waiver is valid for agricultural products: market access may be restricted by import regulations and exports can be strengthened by subsidies. In the Uruguay Round variable levies and quantitative import restrictions were partly replaced by tariffs. This tariffication of quantitative restraints will allow the reduction of tariffs by a flat rate later on. In this round, agricultural tariffs have been reduced by 38 percent in industrial countries and by 24 percent in developing countries.

The third waiver was the world textile agreement (Multi Fiber Agreement). Bilateral agreements between individual countries (including tariffs, quantitative restrictions, and voluntarily export restraints) and trade restraints have been allowed internationally. Since January 1, 2005, the world agreement on textiles and clothing is discontinued.

Anti-dumping and countervailing duty measures

Though defensible in a framework of theoretical models, these instruments can easily develop into a severe impediment for trade (administered protection).

They are defined by national legislation and can be captured by national interest groups. They represent a way around bound tariffs and (now) forbidden quantitative restraints. Even if they are not actually applied, the threat of using them entails uncertainty and may already lead to the 'appropriate' export behavior. In economic categories, contingent protection represents effective protection. This 'administered protection' (Krueger 1998: 8) seems to have become more important as a protectionist device of US trade policy. The task for the WTO will be to contain the protectionist impact of this approach. Standards have to be defined that must be respected by national anti-dumping laws.

Country-of-origin versus country-of-destination

When product norms are applied, we distinguish between country-of-origin rules and country-of-destination rules. The country-of-origin principle accepts the rule of the country of origin whereas the country-of-destination principle leaves it to the importing country to set the domestic standard as the yardstick for its imports. The result would be a myriad of diverging standards representing barriers to trade. Moreover, such regulations can easily be captured by interest groups. The aim of GATT and the WTO has been to push back the role of the country-of-destination principle. Which regulations are set for the production of goods should be left to the discretion of the country of origin. The different regulations of national countries of origin should rather have equal standing competing with each other. A weakening of the country-of-origin principle and a strengthening of the country-of-destination principle will inevitably harm the multilateral order. The goal of the world trade order is therefore that countries mutually accept the regulations of the country of origin for product quality and production processes in order to minimize transaction costs. Thus, competition between rules can thrive. Only in precisely demarcated cases, for example, public health protection, should the country of destination and its standards take precedence over the norms of the country of origin. But even then the measures adopted should involve neither discrimination nor protection.

National treatment

For services, the principle of national treatment is applied. Foreign suppliers have to be treated in the same way as domestic suppliers. This principle is much weaker than the principles applied in trade of products. For services, the country-of-origin principle has not been acceptable so far. An example for this principle is the home rule principle applied in the EU's banking industry. However, even in the European Union, the country-of-origin principle has not been accepted politically after the Eastern enlargement if natural persons cross borders in order to provide a service.

Dispute settlement

The member countries of the WTO have voluntarily agreed to a dispute-settlement system. If a country violates the rules, the WTO is allowed to demand a change in the trade policy decisions and to impose sanctions.

Relative to GATT, the dispute-settlement procedure has been strengthened. Whereas the ruling of a Dispute Panel can be appealed before the Appellate Body, the decision of the Appellate Body is binding unless all parties are against its adoption. When the Dispute Settlement Body has adopted the panel's or the appellate body's report, the losing party must either propose a suitable implementation of the report's recommendations or negotiate compensation payment with the complaining party. If there is no agreement on compensation or if the losing party does not implement the proposed changes, the Dispute Settlement Body can authorize the other party to impose retaliatory measures such as counter-tariffs. The retaliation can occur in the same sector, in other sectors or even in other agreements.

The dispute settlement mechanism seems to have found acceptance. Since the formation of the dispute settlement mechanism, WTO members have requested consultation 338 times, in 153 distinct matters. This compares to 300 cases during the entire life of the GATT (1947–1997). If India, Malaysia, Pakistan, and Thailand file a complaint about the import prohibition of shrimp products by the US, this is counted as four requests and one distinct matter.

Both developed and developing countries rely on the WTO settlement procedure. Developing countries file a rising share of cases. 133 of these consultations requests in seventy distinct matters were made by developing countries. The cotton case won by Brazil against the US in 2005 before the Appellate Body of the WTO Dispute Settlement Mechanism and the sugar case won by Brazil, Thailand, and Australia against the EU (also in 2005) have demonstrated that countries can successfully prove damage done by subsidies of other countries.

The US and the EU have to change their subsidy regimes. The US (eighty-two cases) and the European Union (seventy cases) are the most frequent complainants to the WTO, often filing complaints against each other (forty-five cases among which in twenty-nine cases the EU is the complainant and in sixteen cases the US is the complainant). Thus, the WTO plays an important role in resolving conflicts in the transatlantic relationship. By and large, the dispute settlement system has proved to be a successful device to address trade conflicts and enforce the rights and obligations of WTO members. Nevertheless, some conflicts, in which panel or appellate reports have been adopted by the Dispute Settlement Body (which would have required some kind of action to be taken by the respondent WTO member) have not been resolved. Eight such cases have been filed with the Dispute Settlement Body, since the complainant has not agreed with the actions taken by the respondent. The conflict between the US and the EU about the EU import system for bananas is one of these cases. In the 'banana-case,' retaliation was requested by the US. The dispute settlement body authorized the US to suspend tariff concessions on products of a value of

US$191 million. The use of retaliation has been authorized by the Dispute Settlement Body in four instances.

Major trade conflicts in the world are: the closed Japanese internal market, antidumping measures of the EU and the US (for instance in steel) as an impediment for the developing countries (and for exporters in industrial countries as well) and agricultural protection. In the relationship between the US and Europe the major areas of conflict are, for example: the subsidization of airplane production, the US-tax treatment for foreign sales corporation as a hidden subsidy for exports, the US laws, regulations, and methodology for calculating dumping margins, hormone beef, gene food, and EU import restrictions for bananas.

Trade policy review mechanism

The trade policy review mechanism scrutinizes the trade policy of each member state on a regular basis. The report on the four major trading partners (US, EU, Japan, and Canada) is provided more frequently. This review is expected to exercise discipline on the trade policy of member states.

Legitimacy

NGOs have raised the question of legitimacy of the WTO and other international organizations. National governments have agreed to the WTO arrangement, in contrast to GATT it is ratified by national parliaments, most of them from democracies. The WTO thus has a derived legitimacy. The nation states are the provider of legitimacy. Whereas it is appropriate that the WTO increases transparency in response to the legitimacy demand, in principle the NGOs should have their discourse with the provider of legitimacy, the national governments. Thus, the WTO cannot affect its dependence from and responsibility to the nation states by negotiating with the NGOs (WTO 2004b). The one-country-one-vote principle of the WTO enhances legitimacy, it ensures unanimity, it protects countries from being outvoted and being forced to abide by rule they do not want. Last not least, NGOs only reflect the opinions and preferences of their members; they must accept that their legitimacy through their members directly competes with the legitimacy of democratic governments. They cannot claim to have the same level of legitimacy.

17.5 Issues to be solved for the future world trade order

These are a number of new areas in the international division of labor for which rules have to be developed.

Strategic trade policy and subsidies

While tariffs and quantitative restraints lose importance, governments are tempted to use subsidies in order to lower their producers' production costs, thus establishing an artificial price advantage and distorting the international division of labor. Total subsidies in the world are estimated at US$ 1 billion (Global Subsidy Initiative 2006). Subsidies by one country take market shares away from the corresponding sectors of other countries and lead to political demands for retaliation. Thus their effect resembles those of protectionist measures. Moreover, subsidies intended to protect the small family farm end up over-whelmingly – some say to 80 percent – in the hands of large, well-to-do agricul-tural producers and agribusiness. NGOs have pointed out too many perverse impacts of agricultural subsidies (Oxfam International 2005). Furthermore, with a more international orientation of people in the rich countries – witness the emotional support in the case of the 2004 tsunami – it becomes harder and harder to convince voters that equity and social protection can solely be defined within the national borders. Finally, it is simply inconsistent and unfair to praise the benefits of competition and open markets for the international division of labor, and to shut off the agricultural markets of the rich countries to the exports of developing countries. Export subsidies are especially distorting. They prevent market access and reduce competitiveness of developing countries. In agricul-ture, they are to be abolished by 2013 if the Doha Round succeeds.

Strategic trade theory could, in the future, become more appealing to prac-tical politics and provide a rationale for subsidizing 'new' sectors, albeit on the basis of rather restrictive (and naive) models. We may see more of this interven-tionist approach in some European countries as a reaction to globalization. This may lead to political demands for retaliation. Thus, the effect of subsidies may be as detrimental to international trade as traditional protectionist measures. They may also be part of an aggressive bilateralism.

According to the WTO rules, trade-distorting subsidies for export goods and import substitutes are forbidden and product- and industry-specific subsidies are inadmissible if they harm the trade opportunities of other members. Even so it is difficult to demarcate subsidy practices from other admissible policies such as research assistance and aid in adapting to new environmental technologies. It is likewise difficult to penalize and stop violations in the framework of monitoring processes. Furthermore, important sectors such as agriculture and the aviation industry either explicitly or implicitly still enjoy special treatment. Therefore, the existing subsidy code, of which the core is present in the world trade order, must be further developed in order to prevent subsidy competition between governments.

Free market access and national regulation

The trade order is essentially oriented to deny governments (or integrated regions) tariff and non-tariff instruments with which the governments could directly intervene in trade flows at their borders. Such instruments have been outlawed through a negative catalogue. However, this still does not guarantee that there will be free access to markets. If we want to ensure free market access, it will be necessary that national regulations do not limit access for goods and firms.

Therefore, multinational barriers, resulting from national legislative and informal practices that effectively limit access to markets should be dismantled. These barriers include policy measures in the broadest sense, such as licensing procedures for economic activities, for facilities and for products, technical standards, arrangements for public procurement, and interlocking ties between firms (as with Keiretsu in Japan) on the same or different levels of the vertical production structure, whereby outsiders are excluded (Ostry 1995). By accepting the country-of-origin principle instead of the country-of-destination principle, market access is made easier.

Open services markets

Services comprise an extensive and diverse spectrum. They include cross-border supply, consumption of a service abroad, commercial presence and presence of natural persons. The diversity of services becomes apparent by the WTO classification list with seven main categories and sixty-two subcategories (see Chapter 1). A rule system for the international exchange of services should hold for the whole variety of services. Since the phenomena to which rules are to be applied are so divergent, it is difficult to establish an all-encompassing international rule system. A major distinction is between border-crossing and local services analogous to that between tradable and non-tradable goods. Within these categories, another distinction becomes relevant, namely between 'person-disembodied' and 'person-embodied' services (Bhagwati 1984). Disembodied services are not 'embodied' in persons, for example, detail engineering using computer-supported programs, the development of software, and accounting. For the international trade order, disembodied cross-border services are not very different from material goods. Just as commodities are carried by the transport system, disembodied services cross national borders by means of communication media. As a consequence, markets must be open for them just as they must be open for commodities. Border-crossing disembodied services should be treated like commodities.

National treatment in the case of person-embodied services

In the case of person-embodied services (consumption abroad, commercial presence, presence of natural persons), non-discrimination can be obtained through national treatment, i.e. equal treatment for foreigners and one's own nationals.

The General Agreement on Trade and Services (GATS) establishes for the first time a framework for the notification of existing rules, but it has a long way to go before a rule system for all forms of international services with free market access is fully developed (Snape 1998). As a result of the Hong Kong Declaration plurilateral negotiations started on many services sectors. Markets are yet to be opened in many respects: barriers discriminating against foreigners or non-discriminatory barriers erected by competition policy will have to be torn down; the product coverage must be extended. So far, these are exemptions to the most-favored-nation (MFN) treatment. The conditionality of the most-favored-nation clause prevalent in services must be extended to an unconditional use. National treatment as a central principle only applies to services where a country has made a specific commitment; exemptions are allowed. Moreover, the present approach is to find agreements for specific services. For instance, in financial services a multilateral agreement was reached with seventy WTO members (in December 1997); other sector agreements relate to telecommunications and information technology. This sector-by-sector approach raises the risk that sector-specific aspects will dominate. It has the disadvantage that it does not sufficiently harness the export interests of the economy as a whole in order to dismantle barriers of trade (Krueger 1998).

International competition policy

Markets should not be closed through the market power of firms. Globalization makes markets more contestable, and in this sense free trade is the best competition policy. All measures that improve market access support competition policy. However, firms may try to create monopolistic positions in the global markets, if possible, and to exploit them by setting prices to the disadvantage of buyers.

In the past, competition policy was a national affair (and in the European Union it is an EU matter). In the new global environment, national competition policies face a new challenge. National competition policy should not be oriented towards the advantage of domestic firms or home-based multinationals and should not permit firms to build up or exploit monopolistic positions internationally. Competition policy should also oppose business practices intended to reduce global competition. It should prevent the exploitation of market power, and help to improve the contestability of the world product markets.

Therefore, it is necessary to change the orientation of national competition policies. Interactions between competition policies of different countries have to be taken into consideration. For instance, mergers in one country have an impact on the market structure elsewhere. Therefore, the competition policy of different authorities is involved and mergers need the agreement of different authorities (like the EU and the US). An example is the intended merger of General Electric and Honeywell (in 2001) that was approved by the US antitrust authority but stopped by the competition policy of the EU.

Another issue is the misuse of market power. Thus, the question arises whether a country harmed by another country's competition and antitrust policy should have the right to obtain changes in the objectionable policy or not. An institutional consultation and sanctioning mechanism must be created (Graham 1995). Under consideration are the effects doctrine with an international right to extra-territorial legal application (Immenga 1995), treaty agreements – including already existing bilateral treaties between the US and Europe – on the concession of mutual competencies (Ehlermann 1995), on the harmonization of international competition law (hard law) on the basis of national regulations

(Fikentscher and Immenga 1995), and on the mutual recognition of institutional rules, that is a Cassis-de-Dijon approach with an international interpretation (Nicolaides 1994). An alternative proposal is to give parties injured by anti-competitive practices or competition policies a right to take their case to an international court or an international competition authority empowered to enforce competition rules (Scherer 1994).

Presently, it is not foreseeable that an international institutional framework for competition policy will be established which can effectively restrict the misuse of monopolistic market positions and discourage competition-limiting mergers. Thus, at present we can only expect to establish a few minimal competition policy rules for countries or regional integrations (such as the European Union), either in the framework of the World Trade Organization (Immenga 1995), in the OECD or in multilateral agreements, as between the EU and the US. We also have to consider the option that, initially, only some of the rules would be agreed upon by the most important OECD countries, because there are fundamental differences in their legal systems, as between Anglo-Saxon and Continental European law.

Aggressive trade policy versus the multilateral order

When important trading nations or regions of the world pursue an aggressive trade policy, they endanger the multilateral system. The US and the EU have built up an arsenal of new trade-political instruments, which they can use to open markets or as a retaliatory measure, without considering the mechanisms of the world trade order. The US, for instance, can react immediately on trade-restricting measures of other countries by imposing trade-restricting measures of its own with its powerful instrument 'Super 301.' Trade-barrier reductions already agreed on can be deleted, import restrictions can be imposed and bilateral export-restriction agreements can be pursued. Above all, trade policy restraints are supposed to serve as a lever for opening markets. With the 'Trade Defense Instrument' the European Union has created a similar apparatus, to counter the trade policy of other countries.

By creating these trade policy weapons, the two trading blocs, in the sense of result-oriented bilaterally conceived policies, have exempted themselves from the rules of the multilateral world trade order; they violate the most-favored-nation principle. The risk exists that bilateral measures will escalate. The two large players are forcing other countries to make concessions, and they threaten unilaterally by denying market access in the US and the EU. An aggressive trade policy of one country (unilateralism) and the reaction of other countries, or even the agreement of two countries at the cost of a third country (bilateralism) lead to a destabilization of the multilateral order. Therefore, the trade policy instruments of such an aggressive market opening policy have to be integrated in the rules of the world trade order. An outcome-oriented, bilaterally conceived aggressive trade policy for opening markets must not replace a rule-based multilateral order.

Regional integrations – a threat to the multilateral order

The US and the EU as major players have a political interest to be a hub in their own hub-and-spoke system in which they can extend favors to the members of the network (Chapter 12). Each of them has a set of concentric rings around itself. The risk is that the multilateral order breaks up. Within the WTO world order some 300 free trade arrangement are in force, due to the waiver in article XXIV. Their preferential tariffs undermine the WTO-multilateral tariffs. Thus, the WTO-most favored tariffs of the European Union only apply to nine countries of the world, admittedly among them the US and Japan. Preferential tariffs prevail with respect to all other countries (WTO 2004b). About one-third of all trade flows in regional or more recently in bilateral arrangements. Such arrangements are so much easier to agree on than to conclude a WTO round with a membership of 150. The risk of undermining the WTO becomes clearly visible, if ten years from now China would establish its own economic hub-and-spokes system. It has already concluded a free trade deal with Chile in November 2005 and was negotiating free trade arrangements with twenty-seven countries (as of the end of 2005).

17.6 Rules for factor movements and locational competition

Besides the exchange of goods and services, factor mobility is another important form of interdependence between economies. Countries compete for mobile technological knowledge, for mobile capital, and for mobile qualified labor. This leads to locational competition (Chapter 15). The policy instruments governments can use in order to attract these mobile factors are institutional arrangements, taxes, and infrastructure in the widest sense, including the educational and the university systems.

Property rights for mobile technological knowledge

An emerging new phenomenon for the world economy and its order is the rise of the knowledge economy. It is nearly certain that the knowledge economy needs different rules than the industrial society. The protection of intellectual property is a key point to provide enough incentives to generate new technological knowledge. When countries compete for mobile technological knowledge, property rights become important. These relate to all sorts of intellectual property, copyright and associated rights, trademarks, industrial design, patents, the layout designs of integrated circuits, and geographical indications (like appellations of origin). Issues to be solved (and partly included in the Agreement on Trade-Related Aspects of Intellectual Property Rights (TRIPs)) are minimum standards of protection to be provided by the individual countries, enforcement of intellectual property rights, and dispute settlements.

A global system of rules for new technology has to solve problems, which are similar to those of structuring a national patent system. On the one hand, user rights to new technological knowledge must be secure, since otherwise there will be insufficient incentives to search for and adopt new technological knowledge. This means that property rights to new knowledge must be respected throughout the world. On the other hand, this property protection must not create permanently exclusive positions and make markets uncontestable. Rather, the diffusion of new knowledge must be possible after a certain passage of time. Accordingly, time limits should be set on the protective effect of user rights. The optimal duration of property rights depends among other things on product life-cycles and the timeframe of research and development phases; this can differ greatly from product to product. Since countries may have an interest in protecting their firms' technological knowledge for as long as possible (although this reduces the incentives for their own technological dynamics), the solution cannot consist simply in mutually recognizing national patent laws. Rather, it may be desirable to set time limits on the validity of national patents. With respect to the other types of property right such as trademarks and geographical indications there is no necessity to let protection run out.

National technology policy should be dealt with in the same way as national subsidies. Thus, the international subsidy code must set limits for industry-specific research subsidies. In contrast, there is no need for controlling the improvement of the general conditions for research and development, for example, when countries generally introduce more favorable tax conditions for research and development, innovation, investment, and entrepreneurial activity, as well as organize basic research and further technology transfer so that they can be internationally competitive.

An investment code for capital mobility

It is in the best interest of each country to keep capital at home and to attract more capital from outside. Each country should therefore structure its institutional framework accordingly, i.e. provide for the security of property rights, avoid uncertainty about corporate taxes, develop a tax system and a general economic framework which make the country less risky and more attractive for foreign direct investments.

Even if it is the host country's responsibility to enhance its own attractiveness, it may be helpful to have an investment code in order to minimize disruptions. For instance, foreign direct investments should be protected against expropriation. Capital should be allowed to be repatriated and profits of capital invested should be allowed to be sent to the country of the capital owners. Multilateral agreements can make the direct investments of the sending country more secure. They can make a country appear less risky for direct investments. Moreover, uncertainty for investment may be a cause for uncertainty in trade. Consequently, an investment code is required which goes beyond the trade-related investment measures (TRIMs). It is an open question whether a two-speed approach should be recommended for an investment code, with the OECD countries going ahead and the WTO following, or whether an investment code, has better chances to be accepted if it is initiated by the WTO (Krueger 1998: 408). Eventually, an investment code should be administered by the WTO. So far, the OECD has not succeeded to establish an international investment code (2005).

Another important condition for an efficient international division of labor is that savings should not be prevented from seeking better opportunities abroad. Otherwise countries would force their savers to invest solely at home.

The right of exit for the migration of people

The right of individuals to leave a country, the exit option, can be interpreted as an important element of a liberal order. Every individual should have the right to choose to leave, given living conditions which he or she finds unacceptable. This principle should hold even if the exit option conflicts with the claim that citizens of a state must fulfill their tax duties, when they take their residence abroad. The freedom of the individual should be given priority over the tax claims of the state. A credible right to exit is a limit on the actions of the government and implicitly controls the government.

The exit option does not, however, imply the entry option, i.e. the right to migrate *into* a country. States define their identity by setting their immigration policy. This creates difficult ethical questions, which can be more easily solved if potential countries of immigration – beyond the duty to accept the politically persecuted – are sufficiently open and if regional integrations such as the European Union, although only spatially limited from an international economic perspective, guarantee the freedom of movement within their territory.

For many reasons labor migration should be replaced by the movement of goods and capital mobility. The strengthening of an international economic order for the international exchange of goods and the openness of markets reduces the necessity of migration.

17.7 Social standards

Recently, there have been increased calls to equalize social norms worldwide (see Chapter 14), and this is supposed to be accomplished through trade policy measures. Countries which do not employ these standards are supposed to be denied access to markets elsewhere.

Except for some minimum standards as agreed upon by the members of the International Labor Organization (ILO), this is a misleading idea. By harmonizing social standards the developing countries would be negatively affected. Because of their lower labor productivity these countries are unable to pay the same wages as industrialized countries. For similar reasons, they cannot be expected to adopt the industrialized countries' labor standards or social norms because these standards increase the cost of production in the same way as higher wages do. The industrialized countries have no ethical right to ask the developing countries to implement the social norms of the industrialized countries. Therefore, harmonizing social norms cannot be a promising strategy of the rich countries against globalization. Also in this domain, the country-of-destination principle cannot be practiced in the world trade order. Which regulations are set for the production of goods should consequently be left to the discretion of the country of origin. Besides, trade policy is unsuitable as a means of harmonization. Social norms are not a public good.

17.8 The environment and the world trade order

In the past, international frameworks for environmental issues and for the world trade order have been developed side by side. In the future, it will become increasingly important to consider more strongly the consistency of these frameworks.

National environmental policy and international rules

When the environment is an immobile national endowment factor, the different environmental scarcities of countries can be expressed by different prices of environmental services. This is relevant when the absorptive and regenerative capacities of national environments vary, when a high population density makes it more difficult to spatially separate residential and recreational areas from environmentally degrading transport and production activities and when the preferences of countries for environmental quality differ. Signaling different environmental scarcities by different prices does not require an international rule system but the pricing can be left to national policies. A market economy approach to environmental policy, which taxes emissions or establishes prices for environmental services through licensing, is consistent with an institutional framework for the international division of labor. The more successful the integration of the environment into the economic regulations of individual countries, and the more successful welfare can be defined by also taking into consideration nature and the environment, the better environmental policy can be integrated into the international trade order.

Protecting health and conserving natural resources

If prices for national environmental use are not (or cannot be) applied and other measures such as administrative approaches, emission norms, or product standards are employed by countries in order to protect their citizens' health and life and to conserve natural resources (article XX of the GATT Treaty), those measures must be non-discriminatory. Non-discrimination requires that in the case of market entry restrictions, regulations through production permits, facility permits, and product norms must not give preference to domestic producers and domestic goods. Thus it should not be permissible, for example, with the aim of reducing health hazards, as in the Thailand cigarette case (1990), to restrict the import of goods or to tax them unless the same measures are simultaneously applied to similar domestic goods.

The similarity of products should be defined from the demand side, for example in terms of possible harmful effects, and not from the production side. As in the Mexican–American tuna-fish case (1991), the principle of similarity should not be applied to the production methods (in the tuna-dolphin case, methods of fishing which did not sufficiently protect dolphins). This means that the country-of-origin principle should apply. Non-discrimination should also satisfy the condition that policy instruments should accord to the proportionality principle. Measures must accordingly be necessary in the sense that otherwise environmental policy aims or the protection of natural resources could not be achieved. As a rule, these aims are achieved in a better way through specific environmental policy measures rather than through trade policy.

The territorial principle as a restraint for national measures

Trade policy must not be employed to force national preferences on other countries. Any country's environmental policy should not apply to external effects outside its own territorial area. Externalities elsewhere would be emotional externalities. Since countries have different amounts of environmental resources and also different environmental preferences, those with stronger environmental preferences should not be entitled to impose their environmental preferences on other countries by means of trade-restricting measures (Siebert 1996). Of course, a country is free to offer its financial support for environmental protection abroad. The thesis that the country-of-origin principle should be fundamentally recognized for national environments can be generalized. When harmful effects do not appear outside a country's territorial area, i.e. when there are no cross-border externalities, countries should not have the right to use trade policy to influence the production methods of a country of origin. Also, the protective clauses for health, life, and exhaustible resources found in article XX should in the case of national environmental goods be applied only within a country's own territorial area. Thus, countries should not have the right to employ unilateral measures to protect the environment in other countries. A different matter, however, is when trans-frontier pollution occurs. Then, a Coasian solution has to be found. The Kantian imperative applies (Siebert 2005a).

Global environmental goods

Global environmental goods, i.e. public goods with a worldwide spatial dimension, require an agreement of all countries as to what amount and what quality of these public goods should be supplied. It is not sufficient to decide about which type and quantity of emissions should be reduced, it is also necessary to decide about the appropriate distribution of costs of emission reduction among individual countries (see Chapter 16). Any solution represents de facto an international allocation of emission rights. It is difficult to reach an international consensus, because countries have different preferences and because they have different per capita incomes and thus have different willingness to pay. In addition, the cost functions for disposal differ from country to country. Moreover, a nation can behave as a free-rider. Thus, implementing the polluter-pays principle for global goods runs into difficulties. To what extent a stable international environmental framework with voluntary commitments by states can be created under these conditions using compensatory payments is a complex issue and has been the subject of numerous studies (Siebert 2005a).

Consistency between the international environmental order and the international trade order

Environmental policy aims at protecting the natural living-conditions, i.e. it deals with scarcity. An institutional order for the international division of labor attempts to make it possible to increase the prosperity of all countries through exchange, i.e. it also deals with scarcity. Both orders attempt to do away with distortions and they represent institutional frameworks dealing with allocation. Since environmental policy and international trade intersect at many points, the rules of the two frameworks should not come into conflict. In principle, the aims are not contradictory, since scarcity must be defined by taking the natural living conditions into account. If we start from the premise that the valuation of the goods on which affluence is based as well as the valuation of environmental quality must depend on national preference, a contradiction between the regimes can be avoided. The more successfully the environment as a scarce good is integrated into the economic order of individual countries and the better affluence is defined by taking into account nature and the environment, the sooner congruence of targets will be achieved between the two orders.

Compared to the administrative approach using regulations, the market economy approach to environmental policy using scarcity prices provides more consistency between the two sets of rules. The sooner the polluter-pays principle is accepted as a guideline by all countries, the easier it will be to achieve consistency of the two orders in the case of global environmental concerns. This clearly holds for national environmental goods. For global goods, implementing the polluter-pays principle has to overcome the difficulties mentioned above like the differences in preferences, in willingness-to-pay and free-rider behavior. What would be needed is a consensus on the conditions under which the polluter-pays principle can be applied to global goods; this is equivalent to a consensus regarding the conditions under which compensations must be used.

Inconsistency between the two rules system should be prevented. The following aspects can help to minimize conflicts:

- The group of countries signing international environmental agreements should not be too divergent from those who are members of the WTO.
- Even if the international environmental order and the international trade order have consistent aims in principle, the rules of the two orders should not be contingent upon each other. Making the rules mutually conditional would cause considerable uncertainty, not only in the international division

of labor, but also in the production of environmental goods. Institutional orders should not be uncertain.

- It appears ill-advised to create a temporary waiver for the environment as an exception to the world trade order. One reason is that the previously created exemptions for the agricultural and textile sectors have become resistant to change and have led to a permanent infringement of the most-favored-nation principle. If an exceptional regulation is questionable even in the case of very specific and internationally declining sectors like agriculture, then a similar procedure appears still less desirable for an area like the environment that is pervasive in all sectors of the economy and that will become increasingly important in the future.
- The sets of instruments of the two orders should be kept separate. Trade policy instruments should not be employed for environmental policy purposes. Countries should not have the right to apply their environmental policy outside their own territory. Non-discrimination and the priority of the country-of-origin principle over the country-of-destination principle should be guiding principles.
- A similar mechanism to the WTO dispute settlement mechanism should be developed for the environmental domain.
- In the case of global environmental goods a consensus should be developed regarding the conditions under which the polluter-pays principle or compensations should be applied.

17.9 Stabilizing and strengthening the WTO

The WTO is a multilateral agreement of sovereign states. It is essential that sovereign states abide by the rules to which they have agreed and do not renege. A set of mechanisms stabilizes and strengthens the WTO.

Sanctions

An important mechanism in international contracts are sanctions, which can be taken if rules are violated. The WTO dispute settlement procedure serves this purpose. Unfortunately, sanctions against a country violating WTO rules are not applied by the WTO but by the country which has successfully claimed damage. It can use sanctions against the injuring party but it may hurt itself through this measure.

Positive mechanisms

Besides sanctions in dispute settlement, the world trading order contains mechanisms that attempt to strengthen the institutional arrangement and help to expand it. One such mechanism is the most-favored-nation clause, which extends reductions of trade barriers to third parties and thus multilateralizes liberalizations. Another mechanism is the reciprocity of concessions requiring that the tariff reduction of one country must be answered by other countries (even though the concept of reciprocity has its roots in a mercantilistic philosophy). Yet another mechanism is to bind tariffs so that the results of liberalization rounds are 'chiseled in stone' and countries cannot easily walk away from agreements that have been reached. A country that wants to raise the bound tariff has to negotiate with the countries most concerned. It has to compensate for the trading partners' loss of trade.

Strengthening support from private groups

In order to restrain national interest groups, the World Trade Organization needs the support of the private sector including the NGOs. In the past, export interests were harnessed against protectionist groups. Today, NGOs challenge the basis of the international division of labor by not accepting its mutual benefits for all countries. In order to attract the support of the private sector, it should be made clear what advantages households and enterprises can obtain from the international framework. New rules should be tailored such that they get the support of the private sector. Thus, strengthened intellectual property rights and improved exchange conditions for services can be attractive for the private sector.

The prospect of an increase in future benefits

An essential condition for an international economic order is that the institutional framework should be acceptable to all countries and that all countries can expect to gain from it. For each country the advantages of membership must exceed the advantages of non-membership. It is crucial that benefits are expected in the future. It pays to stick to the rules, because there will be a reward in the future. The individual country's cost–benefit calculations should not shift asymmetrically over time. The net advantage for each country should increase and in no case worsen. If this condition is not fulfilled, there will be an incentive not to honor the treaty, but instead to withdraw from it.

From an intertemporal perspective, the global rule system is a relational contract (MacNeil 1978), in which countries interact along a time axis and in which a strategic gain from non-cooperative behavior today must be confronted with the opportunity costs of retaliation in future periods. Honoring a rule system or violating it must be interpreted as a repeated game in which an agent accumulates or destroys reputation and in which the preparedness of the other agents to cooperate tomorrow is affected by the agent's behavior today. These intertemporal linkages help to prevent reneging on the contract and to give stability to the system.

Preventing institutional domino effects

An economic order may be conceived as existing of several suborders (Eucken 1940). The interdependence of suborders raises other issues. One is that the suborders may contradict each other. Clearly, they must be mutually consistent. One suborder must not lead to behavior on the part of economic agents, which contradicts and undermines some other suborder. As a consequence, suborders must have the same or similar objectives or philosophies. An important example of this consistency issue is the relation between the world trade order and the world environmental order (see above). In any case, the interdependence of suborders must be taken into consideration when an overall rule system is developed.

Another issue is to what extent the withdrawal of benefits from one suborder can be used as a threat or sanction to abide by the rules of the other suborder. In a game-theoretic approach, threatening with the withdrawal of benefits from one rule system may be an effective inducement to join (and to respect) another rule system. However, this approach makes one suborder contingent on another suborder. If one institutional system falls, the other falls too. This raises the risk that the overall rule system is endangered. Therefore, the advantage of threatening with the withdrawal of benefits of one suborder must be weighed against the risk of destroying the overall rule system. If the WTO is understood as a single undertaking, suborders cannot be singled out for strategic purposes.

A possible approach to this question is to explicitly distinguish between two different stages, namely the creation of an institutional arrangement and the implementation of the rule system associated with it. In establishing a new institutional framework, withholding benefits to non-members from another subsystem is a strong sanction that is positive for establishing the new order. Once an institutional arrangement is established, however, the validity of one suborder should – as a principle – not be contingent on the functioning of some other suborder in order to prevent institutional domino effects. This means that suborders should be clearly separated on an instrumental level. As a rule, economic policy instruments available to an international organization should be limited to specific suborders. Trade policy instruments should not be employed for environmental policy purposes. The instrumental level should thus be subdivided into different modules which should be clearly demarcated.

Multilateralizing regional integrations

In order to prevent regionalism from becoming inward looking or degenerating into an aggressive bilateralism (Chapter 12), regional integrations should be multilateralized. An important precondition for multilateralizing regional integrations is to keep regional integrations open to new members. A strong mechanism for this is for members of integrated regions to grant concessions to third countries, in the sense of conditional most-favored-nation treatment where 'conditional' means that the third countries have to grant similar concessions to the integrated region in order to benefit from the trade barrier reductions achieved within the integrated region. This could be done on a voluntary basis, but the WTO could also agree on a timetable for multilateralization (Srinivasan 1998). Another approach is to link regional integrations by agreements going further than the WTO system (see below).

Drawing a line for which areas no rules should be developed

We have discussed several areas into which the WTO has to be expanded: services, investment, and property rights. Other areas are debated such as competition policy, labor and social standards, and the environment. Quite clearly, the rule system has to respond to new issues, at the same time a line must be drawn specifying areas where WTO is not and should not be in charge.

The WTO should stick to its task of establishing rules for the international division of labor, including trade of goods and services, international factor mobility, and trade restrictions arising from national environmental policy for the national environment. Global environmental issues have to be solved by a different institutional arrangement. A basic principle is that differences in endowments are accepted as the starting point for the international division of labor arbitraged by trade and factor flows. This would exclude protectionism, harmonization and worldwide redistribution. The WTO cannot possibly solve the issue of distribution between nation states. Introducing distributional constraints will make the world order ineffective. Such issues, including the alleviation of poverty, have to be solved in other ways. Besides such a discussion in principle, a more practical answer is to look at which areas of rules nation states are prepared to hand over to the WTO and which new areas of rules the WTO can absorb into its rule system without losing efficacy.

Extending to new members

Enlarging the membership of the WTO club will generate additional benefits to the old members. The new members will have benefits as well. Enlargement of the membership is therefore an important mechanism to make the system more attractive.

In the long-run, the optimal size of the WTO is the world as a whole because then all potential benefits of the international division of labor are exploited. In the short-run, however, there is one important condition for the extension of membership. The system of rules should not be weakened but strengthened when a new member enters. China has been admitted in 2001. The pending accessions of Russia illustrate that a new member can have a strong impact on the WTO rule system. New members must accept the rule system as a single undertaking. They must have a track record showing that they have followed the basic WTO philosophy for some time. Moreover, economic conditions in the potential new member countries must be such that the countries are fit to survive in the world market.

Extending the frontier by a WTO-Plus

Another positive mechanism is to allow new problems to be solved by a subset of WTO members. These countries could commit themselves to realize attempted results of the WTO rounds more quickly than planned, liberalize more than agreed, and employ the permitted exceptions less often. Such a WTO-Plus, a two-speed world integration, could advance the integration process in the world economy. This also holds for dovetailing various regional blocks by establishing a free-trade zone between the blocks, for instance in a trans-Atlantic economic area. This mechanism, however, is in conflict with the single-under-taking nature of WTO and the concept of packaging advantages in different areas. Care must be taken where each mechanism should have priority.

17.10 The role of the IMF once more

As discussed in Chapter 9, an institutional arrangement preventing financial crises is an important cornerstone of a multilateral order for the world economy. In this context, the IMF has to play its role. The IMF is caught between its short-term role of helping countries after a currency crisis has broken out its long-term task of establishing incentives that prevent a currency crisis from developing. The IMF has to provide more comprehensive information and to improve the early warning system. By signaling problems to the financial markets early on, larger problems can be prevented. Signaling problems is one way of reducing the moral hazards created by extensive costs of intervention by the IMF. Reducing the moral hazard problem also requires that private creditors (banks, bond-holders) should be adequately involved in the losses of a financial crisis so that they anticipate the risk. The IMF should also address the issue that the size of its operation creates the wrong incentives for sovereign creditors.

17.11 The interdependence of the world institutional order – a summary

The institutional arrangements for the world economy vary with the different types of interdependence among countries. Traditionally, trade policy rules have been intended to facilitate international merchandise trade. Recently, these rules have been extended to services; other areas such as competition policy are dis-cussed. Norms for the mobility of production factors – technology, physical capital, and labor – are receiving increasing attention with locational competi-tion between countries becoming more important. Norms for the use of the environment will also acquire greater significance in the future (Table 17.5). Finally, financial transactions, balance-of-payments disequilibria and exchange rate volatility are a matter of concern.

Looking at these and other problems, the institutional design of the world economy is in a process of continuous development. There has to be a division of labor between the international organizations. Trade and factor mobility is clearly the domain of the WTO. Improving structural conditions for long-run growth is the task of the World Bank. The Bank for International Settlements (BIS) in Basle is in charge of securing the functioning of the payment system. The IMF fluctuates between its short-run role of bridging international liquidity gaps or balance-of-pay-ments crises and its long-run role of improving structural conditions. The assign-ment problem among international organizations seems is a permanent challenge.

Table 17.5 Elements of an institutional order for the world economy

Type of interdependence	Possible distortions, disturbances	Rules
Exchange of:		
Goods	Protectionist trade policy (tariffs, import quotas, 'voluntary' export restraints, strategic trade policy, anti-dumping, subsidies, product standards).	Trade rules, above all against new forms of protectionist trade policy. Country-of-origin principle for product norms.
	Bilateralism, regionalism.	Multilateral arrangements.
	Social norms.	No worldwide standardization possible
	Market power of firms.	Competition rules. Free access to markets. Effects doctrine.
Services	Discrimination against foreign suppliers.	National treatment.
Factor migration		
Capital	Risk of expropriation of foreign investments. Tax competition for mobile capital.	Governments compete using their infrastructure, tax system, and regulations for mobile capital. National self-interest implies countries to make themselves more attractive to outside capital. Investment code.
Technology	Too low incentives for technological progress, due to property rights not respected internationally.	Property rights which protect new knowledge but permit gradual diffusion.
Labor	Abrupt mass migrations.	Free trade and free movements of capital as a substitute for labor migration. A right to emigrate (right of exit). Openness in immigration policy. Not achievable: a universal right of immigration.
Diffusion of pollutants	Transfrontier pollution, free rider behavior of individual countries with regard to global environmental problems.	International rules only for transfrontier and global environmental problems. Transfrontier pollution subject of agreement among countries concerned. National environmental problems are subject to national environmental policy. Separation between environmental policy and trade policy.
Financial transactions	Volatility of exchange rates, currency runs.	Each country must keep the value of its money stable. Discretionary macroeconomic coordination is not possible unless each country submits itself to rules giving up sovereignty similar to the gold standard.

Notes

2 The world product markets

1   The RCA index of a sector i compares exports and imports of a sector i with the exports and imports of all sectors. It is defined as:

$$RCA_i = \left[\frac{x_i - Im_i}{x_i + Im_i} - \frac{\Sigma(x_i - Im_i)}{\Sigma(x_i + Im_i)} \right]$$

A positive value indicates that a sector has a comparative advantage relative to the other sectors of countries which are used as a norm.

3 The factor markets in the world economy

1   In the figure, let BD be equal to DA, i.e. let the straight line have a slope of 45°. Then BC indicates how much of the good is necessary in the future to keep the household indifferent relative to point A. The ratio CB/DA is the preference rate (of consumption) in time. For consumption, the marginal rate of substitution in time results from totally differentiating the utility function:

$$U = U(C_0) + \frac{1}{1+\delta} U(C_1)$$

at a constant utility (the so-called Euler equation):

$$\left| \frac{dC_1}{dC_0} \right| = \frac{U'_0(C_0)(1+\delta)}{U'_1(C_1)}$$

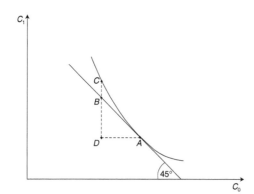

2 From the intertemporal utility-maximizing calculus:

$$\max U = U_0(C_0) + (1 + \delta)^{-1}U_1(C_1)$$

subject to:

$$C_1 = Y/p_1 - (p_0/p_1)C_0$$

It follows that:

$$(1 + \delta)^{-1}U'_1(C_1) - U'_0(C_0)p_1/p_0 = 0$$

or:

$$\frac{p_0}{p_1} = (1 + \delta)U'_0(C_0)/U'_1(C_1)$$

4 Growth processes in the world economy

1 Note that $\delta = 0$ violates the transversality condition; therefore $\delta > 0$ is a necessary condition for a solution to the maximization problem.
2 The production function then becomes $Y = K^{H \alpha + \beta}L^{1-\alpha-\beta}$.
3 When maximizing the present value of the utility:

$$U = \int_0^\infty u(c_t)e^{-\delta t}\, dt$$

under the restrictions:

$$f(k_t) = c_t + \dot{k}_t + nk_t$$

and:

$$k_0 > 0 \text{ given,}$$

maximizing the Hamilton function:

$$H_t = u(c_t) + \lambda_t[f(k_t) - nk_t - c_t]$$

yields:

$$\frac{\partial H_t}{\partial c_t} = u'(c_t) - \lambda_t = 0$$

$$\dot{\lambda}_t = \delta\lambda_t - \frac{\partial H_t}{\partial k_t} = \delta\lambda_t - \lambda_t f_k + \lambda_t n$$

A dot over a variable indicates the derivative with respect to time. Differentiating the first marginal condition with respect to time and substituting the result into the second one yields, with $\lambda_t = u'(c_t)$ and $\dot{\lambda} = u''(c_t)\dot{c}$,

$$\left[-\frac{c_t u''(c_t)}{u'(c_t)} \right]\dot{c} = \delta + n - f_k(k_t)$$

In a growth equilibrium without technical progress, the rate of change in consumption is zero. Consequently, $f_k(k) = \delta + n$ holds. With technical progress, consumption in equilibrium grows with the progress rate ?.

4 For the equation of motion for consumption see the preceding note.
5 See Blanchard and Fischer (1989: 69), in analogy to the closed economy.
6 The empirical analysis shows that factors like population growth and the investment ratios of real and human capital can make a significant contribution to the explanation of country-specific growth rates (Barro and Sala-i-Martin 1995: 382).
7 More precisely, the logarithm of the income relation y_0/y^*_0 is halved.
8 According to the formula $y_t = y^*_t \Leftrightarrow y_0 e^{gt} = 0.8\, y^*_0\, e^{\,g^* t}$
and thus $\ln(y_0) + gt - \ln(0.8) - \ln(y_0^*) - g^* t = 0$ which yields

$$t = \frac{\ln(y_0^*) + \ln(0.8) - \ln(y_0)}{g - g^*}$$

where y^* and y stand for West German and East German GDP respectively.

9 By rewriting this equation, $\ln(y_t) = (1 - e^{-\beta t}) \ln \tilde{y} + e^{-\beta t} \ln(y_0)$ results. The half-life is defined by y_t reaching precisely a medium value between the original level y^0 and the steady-state level $\tilde{y}$. This is the case if $e^{-\beta t} = 0.5$. Solving for t, we obtain $\beta = (1 - \alpha)(x + n + \pi)$ for the half-life which is, in this formulation, independent of the original level. At a rate of convergence of 2 percent (3 percent), it takes thirty-four (twenty-three) years to halve the income difference. The half-life can also be calculated according to the formula $(1 - 0.02)^x = 0.5$.

10 At a constant savings rate (Solow model), $\beta = (1 - \alpha)(x + n + \pi)$ holds. If we insert $\alpha = 0.75$ for the elasticity of production to labor, $x = 0.02$ for the long-term growth rate, $n = 0.01$ for the population growth and $d = 0.05$ for the rate of wear and tear of capital, a value of 2 percent per year results for b.

11 The regression is taken from De Long (1988).

5 Global money and currency markets

1 There is a complete insulation of the home country, if p^*_2 rises proportional to $\tilde{M}^*$ and inversely proportional to e, so that $\tilde{M}$ in the home country as well as p_1 remain unchanged.
2 This assumes that investors are risk neutral.
3 The daily average turnover on the foreign exchange market amounts to US$1.9 trillion (April 2004). The average daily turnover in the over-the-counter derivatives market is US$2.4 trillion (2004).

6 International exchange rate systems

1 The three non-members are Aruba, Hong Kong, and the Netherlands Antilles.
2 For simplification use the nominal exchange rate instead of the real exchange rate. From the equations $S(Y) = I(i) + G + X(e) - eIm^S (Y,e)$ and $L(Y,i) = M$ we have after total differentiation $dY/de = \pi/(s+m + I_i\, L_Y/L_i) > 0$ for $\pi > 0$.
3 Total differentiation of the interest rate parity $i = i^* + (e^e - e)/e^*$ and the monetary equilibrium yields $di = - (e^e/e^2)$ and $L_y\, dY + L_i di = 0$. Hence $dY/de = (L_i\, e^e /L_Y\, e^2) < 0$.
4 The condition for a zero balance in the current account is $CA = X(e) - eIm^S (Y,e)$. The slope is $de/dY = m/\pi > 0$.
5 In a commodity basket currency the value of money is pegged to a basket of commodities. The value of money is determined by the production costs of goods. A possible form of this type of money would be that money is convertible into commodities. If the price of a commodity rises above its value in the basket, market participants could get the commodity from the staple at a pre-announced index price. The monetary authority

must prevent such a case to arise. Problems of such a currency approach are stapling costs of the monetary authority and relative price shifts. Similar arguments hold against a resource basket.
6 Exchange rate volatility between countries i and j is calculated as the standard deviation of the first difference of the log of the exchange rate:

$$Volatility_{ij} = STDEV\,[d(\log(e_{ij}))]$$

For the Bretton Woods system the volatility is calculated from January 1957 to December 1970. For the flexible exchange system the sample January 1975 to December 2005 is used.
7 Note, however, that capital inflows keep the boom alive for some time, providing fresh capital. The capital flow view does not always go together with the trade flow view. For instance, capital inflows may reverse in a recession and aggravate the recession.
8 The theoretical problem is that not all of the n countries of the world can choose the exchange rate as a nominal anchor. Formally, this can also be described as the problem of the $n - 1$ exchange rates. For n countries with n currencies, every single country has $n - 1$ exchange rates. At least one of the currencies (of the nth country) must take the role of the 'numeraire.' As a result, one currency has to be the anchor in a system of fixed exchange rates. In the system of Bretton Woods, the dollar was the anchor; in the European Exchange Rate System, it was the deutsche mark.

7 Financial crises

1 See 'Financial Crises' in *The New Palgrave* (1987).
2 In intertemporal models a transversality condition prevents the emergence of speculative bubbles.

8 Currency crises

1 I use a somewhat different classification than Kaminsky (2003).
2 Assume the home country exports good 1 and the foreign country good 2. Then $e_R = e(p^*_2/p_2)$. Enlarging the right-hand side by p_1, we have $e_R = ep^*_2/p_2p$. From this $\hat{e}_R = [\hat{e} + \hat{p}^*_2 - \hat{p}_2] - \hat{p}$. If purchasing power parity holds, $\hat{e}_R = -\hat{p}$. The current account CA is:

$$CA\,(e\,\frac{p^*_2}{p_2}p^*) = CA(e_Rp)$$

Thus, the curve in Figure 6.3 shifts with a change in the relative price.
3 Appreciation also shows a better competitiveness, if (with unchanged productivity in the foreign country) productivity in tradable goods of the home country increases more than in non-tradables. In this reasoning, the alterative definition of the real exchange rate is used.

9 How to prevent a monetary–financial crisis

1 It now seems to be agreed in the literature that conditionality on fiscal policy and on structural reforms was too tight, for instance in Korea. It is still being debated whether conditionality on monetary policy to keep the interest rate high in order to avoid further devaluation of the won was justified (Ito 1999; Radelet and Sachs 1999).
2 Net uncommitted usable resources are of US$173 billion; balances available under the General Agreement to Borrow and the New Arrangement to Borrow: US$49 billion.

11 China – a new global economic player

1 According to this approach there are three forces affecting the real exchange rate: With respect to trade, productivity growth in the tradable sector relative to non-tradables

(Balasssa Samuelson effect) is a factor leading to an appreciation of the renmimbi. An increase in net foreign assets also implies an appreciation. In this model, only a greater openness means a depreciation.

13 The European Union

1 The multilateral agreement of European integration consists of a set of different treaties. The consolidated versions of the Treaty of the European Union and of the Treaty Establishing the European Community can be found in the Official Journal of the European Communities C 325/2 and C 325/33 dating from December 24, 2002
2 This also would relate to the second-best solution with respect to unanimity, the introduction of the 'unanimity-minus-one rule.' In this model, unanimity is deemed to exist in spite of the veto of one member state. It reflects the idea that no single member state should be in a position to veto a unanimity-based decision.

15 Locational competition

1 Profits are defined as revenue, i.e. price (p) times quantity (Q), minus costs. Costs include capital cost (real interest rate as price of capital times capital input, rK) and labor cost (wage rate times labor input, wL). A company maximizes its profits taking into account taxes ($G = pQ - wL - rK - tK$), subject to the output constraint given by the production function ($Q = F(L, K)$). By differentiating the Lagrangian function $\Lambda = pQ - wL - (r + t)K - \lambda[Q - F(L\ K)]$ with respect to Q, the optimum condition is: $p - \lambda = 0$ which means that the shadow price λ equals the market price. By differentiating with respect to K we have: $F_K(\cdot) = (r + t)/p$.
2 Capital leaves a country if the net marginal productivity is reduced owing to a tax increase, i.e. if:

$$\frac{d\{p \cdot F_K(K,L,G) - t\}}{dt} < 0$$

Because of the budget constraint of the state, $C(G) = t \cdot K$, there is an interrelation between the supply of infrastructure G and tax revenues tK: $G = C^{-1}(t \cdot K)$. The optimal tax rate in the case of capital mobility is characterized by profit maximization subject to tax revenues (tK) and the cost of capital (with r defining the interest rate in the world capital market, which is – for simplicity – supposed to be constant):

$$p \cdot F\{K(t), L, C^{-1}[t \cdot K(t)]\} - t \cdot K(t) - r \cdot K(t)$$

The resulting first-order condition is:

$$[p \cdot F_K - t - r] \frac{dK}{dt} + \frac{p \cdot F_G[K + t \cdot dK / dt]}{C'(G)} - K = 0$$

In the equilibrium of the capital market, the first term equals zero. This yields:

$$F^G = \frac{C'(G) \cdot K}{p \cdot [K + t \cdot dK/dt]}$$

Dividing the denominator and the numerator of the right-hand side of the equation by K, equation 15.2 results.

3 If capital moves out, income of the immobile factor labor will be reduced because labor productivity falls when workers are less well endowed with capital. Lower labor income also implies a lower tax base.

4 If the state redistributes its tax revenues $P'PJI$ among the households, then labor loses only IJH.

5 It is an interesting observation that institutional changes exert considerable influence on the allocation of power. A telling example is the transition from fixed to flexible exchange rates. With the use of flexible exchange rates, the balance of power between fiscal and monetary policy has shifted. Now monetary policy exerts a greater influence than fiscal policy (Siebert and Lorz 2006: Chapter 18).

6 Additionally, it has to be taken into account that the state has to balance its budget. There are tax revenues, but there is also expenditure on infrastructure. With falling average costs of infrastructure (owing to high fixed costs) this creates the problem that the budget might not be balanced with prices equaling marginal costs (Sinn 1997). Note, however, that the immobile factor (labor) also has an indirect advantage arising from the supply of infrastructure, namely if capital is attracted and if consequently labor is better equipped with capital and thus has a higher productivity.

16 Using the national and global environment

1 Cross-border environmental problems are discussed in detail in Siebert 2005a (Chapter 12).

2 With cross-border environmental problems an interdependence exists such that the environment transports emissions from one country to another. The diffusion function is: $E = T(E^*)$ or $E^* = T^*(E)$.

References

Ahearne, A. and J. von Hagen (2005). Global Current Account Imbalances: How to Manage the Risk for Europe. *Bruegel Policy Brief,* 2. Available at: www.bruegel.org/ Repositories/Documents/publications/BPB/EN_Global_Current_Account_Imbalances_ Bruegel_Policy_Brief_2.pdf.

Alonso, W. (1964). *Location and Land Use.* Cambridge: Harvard University Press.

Anderson, K. and H. Norheim (1993). *History, Geography and Regional Economic Integration.* Centre for Economic Policy Research. Discussion Paper No. 795. London.

APEC. www.apecsec.org.sg.

ASEAN. www.aseansec.org.

Axelrod, R. (1986). An Evolutionary Approach to Norms. *American Political Science Review,* 80: 1095–1111.

Balassa, B. A. (1964). The Purchasing Power Parity Doctrine: A Reappraisal. *Journal of Political Economy,* 72 (6): 584-596.

Baldwin, R. E. (2003). *Openness and Growth: What's the Empirical Relationship? National Bureau of Economic Research.* NBER Working Paper No. 9578.

Baldwin, R. E. and Ch. Wyplosz (2004). *The Economics of European Integration.* London: McGraw-Hill Education.

Baldwin, R. E., J. E. Francois, and R. Portes (1997). The Costs and Benefits of Eastern Enlargement: The Impact on the EU and Central Europe. *Economic Policy,* 24: 125–176.

Baldwin R. E., E. Berglöf, F. Giavazzi, and M. Widgrén (2001). Nice Try: Should the Treaty of Nice be Ratified? *Monitoring European Integration,* 11. London: CEPR.

Banga, R. (2005). Trade in Services: A Review. *Global Economy Journal,* 5 (2). Available at: ideas.repec.org/a/bep/glecon/5200523.html.

Bank of International Settlements (2005). *Triennial Central Bank Survey: Foreign Exchange and Derivatives Market Activity in 2004.* Basel, Switzerland.

Barro, R. J. (1992). Convergence. *Journal of Political Economy,* 100: 223–251.

Barro, R. J. and X. Sala-i-Martin (1992). Convergence across States and Regions. In A. Cukierman, Z. Hercowitz, and L. Leiderman (eds), *Political Economy, Growth, and Business Cycles.* Cambridge: MIT Press.

—— (1995). *Economic Growth.* New York: McGraw-Hill.

Bergsten, C. F. (1986). Gearing Up World Growth. *Challenge,* 29 (2): 35–40.

—— (1988). *America in the World Economy: A Strategy for the 1990s.* Washington, DC: Institute for International Economics.

Bhagwati, J. (1984). Splintering and Disembodiment of Services and Developing Nations. *World Economy,* 7 (2): 133–143.

—— (1989). Is Free Trade Passé After All? *Weltwirtschaftliches Archiv*, 125: 17–44.

—— (1991). *The World Trading System at Risk*. New York: Harvester Wheatsheaf.

—— (1992). Regionalism and Multilateralism. *World Economy*, 15 (5): 535–555.

Bhagwati, J., A. Panagariya, and T. N. Srinivasan (1998). *Lectures on International Trade*. 2nd edition. Cambridge: MIT Press.

BIS (Bank for International Settlement) (1998). *The Maturity, Sectoral and Nationality Distribution of International Bank Lending. First Half 1997*. Basle, Switzerland.

Blackhurst, R. (1997). The WTO and the Global Economy. *World Economy*, 20 (5): 527–544.

Blanchard, O. J. and S. Fischer (1989). *Lectures on Macroeconomics*. Cambridge: MIT Press.

Blanchard, O. J. and F. Giavazzi (2005). *Rebalancing Growth in China*. CEPR Discussion Paper No. 5403. London. Available at: www.cepr.org/pubs/new-dps/dplist.asp?dpno=5403.

Blanchard, O. J. and L. F. Katz (1992). Regional Evolutions. *Brookings Papers on Economic Activity*, 1: 1–75.

Blanchard, O. J. and M. Watson (1982). Bubbles, Rational Expectations and Financial Markets. In: P. Wachtel (ed.), *Crises in the Economic and Financial Structure*. Lexington: Lexington Books.

Boss, A. and A. Rosenschon (2006). Subventionen in Deutschland: Eine Bestandsaufnahme. *Kiel Working Papers*, 1267. Kiel, Germany: Institute for World Economy. Available at: opus.zbw-kiel.de/volltexte/2006/3930/pdf/kap1267.pdf.

Bosworth, B. P. (1993). *Saving and Investment in a Global Economy*. Washington, DC: Brookings Institution.

Brander, J. A. and B. J. Spencer (1985). Export Subsidies and International Market Share Rivalry. *Journal of International Economics*, 18 (1/2): 83–100.

British Petroleum Company. *BP Statistical Review of World Energy*. Various Issues. London.

Brown, D. K., A. Deardorff, and R. M. Stern (2003). Multilateral, Regional, and Bilateral Trade-Policy Options for the United States and Japan. *World Economy*, 26 (6): 803–828.

Buch, C. M. (2002). *Globalization of Financial Markets: Causes of Incomplete Integration and Consequences for Economic Policy*. Kiel Studies, Berlin: Springer.

Bucovetsky, S. and J. D. Wilson (1991). Tax Competition with Two Tax Instruments. *Regional Science and Urban Economics*, 21: 333–350.

Bundesanstalt für Geowissenschaften und Rohstoffe (1995). *Reserven, Ressourcen und Verfügbarkeit von Energierohstoffen 1995*. Stuttgart: Schweitzerbart.

Calomiris, C. W. (1998). The IMF's Imprudent Role as a Lender of Last Resort. *Cato Journal*, 17: 275–294.

—— (2000). When Will Economics Guide IMF and World Bank Reforms? *Cato Journal*, 20 (1): 85-103.

Calomiris, C. W. and A. Meltzer (1998). *Reforming the IMF*. New York: Columbia Business School. Unpublished manuscript.

Calvo, G. A. and C. M. Reinhart (2002). Fear of Floating. *Quarterly Journal of Economics*, 117 (2): 379-408.

Caves R. E., J. A. Frankel, and R. W. Jones (1996). *World Trade and Payments: An Introduction*. 7th edition. New York: HarperCollins.

Central Bank of the Russian Federation. *Bulletin of Banking Statistics*. Various Issues. Moscow.

Chinn, M. and J. Frankel (2005). *Will the Euro Eventually Surpass the Dollar as Leading International Reserve Currency?* NBER Working Paper No. 11510. Available at: ksgnotes1.harvard.edu/Research/wpaper.nsf/rwp/RWP05-064/$File /rwp_05_064_frankel.pdf.

Cline, W. (1995). Managing International Debt: How One Big Battle Was Won. *The Economist*, 18 February. London.

Coase, R. H. (1960). The Problem of Social Cost. *Journal of Law and Economics*, 3: 1–44.

Corden, W. M. (2002). *Too Sensational: On the Choice of Exchange Rate Regimes*. Cambridge: MIT Press.

David, P. A. (1999). The Determinants of Long-Run Economic Growth and Wealth Creation. In: OECD (ed.), *21st Century Economic Dynamics: Anatomy of a Long Boom*. Paris.

De Grauwe, P. (1997). *The Economics of Monetary Integration*. 3rd edition. Oxford: Oxford University Press.

De Lisle, J. (2004). *Property Rights Reform in China*. Conference Presentation, The Future of Political Reform in China, 29 January 2004. Available at: www.fpri.org/transcripts/lecture.20040126.delisle.chinapropertyrights.html.

De Long, J. B. (1988). Productivity Growth, Convergence, and Welfare: Comment on W. J. Baumol (1986): Productivity Growth, Convergence, and Welfare. *American Economic Review*, 78 (5): 1138–1154.

Department of the Treasury of the United States Government. *Monthly Treasury Statement of Receipts and Outlays*. Washington, DC.

Deutsche Bundesbank. www.bundesbank.de/index_e.html.

—— *Balance of Payments Statistics*. Various Issues. Frankfurt.

—— *Monthly Reports*. Various Issues. Frankfurt.

Diamond, D. and P. Dybvig (1983). Bank Runs, Deposit Insurance, and Liquidity. *Journal of Political Economy*, 91 (2): 401–419.

Dixit, A. K. and V. Norman (1980). *Theory of International Trade*. Cambridge: Cambridge University Press.

Dollar, D. and A. Kraay (2004). Trade, Growth and Poverty. *Economic Journal*, 114 (493), F22-F49. Available at: www.blackwell-synergy.com/doi/full/10.1111/j.0013-0133.2004.00186.x.

Dooley, M. P. (1995). *A Survey of Academic Literature on Controls over International Capital Transactions*. IMF Working Paper No. 95/127.

Dornbusch, R. (1976). Expectations and Exchange Rate Dynamics. *Journal of Political Economy*, 84 (6): 1161–1176.

—— (1987). The Dollar is Down? Not Nearly for Enough far America's Good. *International Herald Tribune*, 26 March.

—— (2001). Fewer Monies, Better Jobs. *American Economic Review*, 91 (2): 238–242.

Dunaway, S. and X. Li (2005). *Estimating China's 'Equilibrium' Real Exchange Rate*. IMF Working Paper No. 05/202. Available at: www.imf.org/external/pubs/ft/wp/2005/wp05202.pdf.

—— *Economics of Transition*. Various Issues. London.

The Economist (2006). Coming Our: A Survey on China. *The Economist*, 378 (8470). March 25.

Economist Intelligence Unit (1999). *Country Report Brazil*. London.

—— (2006). Country Report China. April. London.

Ehlermann, C.-D. (1995). Ökonomische Aspekte des Subsidiaritätsprinzips: Harmonisierung versus Wettbewerb der Systeme. *Integration*, 18 (1): 11–21.

Eichengreen, B. J. (1997). *European Monetary Unification: Theory, Practice, Analysis.* Cambridge: MIT Press.

—— (1999a). *Involving the Private Sector in Crisis Prevention and Resolution.* IMF Conference on Key Issues in Reform of the International Monetary and Financial Systems, May 28–29, Washington, DC: IMF.

—— (1999b). *Toward A New International Financial Architecture: A Practical Post-Asia Agenda.* Washington, DC: Institute for International Economics.

—— (2001). *The EMS Crisis in Retrospect.* CEPR Discussion Paper No. 2704.

—— (2002). Capital Account Liberalization: What do the Cross-Country Studies Tell Us? *World Bank Economic Review*, 15 (3): 341–365.

—— (2006). *How to Really Reform the IMF.* Speech held on February 23. Available at: www.econ.berkeley.edu/~eichengr/reform.pdf.

Eichengreen, B. J. and N. Sussman (2000). *The International Monetary System in the (Very) Long Run.* IMF Working Paper No. 00/43. Available at: www.imf.org/external/pubs/ft/wp/2000/wp0043.pdf.

Ethier, W. (1995). *Modern International Economics.* 3rd edition. New York: Norton.

Eucken, W. (1940). *Die Grundlagen der Nationalökonomie.* Jena: Fischer. (English Edition: *The Foundations of Economics: History and Theory in the Analysis of Economic Reality.* Berlin, 1992: Springer.)

European Bank for Reconstruction and Development (EBRD). *Transition Report.* Various Issues. London.

European Central Bank. www.ecb.int/stats/html/index.en.htlm.

—— (2006). *Monthly Bulletin.* February. Frankfurt, Germany.

European Union. europa.eu.int.

—— (2005). *Regions: Statistical Yearbook 2005.* Available at: epp.cec.eu.int/cache/ITY_OFFPUB/KS-AF-05-001/EN/KS-AF-05-001-EN.PDF.

—— (2006). *EUROSTAT.* Statistical Database of the European Union. Available at: epp.eurostat.cec.eu.int.

——. *Internal and External Trade of the EU.* Luxembourg.

Federal Reserve Board. www.federalreserve.gov/rnd.htm.

Feldstein, M. (1992). The Case Against EMU. *The Economist*, 13 June: 19–22.

—— (1997a). EMU and International Conflict. *Foreign Affairs,* 76 (6): 60–73.

—— (1997b). The Political Economy of European Monetary Union: Political Reasons for an Economic Liability. *Journal of Economic Perspectives*, 11 (4): 23–42.

—— (1998). Refocusing the IMF. *Foreign Affairs*, 77 (2): 20–33.

Feldstein, M. and C. Horioka (1980). Domestic Saving and International Capital Flows. *Economic Journal*, 90: 314–329.

Fikentscher, W. and U. Immenga (eds) (1995). *Draft International Antitrust Code. Kommentierter Entwurf eines internationalen Wettbewerbsrechts mit ergänzenden Beiträgen.* Baden-Baden: Nomos.

Finger, J. M., M. D. Ingco, and U. Reincke (1996). *The Uruguay Round – Statistics on Tariff Concessions Given and Received.* Washington, DC: World Bank.

Fischer, S. (1998). IMF and Crisis Prevention. *Financial Times*, 30 March.

—— (1999). On the Need for an International Lender of Last Resort. *Journal of Economic Perspectives,* 13 (4): 85–104.

—— (2000). *On the Need for an International Lender of Last Resort.* Princeton: Princeton University.

—— (2001). Distinguished Lecture on Economics in Government: Exchange Rate Regimes: Is the Bipolar View Correct? *Journal of Economic Perspectives,* 15 (2): 3-24.

Forbes, K. (2004). *Capital Controls: Mud in the Wheels of Market Discipline.* NBER Working Paper No. 10284. Available at: papers.nber.org/papers/w10284.pdf.

Frankel, J. A. (1997). *Regional Trading Blocs in the World Economic System.* Washington, DC: Institute for International Economics.

—— (1999). *No Single Currency Regime is Right for all Countries or at All Times.* NBER Working Paper No. 7338. Available at: papers.nber.org/papers/ W7338.pdf.

Freeman, R. B. (1995). Are your Wages Set in Beijing? *Journal of Economic Perspectives*, 9 (3): 15–32.

Garber, P. M. (1989). Tulipmania. *Journal of Political Economy*, 97 (3): 535–560.

—— (1990). Famous First Bubbles. *Journal of Economic Perspectives*, 4 (2): 35–54.

GATT/WTO. *International Trade, Trends and Statistics.* Various Issues. Geneva.

Georgopoulos, G. J. and W. Hejazi (2005). Feldstein-Horioka Meets a Time Trend. *Economic Letters*, 86 (3): 353-357.

Gordon, M. (2005). Foreign Reserves for Crises Management. *Reserve Bank of New Zealand Bulletin*, 68 (1): 4-11.

Government of the Russian Federation. *Russian Economic Trends.* Monthly Update. Various Issues. London.

Graham, E. M. (1995). Competition Policy and the New Trade Agenda. In OECD, *New Dimensions of Market Access in a Globalizing World Economy.* Paris.

Griffith-Jones, S., M. A. Segoviano and S. Spratt (2004). Basel II: Developing Countries and Portfolio Diversification. *CEPAL Review,* 83: 145-160. Available at: www.eclac.cl/publicaciones/SecretariaEjecutiva/1/LCG2231PI/lcg2231iGriffithJones.pdf.

Gros, D. and A. Steinherr (1995). *Winds of Change: Economic Transaction and Central and Eastern Europe.* New York: Longman.

Grossman, G. M. and E. Helpman (1991a). *Innovation and Growth in the Global Economy.* Cambridge: MIT Press.

—— (1991b). Trade, Knowledge Spillovers, and Growth. *European Economic Review*, 35 (2/3): 517–526.

—— (1995). Trade Wars and Trade Talks. *Journal of Political Economy*, 103 (4): 675–708.

Gundlach, E. (1998). Das Wirtschaftswachstum der Nationen im zwanzigsten Jahrhundert. *Die Weltwirtschaft*, 1: 85–107.

Gundlach, E. and P. Nunnenkamp (1998). Some Consequences of Globalization for Developing Countries. In J. H. Dunning (ed.), *Globalization, Trade and Foreign Investment.* Amsterdam: Elsevier.

Haggard, S. and B. A. Simmons (1987). Theories of International Regimes. *International Organization*, 41 (3): 491-517.

Harris, J. and M. Todaro (1970). Migration, Unemployment and Development: A Two-Sector Analysis. *American Economic Review, Papers and Proceedings*, 60 (1): 126–142.

Hayek, F. A. von (1968). Der Wettbewerb als Entdeckungsverfahren. *Kieler Vorträge*, 56. Kiel: Institute for World Economy.

—— (1973). *Law, Legislation and Liberty: A New Statement of the Liberal Principles of Justice and Political Economy. Volume I: Rules and Order.* London: Routledge & Kegan Paul.

Heitger, B. (1993). Comparative Economic Growth: East and West. In B. Heitger and L. Waverman (eds), *German Unification and the International Economy.* London: Routledge.

Helpman, E. (2004). *The Mystery of Economic Growth.* Cambridge: Belknap Press of Havard University.

Helpman, E. and P. R. Krugman (1990). *Market Structure and Foreign Trade.* Cambridge: MIT Press.

Higgins, B. H. (1959). *Economic Development: Principles, Problems and Policies.* London: Constable.

Hillman, A. L. (1989). *The Political Economy of Protection.* Chur: Harwood.

—— (1994). The Political Economy of Migration Policy. In: H. Siebert (ed.), *Migration: A Challenge to Europe.* Tübingen: Mohr.

Hodrick, R. J. and E. C. Prescott (1997). Postwar US Business Cycles: An Empirical Investigation. *Journal of Money, Credit, and Banking,* 29 (1): 1–16.

Hoekman, B. M. and P. C. Mauroidis (1994). Competition, Competition Policy and the GATT. *The World Economy,* 17 (2): 121–150.

Hoggarth, G., R. Reis, and V. Saporta (2002). Costs of Banking System Instability: Some Empirical Evidence. *Journal of Banking & Finance,* 26 (5): 825-855.

Holtfrerich, C. E. and O. Schötz (1988). *Vom Weltgläubiger zum Weltschuldner: Erklärungsansätze zur historischen Entwicklung und Struktur der internationalen Währungsposition der USA.* Frankfurt: Knapp.

Holz, C. A. (2006). Why China's New GDP Data Matters. *Far Eastern Economic Review,* 169 (1): 54-56.

Hornbeck, J. F. (2004). *Argentina's Sovereign Debt Restructuring.* CRS Report of Congress October 19, 2004. Available at: www.cnie.org/NLE/CRSreports/04Oct/RL32637.pdf.

Immenga, U. (1995). Konzepte einer grenzüberschreitenden und international koordinierten Wettbewerbspolitik. *Kiel Working Papers,* 692. Kiel: Institute for World Economy.

International Financial Institution Advisory Commission (IFIAC) (2000). *The Report on the International Financial Institutional Advisory Commission.* (Meltzer Report). Washington, DC.

International Monetary Fund. www.imf.org.

—— *Balance of Payments Statistics.* Various Issuses. Washington, DC.

—— *Currency Composition of Official Foreign Exchange Reserves Database.* Washington, DC. Available at: www.imf.org/external/np/sta/cofer/eng.

—— *International Financial Statistics.* Various Issues. Washington, DC.

—— (1999). *Involving the Private Sector in Forestalling and Resolving Financial Crises.* Washington, DC.

—— (2000). *Country Report Brazil.* Washington, DC.

—— (2002). Managing the Fiscal Impact of Aid. *Finance and Development,* 39 (4). Available at: www.imf.org/external/pubs/ft/fandd/2002/12/bulir.htm.

—— (2003). *Lessons from the Crisis in Argentina.* Prepared by the Policy Development and Review Department. Washington, DC.

—— (2004). *Country Report China.* Washington, DC.

—— (2005a). *Annual Report 2005.* Washington, DC.

—— (2005b). *Annual Report on Exchange Arrangements and Exchange Restrictions 2005.* Washington, DC.

—— (2005c). *Country Report China.* Washington, DC.

—— (2005d). *Direction of Trade Statistics.* Yearbook 2005. Washington, DC.

—— (2005e). *World Economic Outlook: Globalization and External Imbalances.* Washington, DC.

—— (2006). *The Managing Director's Report on Implementing the Fund's Medium-Term Strategy*. Available at: www.imf.org/external/np/pp/eng/2006/040506.pdf.

International Organization for Migration (IOM) (2005). *World Migration 2005: Costs and Benefits of International Migration*. Geneva.

Ito, T. (1999). *The Role of IMF Advice: A Postcrisis Examination*. Paper presented at the Conference on Key Issues in Reform of the International Monetary and Financial System, May 28-29. Washington, DC.

Jones, R. W. and P. B. Kenen (eds) (1984). *Handbook of International Economics*. Amsterdam: North-Holland.

Kaminsky, G. L. (2003). *Varieties of Currency Crises*. NBER Working Paper No. 10193. Available at: papers.nber.org/papers/w10193.pdf.

Kindleberger, Ch. P. (1973). *The World in Depression 1929–1939*. London: Lane.

—— (1993). *A Financial History of Western Europe*. 2nd edition. New York: Oxford University Press.

Klodt, H., J. Stehn, A. Boss, K. Lammers, J. O. Lorz, R. Maurer, A. O. Neu, K. H. Paqué, A. Rosenschon, and C. Walter (1994). Standort Deutschland: Strukturelle Herausforderungen im neuen Europa. *Kieler Studien*, 265. Tübingen: Mohr.

Kornai, J. (1980). *Economics of Shortage*. Amsterdam: North-Holland.

—— (1982). *Growth, Shortage and Efficiency. A Macrodynamic Model of the Socialist Economy*. Oxford: Blackwell.

Krueger, A. O. (1996). *The Political Economy of Trade Protection*. Chicago: University of Chicago Press.

—— (ed.) (1998). *The WTO as an International Organization*. Chicago: University of Chicago Press.

Krugman, P. R. (ed.) (1986). *Strategic Trade Policy and the New International Economics*. Cambridge: MIT Press.

—— (1989). *Exchange-Rate Instability*. Cambridge: MIT Press.

—— (1990). *Rethinking International Trade*. Cambridge: MIT Press.

—— (1991). *Geography and Trade*. Leuven: University Press.

—— (1994). Competitiveness: A Dangerous Obsession. *Foreign Affairs*, 73 (2): 28–44.

Krugman, P. R. and M. Obstfeld (2006). *International Economics, Theory and Policy*. 7th edition. Reading: Addison-Wesley.

Langhammer, R. J. (1995). Regional Integration in East Asia: From Market-Driven Regionalisation to Institutionalised Regionalism? *Weltwirtschaftliches Archiv*, 131 (1): 167–201.

—— (1998). Europe's Trade, Investment and Strategic Policy Interests in Asia and APEC. In P. D. Drysdale, D. Vines (eds), *Europe, East Asia and APEC*. Cambridge: Cambridge University Press.

—— (1999). *The WTO and the Millennium-Round: Between Standstill and Leapfrog*. Kiel Discussion Paper 352. Kiel: Institute for the World Economy.

Langhammer, R. J. and M. Lücke (1999). WTO Accession Issues. *The World Economy*, 22 (6): 837–873.

Levich, R. (2001). *International Financial Markets: Prices and Policies*. 2nd edition. Boston: McGraw-Hill/Irwin.

Lindbeck, A., P. Molander, T. Persson, O. Petersson, A. Sandmo, B. Swedenborg, and N. Thygesen (1994). *Turning Sweden Around*. Cambridge: MIT Press.

Lorz, O. (1997). Standortwettbewerb bei internationaler Kapitalmobilität: Eine modelltheoretische Untersuchung. *Kieler Studien*, 284. Tübingen: Mohr.

—— (1998). Capital Mobility, Tax Competition and Lobbying for Redistributive Capital Taxation. *European Journal of Political Economy*, 14 (2): 265–279.

Lucas, R. E. (1981). Studies in Business Cycle Theory. Oxford: Blackwell.

McKinnon, R. I. (1982). Currency Substitution and Instability in the World Dollar Standard. *American Economic Review*, 72 (3): 320–333.

—— (2005). *Exchange Rates Under the East Asian Dollar Standard: Living with Conflicted Virture.* Cambridge: MIT Press.

MacNeil, I. R. (1978). Contracts. Adjustment of Long-term Economic Relations under Classical, Neoclassical, and Relational Contract Law. *Northwestern University Law Review*, 72 (6): 854–905.

Maddison, A. (1982). *Phases of Capitalist Development.* Oxford: Oxford University Press.

—— (1992). *Dynamic Forces in Capitalist Development.* Oxford: Oxford University Press.

—— (2001). *The World Economy: A Millennial Perspective.* Paris: Development Centre of OECD.

Mankiw, N. G. (1995). The Growth of Nations. *Brookings Papers of Economic Activity*, 1: 275–326.

Marshall, A. (1890). *Principles of Economics. An Introductory Volume.* London.

Mas, I. (1995). Things Governments Do to Money: A Recent History of Currency Reform Schemes and Scams. *Kyklos: International Review for Social Sciences*, 48 (4): 483–512.

Maurer, R. (1998). Economic Growth and International Trade with Capital Goods: Theory and Empiric Evidence. *Kieler Studien*, 289. Tübingen: Mohr.

Meltzer, A. H. (1998). *Asian Problems and the IMF.* Testimony. Prepared for the Joint Committee. February.

Messerlin, P. A. (1989). The EC Antidumping Regulations: A First Economic Appraisal, 1980–85. *Weltwirtschaftliches Archiv*, 125: 563–587.

Minton-Beddoes, Z. (1995). Why the IMF Needs Reform. *Foreign Affairs*, 74 (3): 123–133.

Mishkin, F. S. (1998). *International Capital Movements, Financial Volatility, and Financial Instability.* NBER Working Paper 6390. Cambridge.

Mundell R. A. (1961). A Theory of Optimum Currency Areas. *American Economic Review*, 51 (4): 657–665.

—— (2003). *The International Monetary System and the Case for a World Currency.* Lecture Series. Available at: www.tiger.edu.pl/publikacje/dist/mundell2.pdf.

Mussa, M. (1997). IMF Surveillance. *American Economic Review*, 87 (2): 28–31.

—— (2002). *Argentina and the Fund: From Triumph to Tragedy.* Washington, DC: Institute for International Economics.

Myrdal, G. (1956). *An International Economy.* New York, NY: Harper.

National Bureau of Statistics of China. *China Statistical Yearbook.* Various Issues. Beijing, China.

National Institute of Statistics, Geography, and Informatics. *Mexican Bulletin of Statistical Information.* Aguascalientes.

Neely, C. J. (1999). An Introduction to Capital Controls. *Federal Reserve Bank Review*, 81 (6): 13–30.

Nelson, R. R. (1956). A Theory of the Low-Level Equilibrium Trap in Underdeveloped Economies. *American Economic Review*, 46 (5): 894–908.

Nicolaides, P. (1994). Towards Multilateral Rules on Competition. The Problems in Mutual Recognition of National Rules. *World Competition,* 17 (3): 5–48.

Norheim, H., K.-M. Finger, and K. Anderson (1993). Trends in the Regionalization of

World Trade, 1928 to 1990. In K. Anderson and R. Blackhurst (eds), *Regional Integration and the Global Trading System*. New York: Harvester Wheatsheaf.

North, D. (1990). *Institutions, Institutional Change and Economic Performance*. Cambridge: Cambridge University Press.

Obstfeld, M. and K. Rogoff (1996). *Foundations of International Macroeconomics*. Cambridge, MA: MIT Press.

Obstfeld, M., J. C. Shambaugh, and A. M. Taylor (2005). The Trilemma in History: Tradeoffs among Rates, Monetary Policies, and Capital Mobility. *Review of Economics and Statistics*, 87 (3): 423–438.

OECD. www.oecd.org.

—— *Economic Outlook*. Various Issues. Paris.

—— *International Trade by Commodities Statistics*. Various Issues. Paris.

—— *Main Economic Indicators*. Various Issues. Paris.

—— *National Accounts*. Various Issues. Paris.

—— *Short-Term Economic Indicators, Transition Countries*. Various Issues. Paris.

—— (1998). *Economic Survey: Japan*. Paris.

—— (2005a). *OECD in Figures: Statistics on the Member Countries*. Paris.

—— (2005b). *Science, Technology and Industry Scoreboard*. Paris.

Olson, M. (1969). The Principle of 'Fiscal Equivalence'. *American Economic Review*, 59: 479–487.

—— (1982). *The Rise and Decline of Nations. Economic Growth, Stagflation and Social Rigidities*. New Haven, CT: Yale University Press.

Organization of the Petroleum Exporting Countries (OPEC) (2004). *Annual Statistical Bulletin 2004*. Vienna. Available at: www.opec.org/library/Annual%20Statistical%20Bulletin/pdf/ASB2004.pdf.

Ostry, S. (1995). New Dimensions of Market Access: Challenges for the Trading System. In: OECD, *New Dimensions of Market Access in a Globalizing World Economy*. Paris.

—— (1997). A New Regime of Foreign Direct Investment. Group of Thirty. *Washington Occasional Paper*, 53.

Oxfam International (2005). *Truth or Consequences: Why the EU and the USA must reform their subsidies, or pay the price*. Oxfam Briefing Paper 81. Available at: www.oxfam.ca/news/MakeTradeFair/AgCamp/bp81_truth_or_consequences_amended%20final_no_emb30.11.05.pdf.

Pei, M. (2006). The Dark Side of China's Rise. *Foreign Policy Magazine*, March/April. Available at: www.carnegieendowment.org/publications/index.cfm?fa=view&id=18110&prog=zch.

Ping, H. and Z. Shaohua (2005). *Internal Migration in China: Linking it to Development*. Regional Conference on Migration and Development in Asia. 14–16 March. Available at: www.iom.int/chinaconference/files/documents/bg_papers/China.pdf.

PlanEcon (Annual Reports). *Czech Economic Monitor PlanEcon Report*.

Plummer, M. R. (2004). Creating an ASEAN Economic Community: Lessons from the EU and Reflections on the Roadmap. In Hew, D. Wei-Yen (ed.), *Roadmap to an ASEAN Economic Community*, Singapore: ISEAS: 31–62.

—— (2005). *The ASEAN Economic Community and the European Experience*. Paper presented at the Asian Development Bank, 28 November, 2005

Plummer, M. R. and Jones, E. (2005) Global Economic Regionalism and Asia: The Implications of Intra- and Extra-regional Accords, *Journal of Asian Economics*, (1): pp. 1–3.

Popper, K. R. (1945). *The Open Society and its Enemies*. London: Routledge & Kegan Paul.

Prasad, E. S. (2004). *China's Growth and Integration into the World Economy: Prospects and Challenges*. IMF Occasional Paper 232. Washington, DC: IMF.

Prebisch, R. (1950). *The Economic Development of Latin America and Its Principal Problems*. Economic Commission for Latin America. New York, NY: United Nations Publications.

Radelet, S. and J. Sachs (1999). *What Have We Learned, So Far, From the Asian Financial Crisis?* Unpublished manuscript. Available at: www.ems.bbk.ac.uk/courses/msceconomics/Options/radelet+sachs2.pdf.

Rauscher, M. (1997). *International Trade, Factor Movements, and the Environment*. Oxford: Clarendon.

Rawls, J. (1971). *A Theory of Justice*. Cambridge: Belknap.

Rodrick, D. (1997). *Has Globalization Gone Too Far?* Washington, DC: Institute of International Economics.

Rodrik, D., A. Subramanian, and F. Trebbi (2004). Institutions Rule: The Primacy of Institutions Over Geography and Integration in Economic Development. *Journal of Economic Growth*, 9 (2): 131–165. Available at: ideas.repec.org/a/kap/jecgro/v9y2004i2p131-165.html.

Rogoff, K. (1996). The Purchasing Power Parity Puzzle. *Journal of Economic Literature*, 34 (2): 665–668.

—— (2002). Why not a Global Currency? *American Economic Review,* 91 (2): 243–247.

Romer, P. M. (1986). Increasing Returns and Long-Run Growth. *Journal of Political Economy*, 94 (5): 1002–1037.

Roubini, N. and B. Setser (2005). *China Trip Report.* Available at: pages.stern.nyu.edu/~nroubini/ChinaTripReport-Roubini-Setser.pdf.

Rubin, R. (1999). Remarks on Reform of the International Financial Architecture to the School of Advanced International Studies. *Treasury News*, 21 April, RR-3093.

Rumbaugh, Th. and N. Blancher (2004). International Trade and the Challenges of WTO Accession. In E. Barnett (ed.), *China's Growth and Integration into the World Economy: Prospects and Challenges*. Washington, DC: IMF.

Sachs, J. (1994). *The IMF and Economies in Crisis*. Presented at the London School of Economics. July.

—— (1997). Limits of Convergence. Nature, Nurture and Growth. *The Economist*, 14 June. London.

—— (2003). *Institutions Don't Rule: Direct Effects of Geography on Per Capita Income*. NBER Working Paper 9490. Cambridge.

Sachverständigenrat zur Begutachtung der gesamtwirtschaftlichen Entwicklung. *Annual Reports*. Various Issues. Stuttgart: Metzler-Poeschel.

Samuelson, P. A. (1954). The Pure Theory of Public Expenditure. *Review of Economic and Statistics*, 36 (4): 387–389.

—— (1994). Theoretical Notes on Trade Problems. *Review of Economics and Statistics,* 46 (2): 145–154

Scherer, F. M. (1994). *Competition Policies for an Integrated World Economy*. Washington, DC: Brookings Institution.

Schulze, G. G. and H. W. Ursprung (1999). Globalisation of the Economy and the Nation State. *World Economy*, 22 (3): 295–352.

Schumpeter, J. A. (1934). *The Theory of Economic Development. An Inquiry into Profits, Capital, Credit, Interest and the Business Cycle*. Cambridge: Harvard University Press.

—— (1943). *Capitalism, Socialism and Democracy.* London: Allen & Unwin.

Seidel, M. (1997). Between Unanimity and Majority. Towards New Rules of Decision-Making. In: H. Siebert (ed.), *Quo Vadis Europe?* Tübingen: Mohr:

Shiller, R. J. (2000). *Irrational Exuberance.* Princeton: Princeton University Press.

Siebert, H. (1983). *Ökonomische Theorie natürlicher Ressourcen.* Tübingen: Mohr.

—— (1987). Foreign Debt and Capital Accumulation. *Weltwirtschaftliches Archiv*, 123: 618–630.

—— (1989). The Half and the Full Debt Cycle. *Weltwirtschaftliches Archiv*, 125: 217–229.

—— (1991a). A Schumpeterian Model of Growth in the World Economy: Some Notes on a New Paradigm in International Economics. *Weltwirtschaftliches Archiv*, 127 (4): 800–812.

—— (1991b). German Unification: The Economics of Transition. *Economic Policy*, 13: 287–340.

—— (1991c). The Integration of Germany: Real Economic Adjustment. *European Economic Review*, 35 (2/3): 591–602.

—— (1991d). *The New Economic Landscape in Europe.* Oxford: Basil Blackwell.

—— (1993). Internationale Wanderungsbewegungen: Erklärungsansätze und Gestaltungsfragen. *Schweizerische Zeitschrift für Volkswirtschaft und Statistik*, 129 (3): 229–255.

—— (1995). Eastern Germany in the Fifth Year. Investment Hammering in the Basement? *Kiel Discussion Papers*, 250. Kiel: Institute for World Economy.

—— (1996). Trade Policy and Environmental Protection. *The World Economy: Global Trade Policy*: 183–194.

—— (1997a). *Weltwirtschaft.* Stuttgart: Lucius and Lucius.

—— (1997b). Die Weltwirtschaft im Umbruch: Müssen die Realeinkommen der Arbeitnehmer sinken? *Aussenwirtschaft*, 52: 349–368.

—— (1998a). An Institutional Order for a Globalizing World Economy. In K. Jaeger and K.-J. Koch (eds), *Trade, Growth, and Economic Policy in Open Economies: Essays in Honour of Hans-Jürgen Vosgerau.* Berlin: Springer.

—— (1998b). *The Future of the IMF: How to Prevent the Next Global Financial Crisis.* Kiel Working Paper 870. Kiel: Institute for World Economy.

—— (1999). What Does Globalization Mean for the World Trading System? In: WTO (ed.), *From GATT to the WTO: The Multilateral Trading System in the New Millennium.* The Hague: Kluwer.

—— (2000). *The Paradigm of Locational Competition.* Kiel Discussion Papers 367. Kiel: Institute of World Economics.

—— (2001a). *How the EU Can Move to a Higher Growth Path: Some Considerations.* Kiel Discussion Papers 383. Kiel: Institute of World Economics.

—— (2001b). *Der Kobra Effekt. Wie man Irrwege der Wirtschaftspolitik vermeidet.* Munich: Deutsche Verlags-Anstalt.

—— (ed.) (2001c). *The World's New Financial Landscape: Challenges for Economic Policy.* Heidelberg: Springer.

—— (2002a). Europe: Quo Vadis? Reflections on the Future Institutional Framework of the European Union. *World Economy*, 25 (1): 1-32.

—— (ed.) (2002b). *Economic Policy for Aging Societies.* Heidelberg: Springer.

—— (ed.) (2002c). *Economic Policy Issues of the New Economy.* Heidelberg: Springer.

—— (ed.) (2003). *Global Governance: An Architecture for the World Economy.* Heidelberg: Springer.

——— (ed.) (2004). *Macroeconomic Policies in the World Economy.* Heidelberg: Springer.

——— (2005a). *Economics of the Environment. Theory and Policy.* 6th edition. Berlin: Springer.

——— (2005b). *The German Economy: Beyond the Social Market.* Princeton: Princeton University Press.

——— (2005c). *TAFTA: A Dead Horse or an Attractive Open Club.* Kiel Working Paper No. 1240. Kiel: Institute for the World Economy.

——— (2006a). Locational Competition: A Neglected Paradigm in the International Division of Labour. *World Economy*, 29 (2): 137-159.

——— (2006b). *Jenseits des sozialen Marktes: Eine notwendige Neuorientierung der deutschen Politik.* 3rd edition. Munich: Deutsche Verlags-Anstalt.

——— (2006c). Where Do We Go After Hong Kong? *International Economics and Economic Policy*, 3 (1): 7-10.

Siebert, H. and I. L. Collier (1991). The Economic Integration of Post-Wall Germany. In: *American Economic Review*, 81 (2): 196–201.

Siebert, H. and M. Feldstein (eds) (2002). *Social Security Pension Reform in Europe.* National Bureau of Economic Research Conference Report. Chicago: University of Chicago Press.

Siebert, H. and H. Klodt (1999). Towards Global Competition: Catalysts and Constraints. In: OECD, *21st Century Economic Dynamics: Anatomy of a Long Boom.* Paris.

Siebert, H. and M. Koop (1990). Institutional Competition: A Concept for Europe? *Aussenwirtschaft*, 45: 439–462.

——— (1993). Institutional Competition versus Centralization: Quo Vadis Europe? *Oxford Review of Economic Policy*, 9 (1): 15–30.

Siebert, H. and O. Lorz (2006). *Außenwirtschaft.* 8th edition. Stuttgart: Lucius and Lucius.

Siebert, H., J. Eichberger, R. Gronych, and R. Pethig (1980). *Trade and Environment. A Theoretical Enquiry.* Amsterdam: Elsevier.

Singer, H. W. (1950). The Distribution of Gains between Investing and Borrowing Countries. *American Economic Review*, 40 (2): 473–485.

Sinn, H. – W. (1997). The Selection Principle and Market Failure in Systems Competition. *Journal of Public Economics*, 66 (2): 247–274.

Sinn, S. (1992a). Saving–Investment Correlations and Capital Mobility: On the Evidence from Annual Data. *Economic Journal*, 102 (414): 1162–1170.

——— (1992b). The Taming of Leviathan: Competition among Governments. *Constitutional Political Economy*, 3 (2): 177–196.

Snape, R. H. (1998). Reading Effective Agreements Covering Services. In A. O. Krueger (ed.), *The WTO as an International Organization.* Chicago: University of Chicago Press.

Solow, R. M. (1956). A Contribution to the Theory of Economic Growth. *Quarterly Journal of Economics*, 70 (1): 65–94.

Srinivasan, T. N. (1998). Regionalism and the WTO: Is Nondiscrimination Passé? In A. O. Krueger (ed.), *The WTO as an International Organization.* Chicago: University of Chicago Press.

Statistics Bureau and Statistical Research and Training Institute. *Statistical Handbook of Japan.* Various Issues. Tokyo.

Statistics Canada. www.statcan.ca.

Statistisches Amt der DDR. *Statistisches Jahrbuch der Industrie der Deutschen Demokratischen Republik.* Various Issues. Berlin.

—— *Wirtschaftsbereich Industrie, Produktion und Auftragsbestand.* Berlin.

Statistisches Bundesamt. *Produzierendes Gewerbe* (Fachserie 4, Reihe 2.1/ Reihe S. 17). Wiesbaden.

—— *Volkswirtschaftliche Gesamtrechnung* (Fachserie 18). Wiesbaden.

Stein, J. L. (2001). *The Equilibrium Value of the Euro/$ US Exchange Rate: An Evaluation of Research.* CESifo Working Paper Series 525. Available at: www.cesifo-group.de/pls/guestci/download/CESifo%20Working%20Papers%202001/CESifo%20Working%20Papers%20July%202001/cesifo_wp525.pdf.

Stoeckel, A., D. Pearce, and G. Banks (1990). *Western Trade Blocs: Game, Set or Match for Asia–Pacific and the World Economy?* Canberra: Centre for International Economics.

Stolpe, M. (1995). Technology and the Dynamics of Specialization in Open Economies. *Kieler Studien*, 271. Tübingen: Mohr.

Summers, R. and A. W. Heston (1988). A New Set of International Comparisons of Real Product and Price Level Estimates for 130 Countries, 1950–1985. *Review of Income and Wealth*, 34 (1): 1–25.

—— (1991). The Penn World Table (Mark 5): An Expanded Set of International Comparisons, 1950–1988. *Quarterly Journal of Economics*, 106 (2): 327-368.

Taylor, A. M. and M. P. Taylor (2004). The Purchasing Power Debate. *Journal of Economic Perspectives,* 18 (4): 135-158. Available at: ideas.repec.org/a/aea/jecper/v18y2004i4p135-158.html

Taylor, M. P. (1995). The Economics of Exchange Rates. *Journal of Economic Literature*, 33 (1): 13-47.

Thünen, J. H. von (1826). *Der isolierte Staat in Beziehung auf Landwirtschaft und Nationalökonomie.* Hamburg: Perthes.

Tiebout, C. (1956). A Pure Theory of Local Expenditures. *Journal of Political Economy*, 64 (5): 416–424.

The New Palgrave (1987). *A Dictionary of Economics.* edited by J. Eatwell, M. Nilgate, and P. Newman. London.

Tobin, J. (1978). A Proposal for International Monetary Reform. *Eastern Economic Journal*, 4 (3/4): 153–159.

Tumlir, J. (1979). Weltwirtschaftsordnung: Regeln, Kooperation und Souveränität. *Kieler Vorträge*, 87. Kiel: Institute for World Economy.

—— (1983). International Economic Order and Democratic Constitutionalism. *ORDO*, 34: 71–83.

Uebe, K. (1999). The Japanese Banking Crisis in the 90s. In: Bank for International Settlement (ed.), *Strengthening the Banking System in China: Issues and Experience.* Policy Papers No. 7. Basel. Available at: www.bis.org/publ/plcy07q.pdf.

United Nations Conference on Trade and Development (UNCTAD). *Statistical Databases Online.* www.unctad.org/templates/page.asp?intItemID=1888&lang=1.

—— (2005). *World Investment Report 2005: Transnational Corporations and the Internationalization of R&D.* New York, NT. Available at: www.unctad.org/en/docs/wir2005_en.pdf.

US Census Bureau. *International Data Base.* www.census.gov.

US Department of Commerce. *International Trade Administration.* www.ita.doc.gov/tradestats.

Viner, J. (1950). *The Customs Union Issue.* New York: Carnegie Endowment for International Peace.

Wade, R. (1996). Globalization and its Limits: Reports of the Death of National

Economy are Greatly Exaggerated. In S. Berger and R. P. Dore (eds), *National Diversity and Global Capitalism*. Ithaca, NY: Cornell University Press.

Wang, T. (2004). Exchange Rate Dynamics. In S. A. Barnett and E. S. Prasad (eds), *China's Growth and Integration into the World Economy: Prospects and Challenges*. Washington, DC: IMF.

Williamson, J. (1983). *The Exchange Rate System. Policy Analysis in International Economics*. Cambridge: MIT Press.

—— (1993). Exchange Rate Management. *Economic Journal*, 103 (416): 188-197.

—— (1996). A New Facility for the IMF. *International Monetary and Financial Issues for the 1990s*, 7: 1–9.

—— (2000). What Should the World Bank Think About the Washington Consensus? *World Bank Research Observer*, 15 (2): 251-264.

Winter, A. (2004). Trade Liberalisation and Economic Performance: An Overview. *Economic Journal*, 114 (493), F4-F21. Available at: www.blackwell-synergy.com/doi/pdf/10.1111/j.0013-0133.2004.00185.x#article.

World Bank. www.worldbank.org.

—— *Global Development Finance* (previously: *World Debt Tables*). Various Issues. Washington, DC.

—— *Global Economic Prospects and the Developing Countries*. Various Issues. Washington, DC.

—— *World Data*. Various Issues. Washington, DC.

—— *World Development Indicators*. Various Issues. Washington, DC.

—— *World Development Report*. Various Issues. Washington, DC.

—— (2005a). *Country Fact Sheet: China*. Washington, DC.

—— (2005b). *Global Development Finance 2005: Mobilizing Finance and Managing Vulnerability*. Washington, DC.

—— (2005c). *World Development Indicators* 2005. Washington, DC.

—— (2005d). *World Development Report* 2006. Washington, DC.

—— (2006a). *China Quarterly Update*. February 2006. Available at: siteresources.worldbank.org/intchina/resources/318862-1121421293578/ cqu_feb06.pdf.

—— (2006b). *Corruption & Development Assistance*. Available at: web.worldbank.org/WBSITE/EXTERNAL/TOPICS/EXTPUBLICSECTORANDGOVERNANCE/EXTANTICORRUPTION/0,,contentMDK:20222111~menuPK:1165474~pagePK:148956 ~piPK:216618~theSitePK:384455,00.html.

—— (2006c). Global Economic Prospects: Economic Implications of Remittance and Migration. Washington, DC. Available at: wdsbeta.worldbank.org/external/default/WDSContentServer/IW3P/IB/2005/11/14/000112742_20051114174928/Rendered/PDF/343200GEP02006.pdf.

World Economic Forum (1998). *The Global Competitiveness Report 1998*. Davos.

World Economic Forum (2005). *The Global Competitiveness Report 2005*. Davos.

World Trade Organization. www.wto.org.

—— *Annual Report*. Various Issues. Geneva.

—— (1995). *Regionalism and the World of Trading System*. Geneva.

—— (2004a). *International Trade Statistics 2004*. Geneva.

—— (2004b). *The Future of the WTO*. Report by the Consultative Board to the Director-General Supachai Panitchpakdi. Geneva.

—— (2005). *International Trade Statistics 2005*. Geneva.

Zhao, Z. (2005). Migration, Labor Market Flexibility and Wage Determination in China: A Review. *Developing Economies*, 43 (2): 285–312.

Index

For Product Safety Concerns and Information please contact our EU
representative GPSR@taylorandfrancis.com
Taylor & Francis Verlag GmbH, Kaufingerstraße 24, 80331 München, Germany